W9-CFS-431

Fodor's

SEVILLE, GRANADA & ANDALUSIA

Where to Stay and Eat
for All Budgets

Must-See Sights
and Local Secrets

Ratings You Can Trust

Fodor's Travel Publications   New York, Toronto, London, Sydney, Auckland
www.fodors.com

FODOR'S SEVILLE, GRANADA & ANDALUSIA
Editor: Debbie Harmsen

Editorial Production: Tom Holton
Editorial Contributors: Maria Burwell, Ben Curtis, Michael Kessler, Mary McLean, Norman Renouf, Helio San Miguel, George Semler, Stephen Kip Tobin
Maps & Illustrations: David Lindroth Inc., Mark Stroud and Henry Colomb, Moon Street Cartography, William Wu; Bob Blake and Rebecca Baer, *map editors*
Design: Fabrizio LaRocca, *creative director*; Guido Caroti, Siobhan O'Hare, *art directors*; Tina Malaney, Chie Ushio, Ann McBride, *designers*; Melanie Marin, *senior picture editor*; Moon Sun Kim, *cover designer*
Production/Manufacturing: Angela L. McLean
Cover Photo: (Feria de Abril, Seville): Ruth Tomlinson/Robert Harding

First Edition

ISBN 978-1-4000-1868-0

ISSN 1939–9928

SPECIAL SALES
This book is available at special discounts for bulk purchases for sales promotions or premiums. Special editions, including personalized covers, excerpts of existing books, and corporate imprints, can be created in large quantities for special needs. For more information, write to Special Markets/Premium Sales, 1745 Broadway, MD 6-2, New York, New York 10019, or e-mail specialmarkets@randomhouse.com.

AN IMPORTANT TIP & AN INVITATION
Although all prices, opening times, and other details in this book are based on information supplied to us at press time, changes occur all the time in the travel world, and Fodor's cannot accept responsibility for facts that become outdated or for inadvertent errors or omissions. So **always confirm information when it matters,** especially if you're making a detour to visit a specific place. Your experiences—positive and negative—matter to us. If we have missed or misstated something, **please write to us.** We follow up on all suggestions. Contact the Seville, Granada & Andalusia editor at editors@fodors.com or c/o Fodor's at 1745 Broadway, New York, NY 10019.

PRINTED IN THE UNITED STATES OF AMERICA
10 9 8 7 6 5 4 3 2 1

Be a Fodor's Correspondent

Your opinion matters. It matters to us. It matters to your fellow Fodor's travelers, too. And we'd like to hear it. In fact, we need to hear it.

When you share your experiences and opinions, you become an active member of the Fodor's community. That means we'll not only use your feedback to make our books better, but we'll publish your names and comments whenever possible. Throughout our guides, look for "Word of Mouth," excerpts of your unvarnished feedback.

Here's how you can help improve Fodor's for all of us.

Tell us when we're right. We rely on local writers to give you an insider's perspective. But our writers and staff editors—who are the best in the business—depend on you. Your positive feedback is a vote to renew our recommendations for the next edition.

Tell us when we're wrong. We're proud that we update most of our guides every year. But we're not perfect. Things change. Hotels cut services. Museums change hours. Charming cafés lose charm. If our writer didn't quite capture the essence of a place, tell us how you'd do it differently. If any of our descriptions are inaccurate or inadequate, we'll incorporate your changes in the next edition and will correct factual errors at fodors.com immediately.

Tell us what to include. You probably have had fantastic travel experiences that aren't yet in Fodor's. Why not share them with a community of like-minded travelers? Maybe you chanced upon a beach or bistro or B&B that you don't want to keep to yourself. Tell us why we should include it. And share your discoveries and experiences with everyone directly at fodors.com. Your input may lead us to add a new listing or highlight a place we cover with a "Highly Recommended" star or with our highest rating, "Fodor's Choice."

Give us your opinion instantly at our feedback center at www.fodors.com/feedback. You may also e-mail editors@fodors.com with the subject line "Andalusia Editor." Or send your nominations, comments, and complaints by mail to Andalusia Editor, Fodor's, 1745 Broadway, New York, NY 10019.

You and travelers like you are the heart of the Fodor's community. Make our community richer by sharing your experiences. Be a Fodor's correspondent.

¡Buen Viaje!

Tim Jarrell, Publisher

CONTENTS

CLOSE UPS

ANDALUSIA IN FOCUS

MAPS

ABOUT THIS BOOK

Our Ratings

Sometimes you find terrific travel experiences and sometimes they just find you. But usually the burden is on you to select the right combination of experiences. That's where our ratings come in.

As travelers we've all discovered a place so wonderful that its worthiness is obvious. And sometimes that place is so experiential that superlatives don't do it justice: you just have to be there to know. These sights, properties, and experiences get our highest rating, **Fodor's Choice**, indicated by orange stars throughout this book.

Black stars highlight sights and properties we deem **Highly Recommended**, places that our writers, editors, and readers praise again and again for consistency and excellence.

By default, there's another category: any place we include in this book is by definition worth your time, unless we say otherwise. And we will.

Disagree with any of our choices? Care to nominate a place or suggest that we rate one more highly? Visit our feedback center at www.fodors. com/feedback.

Budget Well

Hotel and restaurant price categories from ¢ to $$$$ are defined in the opening pages of each chapter. For attractions, we always give standard adult admission fees; reductions are usually available for children, students, and senior citizens. Want to pay with plastic? **AE, D, DC, MC, V** after restaurant and hotel listings indicate if American Express, Discover, Diner's Club, MasterCard, and Visa are accepted.

Restaurants

Unless we state otherwise, restaurants are open for lunch and dinner daily. We mention dress only when there's a specific requirement and reservations only when they're essential or not accepted—it's always best to book ahead.

Hotels

Hotels have private bath, phone, TV, and air-conditioning and operate on the European Plan (aka EP, meaning without meals), unless we specify that they use the Continental Plan (CP, with a continental breakfast), Breakfast Plan (BP, with a full breakfast), or Modified American Plan (MAP, with breakfast and dinner) or are all-inclusive (including all meals and most activi-

ties). We always list facilities but not whether you'll be charged an extra fee to use them, so when pricing accommodations, find out what's included.

Many Listings	
★	Fodor's Choice
★	Highly recommended
⊠	Physical address
✛	Directions
⌖	Mailing address
☎	Telephone
⊟	Fax
⊕	On the Web
✍	E-mail
⊠	Admission fee
☉	Open/closed times
Ⓜ	Metro stations
⊟	Credit cards
Hotels & Restaurants	
⊞	Hotel
⇥	Number of rooms
⚲	Facilities
❙❂❙	Meal plans
✕	Restaurant
⌂	Reservations
↘	Smoking
⚵	BYOB
✕⊞	Hotel with restaurant that warrants a visit
Outdoors	
⚐	Golf
⛺	Camping
Other	
♨	Family-friendly
⇨	See also
⊠	Branch address
☞	Take note

WHAT'S WHERE

Bay of Biscay

BASQUE COUNTRY (EUSKADI)

A Coruña
Gijón
Santander
San Sebastián
FRANCE

Santiago de Compostela
Oviedo
ASTURIAS
CANTABRIA
Bilbao

Lugo

Trevino
NAVARRE
PYRENEES

GALICIA
León
Logroño
LA RIOJA
Huesca

Pontevedra
Ourense
Burgos
Palencia
Soria
Zaragoza

Valladolid
Duero
ARAGON

Zamora
CASTILE–LEÓN

Salamanca
Segovia
Tajo
Teruel

Ávila
MADRID
Costellón de la Plana

PORTUGAL
Toledo
Aranjuez
Cuenca

Tajo
CASTILE– LA MANCHA
Requena
Valencia

Cáceres
Trujillo
Alcázar
VALENCIA

EXTREMADURA
Mérida
Guadiana
Ciudad Real
Albacete
Alicante
COSTA BLANCA

Badajóz
Valdepeñas
Segura

Córdoba
Jaén
MURCIA
Murcia

Guadalquivir
ANDALUSIA
Granada
Lorca
Cartagena

Huelva
Seville
Antequera
Almería
COSTA DE ALMERÍA

Jerez
Málaga

COSTA DE LA LUZ
Cádiz
COSTA DEL SOL

Gibraltar
Ceuta

Melilla

MOROCCO

1 Andalusia. Eight provinces, five of which are coastal (Huelva, Cádiz, Málaga, Granada, and Almería) and three that are landlocked (Seville, Córdoba, and Jaén), compose the southern Spain autonomous community of Andalusia. The region is bordered by Portugal to the west, the province of Murcia to the east, Extremadura and Castile–La Mancha to the north, and the Mediterranean Sea and Atlantic Ocean to the south. The region's key cities are Seville and Granada. A fantasy of passionate flamenco, dashing bullfighters, and flower-choked streets winding past whitewashed villas perfumed with orange blossoms, Seville is the setting of Bizet's Carmen. Granada shimmers red-gold and amber in the mind's eye, an indelibly romantic reverie. It is home to the Alhambra, a marvel from the era of Moorish rule every bit as mysterious and inspiring as Washington Irving found it two centuries ago. Other Andalusian destinations worth a day trip or more are the cities of Córdoba (see its mosque, the mezquita) and Jerez de la Frontera (sip some sherry), and outdoor-recreational reserves (don't miss Doñana National Park).

2 Costa del Sol. The allure of sun and sand is never to be underestimated---and the Costa del Sol is perhaps the ultimate proof. With more than 320 days of sunshine a year, this touristy, fun-in-the-sun tour de force buzzes with energy and vacationing Europeans. The main holiday resorts are built up with high-rise hotels, shopping centers, and sprawling housing developments near the beach. In some places, the coast is overdeveloped, with resorts and sunseekers filling every cranny. But villages such as Casares seem immune to the goings-on along the coast (even as it shimmers below). Marbella, a longtime glitterati favorite, has a pristine Andalusian old quarter, while the ancient town of Ronda straddles a giant river gorge. Birdlovers flock to the Cabo de Gata Nature Reserve.

ON THE CALENDAR

WINTER	
January	**Epiphany** (January 6) is when youngsters leave their shoes on the doorstep to be filled with gifts from the Three Kings.
February	**Carnaval** dances through Andalusia and Spain just before Lent, most flamboyant in Cádiz, where satirical street theater mocks local and international figures and phenomena. Reserve lodging far in advance.
SPRING	
March	**Semana Santa** (Holy Week) is the reigning queen of Andalusian festivals, with Seville staging the most elaborate processions. The full week of hauntingly beautiful religious processions is highlighted by spontaneous *saetas*—flamenco song, literally "arrows" to and from the heart. (Note that some years it is in April rather than March. It is always the week leading up to Easter.)
April	Following Semana Santa, Seville's **Feria de Abril (April Fair)** features horses, bulls, and beautiful women. The horseback parades during the fair are particularly photogenic.
May	The Jerez de la Frontera's **Feria del Caballo (Horse Fair)** in May is a pageant of equestrian events, showing off Andalusia's famous equestrian culture with accompanying sherry tasting and flamenco dancing until dawn. In Córdoba, the mid-May **Festival de los Patios** combines flamenco performances with lavish floral displays in the city's finest courtyards.
SUMMER	
June	**El Rocío,** the late-May/early-June pilgrimage from all over Andalusia to the Hermitage of the Vergen del Rocío (Our Lady of the Dew), is one of Spain's most picturesque explosions of gypsy, flamenco, and religious fervor. From mid-June to mid-July, Granada's **International Festival of Music and Dance** brings orchestras, opera companies, and ballet corps to the grounds of the Alhambra.
FALL	
September	Jerez celebrates harvest time with **Fiesta de Otoño** (Autumn Festival).
October	**El Pilar** (Oct. 12) celebrates Virgen del Pilar, patron saint of Spain and of Hispanic culture worldwide. The festivities bring representatives from the Spanish-speaking world around the globe.

ANDALUSIA'S TOP EXPERIENCES

Surf the Seas

On the Atlantic Coast, Tarifa has fast become the wind- and kite-surfing capital of Europe, and every year seems to attract more devotees from all over the world. Silhouetted against a bold blue backdrop, the vivid sails flutter in the breeze like tropical butterflies. The most popular beaches for the sport are just northwest of the town along what is known as the Costa de la Luz (Coast of Light)—wide stretches of silvery white sand, washed by magical rollers and flanked by rolling dunes. The winds here are the eastern Levante and the western Poniente, which can be a gusty problem if you are trying to read the paper under a beach umbrella, but ideal for surfing the waves.

Play Top Chef at the Spanish Market

Markets (*mercados*) are the key to delicious local cuisine and represent an essential part of Spanish life, largely unaffected by competition from supermarkets and hypermarkets. You'll find fabulous produce sold according to whatever is in season: counters neatly piled with shiny purple eggplants, blood-red peppers, brilliant orange cantaloupes and all variety of fruit, including fresh figs, a couple sliced open to show their succulent pink flesh.

Dance in the Streets during the Ferias

Throughout Andalusia, the year revolves around *ferias* (fairs), which are far more than a holiday from work. While city-based *ferias* are rich and glittering affairs attracting millions of visitors, others, such as the *feria* of Casares village near the Costa del Sol, is more an exuberant street party. The most famous fair of all is Seville's Feria de Abril (April Fair), when sultry foot-stomping señoritas wear traditional, brilliantly colored flamenco dresses. From 1 to 5 every afternoon,

Sevillana society parades around in carriages drawn by high-stepping horses. The atmosphere is electric and infectious and, like all *ferias*, the charm lies in the universal spontaneity of enjoyment.

Catch the Carnaval

Second only to Rio in terms of revelry and costumes, the annual *Carnaval* in Andalusia can reach serious partying proportions. Cadíz is famous for its annual extravaganza of drinking, dancing, and dressing up—the more outrageous the better. The celebrations typically carry on for ten days. There are processions of costumed groups and everyone is dressed up, including a number of drag queens. Book your hotel months in advance, because you're not likely to find a single vacancy in town during the celebration.

Spot Celebrities on the Costa

The Monte Carlo of Costa del Sol, Puerto Banús is *the* place to pick up your made-to-measure gold chain or meet up with members of the local Ferrari Club. The buildings reflect a tantalizing combination of Andaluz and Moorish design, while the position, cradled by lofty mountains overlooking the Mediterranean, is suitably stunning. The harbor is the port of call to some of the most lavish yachts in the world, so you may have to shift your credit card into overdrive to eat here.

QUINTESSENTIAL ANDALUSIA

El Paseo

One of the most delightful Andalusian customs is *el paseo* (the stroll), which traditionally takes place during the early evening, and is common throughout the country, but particularly in *pueblos* and towns. Given the modern hamster-wheel pace of life, there is something appealingly old-fashioned about families and friends walking around at a leisurely pace with no real destination or purpose. In fact, if you were to set off for a jog at dusk in a small village here, you would likely be viewed with amusement or even suspicion. Dress is usually formal or fashionable: elderly señoras with their boxy tweed suits, men with jackets slung, capelike, round the shoulders, teenagers in their latest Zara gear, and younger children in their Sunday best. El paseo provides everyone with an opportunity to participate in a lively slice of street theater.

La Siesta

The unabashed Spanish pursuit of pleasure and the unswerving devotion to establishing a healthy balance between work and play is nowhere more apparent than in this midday shutdown. However, as air-conditioning, fitness clubs, and other distractions gain ascendancy in modern Spain, and Mom-cooked lunches, once a universal ritual, become all but extinct in the two-salary, 21st-century Spanish family, the siesta question is increasingly debated. The classic midday snooze described by novelist Camilo José Cela as "de padrenuestro y pyjama" (with a prayer and pajamas) is not often practiced these days, especially in larger cities. Even so, most stores and businesses close from 1:30 to 4:30 or later. Whether they're sleeping, feasting, exercising, or canoodling, one thing is certain: they're not working.

If you want to get a sense of Andalusian culture and indulge in some of its pleasures, start by familiarizing yourself with the rituals of daily life. These are a few things you can take part in with relative ease.

Flamenco

Seductive and spontaneous, flamenco embodies Andalusia's free-spirit culture, an attitude inherited from the Moors and Gypsies who once inhabited southern Spain. This passionate dance form is a tantalizing mix of Arabic, African, Jewish, Hindu, and Spanish influences, and in Andalusia you can see flamenco at its finest.

Bullfighting

While controversy over bullfighting in Spain has grown, it is very much a staple of southern Spain, where a chance to see a renowned matador perform at Seville's Maestranza bullring—the sanctum sanctorum of the art of tauromachy—during the *Feria de Abril* (April Fair) is an exquisitive and riveting memory-making moment.

Sunday Lunch

The Spanish love to eat out, especially on Sundays, the traditional day when families will drive to restaurants for long leisurely lunches. Depending on the time of year, this is most likely to be a seaside *chiringuito* or rural *venta*. The latter thrive, particularly in southern Spain, born from bygone days when much of the region's seasonal work was done by itinerant labor. Cheap, hearty meals were much in demand and some enterprising country housewife saw the opportunity and decided to provide *ventas* (meals for sale); an idea that quickly mushroomed. Ventas are still a wonderfully good value today, not just for the food, but also for the atmosphere: long scrubbed wooden tables, large noisy Spanish families, and a convivial informality. Sundays can be slow. So relax, and remember that all good things are worth waiting for...

IF YOU LIKE

Art

During the Spanish Golden Age (1580–1680), the empire's wealth flowed to the imperial capital of Madrid, and Spanish monarchs used it not only for defense and civil projects but to finance the arts. Painters from El Greco to Rubens, and writers from Lope de Vega to Cervantes, were drawn to the luminous (and solvent) royal court. For the first time in Europe, the collecting of art became an important symbol of national wealth and power. In southern Spain, Andalusia has its share of noteworthy art collections.

■ **Museo de Bellas Artes, Granada.** Set in the Alhambra's Palacio de Carlos V, this art museum features works by Fray Juan Sanchez Cotán.

■ **Museo de Bellas Artes, Seville.** This is the finest museum in Andalusia and one of the top three in Spain. Among the fabulous works are those of Murillo, Zurbarán, Valdés Leal, and El Greco, and there are examples of Seville Gothic art, baroque religious sculptures, and Sevillian art of the 19th and 20th centuries.

■ **Museo Julio Romero de Torres, Córdoba.** The collection offers sensual works by the early-20th-century Córdoban artist.

■ **Museo Picasso, Málaga.** Several worth-seeing works by the Cubist mastermind are on display here. They are from all three of his movements: Blue, Rose, and Cubism.

Architecture

Mudéjar Spain—the Spain built under Christian rule by Moorish architects, engineers, and craftsmen—has been called the most distinctive and characteristic Iberian contribution to western European art and architecture. The staggering variety of architectural treatments throughout Andalusia can be seen in the Renaissance palaces of Úbeba and Baeza, Ronda's bullring, and Córdoba's synagogue, as well as the attractions below.

■ **Mezquita, Córdoba and Alhambra, Granada.** In a sense the two bookends of Moorish architecture, coming as they did at the outset and the sunset of the Moorish empire on the Iberian Peninsula, these are the two best examples of purely Moorish art and architecture. The mesquita (mosque) has a sublime beauty, with materials such as jade, onyx, and marble composing its interior. Don't miss it. Likewise, the Alhambra has an array of architectural elements, from honeycomb-like designs to ornate ceilings.

■ **Seville's Alcázar.** This comes third only because it was built after Fernando III conquered Córdoba and Seville and set about converting Islamic mosques to Christian churches.

■ **Arab Ruins, Huelva.** The ruins of Moorish castles and former mosques in the Huelva's Sierra de Aracena are consistently surprising feasts for the eyes of curious travelers.

Beaches

Virtually surrounded by bays, oceans, gulfs, straits, and seas, the entire country of Spain is a beach-lover's dream, and the Costa del Sol takes the cake for the sunniest spots. August beaches are overcrowded and to be avoided, whereas winter beaches offer solitude and sunshine without the stifling heat.

- **Mar Menor, Costa Blanca.** Known for its warm-water temperatures and the healing properties of its brine and iodine content, the Mar Menor offers year-round beach fun.

- **From Málaga to Estepona.** Beaches from Málaga to Estepona are warm enough for swimming year-round, though the overdeveloped high-rise apartments that have replaced fishing villages along this strip are ugly and depressing.

- **The Costa de La Luz.** Just beyond Algeciras, this coast presents a very different picture with its white sandy beaches and a refreshing lack of concrete, particularly around Tarifa, which is famous for its water sports.

- **Andalusia's West Coast.** Matalascañas, at the western end of the Andalusian coast, and La Antilla, west of Huelva, are fine beaches except in late July and August when there's no towel space on the sand.

- **Cadíz's Atlantic beaches.** South of Huelva are some wild and very windy beaches, appreciated by water-sports fans and by locals fleeing from the Mediterranean clamor and crowds.

Exploring the Outdoors

Composing nearly a fifth of the country in geographic size, Andalusia has a wealth of natural treasures for outdoor enthusiasts. Hiking is excellent in the Alpujarra Mountains southeast of Granada, and in the one of the country's national parks, such as Doñana National Park in the southeast corner of Huelva province. Perhaps the best part of Spain's outdoor space and activities is that they often bring you nearer to some of the finest architecture and cuisine in Iberia.

- **Cabo de Gata Nature Reserve, near San José.** You can hike here, but the primary draw is the birds, including a rare species from Africa.

- **Doñana National Park, Huelva province.** One of Europe's last tracts of true wilderness includes wetlands, beaches, shifting sand dunes, marshes, 150 species of rare birds, and countless kinds of wildlife, including the endangered imperial eagle and Iberian lynx. The park has been designated a UNESCO World Heritage site due to its rare-bird status.

- **Sierra Nevada National Park, Eastern Andalusia.** Dip into its medicinal waters, or, come winter, go skiing high in the Sierra Nevada mountains at this park whose geographic boundaries include parts of Granada and Almería provinces.

GREAT ITINERARIES

ANDALUSIAN UPLANDS
13 to 16 days

More widely known for beaches and the flat and fertile *vega* (farmland), Andalusia has surprising highlands rich in hiking and trekking options as well as varied and interesting architectural and gastronomic treasures. With six national parks to choose from, the mountain resources of southern Spain should not be overlooked.

You can visit all of the following for a two-week excursion, or, if you're staying for awhile in one of the hub cities of Seville, Granada, or Córdoba, then use this overview as a guide for where to go for weekend getaways with a mountain theme. The orange line on the map on the opposite page shows this itinerary.

Sierra de Aracena, Huelva

2 days. This lush mountain retreat in Spain's southwestern corner is home to, among other wildlife, the free-range Iberian pig. Jabugo is synonymous with this acorn-fattened delicacy. Cortegana, Almonaster la Real, and Aracena have lovely Mudéjar churches.

Sierra de Grazalema, Cádiz and Málaga

2 or 3 days. The Cádiz highlands are famous for the pueblos blancos from Arcos de la Frontera up to Grazalema and into the province of Málaga to Ronda.

Sierra de Segura, Jaén

2 days. This mountainous area is rife with flora and fauna from mountain goats to royal eagles. Trout thrive in the clear mountain streams, headwaters of the historic Guadalquivir.

Sierra Nevada and the Alpujarra, Granada

3 or 4 days. Spain's highest peak at Mulhacén, the skiing in the Sierra Nevada, and the hiking trails in the Alpujarra foothills along the Sierra Nevada's southern flanks are some of the Iberian Peninsula's finest mountain resources.

Sierra Morena, Córdoba

2 or 3 days. Northern Andalusia's Sierra Morena is rough up-country that seems closer to Castilla and the Iberian meseta than to Andalusia and the Mediterranean. Belalcázar's castle and Hinojosa del Duque's "Catedral de la Sierra" are highlights.

Sierra Norte, Seville

2 days. Due north of Seville, the mountain villages of Constantina and Cazalla de la Sierra are weekend retreats from the heat and pace of Andalusia's greatest metropolis.

ROMAN, MOORISH & MUDÉJAR HIGHLIGHTS
7 to 10 days

Colonized by Rome, followed from the 4th through 7th centuries by Visigoths, who were then superseded by the Moors in 711, Andalusia offers opportunities to explore Roman, Moorish, and neo-Moorish or Mudéjar sites of various kinds.

In 206 BC, Itálica was the Roman city on the Guadalquivir River before commerce moved closer to the port at Hispalis, now Seville. Nearby Carmona's Roman necropolis contains some 900 tombs dating from the 2nd century BC. The other major Roman site is at Baelo Claudia, near Tarifa in the province of Cádiz.

Córdoba's Mezquita and Granada's Alhambra are the most important manifestations of Moorish architecture on the Iberian Peninsula, although Abderraman III's summer palace at Madinat al-Zahra near Córdoba may have been even more opulent than Granada's Alhambra before Berbers sacked and pillaged it in AD 1010.

Seville's Alcazar is the main example of neo-Moorish construction. The many Mudéjar churches of Córdoba and Seville, as well as more remote chapels in places such as Huelva's Almonaster la Real and Córdoba's Montoro, also each have their own distinct character.

Again, you can visit all of the following for a week or two excursion, or use it as a guide for weekend getaways from a hub city. The gray line on the map shows this itinerary.

Seville, Itálica, and Carmona

2–3 days. The Moorish-style Alacazar, the medieval Barrio de Santa Cruz Jewish quarter, and the city's many Mudéjar churches are Seville's patrimony, but the Roman ruins at Itálica and Carmona's Roman cemetery reverberate with history.

Córdoba and Madinat al-Zahra

2–3 days. Córdoba's Mezquita-Catedral (a mosque with a Gothic cathedral in the middle of it), the Judería with its unique synagogue, and the remains of the Umayyad summer palace at Madinat al-Zahra are all two hours from Madrid by the high-speed AVE train.

Granada and Sierra Nevada

2–3 days. The Alhambra with the snow-capped Sierra Nevada behind it is one of Spain's great sights, but even more unusual is the chance to combine sizzling Granada's urban and cultural resources with the high sierra skiing and trekking opportunities less than an hour away

Cádiz, the Costa de la Luz & Baelo Claudia

1–2 days. The city of Cádiz, western Europe's oldest, and the coast between Cádiz and Tarifa offer a variety of urban and natural opportunities. Baelo Claudia is a well-preserved Roman town to explore.

Gain access to the inner chambers of paradores in Santiago de Compostela (left) and Sigüenza (above).

A NIGHT WITH HISTORY

Spain's nearly 100 paradores all have one thing in common: heritage status. More often than not they also have a killer view. If a visitor plans a trip with stays at a number of paradores, he has the chance to experience an authentic slice of Spanish culture around the country. Spaniards themselves love the paradores and make up about 70 percent of visitors.

Accommodations come in all manner of distinguished settings, including former castles, convents, and Arab fortresses—soon, in Madrid, you'll even be able to check into a former women's prison. Talk about ex-cell-ent sleeping....

Even if you find yourself in a parador that's a (ho-hum) stately historic home, you'll most likely be perched above, or nestled in, some lovely surroundings—from the *pueblos blancos* (whitewashed villages) and verdant golf courses of Andalusia to the rolling fields, mountains, and beaches of northern Spain.

THE PARADOR'S TRUE CHARM: PAY LESS, GET MORE

Why pay top-euro prices when you can get top-notch quality for considerably less? In most cases, the accommodations, interior decoration, and cuisine at paradores are just as good and, in many cases, vastly superior to that of four- and five-star hotels. Just as strong a selling point is that paradores have the luxury of beautiful and peaceful settings. The variety of settings is perhaps what attracts most visitors, from a balcony overlooking the Alhambra or views of snow-peaked mountains to sweeping views of plains in countryside venues.

FROM ROYAL HUNTING LODGE TO FIRST PARADOR

An advocate for Spain tourism in the early 20th century, King Alfonso XIII was eager to develop a countrywide hotel infrastructure that would cater to local and overseas travelers. He directed the Spanish government to set up the Royal Tourist Commission to mull it over, and in 1926, commissioner Marquis de la Vega Inclán came up with the parador ("stopping place") idea and searched for where to build the first such inn. His goal was to find a setting that would reflect both the beauty of Spain and its cultural heritage. He nominated the wild Gredos Mountains, where royalty came to hunt and relax, a few hours west of Madrid.

King Alfonso XIII

By October of 1928, the Parador de Gredos opened at a spot chosen by King Alfonso himself, amid pine groves, rocks, and the clear waters of Avilá. In 1937, this parador is where the fascist Falange party was established, and a few decades later, in 1978, it's where national leaders drafted the Spanish Constitution.

SPAIN'S PARADOR CHAIN

When Alfonso gave his blessing to the establishment of Spain's first parador, he probably didn't realize that he was sitting on a financial, cultural, and historical gold mine. But after it opened, the Board of Paradores and Inns of Spain was formed and focused its energies on harnessing historical, artistic, and cultural monuments with lovely landscapes into a chain—an effort that has continued to this day.

The number of state-run paradores today approaches nearly 100, with the latest two being the Parador La Granja on the grounds of the royal summer home of Carlos III and Isabel de Farnesio in Segovia, and the Parador de Gran Canaria in Cruz in Tejeda in Las Canarias. Three others are scheduled to open in 2008.

Pillow Talk

Grace Kelly

Given that many paradores were once homes and residences to noble families and royalty, it's no surprise that they've continued to attract the rich and famous. Italian actress Sophia Loren stayed at the Parador de Hondarribia, as did distinguished Spanish writer José Cela. Meanwhile, the Cardona's castle and fortress was the backdrop for Orson Welles's movie *Falstaff*.

Topping the list, though, is the Parador de Granada. President Johnson, Queen Elizabeth, actress Rita Hayworth, and even Franco himself have all stayed here. Additionally, Grace Kelly celebrated some of her honeymoon trip with Prince Rainier of Monaco in these hallowed walls, and many a Spanish intellectual and artist also have gotten cozy in this charming, sophisticated abode.

WHAT TO EXPECT

Walk where famous people have walked in the Parador de Granada's courtyard.

Paradores have been restored to provide modern amenities. Depending on the location, some have swimming pools, while others have fitness rooms and/or saunas. Most paradores have access to cable TV, but if they veer more toward four-star status, English channels may be limited to news services such as CNN and BBC World, though films may be available via a pay-for-view service. Some rooms have DVDs and a rental service. Laundry facilities are available at almost all of the paradores. Internet access is limited.

Lodging at the paradores is generally equivalent to a four-star hotel and occasionally a five-star. The dining is what sets the paradores apart—you'd pay considerably more to eat the quality of food they serve at the same caliber restaurant in town. Another advantage of the paradores is that unlike hotels, the room rates do not vary much in the peak months of June, July, and August.

Cost: Prices at the paradores vary, depending on location and time of year. In general, one-night stays range from €95 to €200, though the Parador de Granada will hit your wallet for at least 60 euros more per night. July through September and Easter Week tend to be the most expensive times.

GREAT FOR DAY VISITS, TOO

While paradores are a great means of accommodation, they also attract huge numbers of day visitors. The reasons for this are two-fold. First, the buildings are often spectacular and historically significant and many contain great views. Secondly, the restaurants are consistently excellent but reasonable priced. Each parador strives to use local produce and reproduce the traditional gastronomy found in its region.

FODOR'S CHOICE PARADORES

PARADOR DE GRANADA

Location: Granada, Andalusia

Why Visit: Situated within the walls of the Alhambra, this former 15th-century monastery is Spain's most popular (and most expensive) parador. Originally a Moorish nobleman's house, it later became the first holy place for Christians in Granada. The building has survived abandonment by the monks and French occupation, and at different times has housed the poor and the military. It opened as a parador in 1949.

Lodging & Dining Highlights: Spacious rooms are tastefully decorated in a classic Moorish style, many with patios. An excellent restaurant serves great local cuisine—try the Tortilla de Sacromonte (omelet of eggs, brains, and sweetbreads) and Moraga de Sardinas (oven-baked sardines).

PARADOR DE SIGÜENZA

Location: Sigüenza, Castilla-La Mancha

Why Visit: This sprawling 12th-century Moorish citadel is arguably the finest architectural example of all the parador castles. Its appointments include a splendid courtyard, stately corridors, and elegantly rustic furniture, all of which give the parador a strong medieval ambience. The best thing about the parador is its access to Siguenza, in Don Quixote territory.

Lodging & Dining Highlights: The rooms, many with a terrace, are decked out with traditional furniture from the region. All the local delicacies are here: fried bread crumbs with bacon and fried eggs, roast suckling kid, and cod prepared with manchego cheese. If you like game, there's also deer and partridge.

PARADOR DE CARDONA

Location: Cardona, Catalonia

Why Visit: As you approach Cardona along the highway from Manresa you can see the gigantic, 9th-century castle, church, and tower looming 10 km (6.2 mi) away. Perhaps there are more ornate and architecturally refined castles in Spain, but there is surely not one as towering and omnipresent as Cardona's. What draws crowds to the area are the famous salt mines, where visitors can take underground tours.

Lodging & Dining Highlights: Rooms tend to vary; some are spacious, while others are simple yet still remarkable, due to the lovely views of the valley. The food is nothing short of superb. Shoulder of lamb, salted octopus, seafood bisque, and leg of duck are all equally good, and there's a great selection of wines.

PARADOR DE SANTILLANA GIL BLAS

Location: Santillana del Mar, Cantabria

Why Visit: French philosopher and writer Jean-Paul Sarte once described the village of Santillana de Mar as the most beautiful village in Spain. Few would disagree. If you're after peace and quiet, this is the parador for you. Set in a former noble family's residence in the mountains, the Parador Santillana del Mar has a history as a haven for writers in the 1940s, and later, as a theater, attended by the likes of King Alfonso XIII.

Lodging & Dining Highlights: The rooms are comfortable without being spectacular. Rather, it's the peaceful ambience that's the attraction here—and the mountain food: try the *cocido montañ*, a dish of boiled white beans, vegetables, bacon and sausages; also worth sampling is *sorropotún*, Cantabrian hakefish with green asparagus and the *quesada* cheese pudding.

PARADOR DE HONDARRIBIA

Location: Hondarribia, Pais Vasco

Why Visit: This 10th-century castle-cum-fortress may look severe on the outside, but indoors, plentiful nooks and crannies, spaces adorned with arches, wrought-iron appointments, and coffered ceilings envelop the traveler in an atmosphere of indescribable beauty. Lances, cannons, and armour make up the interior decor, and two terraces, with their sweeping views of the French coastline, top off a stay here. The parador is in the heart of Hondirribia, an elegant and stunning border town renowned for its food.

Lodging Highlights: Rooms are comfortable and elegant, some with stunning views of the sea. There's no dining facilities on the premises.

In the Works: New Paradores to Open Soon

Three new paradores are scheduled to open in 2008 in Madrid, Murcia, and Castellón. Here is a brief description of each:

■ **Pardor de Alcalá de Henares** is set in a former women's prison on Madrid's Calle Colegios, just across the street from the Hostería del Estudiante parador.

■ The 83-room **Parador de Lorca**, in Murcia, has a distinguishing tower and a view of the nearby one-time Arab fortress.

■ Offering a prayerful night's sleep, the 15th-century San Francisco convent is set to open as the **Parador de Morella** in Castellón.

MORE PARADORES WORTH VISITING

With its Spanish plateresque façade, the Parador de León adorns the Plaza de San Marcos.

PARADOR DE CANGAS DE ONIS, *Asturias.* This is a beautiful former monastery set in the lush mountains of Picos de Europa.

PARADOR DE GOMERA, *Canarias.* Great ocean views of Tenerife Island, a pool, and gardens make a visit here a tropical stay.

PARADOR DE LEON, *Castilla y León.* Pure luxury sums up this five-star monastery, with arguably the best restaurant in the parador network.

PLASENCIA, *Extremadura.* Built in Gothic style through and through, this pretty convent lies in the heart of Plasencia's beautiful old quarters.

SANTIAGO DE COMPOSTELA, *Galicia.* Considered to be the world's oldest hotel, this is the meeting point for the many pilgrims who've traveled the long road to Santiago. Set in one of the city's famous squares, Plaza do Obradoiro, the parador boasts beautiful rooms, lots of space, and tantalizing Galician cuisine, including pulpo gallego (octopus) and percebes (gooseneck barnacles).

SANTO DOMINGO DE LA CALZADA, *La Rioja.* This 12th-century hospital, also known for sheltering pilgrims en route to Santiago, is popular for its restaurant (stuffed peppers are a staple) and its wines—it is, after all, situated in La Rioja, Spain's wine capital, and offers good value wines such as Marqués de Vargas and Allende.

■ TIP → **Popular paradores such as the two in Granada and Santiago de Compostela are in huge demand and need to be booked up to six months in advance. Booking can be done by telephone or via the Internet.**

PARADOR INFORMATION

For more information about paradores, consult the official parador Web site, ⊕ www.paradores.es/english, e-mail ✉ reservas@parador.es, or call ☎ 34 902/547979.

Seville, Granada & Mainland Andalusia

The Mosque of Cordoba

WORD OF MOUTH

"Andalusia feels, looks, sounds, and tastes so different from Catalonia that I thought I had arrived in another world. Until you hear flamenco and see the Moorish architecture and taste the cumin seed in the cooking, you don't fully understand how diverse Spain is."

—Eyecandy

WELCOME TO SEVILLE, GRANADA & MAINLAND ANDALUSIA

Cordoba's Great Mosque.

TOP REASONS TO GO

★ **Arabian Romance:** Soak in the history and drama of the mighty Alhambra in Granada.

★ **Enchanted Dancing:** Olé the night away at a heel-stomping flamenco show. Jerez de la Frontera is the "cradle of flamenco."

★ **Priceless Paintings:** Bask in the golden age of Spanish art at Seville's Museo de Bellas Artes.

★ **Exquisite Architecture:** Marvel at the jasper, marble, granite, and onyx of Córdoba's Mezquita.

★ **Tempting Tapas:** Try a little bit of everything on an evening tapas crawl.

★ **Tumultuous Fiestas:** Celebrate Semana Santa (Holy Week) with rich festivities in Granada, Córdoba, or Seville.

★ **Matador Moves:** Witness a bullfight in the historic bullrings of Seville or Ronda.

1 Seville. Long Spain's chief riverine port, the captivating town of Seville sits astride the Guadalquivir River that launched Columbus to the New World and Magellan around the globe. South of the capital is fertile farmland; in the north are highland villages.

2 Huelva. Famed as live oak-forested grazing grounds for the treasured *cerdo ibérico* (Iberian pig), the province's Sierra de Aracena is a fresh and leafy mountain getaway on the border of Portugal. Huelva's Doñana National Park is one of Spain's greatest national treasures.

Holy Week procession in Granada.

5 **Málaga.** Pablo Picasso was born in this maritime province, known for its tapas taverns, bullring, and tourist beaches, but also the mountain town of Ronda.

GETTING ORIENTED

Andalusia is infinitely varied and diverse within its apparent unity. Seville and Granada are like feuding sisters, one vivaciously flirting, the other darkly brooding. Córdoba and Cádiz are estranged cousins, one landlocked, the other virtually under sail. Huelva and Almería are universes apart, the first a verdant Atlantic Arcadia and the second a parched Mediterranean sunbelt. And Jaén is an upland country bumpkin—albeit with Renaissance palaces —compared with the steamy cosmopolitan seaport of Málaga.

6 **Jaén.** Andalusia's northwesternmost province is a striking contrast of olive groves, pristine wilderness, and Renaissance towns with elegant palaces and churches.

7 **Granada.** The blend of Christian and Moorish cultures are dramatically counterposed in Granada, especially in the sultry enclave of the Alhambra.

8 **Almería.** Once a textile and commercial giant, Almería today showcases architectural reminders of this past, as well as colorful cave dwellings.

3 **Cádiz.** Cádiz is to Spain what Havana is to Cuba, but with less salsa and more charm. It is well known for its sherries and sherrylike Manzanilla.

4 **Córdoba.** A center of world culture in the 9th and 10th centuries, Córdoba is a living monument to its past glory. Its prized building is the Mezquita (mosque). In the countryside, acorns and olives thrive.

SEVILLE, GRANADA & MAINLAND ANDALUSIA PLANNER

When to Go

The best months to go to Andalusia are October and November, and April and May.

Andalusia is blisteringly hot in the summer. If summer is your only chance to come, plan time in the Sierra de Aracena in Huelva, the Pedroches of northern Córdoba province, Granada's Sierra Nevada and Alpujarra highlands, or the Sierra de Cazorla in Jaén. Autumn catches the cities going about their business, the temperatures are moderate, and you will rarely see a line form. The months between December and April tend to be cool, uncrowded, and quiet. But come spring, it's fiesta time, with Seville's Semana Santa (Holy Week) the most moving and multitudinous. April showcases whitewashed Andalusia at its floral best, every patio and facade covered with everything from bougainvillea to honeysuckle.

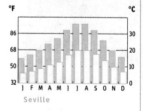

Seville

Getting There & Around

Seville is easily reached by air, although from the U.S. you need to connect in Madrid or London. Domestically, airlines such as Air Europa, Spanair, and Vueling connect Madrid, Barcelona, Valencia, and other major Spanish cities with Seville, Granada, Málaga, and Gibraltar, while Iberia flies from Jerez de la Frontera to Almería, Madrid, Barcelona, Bilbao, Valencia, Ibiza, and Zaragoza.

From Madrid, the best approach to Andalusia is via the high-speed railroad connection, the AVE. In under three hours, the spectacular ride winds from Madrid's Atocha Station through the olive groves and rolling fields of the Castilian countryside to Córdoba and on to Seville. Another option, especially if you plan to go outside Seville, Granada, and Córdoba, is to travel by car. The main road south from Madrid is the A4/E5.

Once in the region, buses are the best way (other than driving) to get around Andalusia. Buses serve most small towns and villages and are faster and more frequent than trains. From Granada, Alsina Gräells serves Alcalá la Real, Almería, Almuñecar, Cazorla, Córdoba, Guadix, Jaén, Lanjarón, Motril, Órgiva, Salobreña, Seville, and Úbeda.

Autocares Bonal operates buses between Granada and the Sierra Nevada. Granada's bus station is on the highway to Jaén. Buses serve Córdoba as well, but the routes are covered by myriad companies. For schedules and details, go to Córdoba's bus station (next to the train station) and inquire with the appropriate company. Alsina Gräells connects Córdoba with Granada, Seville, Cádiz, Badajoz, and Málaga. Alsa long-distance buses connect Seville with Madrid; with Cáceres, Mérida, and Badajoz in Extremadura; and with Córdoba, Granada, Málaga, Ronda, and Huelva in Andalusia. Regional buses connect the towns and villages in this region. The coastal route links Granada, Málaga, and Marbella to Cádiz. From Ronda, buses run to Arcos, Jerez, and Cádiz.

See Andalusia Essentials at the end of this chapter for transportation contact information.

Fiesta Fun

Fiestas, which fill the calendar in Andalusia, can be a great way to combine the themes for which this region is known: flamenco, bullfighting, gastronomy, nature, wines, golf, skiing, and water-based activities.

Cádiz is famous for its January *Carnaval*, while Seville throws the most spectacular fiesta in all of Spain during *Semana Santa* (Holy Week), followed by the decidedly more secular *Feria de Abril*, starring beautiful horses and bountiful bullfights. Córdoba's *Cruces de Mayo* fiesta and its floral patio competition fills the month of May. Early June is the gypsy favorite, the *Romería del Rocío* festival in Huelva, a multitudinous pilgrimage on horseback and carriage to the hermitage of la Virgen del Rocío, Our Lady of the Dew. Early August showcases horse races on the beaches of Sanlúcar de Barrameda, while Málaga's mid-August *feria* (fair) offers top bullfights and flamenco. The second week of October Jaén celebrates the olive harvest.

Planning Your Time

A week in Andalusia should include visits to Córdoba, Seville, and Granada to see, respectively, the Mezquita, the Cathedral and Giralda, and the Alhambra. Two days in each city nearly fills the week, though the extra day would be best spent in Seville, by far Andalusia's most vibrant concentration of art, architecture, culture, and excitement.

A week or more in Seville alone would be well spent, especially during the *Semana Santa* celebration when the city, though crowded, becomes a giant street party. With more time on your hands, Cádiz, Jerez de la Frontera, and Sanlúcar de Barrameda form a three- or four-day cruise through flamenco, sherry, Andalusian equestrian culture, and tapas emporiums.

A three-day trip through the Sierra de Aracena will introduce you to a lovely Atlantic upland, filled with Mediterranean black pigs deliciously fattened on acorns, while the Alpujarra Mountains east of Granada offer anywhere from three days to a week of hiking and trekking opportunities in some of Iberia's highest and wildest reaches. For nature enthusiasts, there's also the highland Cazorla National Park and the wetland Doñana National Park—Andalusia's highest and lowest outdoor treasures. The Pueblos Blancos, whitewashed villages in the mountains, provide a dazzling two-day exploration with a night in Ronda.

WHAT IT COSTS In Euros

	$$$$	$$$	$$	$	¢
RESTAU-RANTS	over €20	€15–€20	€10–€15	€6–€10	under €6
HOTELS	over €180	€100–€180	€60–€100	€40–€60	under €40

Prices are per person for a main course at dinner. Prices are for two people in a standard double room in high season, excluding tax.

By George
Semler

GYPSIES, BULLS, FLAMENCO, HORSES—ANDALUSIA IS the Spain of story and song, the one Washington Irving romanticized in the 18th century. Andalusia is, moreover, at once the least and most surprising part of Spain: least surprising because it lives up to the hype and stereotype that long confused all of Spain with the Andalusian version, and most surprising because it is, at the same time, so much more.

To begin with, five of the eight Andalusian provinces are maritime, with colorful fishing fleets and a wealth of seafood usually associated with the north. Secondly, there are snowcapped mountains and ski resorts in Andalusia, the kind of high sierra resources long thought most readily available in the Alps, or even the Pyrenees, yet the Sierra Nevada is within sight of North Africa. Thirdly, there are wildlife-filled wetlands and highland pine and oak forests rich with game and trout streams, not to mention free-range Iberian pigs. And lastly, there are cities such as Seville that somehow manage to combine all of this natural plenty with the creativity and cosmopolitanism of London or Barcelona.

Andalusia—for 781 years (711–1492) a Moorish empire and named for Al-Andalus (Arabic for "Land of the West")—is where the authentic history and character of the Iberian Peninsula and Spanish culture are most palpably, visibly, audibly, and aromatically apparent.

Though church- and Franco regime–influenced historians endeavor to sell a sanitized, Christians-versus-infidels portrayal of Spanish history, what most distinctively imprinted and defined Spanish culture—and most singularly marked the art, architecture, language, thought, and even the cooking and dining customs of most of the Iberian Peninsula—was the almost eight-century reign of the Arabic-speaking peoples who have become known collectively as the Moors.

All the romantic images of Andalusia, and Spain in general, spring vividly to life in Seville. Spain's fourth-largest city is a cliché of matadors, flamenco, tapas bars, gypsies, geraniums, and strolling guitarists. So tantalizing is this city that many travelers spend their entire Andalusian time here. It's a good start, for an exploration of Andalusia must begin with the cities of Seville, Córdoba, and Granada as the fundamental triangle of interest and identity. But there's so much more than these urban treasures. A more thorough Andalusian experience includes such unforgettable natural settings as Huelva's Sierra de Aracena and Doñana wetlands, Jaén's Parque Natural de Cazorla, Cádiz's *pueblos blancos* (white villages), and Granada's Alpujarras. The smaller cities of Cádiz—the Western world's oldest metropolis, founded by Phoenicians more than 3,000 years ago—and Jerez, with its sherry cellars and purebred horses, have much to recommend themselves as well. And in between the urban and rural attractions is another entire chapter of Andalusian life: the noble towns of the countryside, ranging from Carmona—Alfonso X's "Lucero de España" (Morning Star of Spain)—to Jaén's Renaissance gems of Úbeda and Baeza, Córdoba's Priego de Córdoba, Málaga's Ronda, and Cádiz's Arcos de la Frontera.

EXPLORING ANDALUSIA

ABOUT THE RESTAURANTS

Spaniards drive for miles to sample the succulent seafood of Puerto de Santa María and Sanlúcar de Barrameda and to enjoy *fino* (a dry and light sherry from Jerez) and Manzanilla (a dry and delicate Sanlúcar sherry with a hint of saltiness). Others come to feast on tapas in Seville or Cádiz. The village of Jabugo, in Huelva, is famous for its cured ham from the free-ranging Iberian pig. Look for Spain's top dining delicacy *jamon ibérico de bellota* (Ibérico acorn-fed ham) on the menu. Córdoba's specialties are *salmorejo* (a thick version of gazpacho topped with hard-boiled egg) and *rabo de toro* (bull's-tail or oxtail stew). A glass of *fino de Moriles,* a dry, sherrylike wine from the Montilla-Moriles district, makes a good aperitif.

Moorish dishes such as *bstella* (from the Moorish *bastilla,* a salty-sweet puff pastry with pigeon or other meat, pine nuts, and almonds) and spicy *crema de almendras* (almond cream soup) are not uncommon on Granada menus. *Habas con jamón de Trevélez* (broad beans with ham from the Alpujarran village of Trevélez) is Granada's most famous regional dish, with *tortilla al Sacromonte* (an omelet made of calf's brains, sweetbreads, diced ham, potatoes, and peas) just behind. *Sopa sevillana* (tasty fish and seafood soup made with mayonnaise), surprisingly named for Granada's most direct rival city, is another staple, and *choto albaicinero* (braised kid with garlic, also known as *choto al ajillo*), is also a specialty.

Note that many restaurants are closed on Sunday evenings, and several close for all of August.

ABOUT THE HOTELS

Seville has grand old hotels, such as the Alfonso XIII, and a number of former palaces converted into sumptuous hostelrie. The Parador de Granada, next to the Alhambra, is a magnificent way to enjoy Granada. Hotels on the Alhambra hill, especially the parador, must be reserved long in advance. Lodging establishments in Granada's city center, around the Puerta Real and Acera del Darro, are unbelievably noisy, so ask for a room toward the back. Though Granada has plenty of hotels, it can be difficult to find lodging during peak tourist season—Easter to late October. In Córdoba, several pleasant hotels occupy houses in the old quarter, close to the mosque. Other than during Holy Week and the May Patio Festival, it's easy to find a room in Córdoba, even if you haven't reserved one.

In all three cities, hotels fill up fast for Holy Week and major festivals, so book early—six to eight months in advance. Also note that prices in hotels can rise by at least 50% during fiesta time.

Outside the main cities, bed-and-breakfasts and rural lodgings give good access to the countryside and its rich folk traditions.

Numbers in the text correspond to numbers in the margin and on chapter maps.

SEVILLE

550 km (340 mi) southwest of Madrid.

Seville's whitewashed houses, bright with bougainvillea, its ocher-colored palaces, and its baroque facades have long enchanted both sevillanos and travelers. Lord Byron's well-known line, "Seville is a pleasant city famous for oranges and women," may be true, but is far too tame. Yes, the orange trees are pretty enough, but the fruit is too bitter to eat except as Scottish-made marmalade. As for the women, stroll down the swankier pedestrian shopping streets and you can't fail to notice just how good-looking *everyone* is. Aside from being blessed with even features and flashing dark eyes, sevillanos exude a cool sophistication of style about them that seems more Catalan than Andalusian.

This bustling city of almost 800,000 has its downsides: traffic-choked streets, high unemployment, a notorious petty-crime rate, and at times the kind of impersonal treatment you won't find in the smaller cities of Granada and Córdoba.

EXPLORING SEVILLE

The layout of the historic center of Seville makes exploring easy. The central zone—**Centro**—around the cathedral, the Alcázar, Calle Sierpes, and Plaza Nueva is splendid and monumental, but it's not where you'll find Seville's greatest charm. **El Arenal,** home of the Maestranza bullring, the Teatro de la Maestranza concert hall, and a concentration of picturesque taverns, still buzzes the way it must have when stevedores (ship loaders) loaded and unloaded ships from the New World. Just north of Centro, the medieval Jewish quarter, **Barrio de Santa Cruz,** is a lovely, whitewashed tangle of alleys. The **Barrio de la Macarena** to the west is rich in sights and authentic Seville atmosphere. The fifth and final neighborhood to explore, on the far side of the river Guadalquivir, is in many ways the best of all—**Triana,** the traditional habitat for sailors, Gypsies, bullfighters, and flamenco artists, as well as the main workshop for Seville's renowned ceramics artisans.

CENTRO

❶ **Cathedral.** The cathedral can be described only in superlatives: it's the
★ largest and highest cathedral in Spain, the largest Gothic building in the world, and the world's third-largest church, after St. Peter's in Rome and St. Paul's in London. After Ferdinand III captured Seville from the Moors in 1248, the great mosque begun by Yusuf II in 1171 was reconsecrated to the Virgin Mary and used as a Christian cathedral. But in 1401 the people of Seville decided to erect a new cathedral, one that would equal the glory of their great city. They promptly pulled down the old mosque, leaving only its minaret and outer court, and set about constructing the existing building in just over a century—a remarkable feat for the time.

When visiting, head first for the **Patio de los Naranjos** (Courtyard of Orange Trees), on the northern side and part of the original mosque. The fountain in the center was used for ablutions before people entered the mosque. Near the Puerta del Lagarto (Lizard's Gate), in the corner near the Giralda, try to find the wooden crocodile—thought to have been a gift from the emir of Egypt in 1260 as he sought the hand of the daughter of Alfonso the Wise—and the elephant tusk, found in the ruins of Itálica. The cathedral's exterior, with its rose windows and flying buttresses, is a

> ### A CRAZY CHURCH?
>
> In building Seville's cathedral, the clergy renounced their incomes for the cause, and a member of the chapter is said to have proclaimed, "Let us build a church so large that we shall be held to be insane."

monument to pure Gothic beauty. The dimly illuminated interior, aside from the well-lighted high altar, can be disappointing: Gothic purity has been largely submerged in ornate baroque decoration. Enter the cathedral through the Puerta de la Granada or the Puerta Colorada. In the central nave rises the **Capilla Mayor** (Main Chapel) and its intricately carved altarpiece, begun by a Flemish carver in 1482. This magnificent *retablo* (altarpiece) is the largest in Christendom (65 feet by 43 feet). It depicts some 36 scenes from the life of Christ, with pillars carved with more than 200 figures.

Make your way to the opposite (southern) side of the cathedral to see the **monument to Christopher Columbus.** The great explorer's coffin is borne aloft by the four kings representing the medieval kingdoms of Spain: Castile, León, Aragón, and Navarra. Columbus's son Hernando Colón (1488–1539), is also interred here; his tombstone is inscribed with the words A CASTILLA Y A LEÓN, MUNDO NUEVO DIO COLÓN (to Castile and León, Columbus gave a new world).

Between the elder Columbus's tomb and the Capilla Real, at the eastern end of the central nave, the cathedral's treasures include gold and silver, relics, and other works of art. In the **Sacristía de los Cálices** (Sacristy of the Chalices) look for Martínez Montañés's wood carving *Crucifixion, Merciful Christ*; Valdés Leal's *St. Peter Freed by an Angel*; Zurbarán's *Virgin and Child*; and Goya's *St. Justa and St. Rufina*. The **Sacristía Mayor** (Main Sacristy) holds the keys to the city, which Seville's Moors and Jews presented to their conqueror, Ferdinand III. Finally, in the dome of the **Sala Capitular** (Chapter House), in the cathedral's southeastern corner, is Murillo's *Immaculate Conception,* painted in 1668.

One of the cathedral's highlights, the **Capilla Real** (Royal Chapel), is reserved for prayer and concealed behind a ponderous curtain, but you can duck in if you're quick, quiet, and properly dressed (no shorts or sleeveless tops). To do so, enter from the Puerta de los Palos, on Plaza Virgen de los Reyes (signposted ENTRADA PARA CULTO—entrance for worship). Along the sides of the chapel are the tombs of the wife of 13th century's Ferdinand III, Beatrix of Swabia, and his son Alfonso X, called the Wise; in a silver urn before the high altar rest the relics of Ferdinand III himself, Seville's liberator. Canonized in 1671, he was said to have died from excessive fasting. In the (rarely open) vault below lie the tombs of Ferdinand's descendant Pedro the Cruel and Pedro's mistress, María de Padilla.

Before you duck into the Capilla Real, climb to the top of the **Giralda,** which dominates Seville's skyline. Once the minaret of Seville's great mosque, from which the faithful were summoned to prayer, it was built between 1184 and 1196, just 50 years before the reconquest of Seville. The Christians could not bring themselves to destroy this tower when they tore down the mosque, so they incorporated it into their new cathedral. In 1565–68 they added a lantern and belfry to the old minaret and installed 24 bells, one for each of Seville's 24 parishes and the 24 Christian knights who fought with Ferdinand III in the Reconquest. They also added the bronze statue of Faith, which turned as a weather vane—*el giraldillo,* or "something that turns," thus the name Giralda. To give it a rest after 400 years of wear and tear, the original statue was replaced with a copy in 1997. With its baroque additions, the slender Giralda rises 322 feet. Inside, instead of steps, 35 sloping ramps—wide enough for two horsemen to pass abreast—climb to a viewing platform 230 feet up. It is said that Ferdinand III rode his horse to the top to admire the city he had conquered. If you follow his route, you'll be rewarded with a view of tile roofs and the Guadalquivir shimmering beneath palm-lined banks. ⊠ *Pl. Virgen de los Reyes, Centro* ☎ *95/421–4971* 🎟 *Cathedral and Giralda €7.50* ⊙ *Cathedral Mon.–Sat. 11–5, Sun. 2:30–6, and for mass (8:30, 9, 10, noon, 5).*

❸ **Alcázar.** The Plaza Triunfo forms the entrance to the Mudejar palace
★ built by Pedro I (1350–69) on the site of Seville's former Moorish *alcázar* (fortress). Don't mistake the Alcázar for a genuine Moorish palace, like Granada's Alhambra—it may look like one, and it was indeed designed and built by Moorish workers brought in from Granada, but it was commissioned and paid for by a Christian king more than 100 years after the reconquest of Seville. In its construction, Pedro the Cruel incorporated stones and capitals he pillaged from Valencia, from Córdoba's Medina Azahara, and from Seville itself. The palace serves as the official Seville residence of the king and queen.

You enter the Alcázar through the Puerta del León (Lion's Gate) and the high, fortified walls. You'll first find yourself in a garden courtyard, the **Patio del León** (Courtyard of the Lion). Off to the left are the oldest parts of the building, the 14th-century **Sala de Justicia** (Hall of Justice) and, next to it, the intimate **Patio del Yeso** (Courtyard of Plaster), the only part of the original 12th-century Almohad Alcázar. Cross the **Patio de la Montería** (Courtyard of the Hunt) to Pedro's Mudejar palace, arranged around the beautiful **Patio de las Doncellas** (Court of the Damsels), resplendent with delicately carved stucco. Opening off this patio, the **Salón de Embajadores** (Hall of the Ambassadors), with its cedar cupola of green, red, and gold, is the most sumptuous hall in the palace. It was here that Carlos V married Isabel of Portugal in 1526.

Other royal rooms include the three baths of Pedro's powerful and influential mistress, María de Padilla. María's hold over her royal lover—and his courtiers, too—was so great that legend says they all lined up to drink her bathwater. The **Patio de las Muñecas** (Court of the Dolls) takes its name from two tiny faces carved on the inside of one of its arches, no doubt as a joke on the part of its Moorish cre-

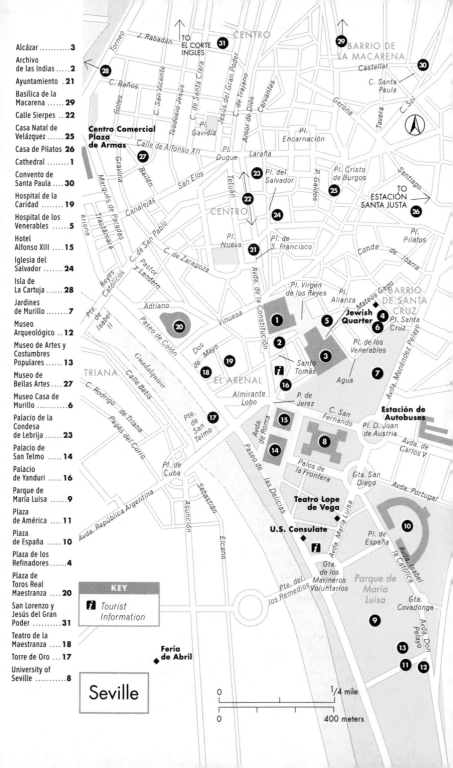

KEY

ℹ *Tourist
Information*

Seville

0   1/4 mile

0   400 meters

ators. Here Pedro reputedly had his half brother, Don Fadrique, slain in 1358; and here, too, he murdered guest Abu Said of Granada for his jewels—one of which is now among England's crown jewels. (The huge ruby came to England by way of the Black Prince—Edward, Prince of Wales [1330–76], eldest son of Edward III. Pedro gave the ruby to him for helping in the revolt of his illegitimate brother in 1367.)

Next is the Renaissance **Palacio de Carlos V** (Palace of Charles V), endowed with a rich collection of Flemish tapestries depicting Carlos's victories at Tunis. Look for the map of Spain: it shows the Iberian Peninsula upside down, as was the custom in Arab mapmaking. There are more goodies—rare clocks, antique furniture, paintings, and tapestries—on the upper floor, in the **Estancias Reales** (Royal Chambers), used by King Juan Carlos I and his family when in town.

In the **gardens,** inhale jasmine and myrtle, wander among terraces and baths, and peer into the well-stocked goldfish pond. From the gardens, a passageway leads to the **Patio de las Banderas** (Court of the Flags), which has a classic view of the Giralda.

Tours depart in the morning only, every half hour in summer and every hour in winter. ⊠ *Pl. del Triunfo, Santa Cruz* ☎ *95/450–2323* ⊕ *www. patronato-alcazarsevilla.es* ⊠ *€7* ⊙ *Tues.–Sat. 9:30–7, Sun. 9:30–5.*

WHERE'S COLUMBUS?

Christopher Columbus knew both triumph and disgrace, yet he found no repose—he died, bitterly disillusioned, in Valladolid in 1506. No one knows for certain where he is buried; he was reportedly laid to rest for the first time in the Dominican Republic and then moved over the years to other locations. His remains are thought to be in Seville's Cathedral.

❷ Archivo de las Indias (Archives of the Indies). Opened in 1785 in the former Lonja (Merchants' Exchange), this dignified Renaissance building stores archives of more than 40,000 documents, including drawings, trade documents, plans of South American towns, even the autographs of Columbus, Magellan, and Cortés. ⊠ *Av. de la Constitución, Santa Cruz* ☎ *95/421–1234* ⊠ *Free* ⊙ *Mon.–Sat. 10–4, Sun. 10–2.*

㉑ Ayuntamiento (City Hall). This Diego de Riaño original, built between 1527 and 1564, is in the heart of Seville's commercial center. A 19th-century, plateresque facade overlooks the Plaza Nueva. The other side, on the Plaza de San Francisco, has Riaño's work. ⊠ *Pl. Nueva 1, Centro* ☎ *95/459–0101* ⊠ *Free* ⊙ *Tours Tues.–Thurs. at 5:30.*

㉒ Calle Sierpes. This is Seville's classy main shopping street. Near the southern end, at No. 85, a plaque marks the spot where the Cárcel Real (Royal Prison) once stood (now a bank). Miguel de Cervantes began writing *Don Quijote* in one of its cells.

㉕ Casa Natal de Velázquez. Spanish painter Diego de Velázquez was born in this *casa de vecinos* (town house shared by several families) in 1599. The house fell into ruin, but was bought in the 1970s by fashion designers Victorio and Lucchino, who restored it for use as their studio. It is not open to the public. ⊠ *Calle Padre Luis María Llop 4, Centro.*

1

A GOOD WALK: SEVILLE

Allow at least a day to tour Seville.

Start with the **cathedral ❶** and a climb up the Giralda, the earlier Moorish mosque's minaret. Down Avenida de la Constitución is the **Archivo de las Indias ❷**, with the walled **Alcázar ❸** fortress and palace behind.

From the Giralda, plunge into the Barrio de Santa Cruz, a tangle of narrow streets and squares that was Seville's medieval Jewish Quarter, near the **Plaza de los Refinadores ❹**. Don't miss the baroque **Hospital de los Venerables ❺**, a hospice with a leafy patio and several notable paintings. On Calle Santa Teresa is the **Museo Casa de Murillo ❻** and the **Jardines de Murillo ❼**. At the far end of the gardens is the **University of Seville ❽**, once the tobacco factory where Bizet's Carmen rolled stogies.

Across the Glorieta de San Diego is the **Parque de María Luisa ❾**, with **Plaza de España ❿** at its northwest end and **Plaza de América ⓫** on its southeast flank, site of the **Museo Arqueológico ⓬**, displaying Roman sculpture and mosaics. Opposite is the **Museo de Artes y Costumbres Populares ⓭**.

Back toward the center along the Paseo de las Delicias on Avenida de Roma is the baroque **Palacio de San Telmo ⓮**, seat of Andalusia's autonomous government, with the neo-Mudéjar **Hotel Alfonso XIII ⓯** behind it. On the north side of Puerta de Jerez is **Palacio de Yanduri ⓰**, birthplace of the Nobel Prize–winning poet Vicente Aleixandre (1898–1984).

South along Calle Almirante Lobo, stands the riverside **Torre de Oro ⓱** opposite the **Teatro de la Maestranza ⓲**. Behind the theater is the **Hospital de la Caridad ⓳**, exhibiting Seville's leading painters. Downriver is the **Plaza de Toros del Real Maestranza ⓴**. Finally, head away from the river toward the Plaza Nueva, in the heart of Seville to see the **Ayuntamiento ㉑**.

North of the town hall is **Calle Sierpes ㉒**, Seville's famous shopping street. Backtrack down Calle Cuna, parallel to Sierpes, to No. 8 to see the **Palacio de la Condesa de Lebrija ㉓**. Continue down Calle Cuna to Plaza del Salvador and the **Iglesia del Salvador ㉔**, a former mosque. Walk up Alcaicería to Plaza de la Alfalfa and along Sales y Ferrer toward Plaza Cristo del Burgos—in an alley off the square is the **Casa Natal de Velázquez ㉕**, the painter's 1599 birthplace. From Plaza Cristo de Burgos follow Descalzos and Caballerizas to the **Casa de Pilatos ㉖**, modeled on Pontius Pilate's house in Jerusalem.

Several Seville visits may require separate trips: if you're an art lover, set aside half a day for the **Museo de Bellas Artes ㉗**. Across the Pasarela de la Cartuja bridge is the island of **La Cartuja ㉘**, a Carthusian monastery now the Andalusian Center of Contemporary Art. To visit the **Basílica de la Macarena ㉙**, home of the beloved Virgen de la Macarena, either walk an hour or taxi from the center.

Other key sites in the Macarena area are the Gothic **Convento de Santa Paula ㉚** and the church of **San Lorenzo y Jesús del Gran Poder ㉛**, where Holy Week floats are on display.

㉔ Iglesia del Salvador. Built between 1671 and 1712, the Church of the Savior stands on the site of Seville's first great mosque, and remains can be seen in the Courtyard of the Orange Trees. Also of note are the sculptures of *Jesus de la Pasión* and St. Christopher by Martínez Montañés. In 2003 archaeologists discovered an 18th-century burial site here; digs are still being carried out with walkways installed to facilitate visits. ⊠ *Pl. del Salvador, Centro* ☎95/459–5405 ⌧€2 *with guide* ⊗ *Weekends only 10–2 and 4–8.*

㉓ Palacio de la Condesa de Lebrija. This lovely palace has three ornate patios, including a spectacular courtyard graced by a Roman mosaic taken from the ruins in Itálica, surrounded by Moorish arches and fine azulejos. The side rooms house a collection of archaeological items. ⊠ *Calle Cuna 8, Centro* ☎95/422–7802 ⌧€7, €4 *for ground floor only* ⊗ *Weekdays 10:30–1:30 and 4:30–7:30, Sat. 10–2.*

BARRIO DE SANTA CRUZ

★ The twisting alleyways and traditional ocher houses add to the tourist charm of this barrio, which is the old **Jewish Quarter.** On some streets, bars alternate with antiques stores and souvenir shops, but most of the quarter is quiet and residential. The Callejón del Agua, beside the wall of the Alcázar's gardens, has some of the quarter's finest mansions and patios. On the Plaza Alianza, pause to enjoy the antiques shops and outdoor cafés. In the Plaza de Doña Elvira, with its fountain and *azulejo* (painted tile) benches, young sevillanos gather to play guitars. Just around the corner from the hospital, at Callejón del Agua and Jope de Rueda, Rossini's Figaro serenaded Rosina on her Plaza Alfaro balcony. Adjoining the Plaza Alfaro, in the Plaza Santa Cruz, flowers and orange trees surround a 17th-century filigree iron cross, which marks the site of the erstwhile church of Santa Cruz, destroyed by Napoléon's General Soult. The painter Murillo was buried here in 1682, though his current resting place is unknown.

㉖ Casa de Pilatos. This palace was built in the first half of the 16th century by the dukes of Tarifa, ancestors of the present owner, the Duke of Medinaceli. It's known as Pilate's House because Don Fadrique, first marquis of Tarifa, allegedly modeled it on Pontius Pilate's house in Jerusalem, where he had gone to on a pilgrimage in 1518. With its fine patio and superb azulejo decorations, the palace is a beautiful blend of Spanish Mudejar and Renaissance architecture. The upstairs apartments, which you can see on a guided tour, have frescoes, paintings, and antique furniture. ⊠ *Pl. Pilatos 1, Santa Cruz* ☎95/422–5298 ⌧€8; *lower floor only, €5* ⊗ *Daily 9–6.*

❺ Hospital de los Venerables. Once a retirement home for priests, this baroque building now has a cultural foundation that organizes on-site art exhibitions. The required 20-minute guided tour takes in a splendid azulejo patio with an interesting sunken fountain (designed to cope with low water pressure) and upstairs gallery, but the hospital's highlight is its chapel, featuring frescoes by Juan Valdés Leal. ⊠ *Pl. de los Venerables 8, Santa Cruz* ☎95/456–2696 ⌧€4.75 *with guide* ⊗ *Daily 10–1:30 and 4–7:30.*

DON JUAN: LOVER OF LEGENDS

Originally brought to literary life by the Spanish Golden Age playwright Fray Gabriel Téllez (better known as Tirso de Molina) in 1630, the figure of Don Juan has been portrayed in countless variations through the years, usually changing to reflect the moral climate of the times. As interpreted by such notables as Molière, Mozart, Goldoni, Byron, and Bernard Shaw, Don Juan has ranged from voluptuous hedonist to helpless victim, fiery lover to coldhearted snake.

The plaques around his effigy in Plaza de los Refinadores can be translated: "Here is Don Juan Tenorio, and no man is his equal. From haughty princess to a humble fisherwoman, there is no female he doesn't desire, nor affair of gold or riches he will not pursue. Seek him ye rivals; surround him players all; may whoever values himself attempt to stop him or be his better at gambling, combat, or love."

7 **Jardines de Murillo** (Murillo Gardens). From the Plaza Santa Cruz you can embark on a stroll through these shady gardens, where you'll find a statue of Christopher Columbus. ⊠*Pl. Santa Cruz, Santa Cruz.*

6 **Museo Casa de Murillo.** Bartolomé Estéban Murillo (1617–82) lived here for a time; there's a small museum here dedicated to the painter's life, but it's open only for special exhibitions. ⊠*C. Santa Teresa 8, Santa Cruz* 🕮*95/422–9415* 🎟*Free* ⊙*Weekdays 10–2 and 4–7.*

16 **Palacio de Yanduri.** Nobel Prize–winning poet Vicente Aleixandre was born here. ⊠ *Puerta de Jerez (north side) s/n, Santa Cruz.*

4 **Plaza de los Refinadores.** This shady square filled with palms and orange trees is separated from the Murillo gardens by an iron grillwork and ringed with stately glass balconies. At its center is a monument to Don Juan Tenorio, the famous Don Juan known for his amorous conquests. ⊠*Santa Cruz.*

EL ARENAL & PARQUE MARIA LUISA

Parque María Luisa is part shady midcity forestland and part monumental esplanade. El Arenal, named for its sandy riverbank soil, was originally a neighborhood of shipbuilders, stevedores, and warehouses. The heart of Arenal lies between the Puente de San Telmo just upstream from the Torre de Oro and the Puente de Isabel II (Puente de Triana). El Arenal extends as far north as Avenida Alfonso XII to include the Museo de Bellas Artes. Between the park and Arenal is the university.

19 **Hospital de la Caridad.** Behind the Maestranza Theater is this almshouse for the sick and elderly, where six paintings by Murillo (1617–82) and two gruesome works by Valdés Leal (1622–90) depicting the Triumph of Death are displayed. The baroque hospital was founded in 1674 by Seville's original Don Juan, Miguel de Mañara (1626–79). A nobleman of licentious character, Mañara was returning one night from a riotous orgy when he had a vision of a funeral procession in which the partly decomposed corpse in the coffin was his own. Accepting the apparition as a sign from God, Mañara renounced his worldly goods and joined the Brotherhood of Charity, whose unsavory task was to collect the bodies of executed criminals and bury them. He devoted his fortune to building this hospital and is buried before the high altar in the chapel. ⊠*C. Temprado 3, El Arenal* 🕾*95/422–3232* 🖃*€5* ⊙*Mon.–Sat. 9–1:30 and 3:30–7:30, Sun. 9–1.*

🚺 **Hotel Alfonso XIII.** Seville's most emblematic hotel, this grand, Mudejar-style building next to the university was built—and named—for the king's visit to the 1929 fair. Nonguests are welcome to admire the gracious Moorish-style courtyard, best appreciated while sipping an ice-cold *fino* (dry sherry) from the adjacent bar. ⊠*Calle San Fernando 2, El Arenal* 🕾*95/491–7000.*

Fodor'sChoice
★

🚺 **Museo Arqueológico** (Museum of Archaeology). This fine Renaissance-style building has artifacts from Phoenician, Tartessian, Greek, Carthaginian, Iberian, Roman, and medieval times. Displays include marble statues and mosaics from the Roman excavations at Itálica and a faithful replica of the fabulous Carambolo treasure found on a hillside outside Seville in 1958: 21 pieces of jewelry, all 24-karat gold, dating from the 7th and 6th centuries BC. ⊠*Pl. de América, El Arenal/Porvenir* 🕾*95/423–2401* 🖃*€1.50, free for EU citizens* ⊙*Tues. 2:30–8:30, Wed.–Sat. 9–8:30, Sun. 9–2:30.*

🚺 **Museo de Artes y Costumbres Populares** (Museum of Folklore). The Mudejar pavilion opposite the Museum of Archaeology is the site of this museum of mainly 19th- and 20th-century Spanish folklore. The first floor has re-creations of a forge, a bakery, a wine press, a tanner's shop, and a pottery studio. Upstairs, exhibits include 18th- and 19th-century court dress, stunning regional folk costumes, carriages, and musical instruments. ⊠*Pl. de América 3, El Arenal/Porvenir* 🕾*95/423–2576* 🖃*€1.50, free for EU citizens* ⊙*Tues. 3–8, Wed.–Sat. 9–8, Sun. 9–2.*

🚺 **Museo de Bellas Artes** (Museum of Fine Arts). This museum is second only to Madrid's Prado in Spanish art. It's in the former convent of La Merced Calzada, most of which dates from the 17th century. The collection includes Murillo, Zurbarán, Valdés Leal, and El Greco; outstanding examples of Seville Gothic art; and baroque religious sculptures in wood (a quintessentially Andalusian art form). In the rooms dedicated to Sevillian art of the 19th and 20th centuries, look for Gonzalo Bilbao's *Las Cigarreras*, a group portrait of Seville's famous cigar makers. ⊠*Pl. del Museo 9, El Arenal/Porvenir* 🕾*95/478–6482* ⊕*www.museosdeandalucia.es* 🖃*€1.50, free for EU citizens* ⊙*Tues. 2:30–8:15, Wed.–Sat. 9–8:15, Sun. 9–2:15.*

Fodor'sChoice
★

🚺 **Palacio de San Telmo.** This splendid baroque palace is largely the work of architect Leonardo de Figueroa. Built between 1682 and 1796, it was first a naval academy and then the residence of the Bourbon dukes of Montpensier, during which time it outshone Madrid's royal court for sheer brilliance. The palace gardens are now the Parque de María Luisa, and the building itself is the seat of the Andalusian government. The main portal, vintage 1734, is a superb example of the fanciful

Churrigueresque style. ■TIP→ **Call in advance if you want to arrange a visit.** ⊠ *Av. de Roma, El Arenal* ☎95/503–5500.

9 **Parque de María Luisa.** Formerly the garden of the Palacio de San Telmo, the park is a blend of formal design and wild vegetation. In the burst of development that gripped Seville in the 1920s, it was redesigned for the 1929 Exhibition, and the impressive villas you see now are the fair's remaining pavilions, many of them consulates or schools. Note the statue of El Cid by Rodrigo Díaz de Vivar (1043–99), who fought both for and against the Muslim rulers during the Reconquest. ⊠ *Main entrance: Glorieta San Diego, El Arenal.*

11 **Plaza de América.** Walk to the south end of the Parque de María Luisa, past the Isla de los Patos (Island of Ducks), to find this plaza, typically carpeted in white doves and designed by Aníbal González. It's a blaze of color, with flowers, shrubs, ornamental stairways, and fountains tiled in yellow, blue, and ocher. The three impressive buildings surrounding the square—in neo-Mudejar, Gothic, and Renaissance styles—were built by González for the 1929 fair. Two of them now house Seville's museums of archaeology and folklore.

10 **Plaza de España.** This grandiose half-moon of buildings on the eastern edge of the Parque de María Luisa was Spain's centerpiece pavilion at the 1929 Exhibition. The brightly colored azulejo pictures represent the 50 provinces of Spain, while the four bridges symbolize the medieval kingdoms of the Iberian Peninsula. You can rent small boats for rowing along the arc-shape canal.

20 **Plaza de Toros Real Maestranza** (Royal Maestranza Bullring). Sevillanos have spent many a thrilling Sunday afternoon in this bullring, built between 1760 and 1763. Painted a deep ocher, the stadium is the one of the oldest and loveliest *plazas de toros* in Spain. An adjoining museum has prints and photos. ⊠ *Paseo de Colón 12, El Arenal* ☎95/422–4577 ⊑ *Plaza and bullfighting museum €5 with English-speaking guide* ⊙ *Daily 9:30–7 (bullfighting days 9:30–3).*

18 **Teatro de la Maestranza** (Maestranza Theater). Opposite the Torre de Oro is Seville's opera house. One of Europe's leading halls, the Maestranza presents opera, zarzuela (Spanish light opera), classical music, and jazz. ⊠ *Paseo de Colón 22, El Arenal* ☎95/422–6573 or 95/422–3344 ⊕ *www.teatromaestranza.com.*

17 **Torre de Oro** (Tower of Gold). A 12-sided tower on the banks of the Guadalquivir built by the Moors in 1220 to complete the city's ramparts, it served to close off the harbor when a chain was stretched across the river from its base to another tower on the opposite bank. In 1248, Admiral Ramón de Bonifaz broke through this barrier, and Ferdinand III captured Seville. The tower houses a small naval museum. ⊠ *Paseo Alcalde Marqués de Contadero s/n, El Arenal* ☎95/422–2419 ⊑ €1 ⊙ *Tues.–Fri. 10–2, Sat.–Sun. 11–2.*

8 **University of Seville.** At the far end of the Jardines de Murillo, opposite Calle San Fernando, stands what used to be the **Real Fábrica de Tabacos** (Royal Tobacco Factory). Built in the mid-1700s, the fac-

Seville's Long and Noble History

Conquered in 205 BC by the Romans, Seville gave the world two great emperors, Trajan and Hadrian. The Moors held Seville for more than 500 years and left it one of their greatest works of architecture—the iconic Giralda tower that served as the minaret over the main city mosque. Saint King Ferdinand (Fernando III) lies enshrined in the glorious cathedral; and his rather less saintly descendant, Pedro the Cruel, builder of the Alcázar, is buried here as well.

Seville is justly proud of its literary and artistic associations. The painters Diego Rodríguez de Silva Velázquez (1599–1660) and Bartolomé Estéban Murillo (1617–82) were sons of Seville, as were the poets Gustavo Adolfo Bécquer (1836–70), Antonio Machado (1875–1939), and Nobel Prize–winner Vicente Aleixandre (1898–1984). The tale of the ingenious knight of La Mancha was begun in a Seville jail—Don Quixote's creator, Miguel de Cervantes, twice languished in a debtors' prison. Tirso de Molina's Don Juan seduced in Seville's mansions, and Rossini's barber, Figaro, was married in the Barrio de Santa Cruz. It was at the old tobacco factory where Bizet's sultry Carmen first met Don José.

tory employed some 3,000 *cigarreras* (female cigar makers) less than a century later, including Bizet's opera heroine *Carmen,* who reputedly rolled her cigars on her thigh. ✉*C. San Fernando s/n, Parque Maria Luisa* ☎*95/455–1000* 💲*Free* ⊙*Weekdays 9–8:30.*

BARRIO DE LA MACARENA
This immense neighborhood covers the entire northern half of historic Seville and deserves to be walked not once but many times. Most of the best churches, convents, markets, and squares are concentrated around the center of this barrio in an area delimited by the Arab ramparts to the north, the Alameda de Hercules to the west, the Santa Catalina church to the south, and the Convento de Santa Paula to the east. The area between the Alameda de Hercules and the Guadalquivir is known to locals as the Barrio de San Lorenzo, a Barrio de la Macarena subdivision that's ideal for an evening of tapas grazing.

㉙ Basílica de la Macarena. This church holds Seville's most revered image, the Virgin of Hope—better known as La Macarena. Bedecked with candles and carnations, her cheeks streaming with glass tears, the Macarena steals the show at the procession on Holy Thursday, the highlight of Seville's Holy Week pageant. She's the patron of gypsies and the protector of the matador. So great are her charms that young Sevillian bullfighter Joselito spent half his personal fortune buying her emeralds. When he was killed in the ring in 1920, the Macarena was dressed in widow's weeds for a month. There's a small adjacent museum devoted to her costumes and jewels. ✉*C. Bécquer 1, La Macarena* ☎*95/490–1800* 💲*Basilica free, museum €3.50* ⊙*Basilica daily 9:30–2 and 5–9, museum daily 9:30–2 and 5–8.*

30 **Convento de Santa Paula.** This 15th-
Fodor'sChoice century Gothic convent has a fine
★ facade and portico, with ceramic
decoration by Nicolaso Pisano.
The chapel has some beautiful
azulejos and sculptures by Martínez Montañés. There's a small
museum and shop selling delicious
cakes and jams made by the nuns.
⊠ *C. Santa Paula 11, La Macarena*
☎ *95/453–6330* ⬛ *€2* ☉ *Tues.–
Sun. 10:30–1.*

31 **San Lorenzo y Jesús del Gran Poder.**
This 17th-century church has many
fine works by such artists as Mon-
tañés and Pacheco, but its outstand-
ing piece is Juan de Mesa's *Jesús del
Gran Poder* (*Christ Omnipotent*).
⊠ *C. Jesús del Gran Poder, La
Macarena* ☎ *95/438–4558* ⬛ *Free* ☉ *Daily 8–1:30 and 6–9.*

> **FIESTA TIME!**
>
> Seville's color and vivacity is most intense during Semana Santa, when lacerated Christs and bejeweled, weeping Mary statues are paraded through town on floats borne by often barefooted penitents. A week later, sevillanos throw April Fair, featuring midday horse parades with men in broad-brim hats and Andalusian riding gear astride prancing steeds, and women in ruffled dresses riding sidesaddle behind them. Bullfights, fireworks, and all-night singing and dancing complete the spectacle.

TRIANA
Across the Guadalquivir from central Seville, Triana used to be the gypsy quarter. Today it has a tranquil, neighborly feel by day, while its atmospheric clubs and flamenco bars throb at night. Enter Triana by the **Puente Isabel II** (better known as the Puente de Triana), built in 1852, the first bridge to connect the city's two sections. Walk across Plaza Altozano up Calle Jacinto and turn right at **Calle Alfarería** (Pottery Street) to see a slew of pottery stores and workshops. Return to Plaza Altozano and walk down Calle Pureza as far as the small **Capilla de los Marineros** (Seamen's Chapel), home to a venerated statue of Mary called the Esperanza de Triana. Head back toward the river and **Calle Betis** for some of the city's most colorful bars, clubs, and restaurants.

28 **Isla de La Cartuja.** Named after its 14th-century Carthusian monas-
☪ tery, this island, across the river from northern Seville, was the site of the decennial Universal Exposition (Expo) in 1992. The island has the Teatro Central, used for concerts and plays; Parque del Alamillo, Seville's largest and least-known park; and the Estadio Olímpico, a 60,000-seat covered stadium. The best way to get to La Cartuja is by walking across one or both (one each way) of the superb Santiago Cala-trava bridges spanning the Guadalquivir. The Puente de la Barqueta crosses to La Cartuja while, downstream, the Puente del Alamillo con-nects la Isla Mágica with Seville. Buses C1 and C2 also serve La Car-tuja. ⊠ *Av. Americo Vespucci 2, La Cartuja* ☎ *95/503–7070* ⬛ *€3.30* ☉ *Daily 10–8.*

The eastern shore holds the **Isla Mágica,** (☎ *902/161716* ⊕ *www. islamagica.es* ⬛ *Apr. and May €21, June–Oct. €23.50* ☉ *Apr. and May, weekends 11* AM*–midnight; June–Oct., daily 11* AM*–midnight*) with 14 attractions, including the hair-raising Jaguar roller coaster. The

14th century **Monasterio de Santa María de las Cuevas** (Monasterio de La Cartuja, ⊠*Isla de la Cartuja* ☎*95/503–7070* €3, *free Tues. for EU citizens* ☉*Tues.–Fri. 10–7:30, Sat. 11–8, Sun. 10–2:30*) was regularly visited by Christopher Columbus, who was buried here for a few years. Part of the building houses the Centro Andaluz de Arte Contemporáneo, which has an absorbing collection of contemporary art.

WHERE TO STAY & EAT

TAPAS BARS

Bar Estrella. This prizewinning tapas emporium does excellent renditions of everything from *paté de esparragos trigueros* (wild asparagus paté) to *fabas con pringá* (stewed broad beans). ⊠*C. Estrella 3, Santa Cruz* ☎*95/422–7535*.

Bar Gran Tino. Named for the giant wooden wine cask that once dominated the bar, this busy spot on the funky Plaza Alfalfa serves an array of tapas, including *calamares fritos* (fried squid) and wedges of crumbly Manchego cheese. ⊠*Pl. Alfalfa 2, Centro* ☎*95/421–0883*.

Bar Rincón San Eloy. This place is always heaving with a happy mix of shoppers and students. You can buy stacked mini-sandwiches, as well as tapas and sherry from the barrel. If no tables are left, grab a pew on the tiled steps. ⊠*Calle San Eloy 2, Centro* ☎*95/421–8079*.

Bodega Santa Cruz. A young college crowd frequents this spot in Seville's famous former Jewish quarter. There's an excellent selection of traditional tapas, including a mini-tortilla. Your bill is chalked up at your place at the bar. ⊠*Calle Mateo Gago 8, Santa Cruz* ☎*95/421–3246*.

Bodega San Jose. At this funky old 1893 bar decorated with faded Semana Santa posters and shelves of dusty bottles, the wine and sherry is served straight from the barrel and accompanied by *gambas* (prawns), the house specialty, prepared in several delicious ways. ⊠*Calle Adriano 10, El Arenal* ☎*95/422–4105*.

El Rinconcillo. Founded in 1670, this lovely spot serves a classic selection of dishes, such as the *caldereta de venado* (venison stew), a superb *salmorejo* (thick gazpacho-style soup), and *espinacas con garbanzos* (creamed spinach with chickpeas). The views of the Iglesia de Santa Catalina out the front window are unbeatable. Your bill is chalked up on the wooden counters. ⊠*C. Gerona 40, La Macarena* ☎*95/422–3183* ☉*Closed Wed.*

WHERE TO EAT

$$$$ ✕**Egaña-Oriza.** Owner José Mari Egaña is Basque, but he is considered one of the fathers of modern Andalusian cooking. The restaurant, ★   on the edge of the Murillo Gardens opposite the university, has spare contemporary decor with high ceilings and wall-to-wall windows. The menu might include *lomos de lubina con salsa de erizos de mar* (sea bass with sea urchin sauce) or *solomillo con foie natural y salsa de ciruelas* (fillet steak with foie gras and plum sauce). On the downside, the service can be slow. You can always drop into the adjoining Bar España for an hors d'oeuvre tapa such as stuffed mussels with béchamel sauce. ⊠*San Fernando 41, Santa Cruz Jardines de Murillo* ☎*95/422–7211* ▭*AE, DC, MC, V* ☉*Closed Sun. and Aug. No lunch Sat.*

$$$-$$$$ ✕ **La Albahaca.** Overlooking one of Seville's prettiest small plazas in the
★ Barrio de Santa Cruz, this wonderful old family manor house was built
by the celebrated architect Juan Talavera as a home for his own family;
inside, four dining rooms are decorated with tiles, antique oil paintings,
and leafy plants. There's a Basque twist to many of the dishes—con-
sider the *lubina al horno con berenjenas y yogur al cardamomo* (baked
sea bass with eggplant in a yogurt-and-cardamom sauce) or *foie de
oca salteado* (lightly sautéed goose liver) followed by the delicious fig
mousse. There's an excellent €27 daily menu. ⊠*Pl. Santa Cruz 12,
Santa Cruz* ☎*95/422–0714* ⌥*Reservations essential* ▭*AE, DC, MC,
V* ⊘*Closed Sun.*

$$$-$$$$ ✕ **Poncio.** In the three small, comfortable dining rooms, diners enjoy
Fodor's Choice dishes based on Andalusian tradition with a French flair. Chef Willy
★ Moya trained in Paris and blends local and cosmopolitan cuisine
flawlessly. Try the *salmorejo encapotado* (thick, garlic-laden gazpa-
cho topped with diced egg and ham), or the *besugo con gambitas* (sea
bream with shrimp). Desserts include a delectable version of French
toast, showered with slivered almonds and garnished with rich cinna-
mon ice cream. The restaurant is around the corner from the Iglesia de
Santa Ana, Seville's oldest church. ⊠*C. Victoria 8, Triana* ☎*95/434–
0010* ▭*AE, DC, MC, V* ⊘*Closed Sun. No dinner Mon.*

$$-$$$$ ✕ **Becerrita.** The affable Jesus Becerra runs this cozy—verging on
cramped—establishment. Diligent service and tasty modern treatments
of such classic Spanish dishes as *lomo de cordero a la miel* (loin of
lamb in a honey sauce) and *rape con salsa de manzana* (monk fish
with applesauce) have won the favor of sevillanos. ⊠*Calle Recaredo
9, Santa Cruz/Santa Catalina* ☎*95/441–2057* ⊕*www.becerrita.com*
⌥*Reservations essential* ▭*AE, MC, V* ⊘*No dinner Sun. and Aug.*

$$-$$$$ ✕ **Enrique Becerra.** Excellent tapas and a lively bar await at this res-
★ taurant run by the fifth generation of a family of celebrated restau-
rateurs (Enrique's brother Jesus owns Becerrita). The menu focuses
on traditional, home-cooked Andalusian dishes, such as *pez espada
al amontillado* (swordfish cooked in dark sherry) and *cordero a la
miel con espinacas* (honey-glazed lamb stuffed with spinach and pine
nuts). Don't miss the cumin seed–laced *espinacas con garbanzos* (spin-
ach with chickpeas). ⊠*Calle Gamazo 2, El Arenal* ☎*95/421–3049*
▭*AE, DC, MC, V* ⊘*Closed Sun. and last 2 wks of July.*

$$$ ✕ **San Marco.** In a 17th-century palace in the shopping district, this
Italian restaurant has original frescoes, a gracious patio, and a menu
that combines Italian, French, and Andalusian cuisine. Pasta dishes,
such as ravioli stuffed with shrimp and pesto sauce, are notable. The
restaurant has four satellites, but this one, the original, is the most
charming. ⊠*Calle Cuna 6, Centro* ☎*95/421–2440* ⌥*Reservations
essential* ▭*AE, DC, MC, V.*

$$-$$$ ✕ **La Isla.** Using fresh fish from Cádiz and Huelva, La Isla serves won-
derful *parrillada de mariscos y pescados*, a fish and seafood grill for
two people. *Zarzuela,* the Catalan seafood stew, is another favorite,
and simple meat dishes are also served. The dining room and tapas bar
are adorned with traditional Sevillano tiles. ⊠*Calle Arfe 25, El Arenal*
☎*95/421–2631* ▭*AE, DC, MC, V* ⊘*Closed Aug.*

$-$$$ ✕**El Corral del Agua.** Abutting the outer walls of the Alcázar on a narrow pedestrian street in the Santa Cruz neighborhood is a restored 18th-century palace, with a patio filled with geraniums and a central fountain. Andalusian specialties, such as *cola de toro al estilo de Sevilla* (Seville-style bull's tail), are prepared with contemporary flair. ⊠*Callejón del Agua 6, Santa Cruz* ☎*95/422–4841* ⊟*AE, DC, MC, V* ⊘*Closed Sun. and Jan. and Feb.*

$-$$$ ✕**Modesto.** The downstairs is a lively, crowded tapas bar; upstairs is the dining room, which has stucco walls decorated with blue-and-white tiles. The house specialty is a crisp *fritura Modesto* (a selection of small fish fried in top-quality olive oil); another excellent choice is the *cazuela al Tío Diego* (Uncle Diego's casserole—ham, mushrooms, and shrimp simmering in an earthenware dish). You can dine cheaply here, but beware: *mariscos* (shellfish) take the bill to another level. ⊠*Calle Cano y Cueto 5, Santa Cruz* ☎*95/441–6811* ⊟*AE, DC, MC, V.*

$-$$ ✕**Habanita.** A vegetarian restaurant in the buzzing Alfalfa barrio is a rarity. The vast menu emphasizes Mediterranean and Cuban fare. Dishes might include yucca with garlic, black beans with rice, tamales, and strict vegan fare. There are girth-expanding desserts and a good wine list. Some meat dishes are available. ⊠*Calle Golfo 3, Santa Cruz/Alfalfa* ☎*606/716456* ⊟*MC, V* ⊘*No dinner Sun.*

$-$$ ✕**Mesón Don Raimundo.** Tucked into an alleyway off Calle Argote de Molina near the cathedral, this former 17th-century convent with its eclectic decor of religious artifacts tends to attract the tour buses. Still, it's worth the trip for its generous portions of traditional fare, including Mozarab-style wild duck (braised in sherry) and solomillo *a la castellana* (Castilian-style steak). Start with the crisp *tortillitas de camarones* (batter-fried shrimp pancakes) or stuffed peppers. ⊠*Argote de Molina 26, Santa Cruz* ☎*95/422–3355* ⊟*AE, DC, MC, V.*

WHERE TO STAY

$$$$ ✕▣**El Bulli Hotel Hacienda Benazuza.** This five-star luxury hotel is in a
★ rambling country palace near Sanlúcar la Mayor, 15 km (9 mi) outside Seville off the main road to Huelva. Surrounded by olive and orange trees and in a courtyard with towering palms, the building incorporates an 18th-century church. The interior has clay-tile floors and ocher walls. The acclaimed restaurant, La Alquería, serves Spanish and international dishes, creative variations on the recipes of superstar Catalan chef (and hotel owner) Ferrán Adrià. ⊠*C. Virgen de las Nieves, Sanlúcar la Mayor 41800* ☎*95/570–3344* 🖷*95/570–3410* ⊕*www.elbullihotel.com* ⇗*41 rooms, 3 suites* ⚙*In-room: public Wi-Fi. In-hotel: 2 restaurants, tennis court, pool, Wi-Fi, public Internet, parking (no fee), some pets allowed* ⊟*AE, DC, MC, V* ⊘*Closed Jan.*

$$$$ ▣**Alfonso XIII.** Inaugurated by King Alfonso XIII in 1929, this grand
Fodor'sChoice hotel is a splendid, historical Mudejar-style palace, built around a huge
★ central patio and surrounded by ornate brick arches. The public rooms have marble floors, wood-panel ceilings, heavy Moorish lamps, stained glass, and ceramic tiles in the typical Seville colors. There is a Spanish and Japanese restaurant, as well as an elegant bar. ⊠*San Fernando 2, El Arenal, 41004* ☎*95/491–7000* 🖷*95/491–7099* ⊕*www.westin.*

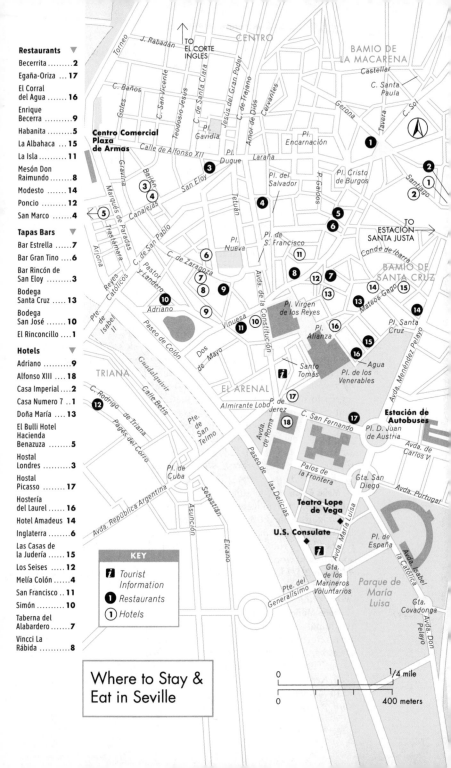

Restaurants ▼

Becerrita **2**
Egaña-Oriza ... **17**
El Corral
del Agua **16**
Enrique
Becerra **9**
Habanita **5**
La Albahaca ... **15**
La Isla **11**
Mesón Don
Raimundo **8**
Modesto **14**
Poncio **12**
San Marco **4**

Tapas Bars ▼

Bar Estrella **7**
Bar Gran Tino **6**
Bar Rincón de
San Eloy **3**
Bodega
Santa Cruz **13**
Bodega
San José **10**
El Rinconcillo **1**

Hotels ▼

Adriano **9**
Alfonso XIII **18**
Casa Imperial **2**
Casa Numero 7 ..**1**
Doña María **13**
El Bulli Hotel
Hacienda
Benazuza **5**
Hostal
Londres **3**
Hostal
Picasso **17**
Hostería
del Laurel **16**
Hotel Amadeus **14**
Inglaterra **6**
Las Casas de
la Judería **15**
Los Seises **12**
Melía Colón **4**
San Francisco .. **11**
Simón **10**
Taberna del
Alabardero **7**
Vincci La
Rábida **8**

Where to Stay & Eat in Seville

KEY

🛈 Tourist Information
❶ Restaurants
① Hotels

com/hotelalfonso 🛏127 *rooms, 19 suites* ☆*In-room: Wi-Fi. In-hotel: 2 restaurants, bar, Wi-Fi, pool, parking (fee)* ⊟*AE, DC, MC, V.*

$$$$ ☷**Casa Imperial.** Adjoining the Casa de Pilatos, and once connected to it via underground tunnel, this 16th-century palace is the former residence of the marquis of Tarifa. Public areas surround four plant-filled patios. The 24 suites are approached by a stairway adorned with trompe l'oeil tiles. Each suite is different—one has a private courtyard with a trickling fountain—but all have kitchenettes. There's a roof terrace with gorgeous views. ⊠*Calle Imperial 29, Santa Cruz/ Santa Catalina, 41003* ☎*95/450–0300* 🖷*95/450–0330* ⊕*www.casa imperial.com* 🛏24 *suites* ☆*In-room: kitchen, Wi-Fi. In-hotel: restaurant, bar, public Wi-Fi, parking (no fee)* ⊟*AE, DC, MC, V* ⦿❘*BP.*

$$$$ ☷**Casa Numero 7.** Voted by *Tatler* magazine as Best Small Hotel in Europe, this exquisite mansion-hotel is owned by a director of González Byass, the famous sherry producer. Dating from 1847, the interior retains a homey, lived-in feel with family-owned antiques, original oil paintings, and plush furnishings throughout. Each room is individually designed, and there is an elegant salon with fireplace and comfy chairs. The roof terrace has Giralda views, and breakfast is excellent, with fluffy scrambled eggs an agreeable option. ⊠*C. Virgenes 7, Santa Cruz, 41003* ☎*95/422–1581* 🖷*95/421–4527* ⊕*www.casanumero7. com* 🛏6 *rooms* ☆*In-hotel: bar* ⊟*AE, V* ⦿❘*BP.*

$$$$ ☷**Los Seises.** This hotel is in a section of Seville's 16th-century Palacio Episcopal (Bishop's Palace), and the combination of modern and ★ Renaissance architecture is striking: Room 219, for instance, is divided by a 16th-century brick archway, and breakfast (for an extra €16) is served in the old chapel. A pit in the center of the basement restaurant reveals the building's foundations and some archaeological finds, including a Roman mosaic. The rooftop pool and summer restaurant are in full view of the Giralda. ⊠*Calle Segovias 6, Santa Cruz, 41004* ☎*95/422–9495* 🖷*95/422–4334* ⊕*www.hotellosseises.com* 🛏42 *rooms, 2 suites* ☆*In-room: Wi-Fi. In-hotel: restaurant, pool, public Wi-Fi, parking (fee)* ⊟*AE, DC, MC, V* ⦿❘*BP.*

$$$$ ☷**Meliá Colón.** A white-marble staircase leads up to the central lobby, which has a magnificent stained-glass dome and crystal candelabra. Downstairs is the El Burladero restaurant, with a bullfight theme, and La Tasca tavern, packed midday with slick local businessmen. The old-fashioned rooms are elegantly furnished with silk drapes and bedspreads, and wood fittings. ⊠*Calle Canalejas 1, El Arenal/San Vicente, 41001* ☎*95/450–5599* 🖷*95/422–0938* ⊕*www.solmelia.com* 🛏204 *rooms, 14 suites* ☆*In-room: public Wi-Fi. In-hotel: restaurant, bar, Wi-Fi, public Internet* ⊟*AE, DC, MC, V* ⦿❘*BP.*

$$$–$$$$ ☷**Doña María.** In a 14th-century former mansion, one of Seville's most charmingly old-fashioned hotels is near the cathedral. Some rooms have been refurbished in minimalist contemporary chic, but most are more ornate and furnished with antiques. Bathrooms throughout are spacious. There's also a rooftop pool with a view of the Giralda. ⊠*Calle Don Remondo 19, Santa Cruz, 41004* ☎*95/422–4990* 🖷*95/421– 9546* ⊕*www.hdmaria.com* 🛏64 *rooms* ☆*In-room: Wi-Fi. In-hotel: pool, public Wi-Fi* ⊟*AE, DC, MC, V.*

1

$$$–$$$$ ▣ **Inglaterra.** This longtime favorite with British visitors to Seville is elegantly run by third generation owner Manolo Otero. The downstairs Trinity pub is a fine hotel bar in the grand tradition, while Galería, the gourmet restaurant upstairs in the mezzanine serves traditional Seville cuisine with creative and contemporary touches. The rooms are traditionally decorated but extremely comfortable. ✉*Pl. Nueva 7, Centro, 41001* ☎*95/422–4970* 🖷*95/456–1336* ⊕*www.hotelinglaterra.es* ⤶*94 rooms* ♿*In-room: Wi-Fi* ▭*AE, DC, MC, V.*

$$$–$$$$ ▣ **Vincci La Rábida.** Rooms in this 18th-century palace are elegant yet traditional, with terra-cotta tiling and wrought-iron bed frames with en suite marble bathrooms. The lounge areas and stunning central patio are sumptuous, and the large sun terrace—complete with outdoor hot tub—has superb city and cathedral views. ✉*Castelar 24, Santa Cruz, 41001* ☎*95/450–1280* 🖷*95/421–6600* ⊕*www.vinccihoteles.com* ⤶*79 rooms, 2 suites* ♿*In-room: dial-up, Wi-Fi. In-hotel: restaurant, public Wi-Fi, parking (fee)* ▭*AE, MC, V.*

$$$ ▣ **Hostería del Laurel.** A small tree-lined square in the heart of the Barrio de Santa Cruz is an unbeatable position for this hotel. It's known for its bodega, which is mentioned in Zorilla's popular 19th-century play *Don Juan Tenorio*, as well as for the adjoining restaurant, which specializes in traditional local cuisine, such as *pollo a la Sevillana* (chicken in a rich gravy sauce) and *espinacas* (spinach) and squid in garlic. The rooms are a relatively recent addition, spread between two floors. They are spotlessly clean and simply furnished. ✉*Pl. de los Venerables 5, Santa Cruz, 41004* ☎*95/422–0295* 🖷*95/421–0450* ⊕*www.hosteriadellaurel.com* ⤶*21 rooms* ♿*In-hotel: restaurant, bar* ▭*MC, V* ⦿*BP.*

$$$ ▣ **Las Casas de la Judería.** This labyrinthine hotel occupies three of the barrio's old palaces, each arranged around inner courtyards. The spacious guest rooms are painted in subdued pastel colors and decorated with prints of Seville. The hotel is tucked into a passageway off the Plaza Santa María. ✉*Callejón de Dos Hermanas 7, Santa Cruz, 41004* ☎*95/441–5150* 🖷*95/442–2170* ⊕*www.casasypalacios.com* ⤶*103 rooms, 3 suites* ♿*In-room: dial-up. In-hotel: restaurant, bar, parking (fee)* ▭*AE, DC, MC, V.*

$$$ ✕▣ **Taberna del Alabardero.** Near the Plaza Nueva, this highly regarded mansion-hotel and restaurant is a superb mid-Seville retreat in a traditional setting. A courtyard and bar precede the dining area, which is decorated in Sevillian tiles. Modern dishes include *bacalao a la parrilla triija de hongos sobre pil-pil y aceite de jamón* (grilled cod with mushrooms in a spicy chili-and-ham sauce). ✉*Calle Zaragoza 20, El Arenal* ☎*95/456–0637* 🖷*95/456–3666* ⊕*www.tabernadelalabardero.com* ⤶*7 rooms* ▭*AE, DC, MC, V* ⊘*Closed Aug.*

$$–$$$ ▣ **Adriano.** Opened in 2004 in an 18th-century mansion, this small hotel has good-size rooms centered around three patios. A short stroll from the cathedral, the river, and the sophisticated shops on Calle Sierpes, Adriano has rooms decorated in a straightforward style with striped burgundy-and-cream fabrics and shiny marble on the floors and in the bathroom. There's a bar downstairs, just one of many on the street. ✉*Calle Adriano 12, El Arenal, 41001* ☎*95/4293800* ⊕*www.hoteladriano.net* ⤶*34 rooms* ♿*In-hotel: bar, parking (fee).*

$$–$$$ ⚆ **Hotel Amadeus.** With pianos in the soundproof rooms and a music
★ room off the central patio and lobby, this acoustical oasis is ideal for touring professional musicians and music fans in general. Classical concerts are regularly held on the patio. The 18th-century manor house has been equipped with such modern amenities as in-room data ports and a small glass-wall elevator that whips quietly up and down a corner of the central patio. You can enjoy breakfast (an extra €7) on the roof terrace overlooking the Judería and Giralda. ⊠ *Calle Farnesio 6, Santa Cruz, 41004* ☎ *95/450–1443* 🖷 *95/450–0019* ⊕ *www.hotelamadeus sevilla.com* ⏎ *14 rooms* 👌 *In-room: ethernet. In-hotel: restaurant, parking (fee)* ☰ *AE, DC, MC, V.*

$$ ⚆ **Hostal Londres.** Near the Museo de Bellas Artes and in the thick of the lively Barrio de San Lorenzo nightlife, this simple, comfortable place is a real find. Rooms are plain but clean and cheery, and some have balconies. ⊠ *San Pedro Mártir 1, El Arenal, 41001* ☎ *95/421–2896* 🖷 *95/450–3830* ⏎ *22 rooms* ☰ *MC, V.*

$$ ⚆ **Hostal Picasso.** You can't beat this situation for the price, within confessional distance of the cathedral and a few minutes' walk from the shopping district in the center of town and the Barrio de Santa Cruz. In this traditional building festooned with potted plants, the rooms vary in size but they are all bright and tidy, with sunny yellow paintwork. Several have small balconies. The same management owns the nearby Van Gogh, of comparable quality and price. ⊠ *C. San Gregorio 1, El Arenal, 41001* ☎ *95/4210864* ⊕ *www.grupo-piramide.com* ⏎ *17 rooms* ☰ *AE, V.*

$$ ⚆ **San Francisco.** An 18th-century town house near the cathedral and the main shopping area houses this modest hotel. A central patio enlivens the entrance, and the simple rooms have en suite marble bathrooms. The upstairs terrace has five-star cathedral views. The friendly owner speaks some English. ⊠ *Calle Álvarez Quintero 38, Santa Cruz, 41004* ☎ *95/450–1541* ⏎ *17 rooms* ☰ *MC, V.*

$$ ⚆ **Simón.** In a rambling turn-of-the-19th-century town house, this hotel is a good choice for inexpensive, comfortable accommodations near the cathedral. The spacious, fern-filled, azulejo-tile patio makes a fine initial impression; the marble stairway and high-ceiling and pillared dining room are cool, stately spaces. The rooms are less grand, but the mansion's style permeates the house. ⊠ *Calle García de Vinuesa 19, El Arenal, 41001* ☎ *95/422–6660* 🖷 *95/456–2241* ⊕ *www.hotel simonsevilla.com* ⏎ *29 rooms* 👌 *In-hotel: restaurant, some pets allowed* ☰ *AE, DC, MC, V.*

NIGHTLIFE & THE ARTS

Seville has lively nightlife and plenty of cultural activity. The free monthly magazine *El Giraldillo* (⊕ *www.elgiraldillo.es*) lists classical and jazz concerts, plays, dance performances, art exhibits, and films in Seville and all major Andalusian cities. (For American films in English, look for the designation *v.o.*, for *versión original*.)

NIGHTLIFE

FLAMENCO CLUBS

Seville has a handful of commercial *tablaos* (flamenco clubs), patronized more by tourists than locals. They offer, generally, somewhat mechanical flamenco at high prices, with mediocre cuisine as the icing on the cake. Check local listings and ask at your hotel for performances by top artists. Spontaneous flamenco is often found for free in *peñas flamencas* (flamenco clubs) and flamenco bars in Triana.

Casa Anselma is a semi-secret (unmarked) bar on the corner of Antillano Campos where Anselma and her friends sing and dance for the pure joy and catharsis that is at the heart of flamenco. ✉*Calle Pagés del Corro 49, Triana* 🕿*No phone* 💶*Free* 🕑*Shows nightly after 11.*

★ **Casa de la Memoria de Al-Andaluz,** housed in an 18th-century palace, has a nightly show plus classes for the intrepid. ✉*Calle Ximenez de Enciso 28, Santa Cruz* 🕿*95/456–0670* 💶*€12* 🕑*Shows nightly at 9.*

Casa del Carmen is a newcomer to the Seville flamenco scene. The flamenco here is generally as passionate and raw as it needs to be to retain credibility. ✉*Calle Marqués de Paradas 30, Santa Cruz* 🕿*95/421–2889* 💶*€12* 🕑*Shows nightly at 8:30 and 10.*

El Tamboril is a late-night bar in the heart of the Barrio de Santa Cruz noted for its great glass case in which the Virgin of Rocío sits in splendor. At 11 each night, locals pack in to sing the *Salve Rociera,* an emotive prayer to her. Afterward everything from flamenco to salsa continues until the early hours. ✉*Pl. Santa Cruz, Santa Cruz* 💶*Free.*

La Carbonería—when it gets packed, which is most Thursdays, the flamenco is spontaneous. ✉*C. Levíes 18, Santa Cruz* 🕿*95/421–4460.*

Los Gallos is an intimate club in the heart of the Barrio de Santa Cruz. Performances are good and reasonably authentic. ✉*Pl. Santa Cruz 11, Santa Cruz* 🕿*95/421–6981* 🌐*www.tablaolosgallos.com* 💶*€30 with 1 drink* 🕑*Shows nightly at 8 and 10:30. Closed Jan.*

THE ARTS

🕑 Long prominent in the opera world, Seville is particularly proud of its opera house, the **Teatro de la Maestranza** (✉*Paseo de Colón 22, Arenal* 🕿*95/422–3344* 🌐*www.teatromaestranza.com*). Classical music and ballet are performed at the **Teatro Lope de Vega** (✉*Av. María Luisa s/n, Parque de María Luisa* 🕿*95/459–0853*). The modern **Teatro Central** (✉*José de Gálvez s/n, Isla de la Cartuja* 🕿*95/503–7200* 🌐*www.teatrocentral.com*) stages theater, dance, and classical and contemporary music.

BULLFIGHTING

Bullfighting season is Easter through Columbus Day; most *corridas* (bullfights) are held on Sunday. The highlight is the April Fair, with Spain's leading toreros; other key dates are Corpus Christi (date varies; about seven weeks after Easter), Assumption (August 15), and the last weekend in September. Bullfights take place at the **Maestranza Bullring** (✉*Paseo de Colón 12, Arenal* 🕿*95/422–4577*). Bullfighting tickets are expensive; buy them in advance from the official *despacho de entradas* (*ticket office* ✉*Calle Adriano 37, Arenal* 🕿*95/450–1382*), alongside the bullring. Other despachos sell tickets on Calle Sierpes, but these are unofficial and charge a 20% commission.

Continued on page 56

FLAMENCO
THE HEARTBEAT OF SPAIN

Palmas, the staccato clapping of flamenco.

Rule one about flamenco: You don't see it. You feel it. There's no soap opera emoting here. The pain and yearning on the dancers' faces and the eerie voices —typically communicating grief over a lost love or family member—are real. If the dancers manage to summon the supernatural *duende* and allow this inner demon to overcome them, then they have done their jobs well.

DUENDE HEAD TO TOE

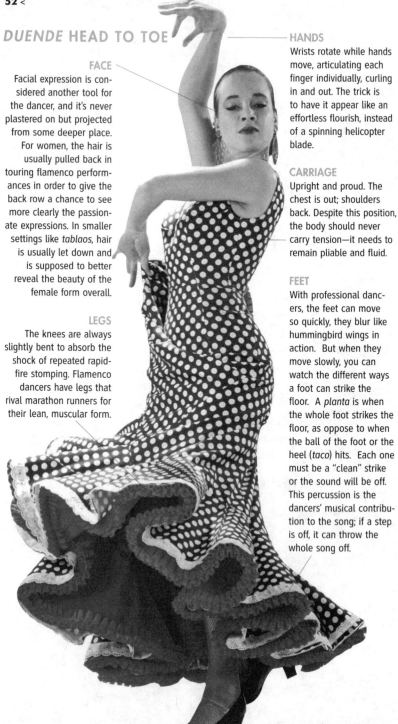

FACE

Facial expression is considered another tool for the dancer, and it's never plastered on but projected from some deeper place. For women, the hair is usually pulled back in touring flamenco performances in order to give the back row a chance to see more clearly the passionate expressions. In smaller settings like *tablaos*, hair is usually let down and is supposed to better reveal the beauty of the female form overall.

LEGS

The knees are always slightly bent to absorb the shock of repeated rapid-fire stomping. Flamenco dancers have legs that rival marathon runners for their lean, muscular form.

HANDS

Wrists rotate while hands move, articulating each finger individually, curling in and out. The trick is to have it appear like an effortless flourish, instead of a spinning helicopter blade.

CARRIAGE

Upright and proud. The chest is out; shoulders back. Despite this position, the body should never carry tension—it needs to remain pliable and fluid.

FEET

With professional dancers, the feet can move so quickly, they blur like hummingbird wings in action. But when they move slowly, you can watch the different ways a foot can strike the floor. A *planta* is when the whole foot strikes the floor, as oppose to when the ball of the foot or the heel (*taco*) hits. Each one must be a "clean" strike or the sound will be off. This percussion is the dancers' musical contribution to the song; if a step is off, it can throw the whole song off.

FLAMENCO 101

All the elements of flamenco working in harmony.

ORIGINS

The music is largely Arabic in its beginnings, but you'll detect echoes of Greek dirges and Jewish chants, with healthy doses of Flemish and traditional Castillian thrown in. Hindu sways, Roman mimes, and other movement informs the dance, but we may never know the specific origins of flamenco.

The dance, along with the nomadic Gypsies, spread throughout Andalusia and within a few centuries had developed into many variations and styles, some of them named after the city where they were borne (such as Malagueñas, Sevillanas) and others taking on the names after people, emotions, or bands. In all, there are over 50 different styles (or *palos*) of flamenco, four of which are the stylistic pillars others branch off from—differing mainly in rhythm and mood: *Toná, Soleá, Fandango,* and *Seguiriya.*

CLAPPING AND CASTANETS

The sum of its parts are awe-inspiring, but if you boil it down, flamenco is a combination of music, singing, and dance. Staccato hand-clapping almost sneaks in as a fourth part—the sounds made from all the participants' palms, or *palmas* is part of the *duende*—but this element remains more of a

continued on following page

THE FLAMENCO HOOK-UP

When *duende* leads to love.

That cheek-to-cheek chemistry that exists between dance partners isn't missing in flamenco—it's simply repositioned between the dancer and the musicians. In fact, when you watch flamenco, you may feel what seems like an electric wire connecting the dancer to the musicians. In each *palo* (style) of music there are certain *letras* (lyrics) inherent within the song that tip off dancers and spark a change in rhythm. If the cues are off, the dancer may falter or simply come off flat. At its best, the dancer and the guitarist are like an old married couple that can musically finish each other's sentences. This interconnectedness has been known to lead into the bedroom, and it's not unusual for dancers and musicians to hook up offstage as well. Two famous couples include dancer Eva La Yerbabuena with guitarist Paco Jarano and dancer Manuela Carrasco with guitarist Joaquín Amador.

connector that all in the performance take part in when their hands are free.

Hand-clapping was likely flamenco's original key instrument before the guitar, *cajón* (wooden box used for percussion), and other instruments arrived on the scene. Perhaps the simplest way to augment the clapping is to add a uniquely designed six-string guitar, in which case you've got yourself a *tablao*, or people seated around a singer and clapping. Dance undoubtedly augments the experience, but isn't necessary for a *tablao*. These exist all throughout Andalusia and are usually private affairs with people who love flamenco. One needn't be a Gypsy in order to take part in it. But it doesn't hurt.

Castanets (or *palillos*) were absorbed by the Phoenician culture and persevered by the Spanish, now part of their own folklore. They accompany other traditional folk dances in Spain and are used pervasively throughout flamenco (though not always present in some forms of dance).

Castanets can be secured in any number of ways. The most important thing is that they are securely fastened to the hand (by thumb or any combination of fingers) so that the wrist can snap it quickly and make the sound.

FLAMENCO NOW

Flamenco's enormous international resurgence has been building for the past few decades. Much of this revival can be attributed to pioneers like legendary singer Camarón de la Isla, guitarist Paco de Lucía, or even outsiders like Miles Davis fusing flamenco with other genres like jazz and rock. This melding brought forth flamenco pop—which flourished in the 80s and continues today—as well as disparate fusions with almost every genre imaginable, including heavy metal and hip-hop. Today the most popular flamenco fusion artists include Ojos de Brujo and Chambao—all of which have found an audience outside of Spain.

IT'S A MAN'S WORLD

Joaquín Cortés

In the U.S., our image of a flamenco dancer is usually a woman in a red dress. So you may be surprised to learn that male dancers dominate flamenco and always have. In its beginnings, men did all the footwork and only since the 40s and 50s have women started to match men step-for-step and star in performances. And in the tabloids, men usually get the sex symbol status more than women (as seen through Farruquito and Cortés). Suits are the traditional garb for male dancers, and recent trends have seen female dancers wearing them as well—presumably rebelling against the staid gender roles that continue to rule Spain. Today, male dancers tend to wear a simple pair of black trousers and a white button-down shirt. The sex appeal comes for unbuttoning the shirt to flash a little chest and having the pants tailor-made to a tightness that can't be found in any store. In traditional *tablaos*, male dancers perform without accessories, but in touring performances—upping the razzle dazzle—anything goes: canes, hats, tuxedos, or even shirtless (much to the delight of female fans).

DANCING WITH THE STARS
SEX, MANSLAUGHTER, EVEN MONOGAMY

Farruquito was born into a flamenco dynasty. He started dancing when he was 8 years old and rose very high in the flamenco and celebrity world (*People* magazine named him one of the 50 most beautiful people in the world) until September 2003 when he ran two lights in an unlicensed, uninsured BMW, hitting and killing a pedestrian.

EVA LA YERBABUENA, The Pro

FARRUQUITO, The Wild Child

This young dancer from Granada has won numerous prizes, including the coveted Flamenco Hoy's Best Dancer award in 2000. In 2006, she took her tour around Asia and New Zealand. She keeps herself out of the tabloids because she doesn't run red lights and enjoys a stable relationship with flamenco guitarist Paco Jarano.

JOAQUÍN CORTÉS, The Lady's Man

Stateside, we're still swooning over her Oscar-nominated sister, Penélope, but in Spain, Mónica also captures the spotlight. With the same dark hair and pillowy lips as her sibling, Mónica works as a flamenco dancer and actress. Most recently she stared in a Soap Opera in Spain called *Paso Adelante*, a Spanish version of *Fame*.

MÓNICA CRUZ, The Bombshell

He's considered a visionary dancer, easily the most famous worldwide for the past 15 years. Despite this, he's often in the press for the hotties he's dated versus his talent; former flames include Oscar-winner Mira Sorvino and supermodel Naomi Campbell. Even *Sports Illustrated* cover girl Elle MacPherson labeled him "pure sex."

SHOPPING

Seville is the region's main shopping area and the place for archetypal Andalusian souvenirs, most of which are sold in the Barrio de Santa Cruz and around the cathedral and Giralda, especially on Calle Alemanes. The shopping street for locals is Calle Sierpes, along with neighboring Cuna, Tetuan, Velázquez, Plaza Magdalena, and Plaza Duque—boutiques abound here. A permanent arts-and-crafts market near the cathedral is **El Postigo** (⊠ *Calle Arfe s/n, Arenal* ☎ *95/456–0013*).

ANTIQUES

For antiques, try Mateos Gago, opposite the Giralda, and in the Barrio de Santa Cruz on Jamerdana and Rodrigo Caro, off Plaza Alianza.

CERAMICS

In the Barrio de Santa Cruz, browse along Mateos Gago; Romero Murube, between Plaza Triunfo and Plaza Alianza, on the edge of the barrio; and between Plaza Doña Elvira and Plaza de los Venerables. Look for traditional azulejo tiles and other ceramics in the Triana **potters' district,** on Calle Alfarería and Calle Antillano Campos. **Cerámica Santa Isabel** (⊠ *Calle Alfarería 12, El Zurraque* ☎ *95/434–4608*) is one of a string of Triana ceramics shops. In central Seville, **Martian Ceramics** (⊠ *Calle Sierpes 74, Centro* ☎ *95/421–3413*) has high-quality dishes, especially the flowers-on-white patterns native to Seville.

FLAMENCO WEAR

Flamenco wear can be expensive; local women will gladly spend a month's grocery money, or more, on their frills, with dresses ranging from €100 to €400 and up. Try recommended shops **María Rosa** (⊠ *Calle Cuna 13, Centro* ☎ *95/422–2143*) and **Molina** (⊠ *Sierpes 11, Centro* ☎ *95/422–9254*), which also sells the traditional foot-tapping shoes. For privately fitted and custom-made flamenco dresses, try **Juan Foronda** (⊠ *Calle Virgen de los Reyes 3, Centro* ☎ *95/421–1856*).

PASTRIES

Seville's most celebrated pastry outlet is **La Campana** (⊠ *Sierpes 1, Centro* ☎ *95/422–3570*), founded in 1885. Andalusia's convents are known for their homemade pastries—sample sweets from several convents at **El Torno** (⊠ *Pl. del Cabildo s/n, Santa Cruz* ☎ *95/421–9190*).

STREET MARKETS

A few blocks north of Plaza Nueva, **Plaza del Duque** has a crafts market on Friday and Saturday. The flea market **El Jueves** is held on Calle Feria in the Barrio de la Macarena on Thursday morning. A Sunday morning crafts market is a weekly happening at the northern Barrio de la Macarena's **Alameda de Hercules.** There's a Sunday pet market in the upper Barrio de Santa Cruz's **Plaza Alfalfa.**

TEXTILES

You can find blankets, shawls, and embroidered tablecloths woven by local artisans at the three shops of **Artesanía Textil** (⊠ *Calle García de Vinuesa 33, Arenal* ☎ *95/456–2840* ⊠ *Sierpes 70, Centro* ☎ *95/422–0125* ⊠ *Pl. de Doña Elvira 4, Santa Cruz* ☎ *95/421–4748*).

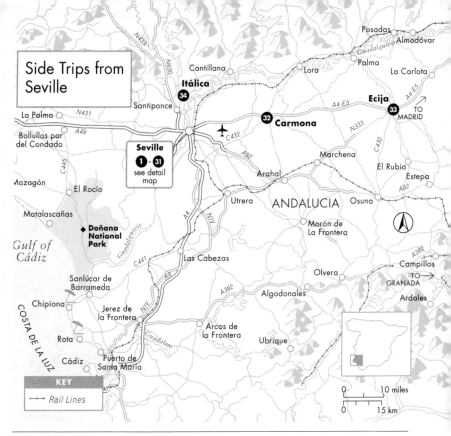

SIDE TRIPS FROM SEVILLE

CARMONA

32 *32 km (20 mi) east of Seville off NIV.*

Claiming to be one of the oldest inhabited places in Spain (the Phoenicians and Carthaginians had settlements here), Carmona, on a steep, fortified hill, became an important town under both the Romans and the Moors. As you wander its ancient, narrow streets, you can see many Mudejar and Renaissance churches, medieval gateways, and simple whitewashed houses of clear Moorish influence, punctuated here and there by a baroque palace. Local fiestas are held in mid-September.

WHAT TO SEE

Park your car near the Puerta de Sevilla in the imposing **Alcázar de Abajo** (Lower Fortress), a Moorish fortification built on Roman foundations. Grab a map at the tourist office, in the tower beside the gate. On the edge of the "new town," across the road from the Alcázar de Abajo, is the church of **San Pedro** (⊠*Calle San Pedro*), begun in 1466. Its interior is an unbroken mass of sculptures and gilded surfaces, and its baroque tower, erected in 1704, is an unabashed imitation of Seville's Giralda.

Up Calle Prim is the **Plaza San Fernando,** in the heart of the old town; its 17th-century houses have Moorish overtones.

☾ The Gothic church of **Santa María** (⊠ *Calle Martín*) was built between 1424 and 1518 on the site of Carmona's former Great Mosque. It retains its beautiful Moorish courtyard, studded with orange trees. Behind Santa María is the **Museo de la Ciudad,** with exhibits on Carmona's history. There's plenty for children; interactive exhibits are labeled in English and Spanish. ⊠ *Calle San Ildefonso 1* ☏ *954/140128* ☞ *€2* ☉ *Mon. 11–2, Tues.–Sun. 11–7.*

Stroll down to the **Puerta de Córdoba** (Córdoba Gate) on the eastern edge of town. This old gateway was first built by the Romans around AD 175, then altered by Moorish and Renaissance additions. The Moorish **Alcázar de Arriba** (Upper Fortress) was built on Roman foundations and later converted by King Pedro the Cruel into a fine Mudejar palace. Pedro's summer residence was destroyed by a 1504 earthquake, but the parador amid its ruins has a breathtaking view.

★ At the western end of town lies the splendid **Roman necropolis.** Here, in huge underground chambers, some 900 family tombs were chiseled out of the rock between the 2nd and 4th centuries BC. The walls, decorated with leaf and bird motifs, have niches for burial urns. The most spectacular tombs are the **Elephant Vault** and the **Servilia Tomb,** which resembles a complete Roman villa with its colonnaded arches and vaulted side galleries. ⊠ *C. Enmedio* ☏ *95/414–0811* ☞ *€2* ☉ *Mid-Sept.–mid-June, Tues.–Fri. 9–4:45, weekends 10–1:45; mid-June–mid-Sept., Tues.–Fri. 8:30–1:45, Sat. 10–2.*

WHERE TO STAY & EAT

$$–$$$ ✕ **San Fernando.** You enter from a side street, but this second-floor restaurant looks out onto the Plaza de San Fernando. Set in an 18th-century palace, the beige dining room is pleasant in its simplicity. The kitchen serves Spanish dishes with flair—as in cream of apple soup or light fried potato slivers shaped like a bird's nest. Game, including partridge, are perennial favorites. ⊠ *Calle Sacramento 3* ☏ *95/414–3556* ▤ *AE, DC, MC, V* ☉ *Closed Mon. and Aug. No dinner Sun.*

$$$–$$$$ ✕ 🏨 **Alcázar de la Reina.** Stylish and contemporary, this hotel has public areas that incorporate three bright and airy courtyards, with marble floors and pastel walls. Guest rooms are spacious and comfortable. The elegant Ferrara ($$–$$$) serves a tasty combination of Italian and Spanish dishes, served à la carte or on a *menú de degustación* (gourmet menu) with four courses and dessert. ⊠ *Pl. de Lasso 2, 41410* ☏ *95/419–6200* ▤ *95/414–0113* ⊕ *www.alcazar-reina.es* ↘ *66 rooms, 2 suites* ♿ *In-room: Ethernet (some). In-hotel: restaurant, bar, pool, parking (fee), some pets allowed* ▤ *AE, DC, MC, V* ⧖*BP.*

$$$ 🏨 **Parador Alcázar del Rey Don Pedro.** The Parador de Carmona has
★   superb views from its hilltop position among the ruins of Pedro the Cruel's summer palace. The public rooms surround a central, Moorish-style patio, and the vaulted dining hall and adjacent bar open onto an outdoor terrace overlooking the sloping garden. Spacious rooms have rugs and dark furniture. All but six, which face onto the front

courtyard, look south over the valley; the best rooms are on the top floor. ⊠*Calle del Alcázar s/n, 41410* ☎*95/414–1010* 🖷*95/414–1712* ⊕*www.parador.es* ↩*63 rooms* ⚷*In-room: dial-up, Wi-Fi. In-hotel: restaurant, bar, pool, Wi-Fi, public Internet* ⊟*AE, DC, MC, V.*

ÉCIJA

㉝ *48 km (30 mi) northeast of Carmona.*

Écija is dubbed the "the frying pan," "furnace," or "oven" of Andalusia for midsummer temperatures often reaching 100°F/37°C. On a more positive note, it has more ceramic-tiled baroque church towers per capita (11) than any other town in Spain.

WHAT TO SEE
Écija's most famous ornamented church is the **Iglesia de Santa María** in the palm tree–shaded Plaza de España, an important meeting point on infernally hot summer evenings. The **Iglesia de San Juan** has an intricate and harmoniously crafted Mudéjar bell tower. The **Iglesia de Santiago** assembles Mudéjar windows from an earlier structure with an 18th-century patio and 17th-century nave and side aisles. Important civil structures in Écija begin with the baroque **Palacio de Peñaflor** (⊠*Calle Emilio Castelar 26* ☎*95/483–0273* 🖾*Free* ⊙*Patio only: weekdays 10–1 and 4:30–7:30, weekends 11–1*) with its concave facade and its *trampantojo* (trompe l'oeil) faux-relief paintings. Note the presentation of the stable windows below the false wrought-iron balcony, which is the noblest feature in the facade. The Renaissance **Valdehermoso Palace** (⊠*Calle Emilio Castelar 37*) near the Iglesia de San Juan is an elegant and aristocratic structure. The **Palacio de Benamejí** (⊠*Plaza de la Consitución s/n*) with its two watchtowers is another of Écija's finest houses. The **Palacio del Conde de Aguilar** (⊠*Calle Sor Angela Cruz s/n*) has a lovely baroque portal and a wrought-iron gallery.

WHERE TO STAY & EAT
$$ ✕▢ **Platería.** This little hideaway in the old silversmiths' quarter has breezy rooms with plenty of space and a good restaurant ($–$$$) that serves regional and national dishes. The building is modern, and the rooms are decorated in sleek, spare lines and tones that exert a cooling influence in this hottest of Andalusian towns. Air-conditioned. ⊠*C. Platería 4, 41400* ☎*95/590–2754* 🖷*95/590–4553* ⊕*www.hotelplateria.net* ↩*18 rooms* ⚷*In hotel: Restaurant, bar* ⊟*AE, DC, MC, V.*

ITÁLICA

㉞ *12 km (7 mi) north of Seville, 1 km (½ mi) beyond Santiponce.*

Fodor's Choice
★

One of Roman Iberia's most important cities in the 2nd century with a population of over 10,000, Itálica today is a monument of Roman ruins, complete with admission charge. Founded by Scipio Africanus in 205 BC as a home for veteran soldiers, Itálica gave the Roman world two great emperors, Trajan (52–117) and Hadrian (76–138). About 25% of the site has been excavated, with work still in progress. You can find traces of city streets, cisterns, and the floor plans of several

villas, some with mosaic floors, though all the best mosaics and stat-ues have been removed to Seville's Museum of Archaeology. Itálica was abandoned and plundered as a quarry by the Visigoths, who pre-ferred Seville. It fell into decay around AD 700. The remains you can see include the huge, elliptical **amphitheater,** which held 40,000 spectators, a **Roman theater,** and **Roman baths.** The small town of Santiponce has sprung up nearby. ☎95/599–7376 or 95/599–6583 ⊠€1.50, free for EU citizens ⊘ Tues.–Sat. 9–5:30, Sun. 10–4.

WESTERN ANDALUSIA'S GREAT OUTDOORS: PROVINCE OF HUELVA

When you've had enough of Seville's urban bustle, nature awaits in Huelva—from the Parque Nacional de Doñana to the oak forests of the Sierra de Aracena, nothing is much more than an hour's drive from Seville. If you prefer history, hop on the miners' train at Riotinto, or visit Aracena's spectacular caves. Columbus's voyage to the New World was sparked near here, at the monastery of La Rábida and in Palos de la Frontera. The visitor center at La Rocina has Doñana information.

DOÑANA NATIONAL PARK

③⑤ *100 km (62 mi) southwest of*
Fodor'sChoice *Seville.*
★

DOÑANA TOURS

Jeep tours of the reserve depart twice daily (Tuesday–Sunday at 8:30 and 3) from the park's Acebuche reception center, 2 km (1 mi) from Matalascañas. Tours are limited to 125 people and should be booked well in advance. Passengers can often be picked up from hotels in Matalascañas. Contact **Parque Nacional de Doñana,** ⊠ *Cooperativa Marisma del Rocío, Centro de Recepción, Matalascañas, 21760* ☎ *959/430432* ⊕ *www.donana.es.*

One of Europe's last swaths of wilderness, these wetlands are beside the Guadalquivir estuary. The site was named for Doña Ana, wife of a 16th-century duke, who, prone to bouts of depression, one day crossed the river and wandered into the wetlands, never to be seen alive again. The 188,000-acre park sits on the migratory route from Africa to Europe and is the winter home and breeding ground for as many as 150 species of rare birds. Habitats range from beaches and shifting sand dunes to marshes, dense brushwood, and sandy hillsides of pine and cork oak. Two of Europe's most endangered species, the imperial eagle and the lynx, make their homes here, and kestrels, kites, buzzards, egrets, storks, and spoonbills breed among the cork oaks. A good base of exploration is the hamlet of **El Rocío,** on the park's northern fringe. In spring, during the Romería del Rocío pilgrimage (40 days after Easter Sunday), up to a million people converge on the local *santuario* (shrine) to worship the Virgen del Rocío. The rest of the year, many of El Rocío's pilgrim-brotherhood houses are empty. Most of the streets are unpaved to make them more comfortable for horses, as many of the yearly pilgrimage events are on horseback or involve horse-drawn carts. At the Doñana **La Rocina visitor center** (☎ *959/442340*), less than 2 km (1 mi) from El Rocío, you can peer at the park's many bird species from a 3½-km (2-mi) footpath. It's open daily 9–7. Five kilometers (3 mi) away, an exhibit at the **Palacio de Acebrón** (⊠ *Ctra. de la Rocina s/n* ☎ *959/448–711*) explains the park's ecosystems. It's open daily 9–6:30; last entrance is one hour before closing.

Two kilometers (1 mi) before Matalascañas, you can find **Acebuche** (⊠ *El Acebuche s/n* ☎ *959/448640* ⊕ *www.parquenacionaldonana. com*), the park's main interpretation center and the departure point for jeep tours, which must be reserved in advance. The center is open June–September, daily 8 AM–9 PM and October–May, daily 9–7. Tours leave daily June–September at 8:30 and 5 and October–May at 8:30 and 3 and last four hours; they cover a 70-km (43-mi) route across beaches, sand dunes, marshes, and scrub. Cost is €24. Off-season (November–February) you can usually book a tour with just a day's notice; at other times, book as far in advance as possible.

WHERE TO STAY

$$$ 🏠 **El Cortijo de Los Mimbrales.** On the Rocío–Matalascañas road, this convivial, one-story Andalusian farm-hacienda is perched on the park's edge, a mere 1 km (½ mi) from the visitor center at La Rocina. Spend a relaxed evening with fellow nature lovers in comfy chairs by the fireplace in the large common lounge. Pick a colorfully decorated room, or a bungalow that sleeps two to four, with a kitchenette and small private garden. Some rooms and bungalows have fireplaces. There are stables on the premises, and the hotel can arrange horseback rides on the fringes of the park. ⊠*Ctra. del Rocío a Matalascañas (A483), Km 30, 21750* ☎*959/442237* 🖷*959/442443* ⊕*www.cortijomimbrales. com* ⤴*24 rooms, 2 suites, 5 bungalows* ☝*In-room: no a/c. In-hotel: restaurant, bar, pool, some pets allowed* ▭*AE, DC, MC, V* ⦿|*BP.*

$$ ⛉**Toruño.** Despite its location behind the famous Rocío shrine, the theme at this simple, friendly hotel is nature: it's run by the same cooperative that leads official park tours and has become a favorite of birdwatchers. Each room is named after a local bird species. Those on the first floor have balconies and priceless views over the marshes. ⊠*Pl. del Acebuchal 22, 21750* ☎*959/442323* 🖷*959/442338* ⤴*30 rooms* ☝*In-hotel: restaurant* ▭*MC, V* ⦿|*BP.*

MATALASCAÑAS

❸❻ *3 km (2 mi) south of Acebuche, 85 km (53 mi) southwest of Seville.*

Its proximity to Acebuche, Doñana's main reception center, makes Matalascañas a convenient lodging base for park visitors. In general though, it's a rather incongruous and ugly sprawl of hotels and vacation homes, very crowded at Easter and in summer, and eerily deserted the rest of the year (most hotels close November–March). There are some nice beaches for relaxation, and the local ocean waters are good for windsurfing.

WHERE TO STAY

$$$ ⛉**Hotel Tierra Mar Golf.** Try this large beachfront hotel if you want to combine Doñana with the seashore. The nearby 18-hole Dunes golf course (€30 greens fee) is windy and challenging year-round; the more gentle prospect of lawn bowling is available within the hotel's grounds. The rooms are modern, spacious, and have balconies. ⊠*Matalascañas Parcela 120, Sector M, 21760* ☎*959/440300* 🖷*959/440720* ⊕*www. atlanticclub-hoteles.com* ⤴*250 rooms* ☝*In-room: dial-up. In-hotel: restaurant, tennis court, pool, gym* ▭*AE, DC, MC, V.*

MAZAGÓN

❸❼ *22 km (14 mi) northwest of Matalascañas.*

There isn't much to see or do in this coastal town, but its parador makes a good base for touring La Rábida, Palos de la Frontera, and Moguer. Mazagón's beautiful beach is among the region's nicest, because of its sweeping sandy beach sheltered by steep cliffs.

WHERE TO STAY & EAT

$$$ ✕⛉**Parador de Mazagón.** This peaceful modern parador stands on a cliff surrounded by pine groves, overlooking a sandy beach 3 km (2 mi) southeast of Mazagón. Most rooms have balconies overlooking the garden. The restaurant serves Andalusian dishes and local seafood

specialties, such as stuffed baby squid and hake medallions. ⊠*Playa de Mazagón, 21130* ☎*959/536300* 📠*959/536228* ⊕*www.parador.es* ↵*63 rooms* ⚴*In-room: Wi-Fi. In-hotel: restaurant, bar, tennis courts, pool, public Wi-Fi, bicycles, parking (no fee)* ☰*AE, DC, MC, V.*

LA RÁBIDA

㊳ *8 km (5 mi) northwest of Mazagón.*

You may want to extend your Doñana tour to see the monastery of **Santa María de La Rábida,** "the birthplace of America." In 1485 Columbus came from Portugal with his son Diego to stay in this Mudejar-style Franciscan monastery. Here he discussed his theories with friars Antonio de Marchena and Juan Pérez, who interceded on his behalf with Queen Isabella. The early 15th-century church holds a much-venerated 14th-century statue of the **Virgen de los Milagros** (Virgin of Miracles). The **frescoes** in the gatehouse were painted by Daniel Vázquez Díaz in 1930. ⊠*Camino del Monasterio, Ctra. de Huelva* ☎*959/350411* 🎫*€3 with audio guide, €2.50 without* ☉*Tues.–Sun. 10–1 and 4–7.*

Two kilometers (1 mi) from the monastery, on the seashore, is the **Muelle de las Carabelas** (Caravels' Wharf), a reproduction of a 15th-century port. The star exhibits here are the full-size models of Columbus's flotilla, the *Niña*, *Pinta*, and *Santa María*, built using the same techniques as in Columbus's day. Board each one and learn more about the discovery of the New World in the adjoining museum. ⊠*Paraje de la Rábida* ☎*959/530597 or 959/530312* 🎫*€3.50* ☉*Tues.–Sun. 9–7.*

PALOS DE LA FRONTERA

㊴ *4 km (2½ mi) northwest of La Rábida, 12 km (7 mi) northeast of Mazagón.*

On August 2, 1492, the *Niña*, the *Pinta*, and the *Santa María* set sail from Palos de la Frontera. At the door of the church of **San Jorge** (1473), the royal letter ordering the levy of the ships' crew and equipment was read aloud, and the voyagers took their water supplies from the fountain known as La Fontanilla (fountain) at the town's entrance.

MOGUER

㊵ *12 km (7 mi) northeast of Palos de la Frontera.*

The residents of this old port town now spend more time growing strawberries than seafaring, as you can see from the surrounding fields. While in Moguer, see the **Casa-Museo Zenobia y Juan Ramón Jiménez,** former home of the Nobel Prize–winning poet who penned the much-loved *Platero y Yo*. At this writing, the Casa-Museo was closed for renovations with plans to reopen soon. Guided tours are offered hourly. ⊠*C. Juan Ramón Jiménez 10* ☎*959/372148* ⊕*www.fundacion-jrj.es* 🎫*€2.50* ☉*Tues.–Sat. 10:15–2 and 5–8, Sun. 10–2*

RIOTINTO

41 *74 km (46 mi) northeast of Huelva.*

Heading north from Palos and Huelva on the N435, you can reach the turnoff to Minas de Riotinto, the mining town near the source of the Riotinto (literally, "Red River"). The waters are the color of blood because of the minerals leached from the surrounding mountains; this area has some of the richest copper deposits in the world, as well as gold and silver. In 1873 the mines were taken over by the British Rio Tinto Company Ltd., which started to dig an open-pit mine and build a 64-km (40-mi) railway to the port of Huelva to transport mineral ore. The British left in 1954, but mining activity continues today, albeit on a smaller scale. Riotinto's landscape, scarred by centuries of intensive mining, can be viewed as part of a **tour** conducted by the Fundación Riotinto. The tour's first stop, the **Museo Minero** (Museum of Mining), has archaeological finds and a collection of historical steam engines and rail coaches. Next comes the **Corta Atalaya,** one of the largest open-pit mines in the world (4,000 feet across and 1,100 feet deep), and **Bellavista,** the elegant English quarter where the British mine managers lived. The tour ends with an optional ride on the **Tren Minero** (Miners' Train), which follows the course of the Riotinto along more than 24 restored km (15 mi) of the old mining railway. Opt for the full tour as described (offered the first Sunday of each month, October–May), or just visit individual sights. ☎959/590025 *Fundación Riotinto* ⊕*www. parquemineroderiotinto.com* ⊠*Full tour €15* ☉ *Museum daily 10:30– 3 and 4–8. Miners' Train mid-Apr.–mid-May and mid-Sept.–mid-Oct., weekends at 5* PM; *mid-June–mid-July and mid-Oct.–mid-Apr., week-ends at 4* PM; *mid-July–mid-Sept., daily at 1:30* PM.

ARACENA

42 *105 km (65 mi) northeast of Huelva, 100 km (62 mi) northwest of Seville.*

Stretching north of the Riotinto mines is the 460,000-acre Sierra de Aracena nature park, an expanse of hills cloaked in cork and holm oak. This region is known for its cured Ibérico hams, which come from the prized free-ranging Iberian pigs that gorge on acorns in the autumn months before slaughter; the hams are buried in salt and then hung in cellars to dry-cure for at least two years. The best Ibérico hams have traditionally come from the village of **Jabugo.** The capital of the region is Aracena, whose main attraction is the spectacular cave known as the **Gruta de las Maravillas** (Cave of Marvels). The 12 caverns hide long corridors, stalactites and stalagmites arranged in wonderful patterns, and stunning underground lakes. ⊠*Pl. Pozo de Nieves, Pozo de Nieves* ☎959/128355 ⊠*€8* ☉ *Guided tours, if sufficient numbers, weekdays hourly 10:30–3 and 4–6; weekends hourly 10:30–1:30 and 3–6.*

1

WHERE TO STAY & EAT

$–$$ ✕**Casas.** There's not much wall space left in the intimate beamed dining room of this typical Sierra Morena restaurant: plates, pots, pans, mirrors, and religious pictures cover every inch. Specializing in the region's famous ham and pork, the honest, home-style cooking is at its best with dishes prepared according to what is in season. ⊠*Calle Colmenetas 41* ☎*959/128044* ▤*MC, V* ◷*No dinner.*

$$–$$$ ⛺**Finca Buenvino.** This lovely country house inn, nestled in 150 acres of woods, is run by a charming British couple, Sam and Jeannie Chesterton. The room price includes a big breakfast; dinner with tapas is available for a moderate extra sum. Jeannie also conducts Spanish cookery and tapas courses for groups of up to six people. Three woodland self-catering cottages are available, each with its own pool. The house is 6 km (4 mi) from Aracena. ⊠*N433, Km 95, 21293 Los Marines* ☎*959/124034* 🖷*959/501029* ⊕*www.fincabuenvino.com* ⇗*5 rooms, 3 cottages* ♿*In-room: no a/c, no phone, kitchen (some), no TV. In-hotel: restaurant, bar, pools* ▤*MC, V* ◷*Closed mid-July–mid-Sept.* ⛨*MAP.*

$ ⛺**Galaroza Sierra.** The common areas in this stone-clad hotel are done in light wood with rustic furnishings and woven textiles. Rooms have small balconies and views of the mountains, and the four bungalows face the swimming pool. Pork dishes are the restaurant's specialty. Galaroza Sierra is on the outskirts of the village of Galaroza, 3 km (2 mi) from Jabugo; the surrounding countryside is ideal for walking. ⊠*Ctra. Sevilla–Lisboa, Km 69.5, Galaroza, 21291* ☎*959/123237* 🖷*959/123236* ⊕*www.hotelgalaroza.com* ⇗*22 rooms, 7 bungalows* ♿*In-hotel: restaurant, pool* ▤*DC, MC, V.*

THE LAND OF SHERRY: JEREZ DE LA FRONTERA & CÁDIZ PROVINCE

A trip through Cádiz is a trip back in time. Winding roads take you through scenes ranging from flat and barren plains to seemingly endless vineyards, and the rolling countryside is carpeted with blindingly white soil known as *albariza*—unique to this area, and the secret to the grapes used in sherry. Throughout the province, *los pueblos blancos* (the white villages) provide striking contrasts with the terrain, especially at Arcos de la Frontera, where the village sits dramatically on a crag overlooking the gorge of the Guadalete River. In Jerez de La Frontera, you can savor the town's internationally known sherry or delight in the skills and forms of purebred Carthusian horses. Finally, in the city of Cádiz, absorb about 3,000 years of history in what is generally considered the oldest continuously inhabited city in the Western world.

JEREZ DE LA FRONTERA

43 *97 km (60 mi) south of Seville.*

★ Jerez, world headquarters for sherry, is surrounded by vineyards of chalky soil, whose Palomino grapes have funded a host of churches and noble mansions. Names such as González Byass, Domecq, Harvey, and Sandeman are inextricably linked with Jerez. The word "sherry," first used in Great Britain in 1608, is an English corruption of the town's old Moorish name, Xeres. Both sherry and horses are the domain of Jerez's Anglo-Spanish aristocracy, whose Catholic ancestors came here from England centuries ago. At any given time, more than half a million barrels of sherry are maturing in Jerez's vast aboveground cellars.

WHAT TO SEE

The 12th-century **Alcázar** was once the residence of the caliph of Seville. Its small, octagonal **mosque** and **baths** were built for the Moorish governor's private use. The baths have three sections: the *sala fria* (cold room), the larger *sala templada* (warm room), and the *sala caliente* (hot room), for steam baths. In the midst of it all is the 17th-century **Palacio de Villavicencio,** built on the site of the original Moorish palace. A camera obscura, a lens-and-mirrors device that projects the outdoors onto a large indoor screen, offers a 360-degree view of Jerez. ⊠ *Alameda Vieja* ☎ €1.50, €3.50 including camera obscura ☉ *Mid-Sept.–Apr., daily 10–6; May–mid-Sept., daily 10–8.*

Across from the Alcázar and around the corner from the González Byass winery, the **cathedral** (⊠ *Pl. de la Encarnación* ☉ *Weekdays 11–1, 6–8; Sat.11–2 and 6–8, Sun. 11–2*) has an octagonal cupola and a separate bell tower, as well as Zurbarán's canvas *La Virgen Niña* (the Virgin as a young girl). On the **Plaza de la Asunción,** one of Jerez's most intimate squares, you can find the Mudejar church of **San Dionisio** and the ornate **cabildo municipal** (city hall), whose lovely plateresque facade dates from 1575.

The **Centro Andaluz de Flamenco** is a flamenco museum; it includes an audio-and-visual library, and a multimedia show. ⊠ *Palacio Pemartín, Pl. San Juan 1* ☎ *956/322711* ☎ *Free* ☉ *Weekdays 9–2.*

Diving into the maze of streets that form the scruffy San Mateo neighborhood east of the town center, you come to the **Museo Arqueológico,** one of Andalusia's best archaeological museums. The collection is strongest on the pre-Roman period. The star item, found near Jerez, is a Greek helmet dating from the 7th century BC. ⊠ *Pl. del Mercado s/n* ☎ *956/341350* ☎ €2 ☉ *Sept.–mid-June, Tues.–Fri. 10–2 and 4–7, weekends 10–2:30; mid-June–Aug., Tues.–Sun. 10–2:30.*

NEED A BREAK?

Bar Juanito (⊠ *Pescadería Vieja 8 and 10* ☎ *956/334838*) has a flowery patio and is a past winner of the national Best Tapas Bar in Spain award. Jolly Faustino Rodríguez and his family serve 50 different tapas and larger-portion raciones. It's closed Monday and during El Rocó pilgrimage.

☺ Just west of the town center the **Parque Zoológico** is set within lush botanical gardens where you can usually spy up to 33 storks' nests. Primarily a place for the rehabilitation of injured or endangered animals native to Spain, the zoo also houses white tigers, elephants, and a giant red panda. ⊠ *C. Taxdirt* ☎ *956/153164* ⊕ *www.zoobotanicojerez.com* ☎ €7.50 ☉ *June–Sept, Tues.–Sun. 10–8, Oct.–May, Tues.–Sun. 10–6.*

A TOAST TO JEREZ: WINERY TOURS

On a **bodega** (winery) visit, your guide will explain the *solera* method of blending old wine with new, and the importance of the *flor* (a sort of yeast that forms on the surface of the wine as it ages) in determining the kind of sherry.

Most bodegas welcome visitors, but it's advisable to phone ahead for an appointment, if only to make sure you join a group that speaks your language. Cellars usually charge an admission fee of €3–€6, and some close in August. Tours, about an hour, go through the aging cellars, with their endless rows of casks. (You won't see the actual fermenting and bottling, which take place in more modern, less romantic plants outside town.) Finally, you'll be invited to sample generous amounts of pale, dry *fino*; nutty *amontillado*; or rich, deep *oloroso*, and, of course, to purchase a few robustly priced bottles in the winery shop.

If you have time for only one bodega, tour the González Byass (⊠ *Calle Manuel María González* ☎ *956/357000* ⊕ *www.gonzalez-byass.com*), home of the famous Tío Pepe. This tour is well organized and includes La Concha, an open-air aging cellar designed by Gustave Eiffel. Jerez's oldest bodega is **Domecq** (⊠ *Calle San Ildefonso 3* ☎ *956/151500*), founded in 1730. Aside from sherry, Domecq makes the world's best-selling brandy, Fundador. **Harveys** (⊠ *Calle Pintor Muñoz Cebrián s/n* ☎ *956/319650*) is the source of Harvey's Bristol Cream. **Sandeman** (⊠ *Calle Pizarro 10* ☎ *956/301100* ⊕ *www.sandeman.com*) is known for its man-in-a-cape logo. **Museo de Vino** (⊠ *Calle Cervantes 3, La Atalaya* ☎ *956/182100* ☏ €6 ☉ *Tues.–Sun. 10–2*), a sherry museum, offers a multimedia show twice daily at 10 and noon, plus a sherry pouring exhibition, a bar, a restaurant, and a shop.

The **Real Escuela Andaluza del Arte Ecuestre** *(Royal Andalusian School of Equestrian Art)* operates on the grounds of the Recreo de las Cadenas, a 19th-century palace. This prestigious school was masterminded by Alvaro Domecq in the 1970s. Every Thursday (and at various other times throughout the year) the Cartujana horses—a cross between the native Andalusian workhorse and the Arabian—and skilled riders in 18th-century riding costume demonstrate intricate dressage techniques and jumping in the spectacular show "Cómo Bailan los Caballos Andaluces" (roughly, "The Dancing Horses of Andalusia"). Reservations are essential. Admission price depends on how close to the arena you sit; the first two rows are the priciest. The rest of the week, you can visit the stables and tack room, watch the horses being schooled, and see rehearsals. ⊠ *Av. Duque de Abrantes s/n* ☎ *956/319635* ⊕ *www.realescuela.org* ☏ *€17–€25, €8 for rehearsals* ☉ *Shows, Nov.–Feb., Thurs. at noon; Mar.–July 14, Tues. and Thurs. at noon; July 15–Oct., Fri. at noon; Mar., fair nightly at 10:30. Rehearsals, Mon.–Wed. and Thurs. 10–1.*

Just outside Jerez de la Frontera is **Yeguada de la Cartuja,** the largest state-run stud farm in Spain, specializing in Carthusian horses. In the 15th century, a Carthusian monastery on this site started the breed for which Jerez and the rest of Spain are now famous. Every Saturday at 11 AM a full tour and show begin. Book ahead. ⊠ *Finca Fuente El Suero, Ctra. Medina–El Portal, Km 6.5* ☎ *956/162809* ⊕ *www.yeguada-cartuja.com* ⊠ *€13–€18, according to seating* ☉ *Shows Sat. at 11 AM.*

Jerez's **bullring** is on Calle Circo, northeast of the city center. Tickets are sold at the official ticket office on Calle Porvera, though only about five bullfights are held each year, in May and October. Six blocks from the bullring is the **Museo Taurino**, a bullfighting museum where admission includes a drink. ⊠ *Calle Pozo del Olivar 6* ☎ *956/319000* ⊠ *€3* ☉ *Weekdays 9–2.*

> **SPRING IN JEREZ**
>
> May and September are the most exciting times to visit Jerez, as spectacular fiestas transform the town. For the Feria del Caballo (Horse Fair), in early May, carriages and riders fill the streets, and purebreds from the School of Equestrian Art compete in races and dressage displays. September brings the Fiesta de Otoño (Autumn Festival), when the first of the grape harvest is blessed on the steps of the cathedral.

WHERE TO STAY & EAT

$$–$$$ ✕ **La Carboná.** This cavernous restaurant in a former bodega has a suitably rustic atmosphere with arches, original beams, and a central fireplace for winter nights. During the summer you can often enjoy live music, and sometimes flamenco, too, while you dine. The chef has worked at several top-grade restaurants; his menu provides an innovative twist to classic dishes, such as *pechuguitas de cordorniz rellenas de pétalos de rosa y foié* (quail stuffed with rose petals and liver pâté). There's an excellent wine list as well. ⊠ *C. San Francisco de Paula 2* ☎ *956/347475* ⊟ *MC, V* ☉ *Closed Tues.*

$–$$$ ✕ **El Bosque.** Housed in a modern villa with contemporary paintings of bullfighting themes, this is one of the most stylish dining spots in town. Most tables are round and seat four; the smaller of the two dining rooms has picture windows overlooking a park. The food is contemporary Spanish. *Sopa de galeras* (soup of mantis shrimp) makes a rich appetizer; follow up with *confit de pato de laguna* (leg of wild duck) or *perdiz estofado con castañas* (stewed partridge with chestnuts). ⊠ *Av. Alcalde Alvaro Domecq 26* ☎ *956/307030* ⊟ *AE, DC, MC, V* ☉ *Closed Mon. No dinner Aug.*

$–$$$ ✕ **Gaitán.** Within walking distance of the riding school, this restaurant has brick arches and white walls decorated with colorful ceramic plates and photos of famous guests. It's crowded with businesspeople at lunchtime. The menu is Andalusian, with a few Basque dishes thrown in. When in season, *setas* (wild mushrooms) make a delicious starter; follow with *cordero asado* (roast lamb) in a sauce of honey and brandy. ⊠ *Calle Gaitán 3* ☎ *956/168021* ⊟ *AE, DC, MC, V* ☉ *Closed Sun.*

$–$$ ✕ **Venta Antonio.** Crowds come to this roadside inn for superb, fresh seafood cooked in top-quality olive oil. You enter through the busy bar, where lobsters await their fate in a tank. Try the specialties of the Bay of Cádiz, such as *sopa de mariscos* (shellfish soup) followed by succulent *bogavantes de Sanlúcar* (local lobster). ⊠*Ctra. de Jerez–Sanlúcar, Km 5* ☎*956/140535* ☐*AE, DC, MC, V* ⊘*No dinner Sun.*

$–$$ ✕**La Mesa Redonda.** Owner José Antonio Valdespino spent years
★ researching the classic recipes once served in aristocratic Jerez homes, and now his son, José, presents them in this small, friendly restaurant off Avenida Alcalde Alvaro Domecq, around the corner from the Hotel Avenida Jerez. Don't be put off by the bland exterior—within, the eight tables are surrounded by watercolors and shelves are lined with cookbooks. Ask the chef's mother, Margarita—who has an encyclopedic knowledge of Spanish wines—what to order. ⊠*Calle Manuel de la Quintana 3* ☎*956/340069* ☐*AE, DC, MC, V* ⊘*Closed Sun. and mid-July–mid-Aug.*

$$$–$$$$ ⊡**Montecastillo Hotel and Golf Resort.** Outside Jerez near the racetrack, the sprawling, modern Montecastillo adjoins a golf course designed by Jack Nicklaus—ask for a room with a terrace overlooking the course. The common areas are spacious and have marble floors. Rooms are cheerfully decorated, with bright floral bedspreads and rustic clay tiles. ⊠*Ctra. de Arcos, Km 9.6, 11406* ☎*956/151200* ☐*956/151209* ⊕*www.montecastillo.com* ⟿*119 rooms, 2 suites, 20 villas* ⟳*In-room: dial-up, Wi-Fi. In-hotel: restaurant, golf course, tennis court, pools, gym, spa* ☐*AE, DC, MC, V* ⊙❘*BP.*

$$$ ⊡**Hotel Sherry Park.** Set back from the road in an unusually large, tree-
★ filled garden, this modern hotel is designed around several patios filled with exotic foliage. The sunny hallways are hung with contemporary paintings. Rooms are bright and airy and decorated in sunny peach and blue; most have balconies overlooking the garden and pool. There are good deals out of season, as well as special weekend packages. ⊠*Av. Alvaro Domecq 11, 11407* ☎*956/317614* ☐*956/311300* ⊕*www. hipotels.com* ⟿*172 rooms* ⟳*In-hotel: restaurant, bar, pools, gym* ☐*AE, DC, MC, V* ⊙❘*BP.*

$$$ ⊡**Hotel Villa Jerez.** This hacienda-style, tastefully furnished hotel has luxury to offer in the historic part of town. The mature gardens surround a traditional courtyard and are lushly landscaped with palm trees and a dazzle of colorful plants and flowers. Facilities include an elegant restaurant with terrace, a saltwater swimming pool, and a gym. Bedrooms are plush and well equipped, and the staff is friendly and efficient. ⊠*Av. de la Cruz Roja 7, 11407* ☎*956/153100* ☐*956/304300* ⊕*www.villajerez.com* ⟿*14 rooms, 4 suites* ⟳*In-room: ethernet. In-hotel: restaurant, bar, pool* ☐*AE, DC, MC, V.*

$$ ⊡**Ávila.** This friendly, inexpensive hotel on a side street off Calle Arcos offers affordable central lodgings. The rooms have basic furnishings and tile floors; beds are European twin-size. A TV lounge and a small bar/breakfast room adjoin the lobby. ⊠*Calle de Ávila 3, 11401* ☎*956/334808* ☐*956/336807* ⟿*32 rooms* ⟳*In-hotel: bar, parking (fee)* ☐*AE, DC, MC, V.*

$–$$ ⊡**El Ancla.** With yellow-and-white paintwork, wrought-iron balconies, and wooden shutters, El Ancla's architecture is classic Jerez. The hotel doubles as a popular bar, which is good for atmosphere but means it can be noisy at night. Rooms are plainly furnished but comfortable. The underground parking lot across the street is a bonus. ⊠*Pl. del*

Mamelón, 11405 ☎*956/321297* 🖨*956/325005* ⇔*20 rooms* ₫*In-hotel: parking (fee)*.

SPORTS

Formula One Grand Prix races—including the Spanish motorcycle Gran Prix on the first weekend in May—are held at Jerez's racetrack, the **Circuito Permanente de Velocidad** (⊠*Ctra. Arcos, Km 10* ☎*956/151100* ⊕*www.circuitodejerez.com*).

SHOPPING

Browse for wicker and ceramics along **Calle Corredera** and **Calle Bodegas. Duarte** (⊠*Calle Lancería 15* ☎*956/342751*) is the best-known saddle shop in town. It sends its beautifully wrought leather all over the world, including even to the British royal family.

ARCOS DE LA FRONTERA

44
★ *31 km (19 mi) east of Jerez.*

Its narrow and steep cobblestone streets, whitewashed houses, and finely crafted wrought-iron window grilles make Arcos the quintessential Andalusian *pueblo blanco* (white village). Make your way to the main square, the Plaza de España, the highest point in the village; one side of the square is open, and a balcony at the edge of the cliff offers views of the Guadalete Valley. On the opposite end is the church of **Santa María de la Asunción,** a fascinating blend of architectural styles: Romanesque, Gothic, and Mudejar, with a plateresque doorway, a Renaissance retablo, and a 17th-century baroque choir. The *ayuntamiento* (town hall) stands at the foot of the old castle walls on the northern side of the square; across from here is the Casa del Corregidor, onetime residence of the governor and now a parador. Arcos is the most western of the 19 pueblos blancos, whitewashed towns dotted around the Sierra de Cádiz.

WHERE TO STAY & EAT

$$–$$$ ✕ **El Convento.** With tables set around a graceful Andalusian patio, this rustic-style restaurant (owned by but separate from the hotel on Calle Maldonado) is known for its fine regional cooking. The *sopa de tagarninas* (wild asparagus soup) is one of the town treasures, as are the *garbanzos con tomillo* (chickpeas with thyme) and the *abajado* (wild rabbit or lamb stew). ⊠*Calle Marqués de Torresoto 7* ☎*956/703222* ▤*AE, DC, MC, V* ☉*Closed Jan.*

$$$ ✕▣ **Parador Casa del Corregidor.** Expect a spectacular view from the
★ terrace—the parador clings to the cliff side, overlooking the rolling valley of the Guadalete River. Public rooms include a popular bar and restaurant that opens onto the terrace, and an enclosed patio. Spacious guest rooms are furnished with dark Castilian furniture, *esparto* (reed) rugs, and abundant tiles. The best are rooms 15–18, which overlook the valley. At the restaurant, try a local dish such as *berenjenas arcenses* (spicy eggplant with ham and chorizo) or sample 10 regional specialties with the *menú degustacíon* (tasting menu; €25). ⊠*Pl. del Cabildo, 11630* ☎*956/700500* 🖨*956/701116* ⊕*www.parador.es* ⇔*24 rooms*

⚐ *In-room: dial-up, Wi-Fi. In-hotel: restaurant, bar, public Wi-Fi, public Internet* ⊟ *AE, DC, MC, V.*

$$ ⊞ **El Convento.** Perched atop the cliff behind the town parador, this tiny hotel (a former convent) shares the same amazing view, though the rooms are much smaller—and cheaper. Some rooms have balconies, and there's a large rooftop terrace on the edge of the cliff. ⊠ *Calle Maldonado 2, 11630* ☎ *956/702333* 📠 *957/704128* ⊕ *www.webdearcos. com/elconvento* ↩ *11 rooms* ⚐ *In-hotel: restaurant* ⊟ *AE, DC, MC, V* ⊗ *Closed Jan.*

$$ ⊞ **La Casa Grande.** Built in 1729, this extraordinary 18th-century man-

Fodor's Choice sion encircles a lushly vegetated central patio and is perched on the

★ edge of the 400-foot cliff to which Arcos de la Frontera clings. Each room has been restored by Catalan owners Elena Posa and Ferran Grau. The artwork, the casually elegant design of the living quarters, and inventive bathrooms are all a delight. The breakfast terrace allows you to look down on falcons circling hundreds of feet above the riverbed below. The rooftop rooms, in El Palomar (The Pigeon Roost) and El Soberao (The Attic), are the best. ⊠ *C. Maldonado 10, 11630* ☎ *956/703930* 📠 *956/703930* ⊕ *www.lacasagrande.net* ↩ *5 rooms, 2 suites* ⚐ *In-room: Wi-Fi. In-hotel: breakfast terrace, no elevator.* ⊟ *AE, DC, MC, V* ⎮⊙⎮ *BP.*

$–$$ ⊞ **Real de Veas.** This tastefully converted 19th-century town house is home to this gem of a hotel. Rooms are set around a central glass-covered patio and are decorated in neutral tones agreeably coupled with rustic furniture. The marble-clad bathrooms have all the extras, including whirlpool baths and hair dryers. The congenial Spanish owners also dish up a more-generous-than-most breakfast, which includes cheese and cold cuts. ⊠ *C. Corredera 12, 11630* ☎ *956/717370* 📠 *956/717269* ⊕ *www.hotelrealdeveas.com* ↩ *12 rooms* ⚐ *In-room: dial-up. In-hotel: restaurant* ⊟ *MC, V* ⎮⊙⎮ *BP.*

SANLÚCAR DE BARRAMEDA

㊺ *24 km (15 mi) northwest of Jerez.*

Columbus sailed from this harbor on his third voyage to the Americas, in 1498. Twenty years later, Magellan began his circumnavigation of the globe from here. Today this fishing town has a crumbling charm and is best known for its *langostinos* (jumbo shrimp) and Manzanilla, an exceptionally dry sherry. The most popular restaurants are in the **Bajo de Guía** neighborhood, on the banks of the Guadalquivir. Here, too, is a visitor center for Doñana National Park.

Boat trips can take you up the river, stopping at various points in the park; the *Real Fernando*, with bar and café, does a four-hour cruise up the Guadalquivir to the Coto de Doñana. ⊠ *Bajo de Guía, Sanlúcar de Barrameda* ☎ *956/363813* ⊕ *www.visitasdonana.com* 💶 *€15.50* ⊗ *Cruises Apr., May, and Oct., daily at 10 AM and 4 PM; Nov.–Mar., daily at 10 AM; June–Sept., daily at 10 AM and 5 PM.*

WHERE TO STAY & EAT

$$–$$$ ✕**Casa Bigote.** Colorful and informal, this spot on the beach is known for its fried *acedias* (a type of small sole) and langostinos, which come from these very waters. The seafood paella is also catch-of-the-day fresh. Reservations are essential in summer. ⊠*Bajo de Guía* ☎956/362696 ⊟*AE, DC, MC, V* ⊘*Closed Sun. and Nov.*

$$–$$$ ✕**Mirador de Doñana.** This Bajo de Guía landmark overlooking the water serves delicious *chocos* (crayfish), shrimp, and the signature dish *mi barca mirador* (white fish in a tomato sauce). The dining area overlooks the large, busy tapas bar. ⊠*Bajo de Guía* ☎956/364205 ⊟*MC, V* ⊘*Closed Jan.*

$–$$ ✕**Casa Balbino.** After the sunset at Bajo de Guía Beach, the serious tapas and tippling begins in the Plaza del Cabildo, Sanlúcar's party nerve center. Balbino is the best of these taverns—though the *patatas aliñá* (potatoes dressed in an olive oil vinaigrette) at nearby Bar Barbiana are noteworthy as well. ⊠*Pl. del Cabildo 14* ☎956/362647 ⊟*AE, DC, MC, V* ⊘*Closed Jan.*

$–$$ ⊡**Los Helechos.** Named for the ferns *(los helechos)* that dominate the patio and entryway, this breezy place with a lovely rooftop terrace has the distinct advantage of being out of earshot but within stumbling distance of the Plaza del Cabildo. ⊠*Pl. Madre de Dios 9, 11540* ☎*956/361349* ⊟*956/369650* ⊕*www.hotelloshelechos.com* ⇆*56 rooms* ⚒*In-hotel: restaurant, bar, parking (fee)* ⊟*AE, DC, MC, V.*

PUERTO DE SANTA MARÍA

46 *12 km (7 mi) southwest of Jerez, 17 km (11 mi) north of Cádiz.*

This attractive, if somewhat dilapidated, little fishing port on the northern shores of the Bay of Cádiz, with lovely beaches nearby, has white houses with peeling facades and vast green grilles covering the doors and windows. The town is dominated by the Terry and Osborne sherry and brandy bodegas. Columbus once lived in a house on the square that bears his name (Cristóbal Colón), and Washington Irving spent the autumn of 1828 at Calle Palacios 57. The marisco bars along the Ribera del Marisco (Seafood Way) are Puerto de Santa María's current claim to fame. Casa Luis, Romerijo, La Guachi, and Paco Ceballos are among the most popular, along with Er Beti, at Misericordia 7. The tourist office has a list of six tapas routes that take in 39 tapas bars.

The **Castillo de San Marcos** was built in the 13th century on the site of a mosque. Created by Alfonso X, it was later home to the Duke of Medinaceli. Among the guests were Christopher Columbus—who tried unsuccessfully to persuade the duke to finance his voyage west—and Juan de la Cosa, who, within these walls, drew up the first map ever to include the Americas. The red lettering on the walls is a 19th-century addition. ⊠*Pl. del Castillo* ☎*965/851751* ⊡*€5, free Tues.* ⊘*Tues., Thurs., and Sat. 10–2.*

This stunning neo-Mudejar **Plaza de Toros** was built in 1880 thanks to a donation from the winemaker Thomas Osborne. It originally had seating for exactly 12,816 people, the population of Puerto at that time.

⊠ *Los Moros* 🎫*Free* ⊙*Apr.–Oct., Thurs.–Tues. 11–1:30 and 6–7:30; Nov.–Mar., Thurs.–Tues. 11–1:30 and 5:30–7. Closed bullfight days plus 1 day before and after each bullfight.*

WHERE TO STAY & EAT

$$–$$$ ✕**El Faro de El Puerto.** In a villa outside town, the "Lighthouse in the Port" is run by the same family that established the classic El Faro in Cádiz. Like its predecessor, it serves excellent fish; also available are such delicacies as veal rolls filled with foie gras in a sweet sherry sauce and several vegetarian options. ⊠*Ctra. Fuentebravia–Rota, Km 0.5* ☎*956/858003 or 956/870952* ⊕*www.elfarodelpuerto.com* ▱*AE, DC, MC, V* ⊙*No dinner Sun. Sept.–July.*

$$$–$$$$ 🏨**Monasterio San Miguel.** Dating from 1733, this monastery is a few
★ blocks from the harbor. There's nothing spartan about the former cells; they're now air-conditioned rooms with all the trappings. The restaurant is in a large, vaulted hall (formerly the nuns' laundry); the baroque church is now a concert hall; and the cloister's gardens provide a peaceful refuge. Beam ceilings, polished marble floors, and huge brass lamps enhance the 18th-century feel. If you're traveling out of season, check the Web site for discounts. ⊠*C. Virgen de los Milagros 27, 11500* ☎*956/540440* 🖨*956/542604* ⊕*www.jale.com* ⇆*139 rooms, 11 suites* ⚘*In-room: Wi-Fi. In-hotel: restaurant, bar, pool, public Wi-Fi, public Internet, parking (fee)* ▱*AE, DC, MC, V.*

CÁDIZ

47 *32 km (20 mi) southwest of Jerez, 149 km (93 mi) southwest of*
★ *Seville.*

Surrounded by the Atlantic Ocean on three sides, Cádiz was founded as Gadir by Phoenician traders in 1100 BC and claims to be the oldest continuously inhabited city in the Western world. Hannibal lived in Cádiz for a time, Julius Caesar first held public office here, and Columbus set out from here on his second voyage, after which the city became the home base of the Spanish fleet. In the 18th century, when the Guadalquivir silted up, Cádiz monopolized New World trade and became the wealthiest port in Western Europe. Most of its buildings—including the cathedral, built in part with gold and silver from the New World—date from this period. The old city is African in appearance and immensely intriguing—a cluster of narrow streets opening onto charming small squares. The golden cupola of the cathedral looms above low white houses, and the whole place has a slightly dilapidated air. Spaniards flock here in February to revel in the carnival celebrations, but in general it's not very touristy.

WHAT TO SEE

Begin your explorations in the Plaza de Mina, a large, leafy square with palm trees and plenty of benches. The tourist office is in the northwestern corner. On the square's western flank, the ornamental facade of the **Colegio de Arquitectos** (College of Architects) is especially beautiful.

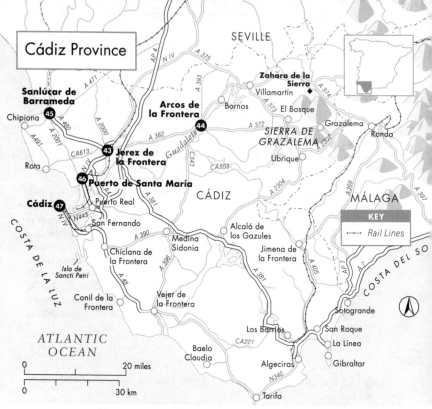

Cádiz Province

On the east side of the Plaza de Mina, is the **Museo de Cádiz** (Provincial Museum). Notable pieces include works by Murillo and Alonso Cano as well as the *Four Evangelists* and set of saints by Zurbarán, which have much in common with his masterpieces at Guadalupe, in Extremadura. The archaeological section contains Phoenician sarcophagi from the time of this ancient city's birth. ✉ *Pl. de Mina* ☎ *956/212281* 🖃 *€1.50, free for EU citizens* ⊙ *Tues. 2:30–8, Wed.– Sat. 9–8, Sun. 9–2.*

A few blocks east of the Plaza de Mina, next door to the Iglesia del Rosario, is the **Oratorio de la Santa Cueva,** an oval 18th-century chapel with three frescoes by Goya. ✉ *C. Rosario 10* ☎ *956/222262* 🖃 *€2.50* ⊙ *Tues.–Fri. 10–1 and 4:30–7:30, weekends 10–1.*

Farther up Calle San José from the Plaza de la Mina is the **Oratorio de San Felipe Neri.** Spain's first liberal constitution was declared at this church in 1812, and here the Cortes (Parliament) of Cádiz met when the rest of Spain was subjected to the rule of Napoléon's brother, Joseph Bonaparte (more popularly known as Pepe Botella, for his love of the bottle). On the main altar is an *Immaculate Conception* by Murillo, the great Sevillian artist who in 1682 fell to his death from a scaffold while working on his *Mystic Marriage of St. Catherine* in Cádiz's Cha-

1

pel of Santa Catalina. ✉ *Calle Santa Inés 38* ☎ *956/211612* 💶 *€2.50* ⏰ *Mon.–Sat. 10–1:30.*

Next door to the Oratorio de San Felipe Neri, the small but pleasant **Museo de las Cortes** has a 19th-century mural depicting the establishment of the Constitution of 1812. Its real showpiece, however, is a 1779 ivory-and-mahogany model of Cádiz, with all of the city's streets and buildings in minute detail, looking much as they do now. ✉ *Santa Inés 9* ☎ *956/221788* 💶 *Free* ⏰ *Oct.–May, Tues.–Fri. 9–1 and 4–7, weekends 9–1; June–Sept., Tues.–Fri. 9–1 and 5–8, weekends 9–1.*

Four blocks west of Santa Inés is the Plaza Manuel de Falla, overlooked by an amazing neo-Mudejar redbrick building, the **Gran Teatro Manuel de Falla.** The classic interior is impressive as well; try to attend a performance. ✉ *Pl. Manuel de Falla* ☎ *956/220828.*

Backtrack along Calle Sacramento toward the city center to **Torre Tavira.** At 150 feet, this tower, attached to an 18th-century palace that's now a conservatory of music, is the highest point in the old city. More than a hundred such watchtowers were used by Cádiz ship owners to spot their arriving fleets. A camera obscura gives a good overview of the city and its monuments; the last show is a half hour before closing time. ✉ *Calle Marqués del Real Tesoro 10* ☎ *956/212910* 💶 *€4* ⏰ *Mid-June–mid-Sept., daily 10–8; mid-Sept.–mid-June, daily 10–6.*

Five blocks southeast of the Torre Tavira are the gold dome and baroque facade of Cádiz's **cathedral,** begun in 1722, when the city was at the height of its power. The Cádiz-born composer Manuel de Falla, who died in 1946 at the age of 70, is buried in the **crypt.** The cathedral **museum,** on Calle Acero, displays gold, silver, and jewels from the New World, as well as Enrique de Arfe's processional cross, which is carried in the annual Corpus Christi parades. The cathedral is known as the New Cathedral because it supplanted the original 13th-century structure next door, which was destroyed by the British in 1592, rebuilt, and renamed the church of **Santa Cruz** when the New Cathedral came along. The entrance price includes the crypt, museum, and church of Santa Cruz. ✉ *Pl. Catedral* ☎ *956/259812* 💶 *€4* ⏰ *Mass Sun. at noon; museum Tues.–Fri. 10–2 and 4:30–7:30, Sat. 10–1.*

Next door to the church of Santa Cruz are the remains of a 1st-century BC **Roman theater** (✉ *Campo del Sur s/n, Barrio del Pópulo* 💶 *Free* ⏰ *Daily 10–2*); it is still under excavation.

The impressive *ayuntamiento (city hall)* (✉ *Pl. de San Juan de Dios s/n*) overlooks the Plaza San Juan de Diós, one of Cádiz's liveliest hubs. The building is attractively illuminated at night. The **Plaza San Francisco,** near the ayuntamiento, is a pretty square surrounded by white-and-yellow houses and filled with orange trees and elegant street lamps. It's especially lively during the evening *paseo* (promenade).

WHERE TO STAY & EAT

$$–$$$$

FodorsChoice ★

✕ **El Faro.** This famous fishing-quarter restaurant is deservedly known as the best in the province. Outside, it's one of many low-rise, white houses with bright-blue flowerpots; inside it's warm and inviting, with half-tile walls, glass lanterns, oil paintings, and photos of old Cádiz. Fish dominates the menu, but alternatives include *cebón al queso de cabrales* (venison in blue-cheese sauce). If you don't want to go for the full splurge, there's an excellent tapas bar as well. ⊠ *Calle San Felix 15* ☎*956/211068* ⊟*AE, DC, MC, V.*

$$–$$$ ✕ **El Ventorrillo del Chato.** Standing on its own on the sandy isthmus con-
★ necting Cádiz to the mainland, this former inn was founded in 1780 by a man ironically nicknamed "El Chato" (pug-nosed) for his prominent proboscis. Run by a scion of El Faro's Gonzalo Córdoba, the restaurant serves tasty regional specialties in charming Andalusian surroundings. Seafood is a favorite, but meat, stews, and rice dishes are also well represented on the menu, and the wine list is very good. ⊠ *Vía Augusta Julia s/n* ☎*956/250025* ⊟*AE, DC, MC, V* ⊙*Closed Sun.*

$–$$ ✕ **Casa Manteca.** Cádiz's most quintessentially Andalusian tavern is just down the street from El Faro restaurant and a little deeper into the La Viña barrio (named for the vineyard that once grew here). *Chacina* (Iberian ham or sausage) served on waxed paper and Manzanilla (sherry from Sanlúcar de Barrameda) are standard fare at this low wooden counter that has served bullfighters and flamenco singers, as well as dignitaries from around the world since 1953. ⊠ *Corralón de los Carros 66* ☎*956/213603* ⊟*AE, DC, MC, V* ⊙*Closed Mon. No lunch Sun.*

$$$ ⊡ **Parador de Cádiz.** Cádiz's modern Parador Atlántico has a privileged position on the headland overlooking the bay and is the only hotel in its class in the old part of Cádiz. The spacious indoor public rooms have gleaming marble floors, and tables and chairs surround a fountain on the small patio. The cheerful, bright-green bar, decorated with ceramic tiles and bullfighting posters, is a popular meeting place for Cádiz society. Most rooms have small balconies facing the sea. ⊠ *Av. Duque de Nájera 9, 11002* ☎*956/226905* ⊟*956/214582* ⊕*www. parador.es* ⥎*143 rooms, 6 suites* �*In-room: dial-up, Wi-Fi. In-hotel: restaurant, bar, pool, gym, parking (no fee), some pets allowed* ⊟*AE, DC, MC, V* ⅙*BP.*

$$ ⊡ **Bahía.** Just off the bustling Plaza de San Juan de Dios, on a tree-lined pedestrian street, this is a budget winner. The beds are firm, and most rooms have small balconies. The lack of dining room is compensated for by the variety and proximity of bars and restaurants. ⊠ *Calle Plocia 5, 11002* ☎*956/259061* ⊟*956/254208* ⥎*21 rooms* ⊟*MC, V.*

NIGHTLIFE & THE ARTS

The **Gran Teatro Manuel de Falla** (⊠ *Pl. Manuel de Falla* ☎*956/220828*) is Cádiz's cultural hub; the tourist office has performance schedules.

CÓRDOBA

166 km (103 mi) northwest of Granada, 407 km (250 mi) southwest of Madrid, 143 km (86 mi) northeast of Seville.

Once a medieval city famed for the peaceful and prosperous coexistence of its three religious cultures—Islamic, Jewish, and Christian—Córdoba is a perfect analogue for the cultural history of the Iberian Peninsula. Strategically located on the north bank of the Guadalquivir

River, Córdoba was the Roman and Moorish capital of Spain, and its old quarter, clustered around its famous mosque (Mezquita), remains one of the country's grandest and yet most intimate examples of its Moorish heritage.

The Romans invaded in 206 BC, later making it the capital of Rome's section of Spain. Nearly 800 years later, the Visigoth king Leovigildus took control. The tribe was soon supplanted by the Moors, whose emirs and caliphs held court here from the 8th century to the early 11th century. At that point Córdoba was one of the greatest centers of art, culture, and learning in the Western world; one of its libraries had a staggering 400,000 volumes. Moors, Christians, and Jews lived together in harmony within Córdoba's walls. Chroniclers of the day put the city's population at around a million, making it the largest city in Europe, though historians believe the real figure was closer to half a million (there are fewer than 300,000 today). In that era, it was considered second in importance only to Constantinople. However, in 1009 Prince Muhammad II and Omeyan led a rebellion that broke up the Caliphate, leading to power flowing to separate Moorish kingdoms.

Córdoba remained in Moorish hands until it was conquered by King Ferdinand in 1236 and repopulated with people from the north of Spain. Later the Catholic Monarchs used the city as a base from which to plan the conquest of Granada. In Columbus's time, the Guadalquivir was navigable as far upstream as Córdoba, and great galleons sailed its waters. Today, the river's muddy water and marshy banks evoke little of Córdoba's glorious past, but the city's bridge—of Roman origin, though much restored by the Arabs and successive generations—and an old Arab waterwheel recall a far grander era.

Córdoba today, with its modest population of just over 300,000, offers a cultural depth and intensity—a direct legacy from the great emirs, caliphs, philosophers, physicians, poets, and engineers of the days of the caliphate—that far outstrips the city's current commercial and political power. The city's artistic and historical treasures begin with the *mezquita-catedral* (mosque-cathedral), as it is ever-more-frequently called, and continue through the winding, whitewashed streets of the Judería (the medieval Jewish quarter); the jasmine-, geranium-, and orange blossom–filled patios; the Renaissance palaces; and the two dozen churches, convents, and hermitages, nearly all of them Mudéjar (built by Moorish artisans) built directly over former mosques.

EXPLORING CÓRDOBA

Córdoba is a very manageable city. It is densely packed with beautiful patios, doorways, streets, rooftops, windows bursting with flowers, and twisting alleyways with surprises around every corner. In general, neighborhoods are known by the parish churches at their center. The main city subdivisions used in this book are the **Judería,** including the Mezquita, the San Basilio neighborhood behind the Jardines de los Reales Alcázares, and the Torre de la Calahorra across the river; the **Plaza de la Corredera,** a historic gathering place for everything from horse

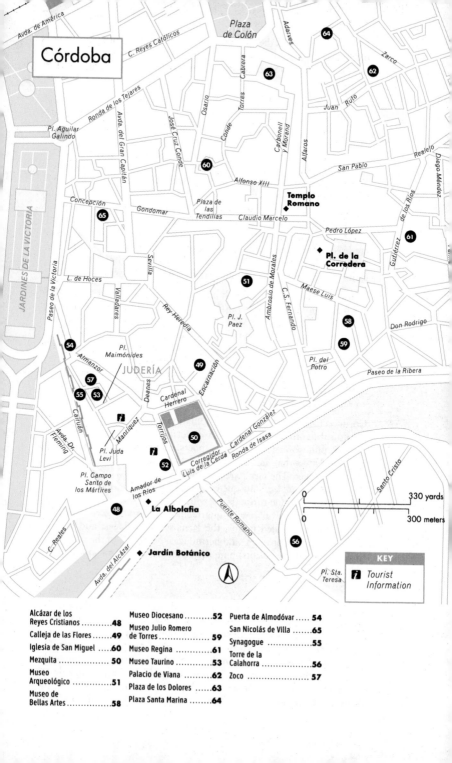

Córdoba

races to bullfights and a neighborhood that, for the purposes of this book, stretches from the Paseo de la Ribera along the Guadalquivir, through the artistically important Plaza del Potro, past the Plaza de la Corredera to the ruins of the Roman Temple; and the **Centro,** from the area around Plaza de las Tendillas to the Iglesia de Santa Marina and the Torre de la Malmuerta. Incidentally, this *centro comercial* (commercial center) is much more than a succession of shops and stores. The town's real life, the everyday hustle and bustle, takes place here, and the general ambience is very different from that of

> ### CÓRDOBA BY BIKE
>
> Never designed to support modern motor traffic, Cordoba's medieval layout is ideal for bicycles. **Cordoba La Llana en Bici** (✉ *Calle Lucano 20* ☎ *639/425884* ⊕ *www.cordobaenbici.com*) offers a variety of tours including half-day excursions, gastronomical tours, rides out to the ruins of the Medina-Azahara palace 8 km (5 mi) outside town, or, farther afield in the Sierra Morena, cycling tours of the Cardeña–Montoro and Hornachuelos nature parks.

the tourist center around the Mezquita. Some of the city's finest Mudéjar churches and best taverns, as well as the Palacio de los Marqueses de Viana, are in this pivotal part of town well back from the Guadalquivir waterfront.

Some of the most characteristic and rewarding places to explore in Córdoba are the parish churches and the taverns that inevitably accompany them. The *iglesias fernandinas* (so-called for their construction after Saint-King Fernando III's conquest of Córdoba) are nearly always built over mosques with stunning horseshoe arch doorways and Mudéjar towers. Taverns tended to spring up around these populous hubs of city life. Examples are the Taberna de San Miguel (aka Casa el Pisto) next to the church of the same name, and the Bar Santa Marina (aka Casa Obispo) next to the Santa Marina Church. Most neighborhoods are built around their parish churches and have a well-known tavern, if not several, nearby, providing an excellent way to explore neighborhoods, see churches, and taste *finos* (montilla-moriles sherry) and *tentempies* (tapas—literally, "keep you on your feet").

■ TIP→ **Córdoba's council authorities and private institutions frequently change the hours of the city's sights; before visiting an attraction, confirm hours with the tourist office or the sight itself.**

WHAT TO SEE

48 **Alcázar de los Reyes Cristianos** *(Fortress of the Christian Monarchs).* Built by Alfonso XI in 1328, the Alcázar is a Mudejar-style palace with splendid gardens. (The original Moorish Alcázar stood beside the Mezquita, on the site of the present Bishop's Palace.) This is where, in the 15th century, the Catholic Monarchs held court and launched their conquest of Granada. Boabdil was imprisoned here in 1483, and for nearly 300 years the Alcázar served as the Inquisition's base. The most important sights here are the Hall of the Mosaics and a Roman stone sacrophagus from the 2nd or 3rd century. ✉*Pl. Campo Santo de los Mártires, Judería* ☎*957/420151* ⊒*€4, free Fri.* ☉*May–Sept.,*

Tues.–Sat. 10–2 and 6–8, Sun. 9:30–3; Oct.–Apr., Tues.–Sat. 10–2 and 4:30–6:30, Sun. 9:30–2:30.

㊾ Calleja de las Flores. You'd be hard pressed to find prettier patios than those along this tiny street, a few yards off the northeastern corner of the Mezquita. Patios, many with ceramics, foliage, and iron grilles, are key to Córdoba's architecture, at least in the old quarter, where life is lived behind sturdy white walls—a legacy of the Moors, who honored both the sanctity of the home and the need to shut out the fierce summer sun. Between the second and the third week of May, right after the early May **Cruces de Mayo**, (Crosses of May) competition when neighborhoods compete at setting up elaborate crosses decorated with flowers and plants, Córdoba throws a **Patio Festival**, during which private patios are filled with flowers, opened to the public, and judged in a municipal competition. Córdoba's council publishes a map with an itinerary of the best patios in town—note that most are open only in the late afternoon during the week and all day on weekends.

OFF THE BEATEN PATH

Jardín Botánico *(Botanical Garden).* Across from Córdoba's modest zoo is its modern botanical garden, with outdoor spaces—including a section devoted to aromatic herbs—as well as greenhouses full of plants from South America and the Canary Islands. The Museo de Etnobotánica explores the way in which humans interact with the plant world. ⊠ *Av. de Linneo s/n, Parque Zoológico* ☎ *957/200018* ☜ *€2* ☉ *Apr.–Oct., Tues.–Sun. 10–2:30 and 5:30–7:30; Nov.–Mar., Tues.–Sat. 10:30–2:30 and 4:30–6:30, Sun. 10:30–6:30.*

㊿ Mezquita *(Mosque).* Built between the 8th and 10th centuries, Córdoba's mosque is one of the earliest and most transportingly beautiful examples of Spanish Muslim architecture. The plain, crenelled walls of the outside do little to prepare you for the sublime beauty of the interior. As you enter through the **Puerta de las Palmas** (Door of the Palms), some 850 columns rise before you in a forest of jasper, marble, granite, and onyx. The pillars are topped by ornate capitals taken from the Visigothic church that was razed to make way for the mosque. Crowning these, red-and-white-stripe arches curve away into the dimness. The ceiling is carved of delicately tinted cedar. The Mezquita has served as a cathedral since 1236, but its origins as a mosque are clear. Built in four stages, it was founded in 785 by Abd ar-Rahman I (756–88) on a site he bought from the Visigoth Christians. He pulled down their church and replaced it with a mosque, one-third the size of the present one, into which he incorporated marble pillars from earlier Roman and Visigothic shrines. Under Abd ar-Rahman II (822–52), the Mezquita held an original copy of the Koran and a bone from the arm of the prophet Mohammed and became a Muslim pilgrimage site second only to Mecca in importance.

Fodors Choice ★

Al Hakam II (961–76) built the beautiful **Mihrab** (prayer niche), the Mezquita's greatest jewel. Make your way over to the **Qiblah,** the south-facing wall in which this sacred prayer niche was hollowed out. (Muslim law decrees that a Mihrab face east, toward Mecca, and that worshippers do likewise when they pray. Because of an error in calculation, the Mihrab here faces more south than east. Al Hakam II spent hours agonizing over a means of correcting such a serious mistake, but he was persuaded by architects to let it be.) In front of the Mihrab is the **Maksoureh,** a kind of anteroom for the caliph and his court; its mosaics and plasterwork make it a masterpiece of Islamic art. A last addition to the mosque as such, the Maksoureh was completed around 987 by Al Mansur, who more than doubled its size.

After the Reconquest, the Christians left the Mezquita largely undisturbed, dedicating it to the Virgin Mary and using it as a place of Christian worship. The clerics did erect a wall closing off the mosque from its courtyard, which helped dim the interior and thus separate the house of worship from the world outside. In the 13th century, Christians had the **Capilla de Villaviciosa** built by Moorish craftsmen, its Mudejar architecture blending with the lines of the mosque. Not so the heavy, incongruous baroque structure of the **cathedral,** sanctioned in the very heart of the mosque by Charles V in the 1520s. To the emperor's credit, he was supposedly horrified when he came to inspect the new construction, exclaiming to the architects, "To build something ordinary, you have destroyed something that was unique in the world" (not that this sentiment stopped him from tampering with the Alhambra to build his Palacio Carlos V). Rest up and reflect in the **Patio de los Naranjos** (Orange Court), perfumed in springtime by orange blossoms. The **Puerta del Perdón** (Gate of Forgiveness), so named because debtors were forgiven here on feast days, is on the north wall of the Orange Court. It's the formal entrance to the mosque. The **Virgen de los Faroles** (Virgin of the Lanterns), a small statue in a niche on the outside wall of the mosque along the north side on Cardenal Herrero, is behind a lantern-hung grille, rather like a lady awaiting a serenade. The **Torre del Alminar,** the minaret once used to summon Moorish faithful to prayer, has a baroque belfry.

Wheelchairs are available, and audio guides can be rented for €3 Monday–Saturday. ⊠ *Calle Torrijos and Cardenal Herrero, Judería* ☎957/470512 ☑€8 ⊙*Jan. and Dec., daily 10–5:30; Feb. and Nov., daily 10–6; Mar. and July–Oct., daily 10–7; Apr.–June, daily 10–7:30.*

NEED A BREAK?

The lively **Plaza Juda Levi,** surrounded by a maze of narrow streets and squares, lies at the heart of the Judería and makes a great spot for indulging in a little people-watching. Sit outside here with a drink or, better still, an ice cream from Helados Juda Levi.

51 **Museo Arqueológico.** In the heart of the old quarter, the Museum of Archaeology has finds from Córdoba's varied cultural past. The ground floor has ancient Iberian statues, and Roman statues, mosaics, and artifacts; the upper floor is devoted to Moorish art. By chance, the ruins of a Roman theater were discovered right next to the museum in 2000—have a look from the window just inside the entrance. The alleys and steps along Altos de Santa Ana make for great wandering. ⊠*Pl. Jerónimo Paez, Judería* ☎957/474011 ☑€1.50, free for EU citizens ⊙*Tues. 2:30–8:30, Wed.–Sat. 9–8:30, Sun. 9–2:30.*

(52) **Museo Diocesano.** Housed in the former Bishop's Palace, facing the mosque, the Diocesan Museum is devoted to religious art, with illustrated prayer books, tapestries, paintings (including some Julio Romero de Torres canvases), and sculpture. The medieval wood sculptures are the museum's finest treasures. *Note that the museum was closed in 2007. At the time of this writing it was due to open soon.* ✉ *Calle Torrijos 12, Judería* ☎ *957/496085* 🎟 *€2, free with ticket for Mezquita* ⏲ *June–Sept., weekdays 9:30–3, Sat. 9:30–1:30; Oct.–Mar., weekdays 9:30–1:30 and 3:30–5:30, Sat. 9:30–1:30.*

(53) **Museo Taurino** (Museum of Bullfighting). Two adjoining mansions on the Plaza Maimónides (or Plaza de las Bulas) house this museum. It's worth a visit, as much for the chance to see a restored mansion as for the posters, Art Nouveau paintings, bull's heads, suits of lights (bullfighter outfits), and memorabilia of famous Córdoban bullfighters including the most famous of all, Manolete. To the surprise of the nation, Manolete, who was considered immortal, was killed by a bull in the ring at Linares in 1947. ✉ *Pl. Maimónides, Judería* ☎ *957/201056* 🎟 *€3, free Fri.* ⏲ *Tues.–Sat. 10–2 and 6–8 (4:30–6:30 Oct.–May), Sun. 9:30–3.*

(54) **Puerta de Almodóvar.** Outside this old Moorish gate at the northern entrance of the Judería is a statue of **Seneca,** the Córdoban-born philosopher who rose to prominence in Nero's court in Rome and was forced to commit suicide at his emperor's command. The gate stands at the top of the narrow and colorful Calle San Felipe.

(55) **Synagogue.** The only Jewish temple in Andalusia to survive the expulsion and inquisition of the Jews in 1492, Córdoba's synagogue is also one of only three ancient synagogues left in all of Spain (the other two are in Toledo). Though it no longer functions as a place of worship, it's a treasured symbol for Spain's modern Jewish communities. The outside is plain, but the inside, measuring 23 feet by 21 feet, contains some exquisite Mudejar stucco tracery. Look for the fine plant motifs and the Hebrew inscription saying that the synagogue was built in 1315. The women's gallery, not open for visits, still stands, and in the east wall is the ark where the sacred scrolls of the Torah were kept. ✉ *C. Judíos, Judería* ☎ *957/202928* 🎟 *€0.30, free for EU citizens* ⏲ *Tues.–Sat. 9:30–2 and 3:30–5:30, Sun. 9:30–1:30.*

(56) **Torre de la Calahorra.** The tower on the far side of the Puente Romano (Roman Bridge) was built in 1369 to guard the entrance to Córdoba. It now houses the **Museo Vivo de Al-Andalus** (Museum of Al-Andalus), with films and audiovisual guides (in English) on Córdoba's history. Climb the narrow staircase to the top of the tower for the view of the Roman bridge and city on the other side of the Guadalquivir. *The museum was closed at the time of this writing but was due to open by press time.* ✉ *Av. de la Confederación, Sector Sur* ☎ *957/293929* 🎟 *€5, €5.50 with audiovisual show* ⏲ *May–Sept., daily 10–2 and 5:30–8:30 with audiovisual shows at 10:30, 11:30, noon, 5, 6, and 7; Oct.–Apr., daily 10–6 with audiovisual shows at 11, noon, 1, 3, and 4.*

(57) **Zoco.** *Zoco* is the Spanish word for the Arab souk, the onetime function of this courtyard near the synagogue. It now is the site of a daily crafts

market, where you can see artisans at work, and evening flamenco in summer. ⊠*Calle Judíos 5, Judería* ☎*957/204033* 🎫*Free.*

NEED A BREAK? **Wander over to the Plaza de las Tendillas, which is halfway between the Mezquita and Plaza Colón. The terraces of the Café Boston and Café Siena are both enjoyable places to relax with a coffee when the weather is warm.**

⑤⑧ Museo de Bellas Artes. Hard to miss because of its deep-pink facade, Córdoba's Museum of Fine Arts, in a courtyard just off the Plaza del Potro, belongs to a former Hospital de la Caridad (Charity Hospice). It was founded by Ferdinand and Isabella, who twice received Columbus here. The collection includes paintings by Murillo, Valdés Leal, Zurbarán, Goya, and Sorolla. ⊠*Pl. del Potro, 1 San Francisco* ☎*957/473345* ⊕*www.juntadeandalucia.es/cultura/museos/MBACO* 🎫*€1.50, free for EU citizens* ☉*Tues. 2:30–8:30, Wed.–Sat. 9–8:30, Sun. 9–2:30.*

⑤⑨ Museo Julio Romero de Torres. Across the courtyard from the Museum of ★ Fine Arts, this museum is devoted to the early-20th-century Córdoban artist Julio Romero de Torres (1874–1930), who specialized in surreal and erotic portraits of demure, partially dressed Andalusian temptresses. Romero de Torres was also a flamenco *cantaor* (singer), died at the age of 56, and is one of Córdoba's greatest folk heroes. ⊠*Pl. del Potro 1, San Francisco* ☎*957/491909* ⊕*www.museojulioromero.com* 🎫*€4, free Fri.* ☉*Tues.–Sat. 10–2 and 4:30–6:30, Sun. 9:30–2:30.*

⑥⓪ Iglesia de San Miguel. Complete with Romanesque doors built around ★ Mudéjar horseshoe arches, the San Miguel Church, the square and café terraces around it, and its excellent tavern, Taberna San Miguel-Casa El Pisto, form one of the city's finest combinations of art, history, and gastronomy. ⊠*Pl. San Miguel Centro.*

⑥① Museo Regina. You can watch craftsmen at work here creating the ★ delicate silver filigree pieces for which Córdoba is famous. Construction unearthed the Roman and Moorish archaeological remains that are on display on the ground floor. ⊠*Pl. Luís Venegas 1, Centro* ☎*957/496889* ⊕*www.museoregina.com* 🎫*€3* ☉*June–mid-Sept., daily 9–2 and 5:30–9; mid-Sept.–May., daily 10–3 and 5–8.*

⑥② Palacio de Viana. This 17th-century palace is one of Córdoba's most splendid aristocratic homes. Also known as the **Museo de los Patios,** it contains 12 interior patios, each one different; the patios and gardens are planted with cypresses, orange trees, and myrtles. Inside the building are a carriage museum, a library, embossed leather wall hangings, filigree silver, and grand galleries and staircases. As you enter, note that the corner column of the first patio has been removed to allow the entrance of horse-drawn carriages. ⊠*Pl. Don Gomé, Centro* ☎*957/496741* 🎫*Patios only €3, patios and interior €6* ☉*Mid-June–Sept., Mon.–Sat. 9–2; Oct.–Apr., Mon.–Sat. 10–1 and 4–6.*

⑥③ Plaza de los Dolores. The 17th-century Convento de Capuchinos surrounds this small square north of Plaza San Miguel. The square is where you feel most deeply the city's languid pace. In its center, a statue

CÓRDOBA FIESTAS

Córdoba parties hard during **Carnival,** on the days leading up to Ash Wednesday, and **Semana Santa** (Holy Week) is always intensely celebrated with dramatic religious processions.

May brings **Las Cruces de Mayo** (The Crosses of May) during the first week of the month, the **Festival de los Patios** (Patio Festival) during the second, and the **Concurso Nacional de Flamenco** (National Flamenco competition) during the second week of May every third year. Córdoba's annual **Feria de Mayo** is the city's main street party, held during the last week of May.

The **International Guitar Festival** brings major artists to Córdoba in early July. Córdoba celebrates **Nuestra Señora de Fuensanta** on the last Sunday in September and the **Romería de San Miguel** (Procession of St. Michael) on September 29.

of **Cristo de los Faroles** (Christ of the Lanterns) stands amid eight lanterns hanging from twisted wrought-iron brackets. ⊠*Centro.*

64 **Plaza Santa Marina.** At the edge of the **Barrio de los Toreros,** a quarter where many of Córdoba's famous bullfighters were born and raised, stands a statue of the famous bullfighter Manolete (1917–47) opposite the lovely *fernandina* church of Santa Marina de Aguas Santas (St. Marina of Holy Waters). Not far from here, on the Plaza de la Lagunilla, is a Manolete bust. ⊠*Pl. Conde Priego Centro.*

65 **San Nicolás de Villa.** This classically dark Spanish church displays the Mudejar style of Islamic decoration and art forms. Córdoba's well-kept city park, the **Jardínes de la Victoria,** with tile benches and manicured bushes, is a block west of here. ⊠*C. San Felipe, Centro.*

WHERE TO EAT

$$$–$$$$
✕ **El Caballo Rojo.** This is one of the most famous traditional restaurants in Andalusia, frequented by royalty and society folk. The interior resembles a cool, leafy Andalusian patio, and the dining room is furnished with stained glass, dark wood, and gleaming marble. The menu mixes traditional specialties, such as *rabo de toro* (oxtail stew) and *salmorejo* (a thick version of gazpacho), with dishes inspired by Córdoba's Moorish and Jewish heritage, such as *alboronia* (a cold salad of stewed vegetables flavored with honey, saffron, and aniseed), *cordero a la miel* (lamb roasted with honey), and *rape mozárabe* (grilled monkfish with Moorish spices). ⊠*Calle Cardenal Herrero 28, Judería* ☎*957/475375* ⊕*www.elcaballorojo.com* ☐*AE, DC, MC, V.*

$$$–$$$$
★
✕ **El Churrasco.** The name suggests grilled meat, but this restaurant in the heart of the Judería serves much more than that. Try tapas such as the *berenjenas crujientes con salmorejo* (crispy fried eggplant slices with thick gazpacho) in the colorful bar. The grilled fish is also supremely fresh, *and* the steak is the best in town. On the inner patio, there's alfresco dining when it's warm outside (covered in winter). ⊠*Calle*

Romero 16, Judería ☎957/290819 ⊕*www.elchurrasco.com* ▭*AE, DC, MC, V* ⊘*Closed Aug.*

\$\$–\$\$\$\$ ✕**Los Marqueses.** Los Marqueses is in the heart of the Judería area, inside a delightful 17th-century palace. It specializes in Mediterranean and Andalusian cuisine; dishes may include fried eggplant with honey, wild mushroom risotto with prawns, and turbot fillets with potato and mascarpone sauce. The lunch menu, served Monday–Saturday, is a bargain at under €30. ⊠*Calle Tomás Conde 8, Judería* ☎957/202094 ▭*AE, DC, MC, V* ⊘*Closed Mon. and 15 days in Sept.*

\$\$\$
★ ✕**Bodegas Campos.** A block east of the Plaza del Potro, this restaurant in a traditional old wine cellar is the epitome of all that is great about Andalusian cuisine and service. The dining rooms are in barrel-heavy and leafy courtyards. Regional dishes include *ensalada de bacalao y naranja* (salad of salt cod and orange with olive oil) and *solomillo con salsa de setas* (sirloin with a wild mushroom sauce). The *menu degustacíon* (taster's menu) is a good value at €35. ⊠*Calle Los Lineros 32, San Pedro* ☎957/497643 ▭*AE, MC, V* ⊘*No dinner Sun.*

\$\$–\$\$\$ ✕**Casa Pepe de la Judería.** Antiques and some wonderful old oil paintings fill this three-floors' labyrinth of rooms just around the corner from the mosque, near the Judería. The restaurant is always packed, noisy, and fun. From May through October, the rooftop opens for barbecues, and there is live Spanish guitar music most nights. A full selection of tapas and house specialties includes *presa de paletilla ibérica con salsa de trufa* (pork shoulder fillet with a truffle sauce). The restaurant also has a fixed-price menu. ⊠*Calle Romero 1, off Deanes, Judería* ☎957/200744 ▭*AE, DC, MC, V.*

\$\$–\$\$\$ ✕**El Blasón.** In an old inn one block west of Avenida Gran Capitán, El Blasón has a Moorish-style entrance bar leading onto a patio enclosed by ivy-covered walls. Downstairs there is a lounge with a red tile ceiling and old polished clay plates on the walls. Upstairs are two elegant dining rooms where blue walls, white silk curtains, and candelabras evoke early 19th-century luxury. The menu includes *salmón fresco al cava* (fresh salmon in cava, Spanish sparkling wine) and *muslos de pato al vino dulce* (leg of duck in sweet wine sauce). ⊠*José Zorrilla 11, Centro* ☎957/480625 ▭*AE, DC, MC, V.*

\$\$–\$\$\$ ✕**El Burlaero.** A block from the front of the Mezquita, El Burlaero—so-named for a bullring's wooden barrier—has wood-beamed ceilings and an antique, traditional charm. The seven different rooms, all decorated with bullfight memorabilia and hunting trophies, can serve as many as 200 diners. There's also a terrace for outdoor dining. Typical dishes include grilled swordfish, meat-and-vegetable brochette, Iberian pork, and partridge with onions. ⊠*Calleja de la Hoguera 5, Judería* ☎957/472719 ▭*MC, V.*

\$\$–\$\$\$ ✕**Taberna Casas Salinas.** This has been an established favorite in Córdoba since 1879: the tiles, paintings, wooden furniture, glassed-in patio, bodega with barrels, and small bar all reflect this era. The cuisine, typical of the Córdobese mountains, might include goat's cheese, meatballs, blood sausage, and lamb chops. ⊠*Calle Tundidores 3, Plaza de la Corredera* ☎957/480135 ▭*AE, DC, MC, V* ⊘*Closed Sun.*

$$–$$$
Fodor'sChoice
★
✕ **Taberna San Miguel-Casa El Pisto.** This central Córdoba hotspot behind Plaza de las Tendillas is always booming with happy diners, most of them Córdobans, enjoying a wide range of typical pinchos and raciones accompanied by chilled glasses of Moriles, the excellent local sherrylike wine. The heavy wooden bar is as good a spot as any, but the tables in the back rooms crackle with conviviality. ⊠ *Pl. de San Miguel 1, Centro* ☎ *957/470166* ⊟ *AE, DC, MC, V* ☉ *Closed Sun.*

$–$$$
✕ **Los Alarifes.** This delightful restaurant serves a fine selection of typical Spanish dishes, including leek salad with Iberian ham, smoked salmon and carrot vinaigrette, cod with red peppers, and partridge. The daily set menu is less than €18. ⊠ *Hotel Alfaros, Calle Alfaros 18, Centro* ☎ *957/491920* ⊟ *AE, DC, MC, V.*

$–$$
✕ **Comedor Árabe Andalussí.** This tiny restaurant is perfect for a romantic dinner for two, in part because of the lack of space but also because of the atmosphere—it's warm and cozy, with Oriental carpets and ornate drapes and cushions. All the Moroccan favorites are here, including tabbouleh, falafel, and couscous, which makes it especially apt for vegetarians. The *tagines* (earthenware vessels with conical tops used for stewing meat and vegetables in Morocco) for two are excellent and will easily feed four, but beware: no wine is served here, in accordance with Islamic religious law. If you ask nicely, the management will allow you to bring in your own wine—try this phrase: *¿Por favor, podemos traer una botella de vino para acompañar nuestra comida?* (May we please bring in a bottle of wine to accompany our meal?) ⊠ *Pl. Abades 4, Judería* ☎ *957/475162* ⊟ *No credit cards.*

$–$$
✕ **El Tablón.** Opened in 1890 as a bodega, El Tablón became a restaurant with simple decor in 1985. From inside or on the pleasing columned patio, you can select from a typical Córdoba-style menu that includes a good choice of two courses plus drink and dessert for just €10.50. Pizzas, tapas, and sandwiches are also available. The small bar, with no seats and a marble counter, retains a 19th-century feel. ⊠ *Calle Cardenal González 69, Judería* ☎ *957/476061* ⊟ *MC, V.*

$–$$
✕ **La Abacería.** By the west side of the Mezquita, close to the tourist office, La Abacerí has a large bar, a pleasing open central patio, and, usually, a full restaurant. It has homemade tapas: *patatas allioli* (potatoes in allioli sauce), *berenjenas fritas* (fried eggplant), *calamares fritos* or *plancha* (squid fried or grilled), and *tortilla de patatas* (Spanish potato omelet), all sold in half or full portions. ⊠ *Corregidor Luis de la Cerda 73, Judería* ☎ *957/487050* ⊟ *MC, V.*

¢
✕ **Bar Santos.** This very small, quintessentially Spanish bar, with no seats and numerous photos of matadors and flamenco dancers, seems out of place surrounded by the tourist shops and overshadowed by the Mezquita. Its appearance—and its prices—are part of its charm. Tapas, such as *morcillo Iberico* (Iberian blood sausage) and *bocadillos* (sandwiches; literally "little mouthfuls") are excellent in quality and value while the Santos *tortilla de patata* (potato omelet) is renowned and celebrated both for its taste and heroic thickness. ⊠ *Calle Magistral González Francés 3, Judería* ☎ *957/479360* ⊟ *MC, V.*

WHERE TO STAY

$$$$ ⊡ **Palacio del Bailío.** Open and thriving since summer 2006, the beautiful 17th-century mansion is built over the ruins of a Roman house in the heart of the historical center of Córdoba. The company specializes in carefully and tastefully renovating impressive and historic buildings to the highest of expected modern standards, and this is another exemplary example of its work. Archaeological remains, mixed with high-tech features (such as Internet access), and a relaxing spa complete the enticing cocktail. ⊠ *Calle Ramírez de las Casas Deza 10–12, Plaza de La Corredera, 14001* ☎ *957/498993* 🖷 *957/498994* ⊕ *www. hospes.es* ⟷ *53 rooms* ♿ *In-room: Ethernet, Wi-Fi. In-hotel: restaurant, bar, pools, spa, bicycles, laundry facilities, public Wi-Fi, public Internet* ▭ *MC, V.*

$$$ ⊡ **Amistad Córdoba.** Two 18th-century mansions that look out on the Plaza de Maimónides in the heart of the Judería are now a stylish hotel. (You can also enter through the old Moorish walls on Calle Cairuán.) There's a cobblestone Mudejar courtyard, carved-wood ceilings, and a plush lounge area; the newer wing across the street is done in blues and grays and Norwegian wood. Guest rooms are large and comfortable. ⊠ *Pl. de Maimónides 3, Judería, 14004* ☎ *957/420335* 🖷 *957/420365* ⊕ *www.nh-hoteles.com* ⟷ *84 rooms* ♿ *In-room: dial-up. In-hotel: restaurant, room service, bar, laundry service, parking (fee)* ▭ *AE, DC, MC, V.*

Fodor'sChoice
★

$$$ ⊡ **Casa de los Azulejos.** Although renovated in 1934, this 17th-century house still has its underground rooms with vaulted ceilings. Decorated with colorful tiles, it mixes Andalusian and Latin American influences. All rooms, painted in warm, pastel colors and filled with antique furnishings, open onto the central patio. There's an Andalusian–Latin American restaurant and a Mexican cantina on the premises. ⊠ *Calle Fernando Colón 5, Centro, 14002* ☎ *957/470000* 🖷 *957/475496* ⊕ *www.casadelosazulejos.com* ⟷ *7 rooms, 1 suite* ♿ *In-hotel: 2 restaurants, public Internet* ▭ *MC, V.*

$$$ ⊡ **Conquistador.** Ceramic tiles and inlaid marquetry adorn the bar and public rooms at this contemporary, Andalusian-Moorish-style hotel next to the Mezquita. The reception area overlooks a colonnaded patio, fountain, and small enclosed garden. Rooms are comfortable and classically Andalusian; those at the front have small balconies overlooking the mosque, which is floodlighted at night. ⊠ *Magistral González Francés 17, Judería, 14003* ☎ *957/481102 or 957/481411* 🖷 *957/474677* ⊕ *www.hotelconquistadorcordoba.com* ⟷ *99 rooms, 3 suites* ♿ *In-room: dial-up. In-hotel: room service, bar, laundry service, parking (fee)* ▭ *AE, DC, MC, V.*

$$$ ⊡ **La Hospedería de El Churrasco.** As should be expected from a place associated with the nearby restaurant of the same name, this small hotel is one of the town's most beautiful and tasteful places to stay. Each room is individually furnished with fine antiques, but also comes with such modern facilities as plasma TVs. The terrace-solarium has fine views of the Mezquita. ⊠ *Calle Romero 38, Judería, 14003* ☎ *957/294808* 🖷 *957/421661* ⊕ *www.elchurrasco.com* ⟷ *9 rooms* ♿ *In-room: dial-up. In-hotel: parking (no fee)* ▭ *AE, DC, MC, V* ⦿ *BP.*

1

$$$　　⌕ **Lola.** Lola, the owner, has decorated the rooms in this former 19th-century palace with decorative flair and attention to detail. There are original beams, woven rugs, antique wardrobes, and art deco decorative pieces. The bathrooms are airy, modern, and marbled. Tucked down a side street, Lola is away from the tour groups, but a short stroll away from all the big-city sights. The roof terrace has Mezquita tower views. There's parking on nearby Plaza Vallinas. ⊠ *Calle Romero 3, Judería, 14003* ☎ *957/200305* 🖷 *957/422063* ⊕ *www.hotelconencantolola.com* ➴ *8 rooms* ⊟ *AE, MC, V* ⓘ⌾*CP.*

$$$　　⌕ **Maciá Alfaros.** One of the advantages of this elegant hotel is that it's in a quieter part of the city but just a 15-minute walk from the Mezquita. The rooms are large, with modern furnishings and a terrace or balcony. The rooms opening onto the inner patio overlook the pool. ⊠ *Alfaros 18, Centro, 14001* ☎ *957/491920* 🖷 *957/492210* ➴ *133 rooms* ♿ *In-room: dial-up. In-hotel: restaurant, bar, pool, laundry service, parking (no fee)* ⊟ *AE, D, MC, V.*

$$$　　⌕ **Maimónides.** The lobby here has a colonnaded sand-color hall with tile floors and a remarkable *mocárabe* (ornamental wood) ceiling. Outside there's a small patio with wrought-iron tables and chairs. Rooms and bathrooms have marble floors and are decorated in light tones. Some of the rooms make you feel like you're so close to the Mezquita you can touch it. ⊠ *Torrijos 4, Judería, 14003* ☎🖷 *957/471500* ⊕ *www.hotusa.es* ➴ *82 rooms* ♿ *In-room: dial-up. In-hotel: restaurant, public Internet, parking (fee)* ⊟ *MC, V.*

$$$　　⌕ **Parador de Córdoba.** A peaceful, leafy garden surrounds this modern parador on the slopes of the Sierra de Co Córdoba, 5 km (3 mi) north of town. Rooms are sunny, with wood or wicker furnishings, and the pricier ones have balconies overlooking the garden or facing Córdoba. ⊠ *Av. de la Arruzafa, El Brillante, 14012* ☎ *957/275900* 🖷 *957/280409* ⊕ *www.parador.es* ➴ *89 rooms, 5 suites* ♿ *In-room: dial-up. In-hotel: restaurant, room service, tennis court, pool, parking (no fee)* ⊟ *AE, DC, MC, V.*

$$　　⌕ **Gonzalez.** A few minutes from the Mezquita, Gonzalez was originally built as a 16th-century palace and has been converted into a small hotel with an elegant marble entrance and a typical Córdobese central patio. Many of the single, double, twin, and triple rooms here overlook the patio. ⊠ *Calle Manrique 3, Judería, 14003* ☎ *957/479819* 🖷 *957/486187* ➴ *17 rooms* ⊟ *AE, DC, MC, V.*

$$　　⌕ **Mezquita.** Across from the mosque, this hotel in a restored 16th-century home is filled with bronze sculptures depicting Andalusian themes, and the public areas are filled with antiques collected by the owner. The best rooms face the interior patio, and one of them is what used to be the house's old chapel. All have elegant dark wooden headboards and matching pink curtains and bedspreads. The only real drawback is the lack of parking; your best bet is nearby Plaza Vallinas. ⊠ *Pl. Santa Catalina 1, Judería, 41003* ☎ *957/475585* 🖷 *957/476219* ➴ *21 rooms* ♿ *In-room: dial-up. In-hotel: bar* ⊟ *AE, DC, MC, V.*

$–$$ ☂ **El Tablón.** Close to the Mezquita, this comfortable hostel has pleasantly decorated rooms in a traditional old-fashioned Spanish style. There's a restaurant and bar across the street. ✉ *Cardenal González 69, Judería, 14003* ☎ *957/476061* ⊕ *www.hostaleltablon.com* 📠 *957/486240* ↩ *8 rooms, 1 suite* ⚐ *In-hotel: restaurant, bar* ▤ *MC, V.*

$ ☂ **Hotel Maestre.** Rooms here overlook a gracious inner courtyard framed by arches. The Castilian-style furniture, gleaming marble, and high-quality oil paintings add elegance to excellent value. The hotel is around the corner from the Plaza del Potro. The management also runs an even cheaper lodging, the Hostal Maestre, and two types of apartments down the street; the best are large and clean and offer one of the best deals in town. ✉ *Calle Romero Barros 4–6, San Pedro, 14003* ☎ *957/472410* 📠 *957/475395* ⊕ *www.hotelmaestre.com* ↩ *26 rooms* ⚐ *In-hotel: parking (fee)* ▤ *AE, MC, V.*

NIGHTLIFE & THE ARTS

NIGHTLIFE

Córdoba locals hang out mostly in the areas of Ciudad Jardín (the old university area), Plaza de las Tendillas, and the Avenida Gran Capitán.

Café Málaga (✉ *Calle Málaga 3, Centro*), a block away from Plaza de las Tendillas, is a laid-back hangout. **Salón de Té** (✉ *Calle del Buen Pastor 13, Judería*), a few blocks away from the Mezquita, is a beautiful place for tea, with a courtyard, side rooms filled with cushions, and a shop selling Moroccan clothing. It closes at midnight. **Sojo** (✉ *Calle Benito Pérez Galdós 3, off Av. Gran Capitán, Centro* ☎ *957/487211* ✉ *José Martorell 12, Judería*) has a trendy crowd. The branch in the Judería has DJs on weekends. **O'Donoghue's** (✉ *Av. Gran Capitán 38, Centro* ☎ *957/481678*) is an Irish pub favored by locals. For some of the best views of Córdoba, drop by **Hotel Hesperia** (✉ *Av. de la Confederación 1, Sector Sur* ☎ *957/421042* ⊕ *www.hesperia-cordoba. com*), across the Guadalquivir. The hotel has a rooftop bar, open only in summer.

Córdoba's most popular flamenco club, the year-round **Tablao Cardenal** (✉ *Calle Torrijos 10, Judería* ☎ *957/483320* ⊕ *www.tablaocardenal. com*) is worth the trip just to see the courtyard of the 16th-century building, which was Córdoba's first hospital. Admission is €20.

THE ARTS

During the **Patio Festival,** on the second and third weeks of May, the city is invaded by flamenco dancers and singers. The **Festival de Córdoba-Guitarra** attracts Spanish and international guitarists for more than two weeks of great music in July, and orchestras perform in the Alcázar's garden on Sunday throughout summer. The **Feria de Mayo** (the last week of May) draws popular performers to the city. See concerts, ballets, and plays year-round in the **Gran Teatro** (✉ *Av. Gran Capitán 3, Centro* ☎ *957/480644* ⊕ *www.teatrocordoba.com*).

SPORTS & OUTDOORS

The top golf course near Córdoba is the 18-hole **Club de Campo y Deportivo de Córdoba** (⊠ *Crta. Antigua de Córdoba–Obejo Km 9, Av. del Brillante* ☎ *957/350208*). For swimming, try the **Piscina Municipal** (⊠ *Av. del Brillante, Polideportivo Ciudad Jardín, Alcalde Sanz Noguer s/n, Av. del Brillante* ☎ *957/484846*).

SHOPPING

Córdoba's main shopping district is around Avenida Gran Capitán, Ronda de los Tejares, and the streets leading away from Plaza Tendillas. **Artesanía Andaluza** (⊠ *Calle Tomás Conde 3, Judería* ☎ *957/203781*), near the Museo Taurino, sells Córdoban crafts, including fine embossed leather (a legacy of the Moors) and jewelry made of filigree silver from the mines of the Sierra Morena. Córdoba's artisans sell their crafts in the **Zoco** (⊠ *C. Judíos, opposite synagogue, Judería* ☎ *957/204033*); note that many stalls are open May–September only. **Meryan** (⊠ *Calleja de las Flores 2 and Encarnación, 12* ☎ *957/475902* ⊕ *www.meryancor.com*) is one of Córdoba's best workshops for embossed leather.

EN ROUTE

Begun in 936, **Medina Azahara (sometimes spelled Madinat Al-Zahra)** was built in the foothills of the Sierra Morena—about 8 km (5 mi) west of Córdoba on C431—by Abd ar-Rahman III for his favorite concubine, az-Zahra (the Flower). Historians say it took 10,000 men, 2,600 mules, and 400 camels 25 years to erect this fantasy of 4,300 columns in dazzling pink, green, and white marble and jasper brought from Carthage. Here, on three terraces, stood a palace, a mosque, luxurious baths, fragrant gardens, fishponds, an aviary, and a zoo. In 1013 the place was sacked and destroyed by Berber mercenaries. In 1944 the Royal Apartments were rediscovered, and the Throne Room was carefully reconstructed. The outline of the mosque has also been excavated. The only covered part of the site is the Salon de Abd Al Rahman III; the rest is a sprawl of foundations, defense walls, and arches that hint at the splendor of the original city-palace. There is no public transport out to here, but the authorities run a daily tourist bus, so check with the tourist offices for hours and place of departure. ⊠ *Off C431; follow signs en route to Almodóvar del Río* ☎ *957/355506* 🎟 *€1.50, free for EU citizens* ⊙ *Tues.–Sat. 10–8:30, Sun. 10–2.*

SIDE TRIPS FROM CÓRDOBA

If you have time to go beyond Córdoba, head west to the ruins and partial reconstruction of the Muslim palace Medina Azahara, site of a once-magnificent complex, or south to the wine country around Montilla, olive oil–rich Baena, and the Subbética mountain range, a cluster of small towns virtually unknown to travelers.

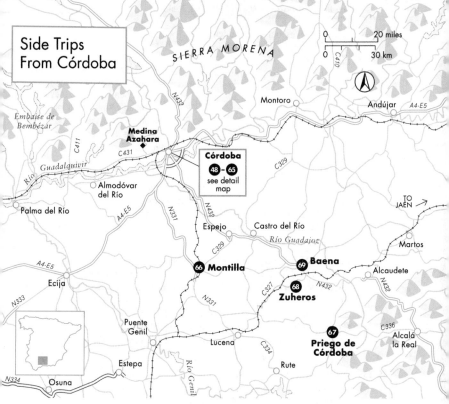

Side Trips
From Córdoba

SIERRA MORENA

0   20 miles
0   30 km

Montoro   Andújar   A4-E5

Embalse de
Bembézar

Medina
Azahara

Córdoba
48 – 65
see detail
map

TO
JAEN

Almodóvar
del Río

Palma del Río

Espejo   Castro del Río

Río Guadajoz

Martos

Ecija

66 Montilla

69 Baena

Alcaudete

68
Zuheros

Puente
Genil

Lucena

67
Priego de
Córdoba

Alcalá
la Real

Estepa

Rute

Osuna

The enitre Subbética region is protected as a natural park. The mountains, canyons, and wooded valleys are stunning. You'll need a car
to explore the area, and in some parts, the roads are rather rough.
To reach these meriting-a-visit towns in *la Campiña* (the countryside),
take the low road (N331) through Montilla, cutting north to Baena
via Zuheros, or take the high road (N432) through Espejo and Baena,
cutting south through Cabra. For park information or hiking advice,
contact the **Mancomunidad de la Subbética** (✉ *Ctra. Carcabuey–Zagrilla,
Km 5.75, Carcabuey* ☎ *957/704106* ∰ *www.subbetica.org*). You can
also pick up handy information, including a pack of maps titled *Rutas
Senderistas de la Subbética,* from any local tourist office. The packet
details 10 walks on handy cards with sketched maps.

Southern Córdoba is also the province's main olive-producing region,
with the town of **Lucena** at its center. By following the Ruta del Aceite
(olive oil route) you pass by some of the province's most picturesque
villages. In Lucena is the Torre del Moral, where Granada's last Nasrid
ruler Boabdil was imprisoned in 1483 after launching an unsuccessful
attack on the Christians; and the Parroquia de San Mateo, a small but
remarkable Renaissance–Gothic cathedral. The town makes furniture
and brass and copper pots. Southeast of Lucena, C334 crosses the
Embalse de Iznájar (Iznájar Reservoir) amid spectacular scenery. On

C334 halfway between Lucena and the reservoir, in **Rute,** you can sample the potent *anís* (anise) liqueur for which this small, whitewashed town is famous.

MONTILLA

 46 km (28 mi) south of Córdoba.

> ### SWEET WINE
>
> Montilla's grapes contain so much sugar (transformed into alcohol during fermentation) that they are not fortified with the addition of extra alcohol. For this reason, the locals claim that Montilla wines do not give you a hangover.

Heading south from Córdoba to Málaga through hills ablaze with sunflowers in early summer, you reach the Montilla-Morilés vineyards of the Córdoban campiña. Every fall, 47,000 acres' worth of Pedro Ximénez grapes are crushed here to produce the region's rich Montilla wines, which are similar to sherry. Recently, Montilla has started developing a young white wine similar to Portugal's Vinho Verde.

Bodegas Alvear. Founded in 1729, this bodega in the center of town is Montilla's oldest. Besides being informative, the fun tour and wine tasting gives you the chance to buy a bottle or two of Alvear's tasty version of the sweet Pedro Ximenez aged sherry. ⊠*Calle María Auxiliadora 1* ☎*957/652939* ⊕*www.alvear.es* ☜*Tour €2, with wine tasting €3–€4.50* ☉*Guided tour and wine tasting Mon.–Sat. 12:30; shop Mon. 4:30–6:30, Tues.–Fri. 10–2 and 4:30–6:30, Sat. 11–1:30.*

WHERE TO STAY & EAT

$$–$$$ ✕**Las Camachas.** The best-known restaurant in southern Córdoba Prov-
★ ince is in an Andalusian-style hacienda outside Montilla—near the main road toward Málaga. Start with tapas in the attractive tiled bar, and then move to one of six dining rooms. Regional specialties include *alcachofas al Montilla* (artichokes braised in Montilla wine), *salmorejo* (a thick version of gazpacho), *perdiz campiña* (country-style partridge), and *cordero a la miel* (lamb with honey). You can also buy local wines here. ⊠*Av. Europa 3* ☎*957/650004* ⊟*AE, DC, MC, V.*

$$ ⬚**Don Gonzalo.** Just 3 km (2 mi) southwest of Montilla is one of Andalusia's better roadside hotels. The wood-beam-covered common areas have a mixture of decorative elements; note the elephant tusks flanking the TV in the lounge. The clay-tile rooms are large and comfortable; some look onto the road, others onto the garden and pool. Ask to see the wine cellar; it's a beauty. ⊠*Ctra. Córdoba–Málaga, Km 47, 14550* ☎*957/650658* ☒*957/650666* ⊕*www.hoteldongonzalo.com* ⇆*35 rooms, 1 suite* ♿*In-room: dial-up. In-hotel: restaurant, bar, tennis court, pool* ⊟*AE, DC, MC, V.*

SHOPPING

On the outskirts of town, coopers' shops produce barrels of various sizes, some small enough to serve as creative souvenirs. On Montilla's main road, **Tonelería J. L. Rodríguez** (⊠*Ctra. Córdoba–Málaga, Km 43.3* ☎*957/650563* ⊕*www.toneleriajlrodriguez.com*) is well worth a stop not just to see the barrels and other things for sale—such as local wines—but also to pop in the back and see them being made.

PRIEGO DE CÓRDOBA

67 ★ *103 km (64 mi) southeast of Córdoba and 37 km (23 mi) northeast of Lucena via C334 going north to Cabra, then east on C340.*

The jewel of Córdoba's countryside is **Priego de Córdoba**, a town of 14,000 at the foot of Mt. Tinosa. Wander down Calle del Río opposite the town hall to see 18th-century mansions, once the homes of silk merchants. At the end of the street is the Fuente del Rey (King's Fountain), with some 130 water jets, built in 1803. Don't miss the lavish baroque churches of La Asunción and La Aurora or the Barrio de la Villa, an old Moorish quarter with a maze of narrow streets of white-wall buildings.

WHERE TO STAY

$$ **Villa Turística de Priego.** Clustered to form an Andalusian pueblo, the semidetached units of this gleaming-white complex sleep between two and six people each. Some have a terrace or balcony. It's in the heart of the Subbética nature park—near Zagrilla, 6 km (4 mi) from Priego de Córdoba. ⊠ *Aldea de Zagrilla, 14816* ☎ *957/703503* 🖶 *957/703573* ⊕ *www.villadepriego.com* 🛏 *47 apartments/villas, 5 rooms* ♨ *In-hotel: restaurant, bar, pool* ▤ *AE, DC, MC, V* ☾ *Closed Jan.*

OFF THE BEATEN PATH

✕▦ **Barceló La Bobadilla**—Standing on its own 1,000-acre estate amid olive and holm-oak trees, this complex ($$$$) 14 km (9 mi) west of the town of Loja resembles a Moorish village, or a rambling *cortijo* (ranch). It has white walls, tile roofs, patios, fountains, and an artificial lake. Guest buildings center around a 16th-century-style chapel that houses a 1,595-pipe organ. Each room has either a balcony, a terrace, or a garden. One restaurant serves highly creative international cuisine, and the other serves more down-to-earth regional items. The hotel is just south of the La Subbética region, technically in Granada Provice, but it has by far the best accommodations in the area. ⊠ *Finca La Bobadilla, Apdo 144 E, Loja18300* ☎ *958/321861* 🖶 *958/321810* ⊕ *www.la-bobadilla.com* 🛏 *52 rooms, 10 suites* ♨ *In-hotel: 2 restaurants, tennis courts, pools, gym* ▤ *AE, DC, MC, V.*

ZUHEROS

68 *80 km (50 mi) southeast of Córdoba.*

At the northern edge of the Subbética and at an altitude of 2,040 feet, Zuheros is one of the most attractive villages in the province of Córdoba. From the road up, it's hidden behind a dominating rock face topped off by the dramatic ruins of a castle built by the Moors over a Roman castle. The view from here back over the valley is immense. Next to the castle is the Iglesia de Santa María, built over a mosque. The base of the minaret is the foundation for the bell tower.

WHAT TO SEE

The **Museo Histórico-Arqueológico Municipal** displays archaeological remains found in local caves and elsewhere; some date back to the Middle Palaeolithic period some 35,000 years ago. You can also visit the remains of the Renaissance rooms in the castle, across the road. Call ahead for tour times. ⊠ *Pl. de la Paz 2* ☎ *957/694545* 🔖 *€2* ☾ *Apr.–Sept., Tues.–Fri. 10–2 and 5–7; weekends 10–7; Oct.–Mar., Tues.–Fri. 10–2 and 4–6; weekends 10–6.*

Opened in 2002, and housed in an impressive square mansion from 1912, the **Museo de Costumbres y Artes Populares Juan Fernandez Cruz** is at the edge of the village. Exhibits here detail the way of life and local customs and traditions. ⊠ *Calle Santo s/n* ☎ *957/694690* 🔖 *€2* ☾ *Tues.–Sun. 11–2 and 4–7.*

Found some 4 km (2½ mi) above Zuheros along a windy, twisty road, the **Cueva de los Murciélagos** *(Cave of the Bats)* runs for about 2 km (1¼ mi), although only about half of that expanse is open to the public. The main attractions are the wall paintings dating from the Neolithic Age (6,000–3,000 BC) and Chalcolithic Age (3,000–2,000 BC), but excavations have identified that the cave was already inhabited 35,000 years ago. Items from the Copper and Bronze ages as well as from the Roman period and the Middle Ages have also been found here. ⊠ *Information and reservations: Calle Nueva 1* ☎ *957/694545 weekdays 10–2:30 and 5–7* ✉ informacion@cuevadelosmurcielagos.com 🔖 *€5.30* ☾ *By appointment only: Apr.–Sept., weekdays noon–5:30, weekends 11–6:30; Oct.–Mar., weekdays 12:30–4:30, weekends 11–5:30.*

WHERE TO STAY & EAT

$–$$$ ✕ **Los Palancos.** Literally built into the cliff face of the towering mountain that Zuheros is built upon, this is a small restaurant and tavern of some charm. Expect local mountain-style cuisine featuring roast young goat, rabbit, partridge, and suckling pig, and choose from many items of local produce to take home with you. ⊠ *Calle Llana 43* ☎ *957/694538* ▤ *MC, V.*

$–$$ ▦ **Señorios de Zuheros.** In a central location, Señorios de Zuheros offers 10 apartments with three or four beds as well as six studios with sleeping accommodations for two people. All rooms are modern and well equipped. ⊠ *Calle Horno 3, 14870* ☎ *957/694527* ⊕ *www.zuherosapartamentos.com* ➹ *10 apartments, 6 rooms* ⚷ *In-hotel: restaurant, bar, laundry facilities* ▤ *MC, V.*

$–$$ ▦ **Zuhayra.** On a narrow street in Zuheros, this small hotel has comfortable large rooms with views over the village rooftops to the valley below. There's a cozy bar and dining room with original beams and an open fireplace. Groups of artists on organized trips often stay here. ⊠ *C. Mirador 10, 14870* ☎ *957/694693* 🖷 *957/694702* ➹ *18 rooms* ⚷ *In-hotel: restaurant, bar* ▤ *AE, DC, MC, V.*

BAENA

🚳 *66 km (43 mi) southeast of Córdoba.*

Outside the boundaries of Subbética and surrounded by chalk fields producing top-quality olives, Baena is an old town of narrow streets, whitewashed houses, ancient mansions, and churches clustered beneath Moorish battlements.

The **Museo del Olivar y el Aceite** is housed in the old olive mill owned and operated by Don José Alcalá Santaella until 1959. The machinery on display dates from the middle of the 19th century, when the mill was capable of processing up to 3 tons a day. The museum aims to demonstrate the most important aspects of olive cultivation, olive-oil production, and the way of life of workers in this most important industry in this region. ⊠ *Calle Cañada 7* ☎ *957/691641* ⊕ *www.museoaceite. com* 💶 *€3* ⊙ *May–Sept., Tues.–Sat. 11–2 and 6–8, Sun. 11–2; Oct.– Apr., Tues.–Fri. 11–2 and 4–6, Sun. 11–2.*

WHERE TO STAY & EAT

$$–$$$ 🏨 **La Casa Grande.** In the center of town just a few steps from the famous Nuñez de Prado olive oil mill, this is the top hotel in Baena and for miles around. The reception hall is high-ceilinged and elegant, the restaurant a good reason for stopping in for a meal, and the professional and friendly staff always helpful. Rooms have antiques and a breezy, comfortable feel to them. ⊠ *Av. De Cervantes 35, 14850* ☎ *957/671905* 🖷 *957/692189* ⊕ *www.lacasagrande.es* 🛏 *38 rooms* ⌂ *In-hotel: restaurant, bar, pool, laundry facilities, laundry service, parking (no fee)* ▤ *AE, DC, MC, V.*

$$ 🏨 **Fuente las Piedras.** This stylish hotel 25 km (15 mi) northeast of Baena in the town of Cabra on the A316 road to Jaén is on the edge of the Parque Natural Sierra Subbética. Its rooms are modern and generous in size. A large pool is surrounded by gardens. ⊠ *Av. Fuente de las Piedras s/n, Cabra, 14940* ☎ *957/529740* 🖷 *957/521407* ⊕ *www.mshoteles. com/fuentelaspiedras* 🛏 *61 rooms* ⌂ *In-hotel: restaurant, bar, pool, laundry facilities, laundry service, parking (no fee)* ▤ *MC, V.*

LAND OF OLIVES: JAÉN PROVINCE

Jaén is dominated by its *alcázar* (fortress). To the northeast are the olive-producing towns of Baeza and Úbeda. Cazorla, the gateway to the Parque Natural Sierra de Cazorla Segura y Las Villas, lies beyond.

JAÉN

🚺 *107 km (64 mi) southeast of Córdoba, 93 km (58 mi) north of Granada.*

Nestled in the foothills of the Sierra de Jabalcuz, Jaén is surrounded by towering peaks and olive-clad hills. The Arabs called it Geen (Route of the Caravans) because it formed a crossroad between Castile and Andalusia. Captured from the Moors by Saint King Ferdinand III in 1246, Jaén became a frontier province, the site of many a skirmish

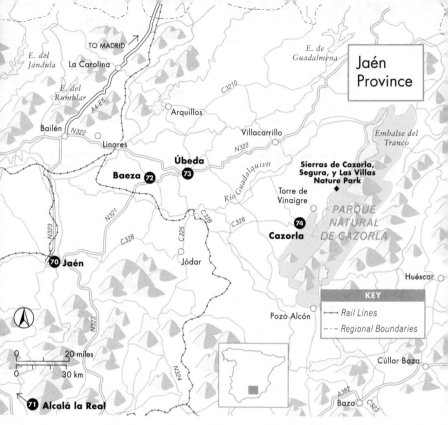

and battle over the next 200 years between the Moors of Granada and Christians from the north and west. Today the province earns a living from its lead and silver mines and endless olive groves.

★ The **Castillo de Santa Catalina**, perched on a rocky crag 400 yards above the center of town, is Jaén's star monument. The castle may have originated as a tower built by Hannibal; the site was fortified continuously over the centuries. The Nasrid king Alhamar, builder of Granada's Alhambra, constructed an *alcázar* here, but King Ferdinand III captured it from him in 1246 on the feast day of Santa Catalina (St. Catherine). Catalina consequently became Jaén's patron saint, so when the Christians built a castle and chapel here, they dedicated both to her. ⊠ *Ctra. del Castillo de Santa Catalina* ☎ *953/120733* 🎟 *€3* ⊘ *June–Sept., Thurs.–Tues. 10–2 and 4:30–7; Oct.–May, Thurs.–Tues. 10–2 and 3:30–6.*

Jaén's **cathedral** is a hulk that looms above the modest buildings around it. Begun in 1492 on the site of a former mosque, it took almost 300 years to build. Its chief architect was Andrés de Vandelvira (1509–75); many more of Vandelvira's buildings can be seen in Úbeda and Baeza. The ornate facade was sculpted by Pedro Roldán, and the figures on top of the columns include San Fernando (King Ferdinand III) surrounded by the four evangelists. The cathedral's most treasured relic is the **Santo Rostro** (Holy Face), the cloth with which, according to tradition, St. Veronica cleansed Christ's face on the way to Calvary, leaving his image imprinted on the fabric. The *rostro* (face) is displayed every Friday. In the underground **museum,** look for *San Lorenzo,* by Martínez Montañés; the *Immaculate Conception,* by Alonso Cano; and a Calvary scene by Jácobo Florentino. ✉*Pl. Santa María* ☎*953/234233* 🖃*Cathedral free, museum €3* ⊙*Cathedral Mon.–Sat. 8:30–1 and 5–8, Sun. 9–1 and 6–8; museum Tues.–Sat. 10–1 and 5–8.*

Explore the narrow alleys of old Jaén as you walk from the cathedral to the **Baños Árabes** (Arab Baths), which once belonged to Ali, a Moorish king of Jaén, and probably date from the 11th century. Four hundred years later, in 1592, Fernando de Torres y Portugal, a viceroy of Peru, built himself a mansion, the **Palacio de Villardompardo,** right over the baths, so it took years of painstaking excavation to restore them to their original form. The palace contains a small museum of folk crafts and a larger museum devoted to native art. There are guided tours of the baths, one of the largest and best conserved in Spain, every 30 minutes. ✉*Palacio de Villardompardo, Pl. Luisa de Marillac* ☎*953/248068* 🖃*Free (bring ID or passport)* ⊙*Tues.–Fri. 9–8, weekends 9:30–2:30.*

Jaén's **Museo Provincial** has one of the best collections of Iberian (pre-Roman) artifacts in Spain. The newest wing has 20 life-size Iberian sculptures discovered by chance near the village of Porcuna in 1975. The museum proper is in a 1547 mansion, on a patio with the facade of the erstwhile Church of San Miguel. The fine-arts section has a roomful of Goya lithographs. ✉*Paseo de la Estación 29* ☎*953/2313339* 🖃*€2, free for EU citizens* ⊙*Sun. 9–2:30; Wed. and Thurs.–Sat. 9–8:30, Tues. 3–8 and 2:30–8:30.*

WHERE TO STAY & EAT

$$$–$$$$ ✕**Casa Vicente.** Locals typically pack this family-run restaurant around the corner from the cathedral. You can have drinks and tapas in the colorful tavern, then move to the cozy courtyard dining room. The traditional Jaén dishes—game casseroles, Jaén-style spinach, and *cordero Mozárabe* (Mozarab-style roast lamb with a sweet-and-sour sauce)— are especially good. ✉*Calle Francisco Martín Mora 1* ☎*953/232222* 🖃*AE, MC, V* ⊙*Closed Aug. and Wed. No dinner Sun.*

$$–$$$ ✕**Casa Antonio.** Exquisite Andalusian food is served at this somber yet elegant restaurant with three small dining rooms, all with cherrywood-panel walls, dark plywood floors, and a few modern-art paintings. Try the *foie y queso en milhojas de manzana verde caramelizada en aceite de pistacho* (goose or duck liver and cheese in julienned green apples caramelized in pistachio oil) or *salmonetes de roca en caldo tibio de molusco y aceite de vainilla* (red mullet in a warm mollusk broth and vanilla oil). ✉*Calle Fermín Palma 3* ☎*953/270262* 🖃*AE, MC, V* ⊙*Closed Aug. and Mon. No dinner Sun.*

$$$ 🏨**Parador de Jaén.** Built amid the mountaintop towers of the Castillo
Fodor'sChoice de Santa Catalina, this is one of the showpieces of the parador chain
★ and a reason in itself to visit Jaén. The parador's grandiose exterior echoes the castle next door, as do the lofty ceilings, tapestries, baro-

nial shields, and suits of armor inside. Comfortable bedrooms, with canopy beds, have balconies overlooking fields stretching toward a dramatic mountain backdrop. ⊠ *Calle Castillo de Santa Catalina, 23001* ☎ *953/230000* 🖷 *953/230930* ⊕ *www.parador.es* 🛏 *45 rooms* ♿ *In-room: dial-up. In-hotel: restaurant, pool* ☰ *AE, DC, MC, V.*

ALCALÁ LA REAL

71 *75 km (46.5 mi) south of Jaén on N432 and A316.*

This ancient city, known to the Iberians and Romans, grew to prominence under the Moors who ruled here for more than 600 years. And it was they who gave it the first part of its name, Alcalá, which originated from a word meaning "fortified settlement."

The **Fortaleza de la Mota.** as it's known today, was started by the Moors in 727 and sits imperiously at an elevation of 3,389 feet, dominating not only the town but the whole area for miles around. From here, you can see spectacular views of the towering peaks of the Sierra Nevada on the southern horizon. During the 12th century the city changed hands frequently as the Moors fought to keep their control of the area. Finally, in 1341 Alfonso XI reconquered the town for good, adding Real (Royal) to its name. It remained of strategic importance until the Catholic Monarchs reconquered Granada—indeed, it was from here that they rode out to accept the keys of the city and the surrender. Hundreds of years later, the French forces left the town in ruins after their retreat in the early 19th century. The town itself was gradually rebuilt, but the fortress, consisting of the *alcazaba* (citadel) and the abbey church that Alfonso XI built, were more or less ignored. Up until the late 1990s, it was possible just to drive up and look around—exposed skeletons were visible in some open tombs on the floor of the church.

These days, things are more organized. To view it, you need a ticket. Then you face a long, uphill climb to the complex, which also has a small archaeology museum. ☎ *639/647796* 🎟 *€2* 🕐 *July–Sept. 10:30–1:30 and 5–8; Oct.–June 10:30–1:30 and 3:30–6:30.*

WHERE TO STAY

$ 🏨**Hospedería Zacatín.** This smallish hideaway in the center of town is an inexpensive and cozy way station for visitors to Alcalá la Real. Rooms are simple but well equipped and outfitted with contemporary facilities. The restaurant is rustic and comfortable. ⊠ *Calle Pradilllo 2, 23680* ☎ *953/580568* 🖷 *953/580301* ⊕ *www.hospederiazacatin.com* 🛏 *15 rooms* ♿ *In-hotel: restaurant, bar, parking (no fee)* ☰ *MC, V.*

BAEZA

72 *48 km (30 mi) northeast of Jaén on N321.*

Fodor'sChoice
★

The historic town of Baeza is nestled between hills and olive groves. Founded by the Romans, it later housed the Visigoths and became the capital of a *taifa* (kingdom) under the Moors. The Saint King Ferdinand III captured Baeza in 1227, and for the next 200 years it stood on the frontier of the Moorish kingdom of Granada. In the 16th and 17th centuries, local nobles gave the city a wealth of Renaissance palaces.

WHAT TO SEE

The **Casa del Pópulo,** in the central paseo—where the Plaza del Pópulo (or Plaza de los Leones) and Plaza de la Constitución (or Plaza del Mercado Viejo) merge to form a cobblestone square—is a beautiful circa 1530 structure. The first Mass of the Reconquest was supposedly celebrated on its curved balcony; it now houses Baeza's tourist office.

In the center of the town square is an ancient Iberian-Roman statue thought to depict Imilce, wife of Hannibal; at the foot of her column is the **Fuente de los Leones** *(Fountain of the Lions).*

To find Baeza's **university,** follow the steps on the south side of the Plaza del Pópulo. The college opened in 1542, closed in 1824, and later became a high school, where the poet Antonio Machado taught French from 1912 to 1919. The building now functions as a cultural center (a new school has been built next door). You can visit Machado's class-room—request the key—and the patio. ⊠ *Calle Beato Juan de Ávila s/n* ☎ *953/740154* ☉ *Thurs.–Tues. 10–2 and 4–6.*

Baeza's **cathedral** was originally begun by Ferdinand III on the site of a former mosque. The structure was largely rebuilt by Andrés de Vandelvira, architect of Jaén's cathedral, between 1570 and 1593, though the west front has architectural influences from an earlier period. A fine 14th-century rose window crowns the 13th-century Puerta de la Luna (Moon Door). Don't miss the baroque silver monstrance (a vessel in which the consecrated Host is exposed for the adoration of the faithful), which is carried in Baeza's Corpus Christi processions—the piece is kept in a concealed niche behind a painting, but you can see it in all its splendor by putting a coin in a slot to reveal the hiding place. Next to the monstrance is the entrance to the clock tower, where a small donation and a narrow spiral staircase take you to one of the best views of Baeza. The remains of the original mosque are in the cathedral's Gothic cloisters. Entrance to the cloister and small museum is €2. ⊠ *Pl. de Santa María* ☎ *953/744157* ☉ *May–Sept., daily 10–1 and 5–7; Oct.–Apr., daily 10:30–1 and 4–6.*

Plaza de Santa María. The main square of the medieval city is surrounded by not just the cathedral but also other palaces. The highlight is the fountain, built in 1564 and resembling a triumphal arch.

Iglesia de Santa Cruz. This rather small and plain church dates from the early 13th century. Not only was it one of the first built here after the Reconquest, but it's also one of the earliest Christian churches in all of Andalusia. It has two Romanesque portals and a curved stone altar. ⊠ *Pl. de Santa Cruz s/n* ☉ *Mon.–Sat. 11–1 and 4–5:30, Sun. noon–2.*

Casa Museo de Vera Cruz. Found immediately behind the Santa Cruz Church, and housed in a building dating from 1540, this museum has religious artifacts from the 16th, 17th, 18th, and 19th centuries. There's also a small shop selling local products. ⊠ *Pl. de Santa Cruz s/n* ☎ *€1.50* ☉ *Daily 11–1 and 4–6.*

Palacio de Jabalquinto. Built between the 15th and 16th centuries by Juan Alfonso de Benavides as a palatial home, this palace has a flamboyant Gothic facade and a charming marble colonnaded Renaissance patio. It's a perfect example of how the old can be retained and incorporated into the new. ⊠*Pl. de Santa Cruz s/n* ⊙ *Weekdays 9–2.*

The ancient student custom of inscribing names and graduation dates in bull's blood (as in Salamanca) is still evident on the walls of the seminary of **San Felipe Neri** (⊠*Cuesta de San Felipe*), built in 1660. It's opposite Baeza's cathedral.

Baeza's **ayuntamiento** (*town hall* ⊠*Pl. Cardenal Benavides, just north of Pl. del Pópulo*) was designed by cathedral master Andrés de Vandelvira. The facade is ornately platteresque; look between the balconies for the coats of arms of Felipe II, the city of Baeza, and the magistrate Juan de Borja. Arrange for a visit to the *salón de plenos,* a major hall with painted, carved woodwork. A few blocks west of the ayuntamiento, the 16th-century **Convento de San Francisco** (⊠*C. de San Francisco*) is one of Vandelvira's architectural religious masterpieces. You can see its restored remains—the building was spoiled by the French army and partially destroyed by a light earthquake in the early 1800s.

WHERE TO STAY & EAT

$$–$$$ ✕ **Vandelvira.** Seldom do you have the chance to eat in a 16th-century convent. The restaurant, within two galleries on the first floor of the Convento de San Francisco, has lots of character and magnificent antiques. Specialties include the *pâté de perdiz con aceite de oliva virgen* (partridge pâté with olive oil) and the *manitas de cerdo rellenas de perdiz y espinacas* (pig's knuckles filled with partridge and spinach). It has a summer terrace that doubles as a tavern. ⊠*C. de San Francisco 14* ☎*953/748172* ▭*AE, DC, MC, V* ⊙*Closed Mon. No dinner Sun.*

$ ✕▤ **Juanito.** Rooms in this small, unpretentious hotel are simple and comfortable. The restaurant's ($–$$$) proprietor is a champion of Andalusian food, and the chef has revived such regional specialties as *alcachofas Luisa* (braised artichokes), *ensalada de perdiz* (partridge salad), and *cordero con habas* (lamb and broad beans); desserts are based on old Moorish recipes. The hotel is next to a gas station on the edge of town, toward Úbeda. ⊠*Paseo Arca del Agua, 23440* ☎*953/740040* ▤*953/742324* ⊕*www.juanitobaeza.com* ⇗*36 rooms, 1 suite* ⌂*In-hotel: restaurant, tennis court, pool* ▭*MC, V* ⊙*No dinner Sun. and Mon.*

ÚBEDA

73 *9 km (5½ mi) northeast of Baeza on N321.*

Fodor'sChoice
★

Úbeda is in the heart of Jaén's olive groves, and olive oil is indeed the main concern here. Although this modern town of 30,000 is relatively dull (it has a reputation as being a serious, religious place), the *casco antiguo* (old town) is one of the most outstanding enclaves of 16th-century architecture in Spain. Follow signs to the *Zona Monumental*

(Monumental Zone), where there are countless Renaissance palaces and stately mansions, most closed to the public.

The Plaza del Ayuntamiento is crowned by the privately owned **Palacio de Vela de los Cobos.** It was designed by Andrés de Vandelvira (1505–75), a key figure in the Spanish Renaissance era for Úbeda's magistrate, Francisco de Vela de los Cobos. The corner balcony has a central white-marble column that's echoed in the gallery above.

WHAT TO SEE

Vandelvira's 16th-century Palacio Juan Vázquez de Molina is better known by its nickname, the **Palacio de las Cadenas** (House of Chains), because decorative iron chains were once affixed to the columns of its main doorway. It's now the town hall and has entrances on both Plaza Vázquez de Molina and Plaza Ayuntamiento. Molina was a nephew of Francisco de los Cobos, and both served as secretaries to emperor Carlos V and king Felipe II.

The Plaza Vázquez de Molina, in the heart of the old town, is the site of the **Sacra Capilla del Salvador.** This building is photographed so often that it has become the city's unofficial symbol. Sacra Capilla was built by Vandelvira, but he based his design on some 1536 plans by Diego de Siloé, architect of Granada's cathedral. Considered one of the masterpieces of Spanish Renaissance religious art, the chapel was sacked in the frenzy of church burnings at the outbreak of the civil war. However, it retains its ornate west front and altarpiece, which has a rare Berruguete sculpture. ⊠*Pl. Vázquez de Molina* ☎953/758150 ⌷€3 ⊙*Mon.–Sat. 10–2 and 4:30–7, Sun. 10:45–2 and 4:30–7.*

The **Ayuntamiento Antiguo** (Old Town Hall), begun in the early 16th century but restored as a beautiful arcaded baroque palace in 1680, is now a conservatory of music. From the hall's upper balcony, the town council watched celebrations and *autos-da-fé* ("acts of faith"—executions of heretics sentenced by the Inquisition) in the square below. On the north side is the 13th-century church of San Pablo, with an Isabelline south portal. ⊠*Pl. Primero de Mayo, off C. María de Molina* ⊙*1-hr tour at 7* PM.

The **Hospital de Santiago,** sometimes jokingly called the Escorial of Andalusia (in allusion to Felipe II's monolithic palace and monastery outside of Madrid), is a huge, angular building in the modern section, and yet another one of Andrés de Vandelvira's masterpieces in Úbeda. The plain facade is adorned with ceramic medallions, and over the main entrance is a carving of Santiago Matamoros (St. James the Moorslayer) in his traditional horseback pose. Inside are an arcaded patio and a grand staircase. Now a cultural center, it holds some of the events at the International Spring Dance and Music Festival. ⊠*Av. Cristo Rey* ☎953/750842 ⊙*Daily 8–3 and 4–10.*

WHERE TO STAY & EAT

¢–$$ ✕ **Libra.** A very pleasant and comfortable combination of cafeteria, pub, and bar, Libra is on a busy plaza on the edge of the older part of town. Combination plates consist of *huevos fritos, calamares, y patatas fritas* (fried eggs, squid, and french fries) and *bacon, huevos fritos, patatas fritas, y asadillo* (bacon, fried eggs, french fries, and red peppers) as well as a tempting selection of sandwiches. ⊠*Pl. Andalucía 3–5* ☎*953/757480* ⊟*MC, V.*

$$$
Fodor'sChoice
★

✕⊞**Parador de Úbeda.** This splendid parador is in a 16th-century ducal palace on the Plaza Vázquez de Molina, next to the Capilla del Salvador. A grand stairway, decked with tapestries and suits of armor, leads up to the guest rooms, which have tile floors, lofty wood ceilings, dark Castilian-style furniture, and large bathtubs. The dining room, specializing in regional dishes, serves perhaps the best food in Úbeda; try one of the *perdiz* (partridge) entrées. There's a bar in the vaulted basement. ⊠*Pl. Vázquez de Molina s/n, 23400* ☎*953/750345* 🖷*953/751259* ⊕*www.parador.es* ⇨*35 rooms, 1 suite* ⚘*In-hotel: restaurant, bar, no elevator* ⊟*AE, DC, MC, V.*

$$$
⊞**Palacio de la Rambla.** In old Úbeda, the wonderfully beautiful 16th-century mansion has been in the same family since it was built, and part of it still hosts the regal Marquesa de la Rambla when she's in town. Eight of the rooms are open to overnighters; each is unique, but all are large and furnished with original antiques, tapestries, and works of art; some have chandeliers. The palace is arranged on two levels, around a cool, ivy-covered patio. ⊠*Pl. del Marqués 1, 23400* ☎*953/750196* 🖷*953/750267* ⇨*7 rooms, 1 suite* ⚘*In-hotel: parking (fee), no elevator* ⊟*AE, MC, V.*

$$–$$$
⊞**María de Molina.** In the heart of the Monumental Zone (Zona Monumental), this hotel is in a large town house formerly known as La Casa de los Curas (The Priests' House), because it once housed two priests who were twins. Each room is different, but all are done in warm pastels and elegant Andalusian furnishings; some have balconies. Rooms 204–207 have the best views over the town's rooftops. The rates go up on weekends and holidays. ⊠*Pl. del Ayuntamiento s/n, 23400* ☎*953/795356* 🖷*953/793694* ⊕*www.hotel-maria-de-molina.com* ⇨*27 rooms* ⚘*In-hotel: restaurant, bar* ⊟*AE, DC, MC, V.*

$$–$$$
⊞**Rosaleda de Don Pedro.** This beautiful 16th-century mansion, in the city's Monumental Zone (Zona Monumental), blends the best of the old with all the comforts a modern traveler would expect. The rooms and public areas are spacious, and the pool offers relief from the summer heat. A unique feature is its parking facility—you drive your car into an elevator to be taken down to the car park. ⊠*Calle Obispo Toral 2, 23400* ☎*953/795147* 🖷*953/795149* ⊕*www.rosaledadedonpedro. com* ⇨*30* ⚘*In-hotel: restaurant, bar, pool, public Internet, parking (no fee)* ⊟*AE, DC, MC, V.*

$$
⊞**Hospedería El Blanquillo.** This hotel is in a small palace from the 16th century, and it's close to the walls and the Hospital Salvador. The simply furnished rooms surround a central patio. The restaurant's specialty is Mediterranean cuisine. ⊠*Pl. del Carmen 1, 23400* ☎*953/795405* 🖷*953/795406* ⇨*16 rooms, 1 suite* ⚘*In-hotel: restaurant, bar, laundry facilities* ⊟*MC, V.*

1

SHOPPING

Little Úbeda is the crafts capital of Andalusia, with workshops devoted to carpentry, basket weaving, stone carving, wrought iron, stained glass, and, above all, the city's distinctive green-glaze pottery. Calle Valencia is the traditional potters' row, running from the bottom of town to Úbeda's general crafts center, northwest of the old quarter (follow signs to Calle Valencia or Barrio de Alfareros). Úbeda's most famous potter was Pablo Tito, whose craft is carried on at three different workshops run by two of Tito's sons (Paco and Juan) and a son-in-law, Melchor, each of whom claims to be the sole true heir to the art.

All kinds of ceramics are sold at **Alfarería Góngora** (⊠ *Calle Cuesta de la Merced 32* ☎ *953/754605*). **Antonio Almazara** (⊠ *Calle Valencia 34* ☎ *953/753692* ⊠ *Calle Fuenteseca 17* ☎ *953/753365*) is one of several shops specializing in Úbeda's green-glaze pottery. The extrovert **Juan Tito** (⊠ *Pl. del Ayuntamiento 12* ☎ *953/751302*) can often be found at the potter's wheel in his rambling shop, which is packed with ceramics of every size and shape. **Melchor Tito** (⊠ *Calle Valencia 44* ☎ *953/753365*) focuses on classic green-glaze items. **Paco Tito** (⊠ *Calle Valencia 22* ☎ *953/751496*) devotes himself to clay sculptures of characters from *Don Quixote*, which he fires in an old Moorish-style kiln. His shop has a small museum as well as a studio.

CAZORLA

74 *48 km (35 mi) southeast of Úbeda.*

Unspoiled and remote, the village of Cazorla is at the east end of Jaén province. The pine-clad slopes and towering peaks of the Cazorla and Segura sierras rise above the village, and below it stretch endless miles of olive groves. In spring, purple jacaranda trees blossom in the plazas.

WHAT TO SEE

For a break from human-made sights, drink in the scenery or watch for wildlife in the **Parque Natural Sierra de Cazorla, Segura y Las Villas** *(Cazorla, Segura and Las Villas Nature Park)*. Try to avoid the summer and late spring months, when the park teems with tourists and locals. It's almost impossible to get accommodations in fall, particularly when it's deer season (September and October). For information on hiking, camping, canoeing, horseback riding, or guided excursions, contact the **Agencia de Medio Ambiente** (⊠ *Tejares Altos, Cazorla* ☎ *953/720125* ⊠ *Fuente de Serbo 3, Jaén* ☎ *953/012400*), or the park visitor center. For hunting or fishing permits, apply to the Jaén office well in advance. Deer, wild boar, and mountain goats roam the slopes of this carefully protected patch of mountain wilderness 80 km (50 mi) long and 30 km (19 mi) wide, and hawks, eagles, and vultures soar over the 6,000-foot peaks. Within the park, at **Cañada de las Fuentes** (Fountains' Ravine), is the source of Andalusia's great river, the Guadalquivir. The road through the park follows the river to the shores of **Lago Tranco de Beas**. Alpine meadows, pine forests, springs, waterfalls, and gorges make Cazorla a perfect place to hike. A short film shown in the **Centro de Interpretación Torre del Vinagre** (⊠ *Ctra. del Tranco, Km 37.8*

🖷*953/713040* 🕒*Daily 11–2 and 4–6*), in Torre de Vinagre, introduces the park's main sights. Displays explain the park's plants and geology and the staff can advise you on camping, fishing, and hiking trails.

There's also a **hunting museum,** with such "cheerful" attractions as the interlocked antlers of bucks who clashed in autumn rutting season, became helplessly trapped, and died of starvation. Nearby are a **botanical garden** and a **game reserve.** Between June and October the park maintains seven well-equipped **campsites.** Past Lago Tranco and the village of Hornos, a road goes to the **Sierra de Segura** mountain range, the park's least crowded area. At 3,600 feet, the spectacular village of **Segura de la Sierra,** on top of the mountain, is crowned by an almost perfect castle with impressive defense walls, a Moorish bath, and a nearly rectangular bullring.

Déjate Guiar-Excursiones organizes four-wheel-drive trips into restricted areas of the park to observe the flora and fauna and photograph the larger animals. ⊠*Paseo del Santo Cristo 17, Bajo, Edificio Parque* 🖷*953/721351* 🌐*www.turisnat.org.*

EN ROUTE   Leave Cazorla Nature Park by an alternative route—the spectacular **gorge** carved by the Guadalquivir River, a rushing torrent beloved by kayak enthusiasts. At the El Tranco Dam, follow signs to Villanueva del Arzobispo, where N322 takes you back to Úbeda, Baeza, and Jaén.

WHERE TO STAY & EAT

\$\$–\$\$\$ ✕🖼 **Parador de Cazorla.** Isolated in a valley at the edge of the nature reserve, 26 km (16 mi) above Cazorla village, lies this white, modern parador with red-tile roof. It's a quiet place, popular with hunters and anglers. The restaurant serves regional dishes such as *pipirrana* (a salad of finely diced peppers, onions, and tomatoes) and, in season, game. ⊠*Calle Sierra de Cazorla, 23470* 🖷*953/727075* 🖷*953/727077* 🌐*www.parador.es* 🛏*33 rooms* ⌂*In-hotel: restaurant, pool, parking (no fee)* ⊟*AE, DC, MC, V* 🕒*Closed Dec. and Jan.*

\$\$ ✕🖼 **Villa Turística de Cazorla.** On a hill with superb views of the village of Cazorla, this leisure complex rents semidetached apartments sleeping one to six. Each has a balcony or terrace as well as a kitchenette—some have a full kitchen—and fireplace. The restaurant (\$–\$\$), done in welcoming warm ocher tones, specializes in trout, lamb, and game. ⊠*Ladera de San Isicio s/n, 23470* 🖷*953/710100* 🖷*953/710152* 🌐*www.villacazorla.com* 🛏*32 apartments* ⌂*In-room: kitchen. In-hotel: restaurant, bar, pool* ⊟*MC, V.*

\$ ✕🖼 **La Hortizuela.** Deep in the heart of Cazorla Nature Park, in what was once a game warden's house, is a small hotel that's the perfect base for exploring the wilderness. Guest rooms are in the back, beyond the central courtyard, and most have unhindered views of the forest-clad mountainside (a few look onto the patio). Wild boar, game, deer, and fresh trout are usually available in the restaurant (\$–\$\$). ⊠*Ctra. del Tranco, Km 50.5, 2 km (1 mi) east of visitor center up dirt track, Coto Ríos 23478* 🖷🖷*953/713150* 🌐*www.lahortizuela.com* 🛏*23 rooms* ⌂*In-hotel: restaurant, pool, parking (no fee)* ⊟*MC, V* 🍽*CP.*

1

$$ ▦**Casa Rural La Calerilla.** Tucked into the mountainside, on the road leading down to Cazorla away from the valley and almost hidden from the road itself, is this rather charming and new stone *casa rural* (rural house). The rooms are bright with a traditional decor, and the garden and pool area is a great place to wind down. ⊠*Ctra. de la Sierra, Km 24.5, Burunchel, 23479* ☎*953/727326* 🖷*953/727034* ⊕*www. casaruralcalerilla.com* ⤚*11 rooms* ⌂*In-hotel: restaurant, bar, pool, parking (no fee), no elevator* ▤*MC, V.*

$$ ▦**Coto del Valle.** This delightful new hotel in Cazorla's foothills is easily recognized by the huge fountain outside. Built in traditional highland stone architecture, the hotel has rooms with a mountain decor and a restaurant with a fireplace and mounted game ranging from mountain goats to redleg partridges. ⊠*Ctra. del Tranco, Km 34.3, 23470* ☎*953/124067* ⊕*www.hotelcotodelvalle.com* ⤚*59 rooms* ⌂*In-hotel: restaurant, bar, pool, parking (no fee)* ▤*AE, DC, MC, V.*

GRANADA

430 km (265 mi) south of Madrid, 261 km (162 mi) east of Seville, and 160 km (100 mi) southeast of Córdoba.

The Alhambra and the tomb of the Catholic Monarchs are the pride of Granada. The city rises majestically from a plain onto three hills, dwarfed—on a clear day—by the Sierra Nevada. Atop one of these hills perches the pink-gold Alhambra palace. The stunning view from its mount takes in the sprawling medieval Moorish quarter, the caves of the Sacromonte, and, in the distance, the fertile *vega* (plain), rich in orchards, tobacco fields, and poplar groves.

Split by internal squabbles, Granada's Moorish Nasrid dynasty gave Ferdinand of Aragón an opportunity in 1491; spurred by Isabella's religious fanaticism, he laid siege to the city for seven months, and on January 2, 1492, Boabdil, the "Rey Chico" (Boy King), was forced to surrender the keys of the city to the Catholic Monarchs. As Boabdil fled the Alhambra via the Puerta de los Siete Suelos (Gate of the Seven Floors), he asked that the gate be sealed forever.

EXPLORING GRANADA

Granada can be characterized by its major neighborhoods. East of the Darro River and up the hill is **La Alhambra.** South of it and around a square and a popular hangout area, Campo del Príncipe, is **Realejo.** To the west of the Darro and going from north to south are the two popular neighborhoods, **Sacromonte** and **Albayzín** (also spelled Albaicín). The latter is the young and trendy part of Granada, full of color, flavor, and charming old architecture and narrow, hilly streets. On either side of Gran Vía de Colón and the streets that border the cathedral (Reyes Católicos and Recogidas—the major shopping areas) is the area generally referred to as **Centro,** the city center. These days much of the Alhambra and Albayzín areas are closed to cars, but starting from

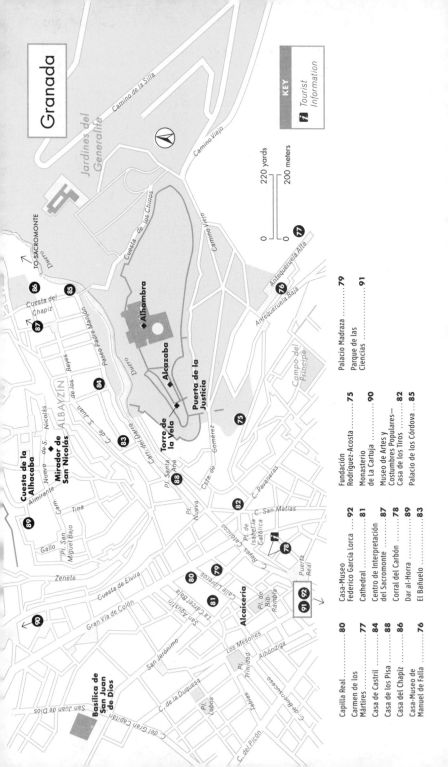

Granada

KEY

ℹ️ Tourist
Information

the Plaza Nueva there are now minibuses—numbers 30, 31, 32, and 34—that run frequently to these areas.

LA ALHAMBRA

Fodor'sChoice With more than 2 million visitors a year, the Alhambra is Spain's most
★ popular attraction. The complex has three main parts: the Alcazaba, the Palacios Nazaríes (Nasrid Royal Palace), and the Generalife. *See the Alhambra in-focus feature for details on visiting the attraction.*

⑰ Carmen de los Mártires. Up the hill from the Hotel Alhambra Palace, this turn-of-the-20th-century Granada *carmen* (private villa), and its gardens—the only area open to tourists—are like a Generalife in miniature. ⊠*Paseo de los Mártires, Alhambra* ☎*958/227953* 🖃*Free* ⊙*Apr.–Oct., weekdays 10–2 and 5–7, weekends 10–7; Nov.–Mar., weekdays 10–2 and 4–6, weekends 10–6.*

⑯ Casa-Museo de Manuel de Falla. The composer Manuel de Falla (1876–1946) lived and worked for many years in this rustic house, tucked into a charming little hillside lane with lovely views of the Alpujarra Mountains. In 1986 Granada paid homage to Spain's classical-music composer by naming its new concert hall (down the street from the Carmen de los Mártires) the Auditorio Manuel de Falla—and from this institution, fittingly, you have a view of his little white house. Note the bust in the small garden: it stands where the composer once sat to enjoy the sweeping view. ⊠ *C. Antequeruela Alta 11, Alhambra* ☎*958/228318* 🖃*€3* ⊙*Open by guided 30-min tour only, Tues.–Sat. 10–1:30.*

REALEJO

⑮ Fundación Rodríguez-Acosta/Instituto Gómez Moreno. A few yards from the impressive Alhambra Hotel, this nonprofit organization was founded at the bequeath of the painter José Marí Rodríguez-Acosta. Inside a typical Granadino *carmen* (private villa), it houses works of art, archaeological findings, and a library collected by the Granada-born scholar Manuel Gómez-Moreno Martínez. Other exhibits include valuable and unique objects from Asian cultures and the prehistoric and classical eras. ⊠*Callejón Niños del Rollo 8, Realejo* ☎*958/227497* ⊕*www. fundacionrodriguezacosta.com* 🖃*€4* ⊙ *Wed.–Sun. 10–2; last entrance 30 min before closing.*

㉒ Museo de Artes y Costumbres Populares–Casa de los Tiros. This 16th-century palace, adorned by the coat-of-arms of the Grana Venegas family who owned it, was named House of the Shots for the musket barrels that protrude from its facade. The stairs to the upper-floor displays are flanked by portraits of miserable-looking Spanish royals, from Ferdinand and Isabella to Philip IV. The highlight is the carved wooden ceiling in the Cuadra Dorada (Hall of Gold), adorned with gilded lettering and portraits of royals and knights. Old lithographs, engravings, and photographs show life in Granada in the 19th and early 20th centuries. ⊠*Calle Pavaneras s/n, Realejo* ☎*958/221072* 🖃*Free* ⊙*Tues. 2:30–8:30, Wed.–Sat. 9–8:30, Sun. 9–2:30.*

A GOOD WALK: GRANADA

Save a full day for the Alhambra and the Alhambra hill sites: the Alcazaba, Generalife, Alhambra Museum, **Fundación Rodríguez–Acosta** ❼❺, **Casa-Museo de Manuel de Falla** ❼❻, and **Carmen de los Mártires** ❼❼. The following walk covers the other major Granada sights.

Begin at Plaza Isabel la Católica (corner of Gran Vía and Calle Reyes Católicos), with its statue of Columbus presenting the Queen with his New World maps. Walk south on Calle Reyes Católicos and turn left into the **Corral del Carbón** ❼❽—the oldest building in Granada.

Cross back over Calle Reyes Católicos to the Alcaicería, once the Moorish silk market and now a maze of alleys with souvenir shops and restaurants. Behind the Alcaicería is Plaza Bib-Rambla, with its flower stalls and historic Gran Café Bib-Rambla, famous for hot chocolate and churros (a deep-fried flour fritter). Calle Oficios leads to **Palacio Madraza** ❼❾, the old Moorish University, and the **Capilla Real** ❽⓪, next to the **cathedral** ❽❶.

Off the cathedral's west side is the 16th-century Escuela de las Niñas Nobles, with its plateresque facade. Next to the cathedral, just off Calle Libreros, are the Curia Eclesiástica, an Imperial College until 1769; the Palacio del Arzobispo; and the 18th-century Iglesia del Sagrario. Behind the cathedral is the Gran Vía de Colón. Cross Gran Vía and head right to Plaza Isabel la Católica.

Make a detour to the **Casa de los Tiros** ❽❷ (on Calle Pavaneras, across Calles Reyes Católicos) before returning to Plaza Isabel la Católica. Follow Reyes Católicos to Plaza Nueva, and the ornate 16th-century Real Cancillería (Royal Chancery), now the Tribunal Superior de Justicia (High Court). Just north is Plaza Santa Ana, and the church of Santa Ana, designed by Diego de Siloé.

Walk through Plaza Santa Ana into Carrera del Darro—recently renovated, with new hotels and restaurants—and you come to the 11th-century Arab bathhouse, **El Bañuelo** ❽❸ and the 16th-century **Casa de Castril** ❽❹, site of Granada's Archaeological Museum.

Follow the river along the Paseo del Padre Manjón (Paseo de los Tristes)—to the **Palacio de los Córdoba** ❽❺. Climb Cuesta del Chapíz to the Morisco **Casa del Chapíz** ❽❻. To the east are the caves of Sacromonte and the **Centro de Interpretación del Sacromonte (Cuevas)** ❽❼. Turn west into the streets of the Albayzín, with the interesting **Casa de los Pisa** ❽❽ and **Dar al-Horra** ❽❾ nearby. Best reached by taxi are the 16th-century **Monasterio de La Cartuja** ❾⓪, the interactive science museum **Parque de las Ciencias** ❾❶, and **Casa-Museo Federico García Lorca** ❾❷.

SACROMONTE

The third of Granada's three hills, the Sacromonte rises behind the Albayzín. The hill is covered with prickly pear cacti and riddled with caverns. These caves may have sheltered early Christians; 15th-century treasure hunters found bones inside and assumed they belonged to San Cecilio, the city's patron saint. Thus the hill was sanctified—*sacro monte* (holy mountain)—and an abbey built on its summit, the **Abadía de**

Continued on page 117

ALHAMBRA

Floating mirage-like on its promontory overlooking Granada, the mighty and mysterious Alhambra shimmers vermilion in the clear mountain air, with the white peaks of the Sierra Nevada rising behind it. This sprawling palace-fortress, named from the Arabic for "red citadel" *(al-Qal'ah al-Hamra)*, was the last bastion of the 800-year Moorish presence on the Iberian Peninsula. Composed of royal residential quarters, court chambers, baths, and gardens, surrounded by defense towers and massive walls, the Alhambra is an architectual gem where Moorish kings worked and played—and even murdered their enemies.

LOOK UP

Among the stylistic
elements you can see
in the Alhambra are
Arabesque geometrical
designs, and elaborate
Mocárabe arches.

Built of perishable materials, the Alhambra was meant to be forever replenished and replaced by succeeding generations. Currently, it is the Patio de los Leones's (above) season for restoration.

INSIDE THE FORTRESS

More than 2 million annual visitors come to the Alhambra today, making it Spain's top attraction. Vistors revel in the palace's architectural wonders, most of which had to be restored after the alterations made after the Christian reconquest of southern Spain in 1492 and the damage from an 1821 earthquake. Incidentally, Napoléon's troops commandeered the site in 1812 with intent to level it; their attempts were foiled.

The courtyards, patios, and halls offer an ethereal maze of Moorish arches, columns, and domes containing intricate stucco carvings and patterned ceramic tiling. The intimate arcades, fountains, and light-reflecting pools throughout are identified in the ornamental inscriptions as physical renderings of paradise taken from the Koran and Islamic poetry. The contemporary visitor to this dream-like space feels the fleeting embrace of a culture that brought its light to a world emerging from medieval darkness.

ARCHITECTURAL TERMS

Arabesque: An ornament or decorative style that employs flower, foliage, or fruit, and sometimes geometrical, animal, and figural outlines to produce an intricate pattern of interlaced lines.

Mocárabe: A decorative element of carved wood or plaster based on juxtaposed and hanging prisms resembling stalactites. Sometimes called *muquarna* (honeycomb vaulting), the impression is similar to a beehive and the honey has been described as light.

Mozárabe: Sometimes confused with Mocárabe, the term Mozárabe refers to Christians living in Moorish Spain. Thus, Christian artistic styles or recourses in Moorish architecture (such as the paintings in the Sala de los Reyes) also are identified as *mozárabe*, or, in English, mozarabic.

Mudéjar: This word refers to Moors living in Christian Spain. Moorish artistic elements in Christian architecture, such as horseshoe arches in a church, also are referred to as Mudéjar.

ALHAMBRA'S ARCHITECTURAL HIGHLIGHTS

The columns used in the construction of the Alhambra are unique, with extraordinarily slender cylindrical shafts, concave base moldings, and carved rings decorating the upper extremities. The capitals have simple cylindrical bases under prism-shaped heads decorated in a variety of vegetal motifs. Nearly all of these columns support false arches constructed purely for decorative purposes. The 124 columns surrounding the Patio de los Leones (Court of the Lions) are the best examples.

Court of the Lions

Cursive epigraphy is used to quote the Koran and Arabic poems. Considered the finest example of this are the Ibn-Zamrak verses that decorate the walls of the Sala de las Dos Hermanas.

Cursive epigraphy

Glazed ceramic tiles covered with geometrical patterns in primary colors cover the walls of the Alhambra with a profusion of styles and shapes. Red, blue, and yellow are the colors of magic in Sufi tradition, while green is the life-giving color of Islam.

The horseshoe arch, widening before rounding off with lower ends extending around the circle until they begin to converge, was the quintessential Moorish architectural innovation, used not only for aesthetic and decorative purposes but because it allowed greater height than the classical, semicircular arch inherited from the Greeks and Romans. The horseshoe arch also had a mystical significance in recalling the shape of the *mihrab*, the prayer niche in the *qibla* wall of a mosque indicating the direction of prayer and suggesting a door to Mecca or to paradise. Horseshoe arches and arcades are found throughout the Alhambra.

Ceramic tiles

The Koran describes paradise as "gardens underneath which rivers flow," and water is used as a practical and ornamental architectural element throughout the Alhambra. Whether used musically, as in the canals in the Patio de los Leones or visually, as in the reflecting pool of the Patio de los Arrayanes, water is used to enhance light, enlarge spaces, or provide musical background for a desert culture in love with the beauty and oasis-like properties of hydraulics in all its forms.

Gate of Justice

Alhambra fountains

The Alcazaba was built chiefly by Nasrid kings in the 1300s.

LAY OF THE LAND

The complex has three main parts: the Alcazaba, the Palacio Nazaríes (Nasrid Royal Palace), and the Generalife. Across from the main entrance is the original fortress, the **Alcazaba**. Here, the watchtower's great bell was once used to announce the opening and closing of the irrigation system on Granada's great plain.

A wisteria-covered walkway leads to the heart of the Alhambra, the **Palacios Nazaríes**. Here, delicate apartments, lazy fountains, and tranquil pools contrast vividly with the hulking fortifications outside. It is divided into three sections: the *mexuar,* where business, government, and palace administration were headquartered; the *serrallo,* a series of state rooms where the sultans held court and entertained their ambassadors; and the harem, which in its time was entered only by the sultan, his family, and their most trusted servants, most of them eunuchs. Nearby is the Renaissance Palacio de Carlos V (Palace of Charles V), featuring a perfectly square exterior but a circular interior courtyard. Designed by Pedro Machuca, a pupil of Michelangelo, it is where the sultan's private apartments once stood. Part of the building houses the free **Museo de la Alhambra**, devoted to Islamic art. Upstairs is the more modest **Museo de Bellas Artes.**

Over on Cerro del Sol (Hill of the Sun) is **Generalife**, ancient summer palace of the Nasrid kings.

TIMELINE

1238 First Nasrid king, Ibn el-Ahmar, begins Alhambra.

1391 Nasrid Palaces is completed.

1492 Boabdil surrenders Granada to Ferdinand and Isabella, parents of King Henry VIII's first wife, Catherine of Aragon.

1524 Carlos V begins Renaissance Palace.

1812 Napoléonic troops arrive with plans to destroy Alhambra.

1814 The Duke of Wellington sojourns here to escape the pressures of the Peninsular War.

1829 Washington Irving lives on the premises and writes *Tales of the Alhambra,* reviving interest in the crumbling palace.

1862 Granada municipality begins Alhambra restoration that continues to this day.

2006 The Patio de los Leones undergoes a multiyear restoration.

ALHAMBRA'S PASSAGES OF TIME

From Columbus's commissioning to a bloody murder, historic events as well as everyday affairs happened between these walls.

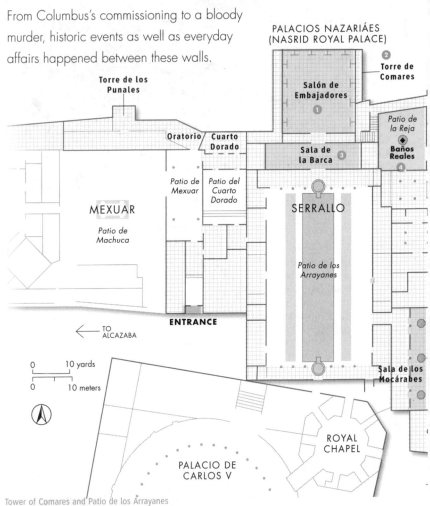

PALACIOS NAZARIÁES (NASRID ROYAL PALACE)

Torre de los Punales

Torre de Comares ②

Salón de Embajadores ①

Oratorio

Cuarto Dorado

Sala de la Barca ③

Patio de la Reja

Baños Reales ④

Patio de Mexuar

Patio del Cuarto Dorado

MEXUAR

Patio de Machuca

SERRALLO

Patio de los Arrayanes

ENTRANCE

← TO ALCAZABA

0 ―― 10 yards
0 ―― 10 meters

Sala de los Mocárabes

PALACIO DE CARLOS V

ROYAL CHAPEL

Tower of Comares and Patio de los Arrayanes

① In **El Salón de Embajadores**, Boabdil drew up his terms of surrender, and Christopher Columbus secured royal support for his historic voyage in 1492. The carved wooden ceiling is a portrayal of the seven Islamic heavens, with six rows of stars topped by a seventh-heaven cupulino or micro-cupola.

② **Torre de Comares**, a lookout in the corner of this hall is where Carlos V uttered his famous line, "Ill-fated the man who lost all this."

③ Mistakenly named from the Arabic word *baraka* (divine blessing), **Sala de la Barca** has a carved wooden ceiling often described as an inverted boat.

⑤ **Peinador de la Reina**

Apartamientos de Carlos V

Patio de Lindaraja

HAREM

⑥ **Mirador de Daraxa**

⑦ **Sala de los Ajimeces**

Sala de las Dos Hermanas

⑧

Patio de los Leones ⑨

Sala de los Reyes

⑪

istern

⑩ **Sala de los Abencerrajes**

TO
JARDINES DEL PARTAL,
GENERALIFE → ⑫

Sala de los Reyes

⑥ Sultana Zoraya often found refuge in this charming little balcony (**Mirador de Daraxa**) overlooking the Lindaraja garden.

⑦ Shhh, don't tell a secret here. In the **Sala de los Ajimeces**, a whisper in one corner can be clearly heard from the opposite corner.

⑧ In the **Sala de las Dos Hermanas**, twin slabs of marble embedded in the floor are the "sisters," though Washington Irving preferred the story of a pair of captive Moorish beauties.

⑨ In the **Patio de Los Leones** (Court of the Lions), a dozen crudely crafted lions support the fountain at the center of this elegant courtyard, representing the signs of the zodiac sending water to the four corners. (The lions are currently not on display while the court undergoes restoration through 2008.)

⑩ In the **Sala de los Abencerrajes**, Muley Hacen (father of Boabdil) murders the male members of the Abencerraje family in revenge for their chief's seduction of his daughter Zoraya. The rusty stains in the fountain are said to be bloodstains left by the pile of Abencerraje heads.

The star-shaped cupola, reflected in the pool, is considered the Alhambra's most beautiful example of stalactite or honeycomb vaulting.

The octagonal dome over the room is best viewed at sunset when the 16 small windows atop the dome admit sharp, low sunlight that refracts kaleidoscopically through the beehive-like prisms.

⑪ In the **Sala de los Reyes**, the ceiling painting depicts the first 10 Nasrid rulers. It was painted by a Christian artist since Islamic artists were not allowed to usurp divine power by creating human or animal figures.

The overhead painting of the knight rescuing his lady from a savage man portrays chivalry, a concept introduced to Europe by Arabic poets.

⑫ The terraces of **Generalife** grant incomparable views of the city.

Generalife gardens

④ The **Baños Reales** is where the sultan's favorites luxuriated in brightly tiled pools beneath star-shape pinpoints of light from the ceiling above. It is open to visitors on certain days. An up-to-date timetable can be obtained from the tourist office.

⑤ **El Peinador de la Reina**, a nine-foot-square room atop a small tower was the Sultana's boudoir. The perforated marble slab was used to infiltrate perfumes while the queen performed her toilette. Washington Irving wrote his *Tales of the Alhambra* in this romantic tree house–like perch.

PLANNING YOUR VISIT

The acoustics in the Palace of Charles V are ideal for the summer symphony concerts at the Alhambra.

GETTING THERE & AROUND

The best approach to the Alhambra is straight up the Cuesta de Gomérez from Plaza Nueva to the Puerta de la Justicia. From hotels up the river Darro in the Albayzín, the walk around the back walls of the palace along the Cuesta de los Chinos is a good hike. Buses 30 and 32 run from Plaza Nueva to the Alhambra. If you're driving, don't park on the street (it leaves your car vulnerable to a break-in). Instead, use the Alhambra parking lot or park underground on Calle San Agustín, just north of the cathedral, and take a taxi or the minibus from Plaza Nueva.

The entrance to the Nasrid Royal Palace is behind Carlos V's Renaissance Palace and leads into the *mexuar*, the chambers of state. The best route through the Alhambra traces an s-shaped path through the *mexuar*, the *serrallo*, and the harem, starting with the Patio de los Leones and ending with the Peinador de la Reina.

Wheelchairs are available on request; inquire at the Entrance Pavilion.

WHEN TO GO

Winter's low, slanting sunlight is best for seeing the Alhambra, and the temperatures are ideal for walking. Spring brings lush floral colors to the gardens. Fall is also sharp, cooler, and clear. July and August are crowded and hot.

The **Festival Internacional de Música y Danza de Granada** (☎ 34 958/276241 ⊕ www.granadafestival.org) held annually from mid-June to mid-July offers visitors an opportunity to hear a concert in the Alhambra or watch a ballet in the Generalife amphitheater.

GETTING TICKETS

Entrance to the Alhambra complex of the Alcazaba, Nasrid Palaces, Mosque Baths, and Generalife is strictly controlled by quotas. There are three types of timed tickets: morning, afternoon, and evening; note that the evening ticket is valid only for the Nasrid Palaces.

Tickets for the Alhambra complex and the Nasrid Palaces cost €12. Tickets can be obtained online at ⊕ www.alhambratickets.com, by phone at ☎ 902/224460 in Spain or ☎ 34 91/537–9178 outside Spain, or at any BBVA (Banco Bilbao Vizcaya Argentaria) branch.

You can visit the Palace of Charles V and its two museums (Museo de la Alhambra and Museo de Bellos Artes) independently of the Alhambra. They're open Tues.–Sat. 9–2:30

HOURS OF OPERATION

The Alhambra is open every day except December 25 and January 1.

November through February, morning visits are daily from 8:30 to 2, with a maximum capacity of 3,300; afternoon visits are daily from 2 to 6, with a maximum capacity of 2,100; and evening visits are Friday and Saturday from 8 to 9:30, with a maximum capacity of 400.

March to October, morning visits are daily from 8:30 to 2, with a maximum capacity of 3,300; afternoon visits are daily from 2 to 8, with a maximum capacity of 3,300; and evening visits are Tuesday through Saturday from 10 to 11:30, with a maximum capacity of 400.

Visits to the main gardens are allowed daily, from 8:30 to 6 year-round; from March through October access is until 8.

CONTACT INFORMATION

Patronato de la Alhambra ☎ 34 958/027900 ✉ informacion.alhambra.pag@juntadeandalucia.es ⊕ www.alhambra-patronato.es.

Sacromonte (✉ *C. del Sacromonte, Sacromonte* ☎ *958/221445* ⌚ *€3* ⊙ *Tues.–Sat. 11–1 and 4–6, Sun. 4–6; guided tours every ½ hr).* The Sacromonte has long been notorious as a domain of Granada's gypsies and a den of pickpocketing, but its reputation is largely undeserved. The quarter is more like a quiet Andalusian *pueblo* (village) than a rough neighborhood. Many of the quarter's colorful *cuevas* (caves) have been restored as middle-class homes, and some of the old spirit lives on in a handful of *zambras*—flamenco performances in caves garishly decorated with brass plates and cooking utensils. These shows differ from formal flamenco shows in that the performers mingle with you, usually dragging one or two onlookers onto the floor for an improvised dance lesson. Ask your hotel to book you a

> ### BICYCLING IN GRANADA
>
> At the foot of the Iberian Peninsula's tallest mountain—the 11,427-foot Mulhacén peak—Granada offers challenging mountain-cycling opportunities, while spinning through the hairpin turns of the Alpujarra mountain range east of Granada is both scenic and hair-raising. For more information about cycling tours around Granada, contact **Cycling Country** (✉ *C/Salmerones 18, Alhama de Granada* ☎ *958/360655* ⊕ *www.cyclingcountry.com*) run by husband-and-wife team Maggi Jones and Geoff Norris in a town about 55 km (33 mi) away.

spot on a cueva tour, which usually includes a walk through the neighboring Albayzín and a drink at a tapas bar in addition to the zambra.

87 **Centro de Interpretación del Sacromonte.** A word of warning: even if you take the 30 or 32 minibus or the city sightseeing bus to get here, you will still be left with a steep, arduous walk to reach the center. The Museo Etnográfico shows how people lived here, and other areas show the flora and fauna of the area as well as cultural activities. ✉ *Calle Barranco de los Negros s/n* ☎ *958/215120* ⊕ *www.sacromontegranada.com* ⌚ *€4 museum, €1 for other areas* ⊙ *Apr.–Oct., Tues.–Fri. 10–2 and 5–9; Nov.–Mar., Tues.–Fri. 10–2 and 4–7, weekends 11–7.*

ALBAYZÍN

Fodor's Choice ★

Covering a hill of its own, across the Darro ravine from the Alhambra, this ancient Moorish neighborhood is a mix of dilapidated white houses and immaculate *carmenes* (private villas in gardens enclosed by high walls). It was founded in 1228 by Moors who fled Baeza after Saint King Ferdinand III captured the city. Full of cobblestone alleyways and secret corners, the Albayzín guards its old Moorish roots jealously, though its 30 mosques were converted to baroque churches long ago. A stretch of the Moors' original city wall runs beside the Cuesta de la Alhacaba. If you're walking—the best way to explore—you can enter the Albayzín from either the Cuesta de Elvira or the Plaza Nueva. Alternatively, on foot or by taxi (parking is impossible), begin in the Plaza Santa Ana and follow the Carrera del Darro, Paseo Padre Manjón, and Cuesta del Chapíz. One of the highest points in the quarter, the plaza in front of the church of San Nicolás—called the **Mirador de San Nicolás**—has one of the finest views in all of Granada: on the hill opposite, the turrets and towers of the Alhambra form a dramatic silhouette against the snowy peaks of the Sierra Nevada. The sight is most magical at dawn, dusk, and on nights when the Alhambra is floodlighted. Interestingly, given the area's Moorish history, the two sloping, narrow streets of Calderería Nueva and Caldería Vieja that meet at the top by the Iglesia San Gregorio have developed into something of a North African bazaar. They are full of shops and stalls selling clothes, bags, crafts, and trinkets. The numerous little teahouses and restaurants here have a decidedly Moroccan flavor. Be warned that there have been some thefts in the Albayzín area, so keep your money and valuables out of sight.

88 **Casa de los Pisa.** Originally built in 1494 for the Pisa family, this house's claim to fame is its relationship to San Juan de Dios, who came to Granada in 1538 and founded a charity hospital to take care of the poor and abandoned. Befriended by the Pisa family, he was taken into the Pisa home when he fell ill in February 1550. A month later, he died there, at the age of 55. Since that time, devotees of the saint have traveled from around the world to this house with a stone Gothic facade, now run by the Hospital Order of St. John. Inside are numerous pieces of priceless religious works of art, an extensive collection of paintings and sculptures depicting St. John, jewelry, and furniture. ⊠ *Calle Convalecencia 1, Albayzín* ☎ *958/222144* 💶 *€3* ⏲ *Mon.–Sat. 10–1.*

84 **Casa de Castril.** Bernardo Zafra, secretary to Queen Isabella, once owned this richly decorated 16th-century palace. Before you enter, notice the exquisite portal, and the facade carvings depicting scallop shells and a phoenix. Inside is the **Museo Arqueológico** (Archaeological Museum), where you can find artifacts from provincial caves and from Moorish times, Phoenician burial urns from the coastal town of Almuñécar, and a copy of the *Dama de Baza* (Lady of Baza) a large Iberian sculpture discovered in northern Granada Province in 1971 (the original is in Madrid). ⊠ *Carrera del Darro 41, Albayzín* ☎ *958/225640* 💶 *€1.50, free for EU citizens* ⏲ *Tues. 2:30–8, Wed.–Sat. 9–8:30, Sun. 9–2:30.*

86 **Casa del Chapíz.** There's a delightful garden in this fine 16th-century Morisco house (built by Moorish craftsmen under Christian rule). It houses the School of Arabic Studies and is not generally open to the public, but if you knock, the caretaker might show you around. ⊠ *C. Cuesta del Chapíz at C. del Sacromonte, Albayzín.*

89 **Dar al-Horra.** Hidden in the back of the upper Albayzín this semi-secret gem was built in the 15th century for the mother of Boabdil, last Nasrid ruler of Granada. After the 1492 conquest of Granada, Dar al-Horra—House of the Honest Woman—was ceded to royal secretary Don Hernando de Zafra. Isabella la Católica later founded the Convent of Santa Isabel la Real here, which continued until the 20th century. Typical of Nasrid art, the interior resembles that of the Alhambra. The north side is the most interesting, with two floors and a tower. The bottom floor is covered with an exquisite flat wooden ceiling decorated with geometric figures. ⊠ *Callejón de las Monjas s/n Albayzín* ☎ *958/077800* 💶 *Free* ⏲ *Weekdays 10–2.*

1

83 **El Bañuelo** *(Little Bath House)*. These 11th-century Arab steam baths might now be a little dark and dank, but try to imagine them filled, some 900 years ago, with Moorish beauties. The dull brick walls were then backed by bright ceramic tiles, tapestries, and rugs. Light comes in through star-shape vents in the ceiling, à la the bathhouse in the Alhambra. ⊠ *Carrera del Darro 31, Albayzín* ☎ *958/227938* ✉ *Free* ⊗ *Tues.–Sat. 10–2.*

NEED A
BREAK? The park at **Paseo Padre Manjón,** along the Darro River—also known as the Paseo de los Tristes (Promenade of the Sad) because funeral processions once passed this way—is a terrific place for a coffee break at one of the cafés or bars along the paseo. Dappled with fountains and stone walkways, the park has a stunning view of the Alhambra's northern side.

85 **Palacio de los Córdova.** At the end of the Paseo Padre Manjón, this 17th-century noble house today holds Granada's municipal archives and is used for municipal functions and art exhibits. You're free to wander about the large garden. ⊠ *Cuesta del Chapiz 4, Albayzín.*

CENTRO

80 **Capilla Real** *(Royal Chapel)*. Catholic Monarchs Isabella of Castile and Ferdinand of Aragón are buried at this shrine. The couple originally planned to be buried in Toledo's San Juan de los Reyes, but Isabella changed her mind when the pair conquered Granada in 1492. When she died in 1504, her body was first laid to rest in the Convent of San Francisco (now a parador), on the Alhambra hill. The architect Enrique Egas began work on the Royal Chapel in 1506 and completed it 15 years later, creating a masterpiece of the ornate Gothic style now known in Spain as Isabelline. In 1521 Isabella's body was transferred to a simple lead coffin in the Royal Chapel crypt, where it was joined by that of her husband, Ferdinand, and later her unfortunate daughter, Juana la Loca (Joanna the Mad), and son-in-law, Felipe el Hermoso (Philip the Handsome). Felipe died young, and Juana had his casket borne about the peninsula with her for years, opening the lid each night to kiss her embalmed spouse good night. A small coffin to the right contains the remains of Prince Felipe of Asturias, a grandson of the Catholic Monarchs and nephew of Juana la Loca who died in his infancy. The underground **crypt** containing the five lead coffins is quite simple, but it's topped by elaborate marble **tombs** showing Ferdinand and Isabella lying side by side (commissioned by their grandson Charles V and sculpted by Domenico Fancelli). The **altarpiece,** by Felipe Viga-rini (1522), comprises 34 carved panels depicting religious and histori-cal scenes; the bottom row shows Boabdil surrendering the keys of the city to its conquerors and the forced baptism of the defeated Moors. The **sacristy** holds Ferdinand's sword, Isabella's crown and scepter, and a fine collection of Flemish paintings once owned by Isabella. ⊠ *Calle Oficios, Centro* ☎ *958/229239* ⊕ *www.capillarealgranada.com* ✉ *€3* ⊗ *Apr.–Oct., Mon.–Sat. 10:30–1 and 4–7, Sun. 11–1 and 4–7; Nov.–Mar., Mon.–Sat. 10:30–1 and 3:30–5:30, Sun. 11–1 and 3:30–6:30.*

⑧ Cathedral. Granada's cathedral was commissioned in 1521 by Charles V, who considered the Royal Chapel "too small for so much glory" and wanted to house his illustrious late grandparents someplace more worthy. Charles undoubtedly had great designs, as the cathedral was created by some of the finest architects of its time: Enrique Egas, Diego de Siloé, Alonso Cano, and sculptor Juan de Mena. Alas, his ambitions came to little, for the cathedral is a grand and gloomy monument, not completed until 1714, and never used as the crypt for his grandparents (or parents). You enter through a small door at the back, off the Gran Vía. Old hymnals are displayed throughout, and there's a museum, which includes a 14th-century gold-and-silver monstrance (used for communion) given to the city by Queen Isabella. Audio guides are available for €3. ⊠ *Gran Vía s/n, Centro* ☎958/222959 ⬚€3 ⊙*Apr.– Oct., Mon.–Sat. 10:30–1:30 and 4–8, Sun. 4–8; Nov.–Mar., Mon.–Sat. 10:45–1:30 and 4–7, Sun. 4–7.*

⑦ Corral del Carbón *(Coal House).* This building was used to store coal in the 19th century, but its history goes further back. Dating from the 14th century, it was used by Moorish merchants as a lodging house, and then later by Christians as a theater. It's one of the oldest Moorish buildings in the city, and is the only Arab structure of its kind in Spain. ⊠ *Pl. Mariana Pineda s/n, Centro* ☎958/221118 ⬚*Free* ⊙*Weekdays 10–1:30 and 5–8, weekends 10:30–2.*

⑦ Palacio Madraza. This building conceals the old Islamic seminary built in 1349 by Yusuf I. The intriguing baroque facade is elaborate; inside, across from the entrance, an octagonal room is crowned by a Moorish dome. There are occasional free art and cultural exhibitions. ⊠ *C. Zacatín s/n, Centro* ☎958/223447.

OUTSKIRTS OF TOWN

㊒ Casa-Museo Federico García Lorca. Granada's most famous native son, the poet Federico García Lorca, gets his due here, in the middle of a park devoted to him on the southern fringe of the city. Lorca's onetime summer home, **La Huerta de San Vicente,** is now a museum—run by his niece Laura García Lorca—with such artifacts as his beloved piano and changing exhibits on specific aspects of his life. ⊠ *Parque García Lorca, Virgen Blanca s/n, Arabial* ☎958/258466 ⊕*www.huertadesanvicente. com* ⬚€3, *free Wed.* ⊙*July and Aug., Tues.–Sun. 10–3; Apr., May, June, and Sept., Tues.–Sun. 10–1 and 5–8; Oct.–Mar. Tues.–Sun. 10–1 and 4–7. Guided tours every 45 min until 30 min before closing.*

㊐ Monasterio de La Cartuja. This Carthusian monastery in northern Granada (2 km [1 mi]) from the center and reached by the number 8 bus) was begun in 1506 and moved to its present site in 1516, though construction continued for the next 300 years. The exterior is sober and monolithic, but inside are twisted, multicolor marble columns; a profusion of gold, silver, tortoiseshell, and ivory; intricate stucco; and the extravagant sacristy—it's easy to see why Cartuja has been called the Christian answer to the Alhambra. ⊠ *C. de Alfacar, Cartuja* ☎958/161932 ⬚€4 ⊙*Apr.–Oct., Mon.–Sat. 10–1 and 4–8, Sun. 10–noon and 4–8; Nov.–Mar., Mon.–Sun. 10–1 and 3:30–6.*

1

㉑ **Parque de las Ciencias** *(Science Park)*. Across from Granada's convention center, and easily reached on either a number 1 or 5 bus, this museum has a planetarium and interactive demonstrations of scientific experiments. The 165-foot observation tower has views to the south and west. This is the most-visited museum in Andalusia. ⊠*Av. del Mediterráneo, Zaidín* ☎*958/131900* ⊕*www.parqueciencias.com* 🎫*Park €4.50, planetarium €2* ⊙*Tues.–Sat. 10–7, Sun. and holidays 10–3. Closed Sept. 15–30.*

WHERE TO STAY & EAT

WHERE TO EAT

$$$–$$$$ ✕**Ruta del Veleta.** It's worth the short drive 5 km (3 mi) out of town to
★ this Spanish restaurant, which serves some of the best food in Granada. House specialties include *carnes a la brasa* (succulent grilled meats) and fish dishes cooked in rock salt, as well as seasonal dishes such as *Solomillo de jabalí con frutos de otoño y salsa de vinagre* (wild boar fillet with autumn fruits in a vinegar-and-honey sauce). Dessert might be *morito de chocolate templado con helado de gachas* (warm chocolate sponge cake with ice cream). ⊠*Ctra. de la Sierra 136, on road to Sierra Nevada, Cenes de la Vega* ☎*958/486134* ⊕*www.rutadelveleta. com* ⊟*AE, DC, MC, V* ⊙*No dinner Sun.*

$$–$$$$ ✕**Azafrán.** It is rather a charming surprise when entering this restaurant, nestled at the foot of the Albayzín by the side of the Darro River and in the shadow of the Alhambra, to find such a bright and modern decor. It is newly opened, and you can expect an interesting and varied menu with fish and meat dishes as well as pasta, couscous, and an enticing rice-and-fish casserole. ⊠*Paseo de los Tristes 1, Albayzín* ☎*958/226882* ⊟*MC, V.*

$$–$$$$ ✕**La Ermita en la Plaza de Toros.** As the name implies, this classy restaurant is under the seats of the Plaza de Toros; the decor, with *carteles* (bullfighting posters), bulls' heads, and bullfighter suits, reflects that fact. Meat selections such as *rabo de toro estofado al vino tinto* (bull's tail cooked in red wine) and *lomo de buey Gallego a la parrilla* (grilled beef tenderloin) dominate, but there are also seafood dishes and daily specials. ⊠*Calle Dr. Olóriz 25, Centro* ☎*958/290257* ⊟*MC, V.*

$$$ ✕**La Yedra Real.** This is a very modern-style restaurant with a terrace that has a good selection of typical Spanish dishes at reasonable prices. Because it is very close to the Alhambra's main entrance, it's an ideal stop for those visiting this amazing monument. ⊠*C. Viejo del Cementerio s/n, Alhambra* ☎*958/229145* ⊟*MC, V* ⊙*Closed Mon.*

$$–$$$ ✕**Bodegas Castañeda.** A block from the Cathedral across Gran Vía, this is a delightfully typical Granadino bodega. In addition to its wines, the specialties here are *jamón ibérico* (acorn-fed Ibérico ham) and *embutidos* (sausages). The extensive list of tapas includes the likes of *queso viejo en aceite* (cured cheese in olive oil), bacon with Roquefort cheese, and *jamón de Trevélez* (ham from the Alpujarran village of Trevélez). Combination plates and *raciónes* (family-style platters) come in two sizes. ⊠*Calle Almireceros 1–3, Centro* ☎*958/223222* ⊟*MC, V.*

$$-$$$ ✕**Carmen Verde Luna.** This intriguingly named restaurant, Carmen (Arabic for "summer cottage") Green Moon, a reference to Federico García Lorca's famous poem "Romance Somnámbulo" (Sleepwalking Ballad), has a terrace with marvelous views across to the Alhambra and Sierra Nevada. Regional dishes here might include toasted and stuffed eggplants with pâté, stuffed sea bass and vegetables, and hake with prawns. ⊠ *Calle Nuevo de San Nicolás 16, Albayzín* 🕾 *958/291794* ⊟ *MC, V.*

$$-$$$ ✕**Cunini.** Around the corner from the cathedral is Granada's best fish house, where seafood, often fresh from the boats at Motril, is displayed in the window at the front of the tapas bar. Both the *pescaditos fritos* (fried) and the *parrillada* (grilled) fish are good choices, and if it's chilly, you can warm up with *caldereta de arroz, pescado y marisco* (rice, fish, and seafood stew). There are tables outdoors in warm weather. ⊠ *Calle Pescadería 14, Centro* 🕾 *958/250777* ⊟ *AE, DC, MC, V* ☉ *Closed Mon. No dinner Sun.*

$$-$$$ ✕**Jardines Alberto.** Spacious and well located near the Alhambra, this restaurant has two outside patios with stunning views of the Generalife, plus a summer bar and barbecue. The interior is cozy and rustic, and the food, classically *granadino* with a choice of five-course menu, includes dishes such as *lomo de cerdo ibérico confitado al ajo y hierbas serranas con puré de castañas* (preserved Ibérico pork with garlic, wild herbs, and chestnut sauce) followed by the diet-defying *mousse de turrón y crema de cafe* (nougat mousse with coffee cream). ⊠ *Av. Alixares del Generalife s/n, Alhambra* 🕾 *958/224818* ⊟ *AE, MC, V* ☉ *Closed Sun. No dinner Mon.*

$$-$$$ ✕**Mirador de Morayma.** Buried in the Albayzín, this place is hard to find
★   and might appear to be closed (ring the doorbell). Once inside, you'll have unbeatable views across the gorge to the Alhambra, particularly from the wisteria-laden outdoor terrace. The adequate menu has some surprises, such as smoked *esturión* (sturgeon) from Riofrío, served cold with cured ham and a vegetable dip, and the *ensalada de remojón granadino*, a salad of cod, orange, and olives. ⊠ *Calle Pianista García Carrillo 2, Albayzín* 🕾 *958/228290* ⊟ *AE, MC, V* ☉ *No dinner Sun.*

$$-$$$ ✕**Sevilla.** Since 1930 this colorful, central two-story restaurant has fed
★   the likes of the composer de Falla and the poet García Lorca. There are four dining rooms and an outdoor terrace overlooking the Royal Chapel and Cathedral. There's a small but superb tapas bar; the dinner menu includes Granada favorites such as *sopa sevillana* (soup with fish and shellfish) and *tortilla al Sacromonte* (with bull's brains and testicles) as well as more elaborate dishes. ⊠ *Calle Oficios 12, Centro* 🕾 *958/221223* ⊟ *AE, DC, MC, V* ☉ *No dinner Sun.*

$$-$$$ ✕**Velázquez.** Tucked into a side street one block west of the Puerta de Elvira and Plaza del Triunfo, this cozy, very Spanish restaurant has long been popular with locals. At street level, the brick-wall bar is hung with hams; the intimate, wood-beam dining room is upstairs. House specialties include *zancarrón cordero a la miel* (lamb with honey) and *lomitos de rape* (braised monkfish medallions). ⊠ *Calle Emilio Orozco 1, Centro* 🕾 *958/280109* ⊟ *MC, V* ☉ *Closed Sun.*

$-$$$ ✕**Taberna Tendido 1.** Also found under the Plaza de Toros, this is next to the La Ermita but more informal. Dishes on the menu of salads, cheeses, smoked fish, and popular tapas are served in three sizes—tapa, half-*ración* (half portion) and *ración* (full portion)—and fit neatly onto the barrel tops. Fixed-price menus are also available. ⊠*Calle Dr. Olóriz 25, Centro* ☎*958/203136* ⊕*www.tendido1.com* ⊟*MC, V.*

$–$$ ✕**Antigua Bodega Castañeda.** This typical and traditional-style bodega, close to Plaza Nueva, is the ideal place to pop into for a snack and a quick drink. It features salads, sandwiches—made with toasted slipper bread—smoked fish, cheeses, pates, stews, tapas, stuffed baked potatoes, and desserts, and an interesting range of wines. ⊠*Calle Elvira 5, Centro* ☎*958/226362* ⊟*MC, V.*

$–$$ ✕**Kasbah Tetería.** On a sloping street that feels very North African, Kasbah Tetería has a menu that's fairly short. Dishes include couscous with chicken, lamb, and vegetables, as well as tasty *pasteles árabes* (cakes). ⊠*Calle Calderería Nueva 4, Centro* ☎*958/227936* ⊟*MC, V.*

$–$$ ✕**Meknes Rahma.** This Moroccan restaurant has an unusual location—on the edge of the Albayzín at the junction of the road to Sacromonte—but can be easily reached on the minibus numbers 31 or 32 from Plaza Nueva. In addition to dishes such as Moroccan soup and shish kebab, there's a selection of Eastern teas, and, for entertainment, belly dancing. ⊠*Peso de la Harina 1, Albayzín* ☎*958/227430* ⊟*MC, V.*

$–$$ ✕**Mesón Blas Casa.** In the choicest square in the Albayzín, this restaurant serves solidly traditional cuisine that includes *rabo de toro* (oxtail) and habas con jamón (ham with broadbeans). There's a cheap and filling *menú del día* (daily menu) and a fireplace for warming the toes when there's snow on the Sierras. ⊠*Pl. San Miguel Bajo 15, Albayzín* ☎*958/273111* ⊟*MC, V* ☉*Closed Mon.*

WHERE TO STAY

$$$$ 🏨**Palacio de los Patos.** This beautiful palace is unmissable, as it sits
★ proudly on its own in the middle of one of Granada's busiest shopping streets. While retaining its 19th-century classical architecture, it also, thanks to remodeling and renovation, incorporates absolutely everything—including a gastronomic restaurant and spa—that even the most discriminating 21st-century traveler could desire. Some consider this Granada's finest hotel. ⊠*Calle Solarillo de Gracia 1, Centrón, 18002* ☎*958/536516* 🖷*958/536517* ⊕*www.hospes.es* ⟿*42 rooms* ⌂*In-room: Ethernet. In-hotel: restaurant, bar, pool, spa, parking (fee)* ⊟*AE, DC, MC, V.*

$$$$ 🏨**Parador de Granada.** This is Spain's most expensive and popular
Fodor'sChoice parador, and it's right in the Alhambra precinct. The building, a former
★ Franciscan monastery built by the Catholic Monarchs after they captured Granada, is soul-stirringly gorgeous. If possible, go for a room in the old section where there are beautiful antiques, woven curtains, and bedspreads. The rooms in the newer wing are also charming but simple. Reserve four to six months in advance. ⊠*Calle Real de la Alhambra s/n, Alhambra, 18009* ☎*958/221440* 🖷*958/222264* ⊕*www.parador. es* ⟿*34 rooms, 2 suites* ⌂*In-room: dial-up. In-hotel: restaurant, bar, parking (no fee)* ⊟*AE, DC, MC, V.*

$$$–$$$$ 🏨**Casa de los Migueletes.** This very attractive 17th-century mansion with patios and galleries is found close to the popular Plaza Nueva. Expect to find antique or handmade furnishings in the individually dec-

orated rooms—some with Alhambra views. It comes by its name from the fact that it was once the headquarters of the Migueletes, a 19th-century rural police force. It is 100% no-smoking. Parking arrangements are at the Plaza Puerta Real garage some distance away. ⊠*Benalua 11, Albayzín, 18010* ☎*958/210700* 🖷*958/210702* ⊕*www.casa-migueletes.com* ⇔*24 rooms, 1 suite* ⚑*In-room: Ethernet. In-hotel: bar, parking (fee)* ⊟*AE, DC, MC, V.*

$$$
Fodor'sChoice
★
🏨 **Alhambra Palace.** Built by a local duke in 1910, this neo-Moorish hotel is on leafy grounds at the back of the Alhambra hill. The interior is very Arabian Nights, with orange-and-brown overtones, multicolor tiles, and Moorish arches and pillars. Even the bar is decorated as a mosque. Rooms overlooking the city have incredible views, as does the terrace, a perfect place to watch the sun set on Granada and its fertile plain. ⊠*Calle Peña Partida 2, Alhambra, 18009* ☎*958/221468* 🖷*958/226404* ⊕*www.h-alhambrapalace.es* ⇔*124 rooms, 11 suites* ⚑*In-room: dial-up. In-hotel: restaurant, bars, parking (no fee)* ⊟*AE, DC, MC, V.*

$$$
🏨 **Carmen.** This hotel has a prized city-center location on a busy shopping street, and is directly across from the El Corte Inglés department store. The rooms are spacious and have a mix of modern and classic decor. The rooftop terrace and pool offer stunning views of the city. ⊠*Acera del Darro 62, Centro, 18005* ☎*958/258300* 🖷*958/256462* ⊕*www.hotelcarmen.com* ⇔*270 rooms, 13 suites* ⚑*In-hotel: restaurant, bar, pool, parking (fee)* ⊟*AE, DC, MC, V.*

$$$
🏨 **Carmen de la Alcubilla del Caracol.** In a traditional Granadino *carmen*–style house, on the slopes of the Alhambra, this is one of Granada's most stylish hotels. The rooms are bright, airy, and furnished with antiques; they also have views over the city and the Sierra Nevada. The traditional terraced garden, with water troughs fed by an irrigation system from the Alhambra itself, is a peaceful oasis. ⊠*Calle Aire Alta 12, Alhambra, 18009* ☎*958/215551* ⊕*www.alcubilladelcaracol.com* ⇔*7 rooms* ⚑*In-room: Wi-Fi. In-hotel: restaurant, bar, parking (no fee), public Wi-Fi* ⊟*MC, V* ⊗*Closed Aug.*

$$$
★
🏨 **Casa Morisca Hotel.** The architect-owner of this 15th-century building transformed it into a hotel and received the 2001 National Restoration Award for the project. The brick building has many original architectural elements, three floors, and a central courtyard with a small pond and well. The rooms aren't large, but they get a heady Moorish feel through wonderful antiques and views of the Alhambra and Albayzín. ⊠*Cuesta de la Victoria 9, Albayzín, 18010* ☎*958/221100* 🖷*958/215796* ⊕*www.hotelcasamorisca.com* ⇔*12 rooms, 2 suites* ⚑*In-room: dial-up. In-hotel: restaurant* ⊟*AE, DC, MC, V.*

$$$
🏨 **El Ladrón de Agua.** Situated by the side of the Darro River, in an interesting area directly under the imposing shadow of the Alhambra, this 16th-century mansion is called the Water Thief—a name inspired from a poem by Juan Ramón Jiménez (winner of the Nobel Prize for Literature in 1956). The rooms, traditionally decorated, are all named after poems by Federico García Lorca and Manuel deFalla, and are found around the galleries of the two floors, with the best found in the tower; eight of the rooms overlook the Alhambra, There is no nearby

1

parking. ⊠*Carrera del Darro 13, Albayzín, 18010* ☎*958/215040* 🖷*958/224345* ⊕*www.ladrondeagua.com* ⤶*15 rooms* ⚬*In-room: Wi-Fi. In-hotel: restaurant, bar* ▤*AE, DC, MC, V.*

$$$ 🏨**Palacio de los Navas.** In the center of the city, this was built by aristocrat Francisco Navas in the 16th century and later became the Casa de Moneda (The Mint). It retains original architectural features while also blending in new features with the old to become a particularly charming hotel. ⊠*Calle Navas 1, Centro, 18009* ☎*958/215760* 🖷*958/215760* ⊕*www.palaciodelosnavas.com* ⤶*19 rooms* ⚬*In-hotel: parking (fee)* ▤*AE, DC, MC, V.*

$$$ 🏨**Reina Cristina.** In the former Rosales family residence, where the
★ poet Lorca was arrested after taking refuge when the Spanish civil war broke out, the Reina Cristina is near the lively and central Plaza de la Trinidad. Plants trail from the windowsills of the reception area and a covered patio with a small marble fountain. A marble stairway leads to the simply but cheerfully furnished (red fabrics on a white background) guest rooms. ⊠*Calle Tablas 4, Centro, 18002* ☎*958/253211* 🖷*958/255728* ⊕*www.hotelreinacristina.com* ⤶*43 rooms* ⚬*In-hotel: restaurant, bar, parking (fee)* ▤*AE, DC, MC, V* ❂*BP.*

$$–$$$ 🏨**Alojamientos con Encanto.** A bargain for groups and families, these elegant, comfortable, and large apartments are on the slopes of the Albayzín. Tiles, wrought-iron headboards, and other local crafts accent the apartments; quarters in the upper reaches of the Albayzín share a pebble patio crowded with plants and a terrace with magnificent views of the Alhambra. ⊠*C. Cuesta del Chapíz 54, Albayzín, 18010* ☎*958/222428* 🖷*958/222810* ⊕*www.granada-in.com* ⚬*In-room: Ethernet. In-hotel: parking (no fee)* ▤*AE, DC, MC, V.*

$$–$$$ 🏨**Guadalupe.** This charming hotel is close to the Alhambra. The rooms, in single, double, and triple sizes, are traditionally styled and of a generous size. ⊠*Paseo de la Sabica 30, Alhambra, 18009* ☎*958/223423* 🖷*958/223494* ⊕*www.hotelguadalupe.es* ⤶*58 rooms* ⚬*In-hotel: restaurant* ▤*AE, DC, MC, V.*

$$–$$$ 🏨**Inglaterra.** The interior of this 19th-century house in the heart of town (two blocks east of the Gran Vía de Colón) is comfortable and modern. Guest rooms are painted in pastel tones and have functional furniture and polished-wood floors. ⊠*Calle Cetti Meriem 4, Centro, 18010* ☎*958/221558* 🖷*958/227100* ⊕*www.nh-hoteles.com* ⤶*36 rooms* ⚬*In-hotel: restaurant, parking (fee)* ▤*AE, DC, MC, V.*

$$–$$$ 🏨**Palacio de Santa Inés.** It's not often you stay in a 16th-century palace, and this one in particular has a stunning location in the heart of the Albayzín. Rooms on the two upper floors are centered on a courtyard with frescoes painted by a disciple of Raphael. Each room is magnificently decorated with antiques and modern art; some have balconies with Alhambra views. ⊠*Cuesta de Santa Inés 9, Albayzín, 18010* ☎*958/222362* 🖷*958/222465* ⊕*www.palaciosantaines.com* ⤶*15 rooms, 20 suites* ⚬*In-hotel: restaurant, parking (fee)* ▤*AE, DC, MC, V.*

$$ 🏨**Hotel Los Tilos.** With a comfortable modern interior and a central location overlooking a pleasant square with a daily flower market, this good-value no-frills hotel is worth a try. Best of all is the fourth-

floor terrace where you can sip a drink, read a book, or just enjoy the panoramic view of the skyline. ⊠ *Pl. Bib-Rambla 4, Centro, 18001* ☎ *958/266712* 🖷 *958/266801* ⊕ *www.hotellostilos.com* 🖘 *30 rooms* ♿ *In-hotel: parking (fee)* ▤ *MC, V.*

¢–$ 🖵 **Britz.** If you plan on spending considerable time at the Alhambra and don't have wads of cash, consider this hostel, which is within walking distance. Rooms are more than adequate, and some have terraces and brightly tiled bathrooms. Its location on the bustling Plaza Nueva means noise can be a problem, but on the other hand there is also a wide choice of sidewalk cafés a short stroll away. ⊠ *Cuesta de Gomérez 1, Centro, 18010* ☎ *958/223652* ⊕ *www.lisboaweb.com* 🖘 *22 rooms, some with bath* ♿ *In-room: no TV* ▤ *MC, V.*

NIGHTLIFE & THE ARTS

THE ARTS

Get the latest on arts events at the **Diputacíon de Cultura** (Department of Culture), in the **Palacio de los Condes de Gabia** (⊠ *Pl. de los Girones 1, Centro* ☎ *958/247383*); free magazines at the tourist offices also have schedules of cultural events. Granada's orchestra performs in the **Auditorio Manuel de Falla** (⊠ *Paseo de los Mártires, Realejo* ☎ *958/222188*). Plays are staged at the **Teatro Alhambra** (⊠ *Calle Molinos 56, Realejo* ☎ *958/220447*). Granada's **Festival Internacional de Teatro** fills 10 days with drama each May; contact the **tourist office** (⊠ *Pl. Mariana Pineda 10, Centro* ☎ *958/247128*) for details. The **Festival Internacional de Música y Danza de Granada** (☎ *958/220691, 958/221844 tickets* ⊕ *www.granadafestival.org*) is held annually from mid-June to mid-July, with some events in the Alhambra itself. Contact the tourist office or visit the Web site for information on November's **Festival Internacional de Jazz de Granada** (⊕ *www.jazzgranada.net*).

FLAMENCO

Flamenco is played throughout the city, especially in the *cuevas* (caves) of the Albayzín and Sacromonte, where *zambra* shows—informal performances by gypsies—take place almost daily. The most popular cuevas are along the Camino de Sacromonte, the major street in the neighborhood of the same name. For any Sacromonte show, prepare to part with lots of money (€18–€20 is average). In August free shows are held at the delightful El Corral del Carbón square—home of the tourist office. The annual Encuentro Flamenco festival held during the first days of December typically attracts some of the country's best performers. If you do not want to show up randomly at the flamenco clubs, join a tour through a travel agent or your hotel, or contact **Los Tarantos** (⊠ *Calle del Sacromonte 9, Sacromonte* ☎ *958/224525*), which has lively nightly shows with midnight performances on Friday and Saturday. **Sala Alhambra** (⊠ *Parque Empresarial Olinda, Edif. 12* ☎ *958/412269 or 958/412287*) runs well-organized, scheduled performances. **La Rocío** (⊠ *Calle del Sacromonte 70, Albayzín* ☎ *958/227129*) is a good spot for authentic flamenco shows. **María La Canastera** (⊠ *Calle del Sacromonte 89, Sacromonte* ☎ *958/121183*) is another one of the cuevas on Camino de Sacromonte with unscheduled zambra shows.

TAPAS BARS

Poke around the streets between the Carrera del Darro and the Mirador de San Nicolás, particularly around the bustling Plaza San Miguel Bajo, for Granada's most colorful twilight hangouts. Also try the bars and restaurants in the arches underneath the Plaza de Toros (Bullfighting Ring), on the west of the city and a bit farther from the city center. For a change, check out some Moroccan-style tea shops, known as *teterías*—these first emerged in Granada and are now equally popular in Seville and Málaga, particularly among students. Tea at such places can be expensive, so be sure to check the price of your brew before you order. The highest concentration of teterías is in the Albayzín, particularly around Calle Calderería Nueva where, within a few doors from each other, you find Tetería Kasbah, Tetería Oriental, and El Jardín de los Sueños, which also sells delicious milk shakes—try the almond and pistachio.

La Trastienda (✉*Calle Cuchilleros 11, Centro* ☎*958/226985*) is named "The Backroom" because of where you eat the tapas—after you get your tapas and drink, take them to the dining area in back. **Le Gran Taberna** (✉*Pl. Nueva 12, Centro* ☎*958/228846*) serves unusual tapas, such as trout with cottage cheese, Roquefort with beets, and goat's-cheese canapés, as well as the more standard selections. **Taberna Salínas** (✉*Elvira 13, Centro* ☎*958/221411*) has a brick-and-beam decor and great wine to accompany its delicious tapas. More filling fare is also available. Off Calle Navas in Plaza Campillo is **Chikito** (✉*Pl. del Campillo 9, Puerta Real* ☎*958/223364*), best known for its tasty sit-down meals, but the bar is an excellent place for tapas. The place is usually packed, so additional tables are set up on the square in summer. Moroccan-run **Al-Andalus** (✉*Elvira 12,, Centro*) serves tasty tapas, including bite-size falafel and other vegetarian options. **La Taberna de Baco** (✉*Campo del Príncipe 22, Realejo* ☎*958/226732*) fuses Ecuadoran and Andalusian flavors. **El Pilar del Toro** (✉*C. Hospital de Santa Ana 12, Albayzín* ☎*958/225470*) is a bar and restaurant with a beautiful patio. The popular **Bodegas Castañeda** (✉*Elvira 6, Centro* ☎*958/226362*) serves classic tapas, as well as baked potatoes with a choice of fillings. **Bodega Peso La Harina** (✉*Placeta del Peso de la Harina, Sacromonte*), on a square right at the entrance of Camino de Sacromonte, prepares reliably good tapas. Southeast of Granada's cathedral, **Café Botánico** (✉*Calle Málaga 3, Centro* ☎*958/271598*) is a modern hot spot with a diverse menu that serves twists on traditional cuisine for a young, trendy crowd.

NIGHTLIFE

Granada's ample student population makes for a lively bar scene. Some of the trendiest bars are in converted houses in the Albayzín and Sacromonte and in the area between Plaza Nueva and Paseo de los Tristes. Calle Elvira and Caldería Vieja, and Nueva are crowded with laid-back coffee and pastry shops. In the modern part of town, Pedro Antonio de Alarcón and Martinez de la Rosa have larger but less glamorous offerings. Another nighttime gathering place is the Campo del Príncipe, a large plaza surrounded by typical Andalusian taverns.

El Eshavira (✉ *Calle Postigo de la Cuna 2, Albayzín* ☎ *958/290829*) is a smoky, dimly lighted club where you can hear sultry jazz and occasional flamenco. **Planta Baja** (✉ *C. Horno de Abad 11, Centro* ☎ *958/207607*) is a funky late-night club that hosts bands playing everything from exotic pop to garage and soul. **Fondo Reservado** (✉ *Calle Santa Inés 4, Albayzín* ☎ *958/222375*) is a hip hangout for mainly students, and has late-night dance music. **Granada 10** (✉ *Calle Carcel Baja 10, Centro* ☎ *958/224001*), with an upscale crowd, in a former theater. **La Industrial Copera** (✉ *Calle de la Paz 7, Ctra. de la Armilla* ☎ *958/258449*) is a popular disco, especially on Friday night. **Zoo** (✉ *C. Mora 2, Puerta Real* ☎ *No phone*) is one of the longest-established and largest discos in town.

SHOPPING

A Moorish aesthetic pervades Granada's silver-, brass- and copperware, ceramics, marquetry (especially the *taraceas,* wooden boxes with inlaid tiles on their lids), and woven textiles. The main shopping streets, centering on the Puerta Real, are the Gran Vía de Colón, Reyes Católicos, Zacatín, Ángel Ganivet, and Recogidas. Most antiques stores are on Cuesta de Elvira, and Alcaicería—off Reyes Católicos—and Cuesta de Gomérez, on the way up to the Alhambra, also has many handicraft shops. **Cerámica Fabre** (✉ *Pl. Pescadería 10, Centro*), near the cathedral, has typical Granada ceramics: blue-and-green patterns on white, with a pomegranate in the center. For wicker baskets and esparto-grass mats and rugs, head off the Plaza Pescadería to **Espartería San José** (✉ *C. Jaudenes 22, Centro*).

SIDE TRIPS FROM GRANADA

The fabled province of Granada spans the Sierra Nevada mountains, with the beautifully rugged Alpujarras, and the highest peaks on mainland Spain—Mulhacén at 11,407 feet and Veleta at 11,125 feet. This is where you can find some of the prettiest, most ancient villages; it is one of the foremost destinations for Andalusia's increasingly popular rural tourism. Granada's plain (known as *la vega*), covered with orchards and tobacco and poplar groves, is covered in snow half the year.

EN ROUTE Eight miles (12 km) south of Granada on N323, the road reaches a spot known as the **Suspiro del Moro** *(Moor's Sigh).* Pause here a moment and look back at the city, just as Granada's departing "Boy King," Boabdil, did 500 years ago. As he wept over the city he'd surrendered to the Catholic Monarchs, his scornful mother pronounced her now legendary rebuke: "You weep like a boy for the city you could not defend as a man."

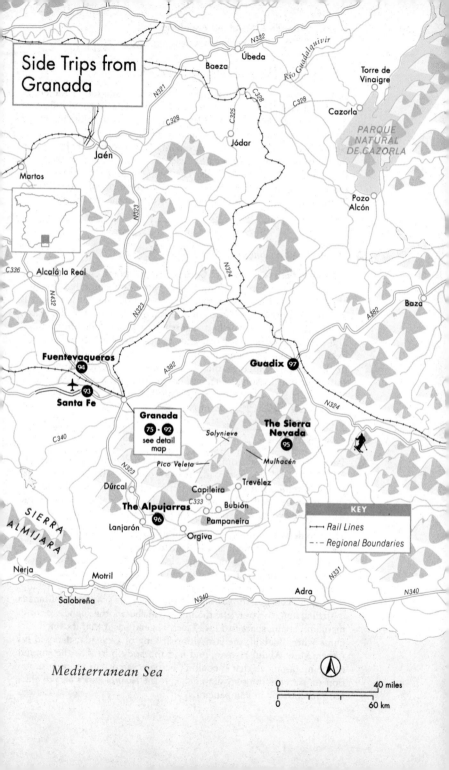

SANTA FE

93 *8 km (5 mi) west of Granada just south of N342.*

Santa Fe was founded in winter 1491 as a campground for Ferdinand and Isabella's 150,000 troops as they prepared for the siege of Granada. It was here, in April 1492, that Isabella and Columbus signed the agreements that financed his historic voyage, and thus the town has been called the Cradle of America. Santa Fe was originally laid out in the shape of a cross, with a gate at each of its four ends, inscribed with Ferdinand and Isabella's initials. The town has long since transcended those boundaries, but the gates remain—to see them all at once, stand in the square next to the church at the center of the old town.

FUENTEVAQUEROS

94 *10 km (6 mi) northwest of Santa Fe.*

The **Museo Casa Natal Federico García Lorca**, the poet's childhood home, opened as a museum in 1986, when Spain commemorated the 50th anniversary of Lorca's assassination and celebrated his reinstatement as a national figure after 40 years of nonrecognition during the Francisco Franco regime. The house has been restored with original furnishings, and the former granary, barn, and stables have been converted into exhibition spaces, with temporary art shows and a permanent display of photographs, clippings, and other memorabilia. A two-minute video shows the only existing footage of Lorca. Tour hours vary; call ahead. ⊠*Calle del Poeta García Lorca 4* ☎*958/516453* ⊕*www.museogarcialorca.org* 🖾*€2* ⊗*Closed Mon.*

THE SIERRA NEVADA

95 The drive southeast from Granada to Pradollano along the N420/A395—Europe's highest road, by way of Cenes de la Vega—takes about 45 minutes. It's wise to carry snow chains from mid-November even as late as April or May. The mountains here make for an easy and worthwhile excursion, especially for those keen on trekking.

The **Pico de Veleta**, Spain's third-highest mountain, is 11,125 feet, and the view from its summit across the Alpujarra range to the sea, at distant Motril, is stunning; on a very clear day you can see the coast of North Africa. In July and August you can drive or take a minibus to within hundreds of yards of the summit—a trail takes you to the top. ■TIP➡ **It's cold up here, so bring a warm jacket and scarf, even if Granada is sizzling hot.** To your left, the mighty **Mulhacén**, the highest peak in mainland Spain, soars to 11,427 feet. Legend has it that it came by its name when Boabdil, the last Moorish king of Granada, deposed his father, Muly Abdul Hassan, and had the body buried at the summit of the mountain so that it couldn't be desecrated. For more information on trails to the two summits, call the **Natural Park's Service office** (☎*958/763127*) in Pampaneira.

1

The Sierra Nevada ski resort's two stations—Pradollano and the higher Borreguiles—draw crowds from December to May. In winter, **buses** (✉ *Autocares Bonal* ☎958/465022) to Pradollano leave Granada's bus station three times a day on weekdays, and four times on weekends and holidays. Tickets are €6 round-trip. As for Borreguiles, you can get there only on skis.

SKIING

The **Estación de Esquí Sierra Nevada** is Europe's southernmost ski resort and one of its best equipped. At the Pradollano and Borreguiles stations there's good skiing from December through May. Both stations have a special snowboarding circuit, floodlighted night slopes, a children's ski school, and après-ski sun and swimming in the Mediterranean less than an hour (33 km [20 mi]) away. There's an **information center** (☎958/249100) at Plaza de Andalucía 4 ⊕*www.cetursa.es.*

WHERE TO STAY

$$$–$$$$ **El Lodge.** A fantastic slope-side location and friendly, professional service adds up to the best hotel in the Sierra Nevada. It's built of Finnish wood—unusual for southern Spain, but perfectly appropriate in this alpine area—and has a warm, cozy quality. Know, however, that accommodations are not particularly large. Rooms are entirely wood—ceiling, walls, and floors. ✉*C. Maribel 8, 18196* ☎*958/480600* 🖷*958/481314* ⊕*www.ellodge.com* ⊷*16 rooms, 4 suites* ♿*In-hotel: restaurant, bar, gym* 🖃*AE, DC, MC, V* ☉*Closed May–Oct.* ❍*BP.*

THE ALPUJARRAS

96 *Village of Lanjarón: 46 km (29 mi) south of Granada.*
★

A trip to the Alpujarras, on the southern slopes of the Sierra Nevada, takes you to one of Andalusia's highest, most remote, and most scenic areas, home for decades to painters, writers, and a considerable foreign population. The Alpujarras region was originally populated by Moors fleeing the Christian Reconquest (from Seville after its fall in 1248, then from Granada after 1492). It was also the final fiefdom of the unfortunate Boabdil, conceded to him by the Catholic Monarchs after he surrendered Granada. In 1568 rebellious Moors made their last stand against the Christian overlords, a revolt ruthlessly suppressed by Philip II and followed by the forced conversion of all Moors to Christianity and their resettlement farther inland and up Spain's eastern coast. The villages were then repopulated with Christian soldiers from Galicia, who were granted land in return for their service against the Moors. To this day the Galicians' descendants continue the Moorish custom of weaving rugs and blankets in the traditional Alpujarran colors of red, green, black, and white, and they sell their crafts in many of the villages. Be on the lookout for handmade basketry and pottery as well.

Houses here are squat and square; they spill down the southern slopes of the Sierra Nevada, bearing a strong resemblance to the Berber homes in the Rif Mountains, just across the sea in Morocco. If you're driving, the road as far as Lanjarón and Orgiva is smooth sailing; after that come steep, twisting mountain roads with few gas stations. Beyond sightseeing, the area is a haven for outdoor activities such as hiking and horseback riding. Inquire at the **Information Point** at Plaza de la Libertad s/n, at Pampaneira.

EN ROUTE

Lanjarón, the western entrance to the Alpujarras some 46 km (29 mi) from Granada, is a spa town famous for its mineral water, collected from the melting snows of the Sierra Nevada and drunk throughout Spain. **Orgiva**, the next and largest town in the Alpujarras, has a 17th-century castle. Here you can leave C348 and follow signs for the villages of the Alpujarra Alta (High Alpujarra), including **Pampaneira**, **Capileira**, and especially Trevélez, which lies on the slopes of the Mulhacén at 4,840 feet above sea level. Reward yourself with a plate of the locally produced *jamón serrano* (cured ham). Trevélez has three levels, the Barrio Alto, Barrio Medio, and Barrio Bajo; the butchers are concentrated in the lowest section (Bajo). The higher levels have narrow cobblestone streets, whitewashed houses, and shops.

WHERE TO STAY & EAT

If you're looking for the unusual—or a slightly longer stay—rural houses scattered throughout the region are an affordable alternative. For information, contact the tourist office of Granada or **Rustic Blue** (⊠*Barrio de la Ermita, Bubión* ☎*958/763381* ⊕*www.rusticblue. com*), which also organizes walking and riding excursions.

$$ ✕⊡ **Taray Botánico.** This hotel has its own farm and makes a perfect base for exploring the Alpujarras. Public areas and guest rooms are in a low, typical Alpujarran building. The sunny quarters are decorated with Alpujarran handwoven bedspreads and curtains; three rooms have rooftop terraces, and there's a pleasant common terrace. Most of the restaurant's ($–$$) food comes from the estate, including trout and lamb; in season, you can even pick your own raspberries or oranges for breakfast. ⊠*Ctra. Tablate–Albuñol, Km 18, Órgiva, 18400* ☎*958/784525* 🖷*958/784531* ⊕*www.turgranada.com/hotel-taray* ⇆*15 rooms* ⌂*In-hotel: restaurant, pool* ☰*AE, DC, MC, V.*

$ ✕⊡ **La Fragua.** Spotless rooms with baths (and some with balconies), fresh air, and views over the rooftops of Trevélez to the valley beyond are the perks at this small, friendly hotel in a typical village house behind the town hall. The restaurant is in a separate house up the street, serving regional dishes such as *arroz liberal* (hunter's rice with sausage and salami), *lomo a los aromas de la sierra* (pork loin with herbs), and *choto al ajillo* (piglet meat in garlic sauce). ⊠*Calle de San Antonio 4, Barrio Medio, Trevélez18417* ☎*958/858626* 🖷*958/858614* ⇆*14 rooms* ⌂*In-hotel: restaurant* ☰*MC, V* ⊗*Closed Mid-Jan.–mid-Feb.*

GUADIX

⓿ *47 km (30 mi) east of Granada on A92.*

Guadix was an important mining town as far back as 2,000 years ago and has its fair share of monuments, including a cathedral (built 1594–1706) and a 9th-century Moorish *alcazaba* (citadel). But Guadix and the neighboring village of Purullena are best known for their cave

1

SPORTS TOURS

Based in the Alpujarras, **Nevadensis** (⊠ *Pl. de la Libertad, Pampaneira* ☎ *958/763127* ⊕ *www.nevadensis. com*) leads guided tours of the region on foot, horseback, and mountain bike.

In Granada, **Sólo Aventura** (⊠ *Pl. de la Romanilla 1, Centro, Granada* ☎ *958/804937* ⊕ *www.soloaventura.com*) offers one- to seven-day outdoor sports—trekking, mountaineering, climbing, mountain biking, and other activities—around the Alpujarras, Sierra Nevada, and the rest of the province.

Kayak Sur (⊠ *Calle Arabial, Urbanizació Parque del Genil, Edificio Topacio, Sur, Granada* ☎ *958/523118* ⊕ *www.kayaksur.com*) organizes kayaking and canoeing trips to the River Guadalfeo. **Granada Romántica/Grupo Al Andalus** (⊠ *Calle Santa Ana 16, Granada* ☎ *958/805481* ⊕ *www.grupoalandalus.com*) takes up to five people in balloon trips above the city and its surroundings. **Excursiones Bujarkay** (☎ *953/721111* ⊕ *www.guiasnativos.com*) leads guided hikes as well as horseback and four-wheel-drive tours. In Zuheros, the **Alúa** (⊠ *Calle Horno 3, Zuheros* ☎ *957/694527* ⊕ *www. aluactiva.com*) can help you with planning and getting the equipment for hiking, rock climbing, mountain biking, caving, and other active sports. Horseback-riding tours, some with English-speaking guides, are offered in the villages of the Alpujarras, Sierra Nevada, and in the Sierra de Cazorla; **Cabalgar Rutas Alternativas** (⊠ *Calle Bubión, Alpujarras* ☎ *958/763135* ⊕ *www.ridingandalucia.com*) is one established Alpujarras agency. **Dallas Love** (⊠ *Ctra. de la Sierra, Bubión, Alpujarras* ☎ *958/763038* ⊕ *www.spainhorse-riding.com*) offers trail rides for up to 10 days in the Alpujarras. The price includes overnight stays and most meals.

communities. Around 2,000 caves were carved out of the soft, sandstone mountains, and most are still inhabited. Far from being troglodytic holes in the wall, they are well furnished and comfortable, with a pleasant year-round temperature; a few serve as hotels. A small cave museum, **Cueva Museo,** is in Guadix's cave district. Toward the town center, the **Cueva la Alcazaba** has a ceramics workshop. A number of private caves have signs welcoming you to inspect the premises, though a tip is expected if you do. Purullena, 6 km (4 mi) from Guadix, is also known for ceramics.

WHERE TO STAY & EAT

$$ ✕⊞ **Comercio.** In the historic center of Guadix is this enchanting little family-run hotel. Rooms in the 1905 building have dark-wood classic furniture, modern bathrooms, and, except for the few that are carpeted, marble floors. The public areas include an art gallery, a jazz concert room, and the best restaurant ($–$$$) in town, with such local specialties as roast lamb with raisins and pine nuts. ⊠ *C. Mira de Amezcua 3, 18500* ☎ *958/660500* 🖷 *958/665072* ⊕ *www.hotelcomercio.com* ⤶ *40 rooms, 2 suites* ⚲ *In-hotel: restaurant, parking (no fee)* ▭ *AE, DC, MC, V.*

$$ ⛏Cuevas Pedro Antonio de Alarcón. If you're looking for a so-called authentic experience, consider staying in a cave. In a "suburb" outside Guadix, this unique lodging consists of 19 adjoining caves and one suite. Each cave sleeps two to five and has a kitchenette; the honeymoon cave has a whirlpool bath. The whitewashed walls and polished clay-tile floors are decorated with charming Granadian crafts and colorful rugs; handwoven Alpujarran tapestries serve as doors between the rooms. The restaurant, also subterranean, serves regional dishes. ✉Barriada San Torcuato, 18500 ☎958/664986 🖷958/661721 ⊕www.andalucia.com/cavehotel 🔑19 rooms, 1 suite ⚒In-room: no a/c, kitchen. In-hotel: restaurant, pool ⊟AE, MC, V ⊘EP.

ANDALUSIA ESSENTIALS

To research prices, get advice, and book travel arrangements, visit www.fodors.com.

TRANSPORTATION

For information on travel to and in Andalusia, see the Andalusia Planner at the beginning of the chapter.

BY AIR

Ryanair operates inexpensive no-frills flights from London to Seville or Jerez de la Frontera for less than €40 round-trip. Air connections to Seville also can be had from other major European cities, including such as Frankfurt, Paris, and Amsterdam. Low-cost flights to Granada from the U.K. include connections on Ryanair and Monarch from London and Liverpool for less than €40. Iberia flies from the U.K. to Granada, Jerez de la Frontera, Seville, and Málaga for about €200. Cheap flights from England and Ireland to Málaga include connections via easyJet, Monarch, First Choice, Air Scotland, Jet2, Excel Airways, Ryanair, and Aer Lingus, flying from such airports as: Manchester, Luton, Gatwick, Birmingham, Dublin, and Shannon.

Andalusian cities you can reach via air include Granada, Jerez de la Frontera, Málaga, and Seville. The region's main airport is in Seville, 7 km (3 mi) east of the city on the A4/E5 highway to Córdoba. There's a bus from the airport to the center of Seville every half hour on weekdays (6:30 AM–8 PM), and every hour on weekends and holidays. It costs €4 one-way. The smaller Aeropuerto de Jerez is 7 km (4 mi) northeast of Jerez on the road to Seville. There's no public transport into Jerez, you will need to take a taxi (approximately €18). Málaga Airport is one of Spain's major hubs (especially for travelers from other European countries) and therefore a possible access point for Granada, Córdoba, and Almería. (These cities are approximately two hours apart by car.)

In Granada, **J. González** buses (€6) run between the center of town and the airport, leaving every 30 minutes from the Palacio de Congresos, and making a few other stops along the way to the airport. Times are listed at the bus stop; service is reduced in winter. **Line 14**

1

(☎950/221422) municipal bus service (€1) operates between the air-port and the city center with buses every 30 minutes.

Airports **Aeropuerto de Almería** (☎950/213700). **Aeropuerto de Granada** (Aeropuerto Federico Garcí Lorca) (☎958/245200). **Aeropuerto Internacional de Málaga** (☎95/204–8484). **Aeropuerto Jerez de la Frontera** (☎956/150000). **Aeropuerto de Sevilla** (Aeropuerto San Pablo) (☎95/444–9000).

Airport Tranfers **J. González** (☎958/490164).

Airlines **Air Europa** (✉*Aeropuerto de Sevilla, Seville* ☎*95/444–9179* ⊕*www. aireuropa.com*). **British Airways** (✉*Aeropuerto de Sevilla, Seville* ☎*902/111333* ⊕*www.ba.com*). **Iberia** (✉*Av. Buhaira 8, Seville* ☎*95/498–7357, 902/400500 at Aeropuerto de Sevilla, 956/150010 at Aeropuerto Jerez de la Frontera airport* ⊕*www.iberia.es*). **Monarch** (✉*Aeropuerto Federico Garcí Lorca, Graanada* ☎*958/245245* ⊕*www.flymonarch.com*). **Ryanair** (☎*0818/303030 fromU.K.* ⊕*www.ryanair.com*). **Spanair** (✉*Aeropuerto de Sevilla, Seville* ☎*902/131415* ⊕*www.spanair.com*). **Vueling** (✉*Aeropuerto Federico Garcí Lorca, Granada* ☎*902/333933* ⊕*www.vueling.com*).

BY BOAT & FERRY

From Cádiz, Trasmediterránea operates ferry services to the Canary Islands with stops at Las Palmas de Gran Canaria (39 hours) and con-necting ferries on to La Palma (8 hours) and Santa Cruz de Tenerife (6.5 hours). There are no direct ferries to Seville.

Contacts **Trasmediterránea** (✉*Estación Marítima* ☎*956/227421 or 902/454645* ⊕*www.trasmediterranea.es*).

BY BUS

Seville has two bus stations: Estación del Prado de San Sebastián, serv-ing the west and northwest, and the Estación Plaza de Armas, which serves central and eastern Spain. Cádiz also has two bus stations: Comes, which serves most destinations in Andalusia, and Los Ama-rillos, which serves Jerez, Seville, Córdoba, Puerto de Santa María, Sanlúcar de Barrameda, and Chipiona. The bus station in Jerez, on Plaza Madre de Dios, is served by two companies: La Valenciana and Los Amarillos. Granada's bus station is at Carretera de Jaen, 3 km northwest of the center of town beyond the end of Avenida de Madrid. All services operate from here except for a few to nearby destinations such as Fuente Vaqueros, Viznar and Sierra Nevada. Luggage lockers (*la consigna*) cost €2. Alsina Gräells buses run to Las Alpujarras, Cór-doba 8 times daily Seville 10 times daily, Malaga 14 times daily and Jaen, Baeza, Ubeda, Cazorla, Almeria, Almuñecar and Nerja several times daily.

Seville's urban bus service is efficient and covers the greater city area. Buses C1, C2, C3, and C4 run circular routes linking the main trans-portation terminals with the city center. The C1 goes east in a clockwise direction, from the Santa Justa train station via Avenida de Carlos V, Avenida de María Luisa, Triana, the Isla de la Cartuja, and Calle de Resolana. The C2 follows the same route in reverse. The C3 runs from the Avenida Menéndez Pelayo to the Puerta de Jerez, Triana, Plaza de Armas, and Calle de Recaredo. The C4 does the same route counter-clockwise. Buses do not run within the Barrio de Santa Cruz because the streets are too narrow, though convenient access points around the periphery of this popular tourist area are amply served.

Seville's city buses operate limited night service between midnight and 2 AM, with no service between 2 and 4 AM. Single rides cost €1, but it is more economical to buy a ticket for 10 rides, which costs €5.30 for use on any bus. A special tourist pass (Tarjeta Turística) valid for one or three days of unlimited bus travel cost (respectively) €3.11 and €7.25. Tickets are on sale at newspaper kiosks and at the main bus station, Prado de San Sebastián.

Granada and Córdoba have extensive public bus networks. The average waiting time usually does not exceed 15 minutes. Normally, buses in both cities start running around 6:30 to 7 AM and stop around 11 PM in Granada and midnight in Córdoba. However, schedules can be slightly reduced for some lines. In Granada, you can buy 6- and 21-trip discount passes on the buses and 10-trip passes at newsstands. In Córdoba, newsstands and the bus office at Plaza de Colón sell 10-trip discount tickets. The single-trip fares are €1 in Granada and Córdoba. Rober and Aucorsa manage the bus networks in Granada and Córdoba, respectively.

Bus Lines **Alsa** (☎ 902/422242 ⊕ www.alsa.es). **Alsina Gräells** (☎ 950/238197 *in Almería, 957/278100 in Córdoba, 958/185480 in Granada, 953/255014 in Jaén, 95/2341738 in Málaga, 95/4418811 in Seville ⊕ www.alsinagraells.es).* **Aucorsa** (☎ 957/764676 ⊕ www.aucorsa.net). **Autocares Bonal** (☎ 958/273100). **Comes** (✉ Pl. Hispanidad, Cádiz ☎ 956/224271). **La Valenciana** (✉ Bus station, Pl. Madre de Dios, Jerez de la Frontera ☎ 956/341063). **Los Amarillos** (✉ Calle Diego Fernández Herreras 34, Cádiz ☎ 956/285852, 956/329347 Jerez). **Rober** (☎ 958/813750 or 900/710900 ⊕ www.transportesrober.com).

Bus Stations **Cádiz–Estación de Autobuses Comes** (✉ Pl. de la Hispanidad 1 ☎ 956/342174). **Córdoba** (✉ Glorieta de las Tres Culturas, Córdoba ☎ 957/404040). **Huelva** (✉ Av. Doctor Rubio s/n ☎ 959/256900). **Granada** (✉ Ctra. Jaén, Granada ☎ 958/185480). **Jerez de la Frontera** (✉ Calle de la Cartuja ☎ 956/345207). **Seville–Estación del Prado de San Sebastián** (✉ Prado de San Sebastián s/n ☎ 95/441-7111). **Seville–Estación Plaza de Armas** (✉ Calle Cristo de la Expiración ☎ 95/490-7737).

BY CAR

The main road from Madrid is the A4/E5 through Córdoba to Seville, a four-lane *autovía* (highway). From Granada or Málaga, head for Antequera; then take A92 *autovía* by way of Osuna to Seville. Road trips from Seville to Córdoba, Granada, and the Costa del Sol (by way of Ronda) are slow but scenic. Along the Costa del Sol, A7/E15 connects Almería with Algeciras in under three hours traveling at the standard Spanish 120–140 kph (72–84 mph) freeway cruising speed. The old coastal N340 highway is useful for slow and panoramic beach touring around Estepona and Motril but has otherwise been replaced by the A7/E15 freeway. Driving within Western Andalusia is easy—the terrain is mostly flat land or slightly hilly, and the roads are straight. From Seville to Jerez and Cádiz, the A4/E5 toll road gets you to Cádiz in under an hour. The only way to access Doñana National Park by road is to take the A49/E1 Seville–Huelva highway, exit for Almonte/Bollullos par del Condado, then follow the signs for El Rocío and Matalascañas. The A49/E1 west of Seville will also lead you to the freeway to Portugal and the Algarve.

With the exception of parts of La Alpujarra, most roads in this region are smooth; touring by car is one of the most enjoyable ways to see the countryside. Local tourist offices can advise about scenic drives. One good route heads northwest from Seville on the N433 passing through stunning scenery; turn northeast on the N435 to Santa Olalla de Cala to the village of Zufre, dramatically set at the edge of a gorge. Backtrack and continue on to Aracena. Return via the Minas de Riotinto (signposted from Aracena), which will bring you back to the N433 heading east to Seville.

Getting in and out of Seville is not difficult thanks to the SE30 ring road, but getting around the city by car is problematic. In Seville and Cádiz, avoid the lunchtime rush hour (around 2–3 PM) and the evening 7:15–8:30 PM rush hour. Bringing a car to Cádiz at Carnival time (pre-Lent) or to Seville during Holy Week or the April Fair can be difficult as processions close most of the streets to traffic. Check with your hotel about access to hotel parking during these ferias.

In the big cities, especially Granada and Córdoba, it's best to park in an underground lot or your hotel garage or parking area. Follow the large blue "P" signs, which will guide you to the city center and the nearest underground lot. You can expect to pay around €1.20 an hour. Blue lines on the street mean you must pay at the nearest meter to park during working hours, around €0.50 an hour. Yellow lines mean no parking. If your car is towed, you will be fined about €150.

Local car-rental agencies can be less expensive than the international chains. *See Spain Essentials in the back of the book for contact information for national rental agencies.*

Rental Agencies Autopro (✉ *Carril de Montañez 49, Málaga* ☎ *952/176030* ⊕ *www.autopro.es*). **Crown Car Hire** (☎ *952/176486* ⊕ *www.crowncarhire.com*). **Niza Cars** (☎ *952/236179* ⊕ *www.nizacars.com*).

BY SUBWAY

The first line of a three-line metro opened in Seville in late 2006. The Seville subway system covers a distance of 19 km (13 mi) and runs from Mairena de Aljarafe to Montequinto with 23 stations, including Puerta de Jerez and Plaza de Cuba. ⊕ *www.metrodesevilla.net.*

BY TAXI

Taxis are plentiful throughout Andalusia and may be hailed on the street or from specified taxi stands marked TAXI. Restaurants are usually obliging and will also call you a taxi, if required. Fares are reasonable, and meters are strictly used; the minimum fare is about €4. Fares are based on the time of the day, and are higher at night and on public holidays. Taxis charge an additional amount (usually about €0.50) for picking up passengers at the train station, as well as for each piece of luggage. You are not required to tip taxi drivers, although rounding off the amount is appreciated.

In Seville and Granada there are taxi stations, or *paradas de taxis,* in almost every major area, or phone Tele Radio Taxi or Asociación de Radio Taxi. In Córdoba there are taxi stations at Avenida de América near the Hotel Gran Capitán, at the corner of El Corte Inglés, and near the hotel Meliá, among other locations; or call Call Radio Taxi. In Seville or Granada, expect to pay around €20 for cab fare from the airport to the city center.

Taxi Companies **Asociació de RadioTaxi** (✉*Granada* ☎*958/132323*). **Radio Taxi** (✉*Córdoba* ☎*957/764444*). **Radio Teléfono Giralda** (✉*Seville* ☎*95/467–5555*). **Tele Radio Taxi** (✉*Granada* ☎*958/280654*). **Tele Taxi** (✉*Jerez de la Frontera* ☎*956/344860*). **Tele Taxi** (✉*Huelva* ☎*959/250022*). **Unitaxi** (✉*Cádiz* ☎*956/212121*).

BY TRAIN

Seville, Córdoba, Jerez, and Cádiz all lie on the main rail line from Madrid to southern Spain. Trains leave from Madrid for Seville (via Córdoba) almost hourly, most of them high-speed ones that reach Seville in 2½ hours. Two of the non-AVE trains continue on to Jerez and Cádiz; travel time from Seville to Cádiz is 1½ to 2 hours. Trains also depart regularly for Barcelona (3 daily, 11 hours), Cáceres (1 daily, 6 hours), and Huelva (4 daily, 1½ hours). From Granada, Málaga, Ronda, and Algeciras, trains go to Seville by way of Bobadilla, where, more often than not, you have to change. A dozen or more local trains each day connect Cádiz with Seville, Puerto de Santa María, and Jerez. There are no trains to Doñana National Park, Sanlúcar de Barrameda, or Arcos de la Frontera, or between Cádiz and the Costa del Sol.

Train Information **RENFE** (☎*902/240202* ⊕*www.renfe.es*).

Train Stations **Cádiz** (✉*Plaza de Sevilla s/n* ☎*956/251010*). **Córdoba** (✉*Glorieta de las Tres Culturas s/n* ☎*957/403480*). **Granada** (✉*Av. de los Andaluces s/n* ☎*958/271272*). **Huelva** (✉*Av. de Italia* ☎*959/246666*). **Jerez de la Frontera** (✉*Pl. de la Estación s/n, off Calle Diego Fernández Herrera* ☎*956/342319*). **Seville–Estación Santa Justa** (✉*Av. Kansas City* ☎*95/454–0202*).

CONTACTS & RESOURCES

BANKS & EXCHANGING SERVICES

Banks are generally in town and city centers; the majority will have an ATM. Banks are open from 8:30 AM to 2 PM weekdays, plus on Saturday from October to April. Currency-exchange offices are also common—however, they generally charge a higher commission than the banks. You can also change money in your hotel, although this again will cost you more than the banks. One of the main banks in Spain is BBVA: www.bbva.es.

EMERGENCIES

In an emergency, call one of the Spain-wide emergency numbers, for police, ambulance, or fire services. The local Red Cross (Cruz Roja) can also dispatch an ambulance in case of an emergency. For nonemergencies, there are private medical clinics throughout the region; they often have staff members who can speak some English. Every town has at least one pharmacy open 24 hours; the address of the on-duty pharmacy is posted on the front door of all pharmacies. You can also dial Spain's general information number (11818) for the location of a doctor's office or pharmacy that's open nearest you.

Emergency Services **Fire, Police or Ambulance** (☎ *112*). **La Cruz Roja (Red Cross)**. (✉ *Calle Amor de Dios 31, Seville* ☎ *954/376613*), (✉ *Cuesta Escoriaza 8, Granada* ☎ *958/221420*), (✉ *Paseo Victoria s/n, Córdoba* ☎ *957/420666*). **Guardia Civil** (☎ *062*). **Insalud** (*Public health service* ☎ *061*). **Policía Local** (*Local police* ☎ *092*). **Policía Nacional** (*National police* ☎ *091*). **Servicio Marítimo** (*Air-Sea Rescue* ☎ *902/202202*).

INTERNET, MAIL & SHIPPING

Internet cafés with competitive prices are plentiful in major cities. In Seville's provincial tourist office between Plaza Nueva and Calle Sierpes there are work stations with free Internet access for an hour; the office can also provide you with a list of local Internet cafés. The main post office in Seville is opposite the cathedral. It's open weekdays 8:30–8:30 and Saturday 9:30–2. Several international courier companies have branches at Seville airport, including DHL. National courier companies include Seur and MRW; both have branches and drop-off locations throughout the country. Granada's main post office is in the Plaza Real. The main office in Córdoba—the only one open in the afternoon—is north of the mosque near the Plaza de las Tendillas.

Internet Cafés **First Centre** (✉ *Av. de la Constitucíon 34, Centro, Seville* ☎ *95/421–5622*). **Hostal "El Pilar del Potro"** (✉ *Calle Lucano, 12, Córdoba* ☎ *957/492966*). **Internet Granada** (✉ *Calle del Pintor Zuloaga 29, Granada* ☎ *958/535025*). **Seville Internet Centre** (✉ *C. Almirantazgo 2, Centro, Seville* ☎ *95/450–0275*). **Turismo de la Provincia** (✉ *Pl. del Triunfo 1, Centro, Seville* ☎ *95/450–1001*).

Couriers **DHL** (✉ *Aeropuerto de Seville* ☎ *902/122–424*). **MRW** (✉ *Aeropuerto de Seville* ☎ *900/300–400*). **SEUR** (✉ *Aeropuerto de Seville* ☎ *902/101–010*).

SAFETY

Seville has long been notorious for petty crime. Tourists continue to be thieves' favored victims, so take common sense precautions. Drive with your doors locked, lock your luggage out of sight in the trunk, and keep a wary eye on scooter riders, who have snatched purses and even smashed windows of moving cars. When walking around, carry only a small amount of cash and one credit card. Leave your passport and other credit cards in the hotel safe.

VISITOR INFORMATION

Seville has both regional and provincial tourist offices and also has branches at the Seville Airport and Santa Justa railway station. Tourist offices are generally open 9–2 and 3–7. Seville's provincial tourist office publishes a monthly events guide, *El Giraldillo*; it is in Spanish but is easy to understand for novice readers. Also in Seville you can pick up the free *Sevilla Welcome and Olé!* The best Web site for the region is andalucia.org.

Regional Tourist Offices Seville (⊠ *Av. de la Constitución 21* ☎ *95/422–1404, 95/421–8157, or 95/444–9128* ⊕ *www.andalucia.org*). **Cádiz** (⊠ *Av. Ramón de Carranza s/n* ☎ *956/258646*).

Provincial Tourist Offices Cádiz (⊠ *Pl. de San Antonio 3, 2nd fl.* ☎ *956/807061*). **Córdoba** (⊠ *Palacio de Exposiciones, Calle Torrijos 10, opposite mosque, Judería* ☎ *957/471235*). **Granada** (⊠ *Pl. Mariana Pineda, 10, Centro* ☎ *958/247146* ⊕ *www.turismodegranada.org*). **Huelva** (⊠ *Av. Alemania 12* ☎ *959/257403*). **Seville** (⊠ *Pl. de Triunfo 1–3, Santa Cruz* ☎ *95/421–0005* ⊕ *www.turismosevilla. org*).

Local Tourist Offices Almonte (⊠ *Calle Alonso Pérez 1* ☎ *959/450419*). **Aracena** (⊠ *Pl. de San Pedro s/n* ☎ *959/128825*). **Arcos de la Frontera** (⊠ *Pl. del Cabildo s/n* ☎ *959/502121*). **Baeza** (⊠ *Pl. del Pópulo* ☎ *953/740444*). **Cádiz** (⊠ *Pl. San Juan de Dios 11* ☎ *956/241001* ⊕ *www.cadizturismo.com*). **Carmona** (⊠ *Arco de la Puerta de Sevilla* ☎ *95/419–0955* ⊕ *www.turismo.carmona.org*). **Córdoba** (⊠ *Pl. Juda Levi, Judería* ☎ *957/200522* 🖷 *957/200277*). **Granada** (⊠ *Pl. Mariana Pineda 10, Centro* ☎ *958/247128*). **El Rocío** (⊠ *Calle La Canalieja s/n* ☎ *959/443908* ⊕ *www.parquenacionaldonana.com*). **Isla Cristina** (⊠ *Calle Ayamonte s/n* ☎ *959/332694*). **Islantilla** (⊠ *Av. de Riofrio s/n* ☎ *959/646013*). **Jaén** (⊠ *C. Maestra, 13-Bajo* ☎ *953/242624*). **Jerez de la Frontera** (⊠ *Calle Larga 39* ☎ *956/331150 or 956/331162* ⊕ *www.turismojerez.com*). **La Rábida** (⊠ *Paraje de la Rábida s/n* ☎ *959/531137*). **Matalascañas** (⊠ *Av. las Adelfas s/n* ☎ *959/430086*). **Mazagón** (⊠ *Av. de los Conquistadores s/n* ☎ *959/376300*). **Moguer** (⊠ *Calle del Castillo s/n* ☎ *959/371898* ⊕ *www.aytomoguer.es*). **Montilla** (⊠ *Capitán Alonso de Vargas 3* ☎ *957/652462* ⊕ *www.turismomontilla.com*). **Puerto de Santa María** (⊠ *Calle Luna 22* ☎ *956/542413* ⊕ *www.elpuertosm. es*). **Rota** (⊠ *Castillo de Luna, Cuna 2* ☎ *956/846345*). **Seville** (⊠ *Av. de la Constitucíon 21, Arenal* ☎ *95/422–1404* ⊕ *www.sevilla.org* ⊠ *Costurero de la Reina, Paseo de las Delicias 9, Arenal* ☎ *95/423–4465*). **Úbeda** (⊠ *Palacio Marqués del Contadero, C. Baja del Marqués 4* ☎ *953/750897*).

The Costa del Sol

Nerja, Málaga province

WORD OF MOUTH

"Málaga is a terrific place to stay as a base for some great day trips as well as some wonderful sights within Málaga itself if you're interested in art and architecture."

—Artlover

WELCOME TO THE COSTA DEL SOL

TOP REASONS TO GO

★ **Sun & Sand:** Relax at the plethora of packed (in summer) beaches; they're all free.

★ **Lovely Strolls:** Spend a morning in Marbella's old town, stopping for a drink at Plaza de los Naranjos (Oranges Square).

★ **Rich Environs:** Bask in the five-star splendor of Puerto Banús, where everything is exclusive, extravagant, and expensive.

★ **Sensational Seafood:** Tuck into a dish of delicious *fritura malagueño* (fried fish, anchovies, and squid) at a beach restaurant in Torremolinos.

★ **Natural Refuges:** Head to Cabo de Gato Nature Reserve, one of the wildest and most beautiful stretches of coast in Spain.

★ **Souvenir Shopping:** Check out the weekly market in one of the Costa resorts—the best place to pick up bargain-price souvenirs, such as ceramics or Spanish music CDs.

1 Almería. Just west of the Murcia Coast, this handsome, underrated city boasts a dynamic and gracious historic center.

2 Ronda. Intrinsically Andalusian, this town is enhanced by the stunning surrounding Serranía de Ronda countryside, which is dotted with *pueblos blancos*.

3 Málaga. This vibrant Spanish city has a fascinating historic center with narrow pedestrian streets flanked by sun-baked ocher buildings and tapas bars.

Horsemen in El Real de la Feria, Fuengirola, Málaga province,

Resort views in Torremolinos.

GETTING ORIENTED

The towns and resorts along the Costa del Sol vary considerably according to whether they lie to the east or to the west of Málaga. To the east lies the Costa del Almería and Costa Tropical, less developed stretches of coastline. Towns such as Nerja also act as a gateway to the dramatic mountainous region of La Axarquía. Heading west from Málaga along the Costa del Sol proper, the strip between Torremolinos and Marbella is the most densely populated. Seamless though it may appear, as one resort merges into the next, each town has a distinctive character, with its own sights, charm, and activities.

ALBACETE

JAÉN

MURCIA

Chirival

Baza

GRANADA

Guadix

Huercal-overa

ALMERÍA

Vera

Gergal

SIERRA NEVADA

▲Mulhacén

Trevélez

Canjarar

Carboneras

apileira Cádiar

Berja

Almería

Adra

0 ——————— 30 mi
0 ——————— 30 km

Winding *pueblo* roads in the Málaga province.

4 Beach resorts. The main ones are Torremolinos, appealing to young families; Fuengirola, with a large foreign resident population; and Marbella, which is more exclusive—and expensive.

5 The Axarquía. This is one of the most agriculturally lush regions in the south of Spain. The bleached dazzle of villages seems almost luminescent against the looming dark backdrop of the Sierra Tejeda mountains.

THE COSTA DEL SOL PLANNER

When to Go

Fall and spring are the best times to visit the coast. There's plenty of sunshine but fewer tourists, although golfers often prefer these cooler times. Winter can have bright sunny days, but you may feel chilled; many hotels in the lower price bracket have heating for only a few hours a day. You can also expect several days of rain. Avoid July and August; it's too hot and crowded. May, June, and the fall are better, with longer days and more space on the beach. Holy Week offers memorable celebrations.

Ferias & Fiestas

Málaga's **Semana Santa** (Holy Week; the week before Easter) processions are dramatic. Nerja and Estepona celebrate **San Isidro** (May 15) with typically Andalusian ferias with plenty of flamenco and *fino* (sherry). The feast of **San Juan** (June 23 and 24), is marked by midnight bonfires on beaches along the coast. Coastal communities honor the **Virgen del Carmen**, the patron saint of fishermen, on her feast day (July 16). The annual **ferias** (more general and usually lengthier celebrations than fiestas) in Málaga (early August) and Fuengirola (early October) are among the best for sheer exuberance.

Getting There & Around

Air Plus Comet operates a weekly direct flight from New York to Málaga, although at press time it had been temporarily suspended. All other flights from the United States connect in Madrid. Iberia and British Airways fly once daily from London to Málaga and numerous British budget airlines, such as easyJet and Monarch, link London with Málaga. There are direct flights to Málaga from most other major European cities on Iberia or other national airlines. Iberia has up to eight flights daily from Madrid (flying time is 1 hour), three flights a day from Barcelona (1½ hours), and regular flights from other Spanish cities.

By far the region's busiest point of entry, Málaga's Pablo Picasso airport is 10 km (6 mi) west of town. Trains from the airport into town run every half hour (7 AM–midnight, journey time 12 minutes, €1.20 single) and from the airport southwest to Fuengirola every half hour (5:45 AM–10:45 PM, journey time 25 minutes, €1.65 single), stopping at several resorts en route, including Torremolinos and Benalmádena. There's a bus service to Málaga every half hour from 6:30 AM to 11:30 PM at a fare of €1. Ten daily buses (more July–September) run between the airport and Marbella, with a journey time of one hour and fare of €4 single. Taxi fares to Málaga, Torremolinos, and other resorts are posted inside the terminal. The trip from the airport to Marbella costs about €45, to Torremolinos €12, to Fuengirola €26. Many of the better hotels and all tour companies will arrange for pickup at the airport.

Buses are the best way to reach the Costa del Sol from Seville or Granada, and the best way to get around once you're here. Larger towns usually have a bus station where all out-of-town buses stop.

Málaga is the main rail terminus in the area, with eight trains a day from Madrid and one from Barcelona and Valencia.

By car you will have the freedom to explore some of Andalusia's mountain villages. Mountain driving can be a hair-raising adventure, but it's getting more manageable as highways are improved.

See The Costa del Sol Essentials at the end of this chapter for more transportation information.

2

Bird-Watching in Costa del Sol

Costa del Sol attracts ornithologists throughout the year; however, the variety of birds increases in spring.

Not surprisingly, the Strait of Gibraltar is a key point of passage for raptors, storks, and other birds migrating between Africa and Europe. Overall, northern migrations take place between mid-February and June, while those birds heading south will set off between late July and early November when there's a westerly wind. Gibraltar itself is generally good for bird-watchers, although when there is not much wind, the Tarifa region on the Atlantic coast can be better.

Soaring birds, such as raptors and storks, cross the Strait of Gibraltar because they rely on thermals and updrafts, which occur only over narrower expanses of water. One of the most impressive sights over the Strait is a crossing of flocks of storks, from August to October, which sometimes numbers up to 3,000.

The more hilly inland parts of the Costa del Sol are the best places to see resident raptor species circling high in the sky.

Planning Your Time

Travelers with their own wheels who want a real taste of the area in just a few days should start by exploring the relatively unspoiled villages of the Costa Tropical. Wander around quaint **Salobreña** before hitting the larger coastal resort of **Nerja** and heading inland for a wander around pretty **Frigiliana.** Move on to **Málaga,** which has plenty on offer—including museums, excellent restaurants, and some of the best tapas bars in the province. Don't miss the stunning mountaintop town of **Ronda** (also on the bus route), which has plenty of atmosphere and memorable sights. Hit the coast at **Marbella,** the Costa del Sol's swankiest resort, followed by a leisurely stroll around **Puerto Banús.** Next head west to **Gibraltar** for a day of shopping and sightseeing before returning to the coast and **Torremolinos** for a night on the town. If you have more time, explore rural Andalusia: **Setenil de las Bodegas, Olvera,** and **Grazalema.**

WHAT IT COSTS In Euros

	$$$$	$$$	$$	$	¢
RESTAURANTS	over €20	€15–€20	€10–€15	€6–€10	under €6
HOTELS	over €180	€100–€180	€60–€100	€40–€60	under €40

WHAT IT COSTS In Pounds in Gibraltar

RESTAURANTS	Over £25	£18–£25	£12–£18	£5–£12	under £5
HOTELS	over £165	£120–£165	£80–£120	£30–£80	under £30

Restaurant prices are per person for a main course at dinner. Hotel prices are for two people in a standard double room in high season, excluding tax.

By Mary
McLean

THE STRETCH OF ANDALUSIAN SHORE known as the Costa del Sol runs west from the Costa Tropical, near Granada, to the tip of Tarifa, the southernmost tip of Europe, just beyond Gibraltar. For most of the Europeans who have flocked here over the past 40 years, though, the Sunshine Coast has been largely restricted to the 70-km (43-mi) sprawl of hotels, vacation villas, golf courses, marinas, and nightclubs between Torremolinos, just west of Málaga, and Estepona, down toward Gibraltar. Since the late 1950s this area has mushroomed from a group of impoverished fishing villages into an overdeveloped seaside playground and retirement haven.

Construction continued unabated along the coast until the early '90s, which saw a brief economic slump caused, in part, by a drop in international airfares. Travelers became more adventurous, and Spain's favorite coast was now competing with seemingly more sophisticated locations. Local municipalities poured money into elaborate landscaping, and better roads and infrastructure. It paid off. In 1997 the prestigious Ryder Cup was held in Sotogrande, seeming to mark the Costa del Sol's return to the world stage. The result was more golf courses, luxury marinas, villa developments, and upscale hotels. The Costa averages some 320 days of sunshine a year, and balmy days are not unknown even in January or February. Despite the hubbub, you *can* unwind here, basking or strolling on mile after mile of sandy beach.

Choose your base carefully. Málaga is a vibrant Spanish city, virtually untainted by tourism. Despite the tour bus trade, Ronda is also intrinsically Andalusian, with the added perk of a stunning inland setting. Back on the coast, Torremolinos is a budget destination catering almost exclusively to the mass market; it appeals to young families, the gay community, and to those who come purely for the sun-bronzing and the late-night scene. Fuengirola is quieter, with a large, and notably middle-aged, foreign resident population; farther west, the Marbella–San Pedro de Alcántara area is more exclusive and expensive.

EXPLORING THE COSTA DEL SOL

ABOUT THE BEACHES

Lobster-pink sun worshippers from northern Europe pack these beaches in summer so that there's little towel space on the sand. Beach chairs can be rented for around €4 a day. Beaches range from shingle and pebbles (Almuñecar, Nerja, Málaga) to fine, gritty sand (from Torremolinos westward). The best—and most crowded—beaches are El Bajondillo and La Carihuela, in Torremolinos; the stretch between Carvajal, Los Boliches, and Fuengirola; and those around Marbella. You may find a secluded beach west of Estepona. Shingle beaches are popular with European vacationers. For wide beaches of fine golden sand, head west past Gibraltar, to Tarifa and the Cádiz coast—though you'll probably find that the winds are quite strong, hence all the sails.

All beaches are free and packed July through August and on Sunday May through October. It's acceptable for women to go topless; if you want to take it *all* off, go to beaches designated *playa naturista*. The most

2

popular nude beaches are in Maro (near Nerja) and near Tarifa.

ABOUT THE RESTAURANTS

Spain's southern coast is known for fresh seafood, breaded with fine flour and fried quickly in sizzling olive oil. Sardines barbecued on skewers at beachside restaurants are another popular and unforgettable treat. Gazpacho and *ajo blanco* (a cold soup based on almonds, grapes, and garlic) are typical cold soups that are refreshing in hot weather. Málaga is best for traditional Spanish cooking, with a wealth of bars and seafood restaurants serving *fritura malagueña,* the city's famous fried fish. Torremolinos' Carihuela district is also a locus for lovers of

SHORT- & LONG-TERM STAYS

There's no shortage of apartments and villas for both short- and long-term stays. Accommodations range from traditional Andalusian farmhouses to luxury villas. An excellent source for apartment and villa rentals is ⊕ *www.andalucia.com.* You can also try **Gilmar** at (⊠ *Av. Ricardo Soriano 56, Marbella, 29600* ☎ *952/861341* ⊕ *www.gilmarinmobiliaria.com*) or **Viajes Rural Andalus** (⊠ *Calle Montes de Oca 18, Málaga, 29007* ☎ *952/276229* ⊕ *www.ruralandalus.es*).

Spanish seafood. The resorts serve every conceivable foreign cuisine as well, from Thai to the Scandinavian smorgasbord. Expect to pay more at the internationally renowned restaurants in Marbella.

At the other end of the scale, and often even more enjoyable, are the *chiringuitos.* Strung out along the beaches, these rough-and-ready, summer-only restaurants serve seafood fresh off the boats. Because there are so many foreigners, meals on the coast are served earlier than elsewhere in Andalusia, with restaurants opening at 1 PM or 1:30 PM for lunch and 7 PM or 8 PM for dinner. Reservations are advisable for the pricier restaurants in Marbella and Málaga; elsewhere, they're rarely necessary. Expect beach restaurants to be packed after 3 PM on Sunday.

ABOUT THE HOTELS

Most hotels on the developed stretch, between Torremolinos and Fuengirola, offer large, functional rooms near the sea at competitive rates. The area's popularity as a budget destination means that most such hotels are booked in high season by package-tour operators. Finding a room at Easter, in July and August, or over holiday weekends can be difficult if you haven't reserved in advance. Málaga has several new lodging establishments, but it's still poorly endowed with high-quality hotels for a city of its size, aside from an excellent but small parador that can be hard to book. Marbella, conversely, has more than its fair share of grand hotels, including some of Spain's most expensive accommodations. Rooms in Gibraltar's handful of hotels tend to be more expensive than most comparable lodgings in Spain.

Numbers in the text correspond to numbers in the margin and on the Costa del Sol and Gibraltar maps.

TAPAS

An Introduction to

Virtually every day, coworkers head to a tapas bar after work for a *caña* (a 4–6 oz beer) that's almost always paired with a tapa or two. On weeknights, families crowd around tables with drinks and tapas, filling up on several *raciones* or small *cazuelas*. In the evenings, couples out on the town do "tapas crawls," the Spanish version of a pub crawl where *croquetas*

Defining tapas as merely a snack is, for a Spaniard, like defining air as an occasional breathable treat. If that sounds a little dramatic, consider how this bite-sized food influences daily life across all regions and classes throughout Spain.

THE HISTORY OF SHRINKING PORTIONS

The origin of tapas is the stuff of heated tapas bar debates. Various reports cloud the history of when and how it started. Some credit Alfonso X's diet for his delicate stomach. However, the most commonly accepted explanation is that a flat object (be it a slice of bread or a flat card with some nuts or sunflower seeds) was used to cover the rim of wine glasses and keep dive-bombing fruit flies out. (To cover something up is "tapar" in Spanish.)

balance out rich wine. And sometimes the spread for a *pica-pica* (a nibbling marathon) with *tortilla de patata, aceitunas, chorizo,* and *jamon* will cause Spaniards to replace their lunch or dinner outright with tapas. These tiny dishes are such a way of life that a verb had to be created for them: *tapear* (to eat tapas) or "*ir a tapeo*" (to go eat tapas). The staff of life in Spain isn't bread. It's finger food.

TAPAS ACROSS SPAIN

MADRID

It is often difficult to qualify what is authentically from Madrid and what has been gastronomically cribbed from other regions thanks to Madrid's melting-pot status for people and customs all over Spain. While *croquetas, tortilla de patata,* and even *paella* can be served as tapas, *patatas bravas* and *calamares* can be found in almost any restaurant in Madrid. The popular *patatas* are a very simple mixture of fried or roasted potatoes with a "Brava" sauce. The sauce is slightly spicy, which is surprising given a country-wide aversion for dishes with the slightest kick. The *calamares*, fried in olive oil, can be served alone or with alioli sauce, mayonnaise, or—and you're reading correctly—in a sandwich. A slice of lemon usually accompanies your serving.

Tortilla de patata

Calamares

ANDALUSIA

Known for the warmth of its climate and its people, Andalusian bars tend to be very generous with their tapas—maybe in spite of the fact that they aren't exactly celebrated for their culinary inventiveness. But tapas here are traditional and among the best. Many times ordering a drink will bring you a sandwich large enough to make a meal, or a bowl of gazpacho that you could swim in. Seafood is also extremely popular in Andalusia, and you will find tapas ranging from sizzling prawns to small anchovies soaked in vinegar or olive oil.

Pescado frito (fried fish) and *albondigas* (meatballs) are two common tapas for the region, and it's worth grazing multiple bars to try the different preparations. The fish usually includes squid, anchovies, and other tiny fish, deep fried and served as is. Since the bones are very small, they are not removed and considered fine for digestion. If this idea bothers you, sip some more wine. The saffron-almond sauce (*salsa de almendras y azafrán*) that accompanies the meatballs might very well make your eyes roll to the back of your head. And since saffron is not as expensive in Spain as it is in the United States, the meatballs are liberally drenched in it.

Fried anchovy fish

Albondigas

Not incidentally, Spain's biggest export, olives, grows in Andalusia, so you can expect many varieties among the tapas served with your drinks.

BASQUE COUNTRY

More than any other community in Spain, the Basque Country is known for its culinary originality. The tapas, like the region itself, tend to be more expensive and inventive. And since the Basques insist on doing things their way, they call their unbelievable bites *pintxos* (or *pinchos* in Spanish) rather than tapas. *Gildas*, probably the most ordered *pintxo* in the Basque Country, is a simple toothpick skewer composed of a special green pepper, (called *Guindilla Vasca*), an anchovy, and a pitted olive. All the ingredients must be of the highest quality, especially the anchovy, which should be marinated in the best olive oil and

Red and green peppers pintxos

not be too salty. Pimientos *Rellenos de Bacalao* (roasted red peppers with cod) is also popular, given the Basque Country's adjacency to the ocean. The festive color of the red peppers and the savoriness of the fish make it a bite-sized Basque delicacy.

A spread of tapas selections

GET YOUR TAPAS ON

Madrid

El Bocaíto. Here you'll find the best *pescaito frito* (deep-fried whitebait) and a huge assortment of *tostas* (toast points with different toppings). ✉ *Libertad 6, Chueca.* ☎ *91/532–1219.*

Estay. You'll find delicious *tortilla Espanola con atun y lechuga* (Spanish omelet with tuna and lettuce) and excellent *rabas* (fried calamari). ✉ *Hermosilla 46, Salamanca* ☎ *91/578–0470.*

Andalusia

El Churrasco. With a name like this, you would expect the meats to be delicious, and they are. But don't miss the *berenjenas crujientes con salmorejo* (crispy fried eggplant slices with thick gazpacho). ✉ *Romero 16, Judería, Córdoba* ☎ *95/729–0819.*

El Rinconcillo. It's great for the view of the Iglesia de Santa Catalina and a *caldereta de venado* (venison stew). ✉ *C. Gerona 40, Barrio de la Macarena, Seville* ☎ *95/422–3183.*

The Basque Country

Aloña Berri Bar. The repeat winner of tapas championships, its *contraste de pato* (duck à l'orange) and *bastela de pichón* (pigeon pie) makes foodies swoon. ✉ *C. Bermingham 24, Gros, San Sebastián* ☎ *94/329–0818.*

Bernardo Etxea. Straight up, freshly prepared classics like fried peppers, octopus, and pimientos with anchovies are served here. ✉ *C. Puerto 7, Parte Vieja* ☎ *94/342–2055.*

Bite-sized food and drink

A wine pairing

THE COSTA DE ALMERÍA

West of Spain's Murcia Coast lie the shores of Andalusia, beginning with the Costa de Almería. Its highlights include the archaeological site of Los Millares, near the village of Santa Fé de Mondújar, and the otherworldly landscape of Tabernas, Europe's only desert, which can mesmerize you with its stark beauty. The mineral riches of the surrounding mountains gave rise to Iberia's first true civilization, whose capital can still be glimpsed in the 4,700-year-old ruins of Los Millares. The towns of Níjar and Sorbas maintain an ages-old tradition of pottery-making and other crafts, and the western coast of Almería has tapped unexpected wealth from a parched land, thanks to modern farming techniques. In contrast to that inhospitable landscape, the mountain-fringed Andarax Valley has a cool climate and gentle landscape, both conducive to making fine wines.

AGUA AMARGA

❶ *22 km (14 mi) north of San José and 55 km (30 mi) west of Almería.*

Agua Amarga is perhaps the most pleasant village on the Cabo de Gata coast. Like other coastal hamlets, it started out in the 18th century as a tuna-fishing port. Today it attracts more visitors, but remains a fishing village at heart, less developed than San José. One of the coast's best beaches is just to the north: the dramatically named **Playa de los Muertos** (Beach of the Dead), a long stretch of fine sand bookended with volcanic outcrops.

SAN JOSÉ & THE CABO DE GATA NATURE RESERVE

2 *40 km (25 mi) east of Almería, 86 km (53 mi) south of Mojácar.*

San José is the largest village in the southern part of the park and has a very nice bay, but these days it has rather outgrown itself and can get busy in the summer months. Those preferring smaller, quieter places should look a little farther north at places such as La Isleta and Agua Amarga and the often-deserted beaches between them. Just south of San José is the **Parque Natural Marítimo y Terrestre Cabo de Gata–Níjar** (⊠*Road from Almería to Cabo de Gata, Km 6* ☎☎*950/160435*). Birds are the main attraction at this nature reserve; it is home to several species native to Africa, including the *camachuelo trompetero* (large beaked bullfinch), which is not found anywhere else outside Africa. The **Centro Las Amuladeras visitor center**, at the park entrance, has an exhibit and information on the region. For beach time, follow signs south to the **Playa Los Genoveses** and **Playa Monsul**. A dirt track follows the coast around the spectacular cape, eventually linking up with the N332 to Almería.

WHERE TO STAY

$$$–$$$$ ⊡ **Mikasa.** Specifically designed for rest and relaxation, this stylish hotel has some rooms with king-size beds and whirlpools as well as sea views; a gourmet breakfast is served on the terrace or in the delightful garden, and the restaurant, exclusively for guests, serves an intriguing mix of local and international cuisine. If you don't fancy the beach, relax at one of the two pools (one is heated) or luxuriate in the spa. ⊠*Ctra. de Carboneras s/n, Agua Amarga, 04149* ☎*950/138073* ⊕*www.mikasasuites.com* ⤴*20 rooms* ⚐*In-hotel: restaurant, bar, pools, spa* ⊟*AE, DC, MC, V.*

ALMERÍA

3 *219 km (136 mi) southwest of Murcia, 183 km (114 mi) east of Málaga.*

Warmed by the sunniest climate in Andalusia, Almería is a youthful Mediterranean city, basking in sweeping views of the sea from its coastal perch. Almería is also a capital of the grape industry, thanks to its wonderfully mild climate in spring and fall. Rimmed by tree-lined boulevards and some landscaped squares, the city's core is still a maze of narrow, winding alleys formed by flat-roof, distinctly Mudéjar houses. Though now surrounded by modern apartment blocks, these dazzling-white older homes give Almería an Andalusian flavor. Dominating the city is its **Alcazaba** *(Fortress)* built by Caliph Abd ar-Rahman I and given a bell tower by Carlos III. From here you have sweeping views of the port and city. Among the ruins of the fortress, damaged by earthquakes in 1522 and 1560, are landscaped gardens of rock flowers and cacti. ⊠ *C. Almanzor* ☎*950/271617* 🎟*€1.50; free for EU citizens* ☉ *Apr.–Oct., Tues.–Sun. 10–8; Nov.–Mar., Tues.–Sun. 9–6:30.* Below the Alcazaba stands the **cathedral,** whose buttressed towers make it look like a castle. It is Gothic in design, but with some classical touches around the doors. 🎟*€3* ☉ *Weekdays 10:30–4:30, Sat. 10–1.*

WHERE TO STAY & EAT

$$ ✕ **Veracruz.** In Almería's beach barrio, El Zapillo, this justly popular seafood restaurant has its own storage tank for oysters, clams, prawns, and lobsters. The specialty is *parillada de pescado,* a mixed grill of everything that swims in the Mediterranean. ⊠ *Av. Cabo de Gata 119* ☎*950/251220* ▤*AE, MC, V.*

$–$$ ✕ **Valentin.** This popular, central spot serves fine regional specialties, such as *cazuela de rape* (monkfish baked in a sauce of almonds and pine nuts). The surroundings are Andalusian: white walls, wood, and glass. Come on the early side (around 9) to get a table. ⊠ *Tenor Iribarne 7* ☎*950/264475* ▤*AE, MC, V* ☉ *Closed Mon. No dinner Sun.*

$$ ✕🏨 **Torreluz III.** Value is the overriding attraction of this comfortable yet elegant modern hotel. Guest rooms are slick and bright, with the kind of installations for which you'd expect to pay more. Its restaurant, Torreluz Mediterráneo, is famous among locals for robust portions and brisk lunchtime service. It serves an excellent cross section of southeastern fare—try the *zarzuela de marisco a la marinera* (mixed seafood in a zesty red marinade). The cheaper Torreluz Hotel, with just 24 rooms ($) next door (with the same phone number) is also good value, as are the nearby apartments, which offer more space for the same price as the main hotel. ⊠ *Plaza Flores 3, 04001* ☎*950/234399* 🖷*950/281428* ⊕*www.torreluz.com* ⇱*94 rooms* ⌂*In-hotel: 2 restaurants, bar* ▤*AE, DC, MC, V.*

$$ 🏨 **NH Ciudad de Almería.** One of the newest hotels in Almería, this has the appealing mix of traditional and modern style—including avantgarde art pieces—often found in NH hotels, and offers larger rooms than is usually expected in the region. It also has a fine strategic location, just to the east of the town center and directly across from the train and bus station. ⊠ *Jardín de Medina s/n, 04006* ☎*950/182500* 🖷*950/273010* ⊕*www.nh-hotels.com* ⇱*139 rooms* ⌂*In-hotel: restaurant, bar, laundry facilities, public Internet* ▤*AE, DC, MC, V.*

$ 🏨 **Hostal Sevilla.** If you want inexpensive comfort, look no further. In the labyrinth of the old town, you'll find healthy doses of Andalusian style and charm. The rooms vary; those on the street side have small terraces, whereas those on the quiet interior look over the courtyards and rooftops of the old town. All have ceramic-tile floors. ⊠ *Granada 25, 04001* ☎🖷*950/230009* ⇱*37 rooms* ▤*MC, V.*

NIGHTLIFE

Nocturnal action centers on **Plaza Flores,** moving down to the beach in summer. In town, try the small **Cajón de Sastre** (⊠ *Plaza Marques de Heredia 8*) for typical *copas* (libations) and a mainly Spanish crowd.

OFF THE
BEATEN
PATH
The Desierto de Tabernas, 25 km (15 mi) north of Almería, is billed as the only true desert in Europe, receiving an average of 8 inches of rainfall a year. The striking, almost lunar landscape of scrub and parched hills bears a similarity to the American desert—a fact not lost on filmmakers. More than 300 westerns were made in the area between 1950 and 1990, most of them of the "spaghetti western" genre. Several of the old film sets still stand, and two of them are open to the public, Mini Hollywood (⊠ *N340, Km 364* ☎ *950/365236* 🎟 *€16* ⊘ *Tues.–Sun. 10–7*) and Western Leone (⊠ *A92, Km 378.9* ☎ *950/165405* 🎟 *€6.50* ⊘ *Daily 10–dusk*).

THE COSTA TROPICAL

East of Málaga and west of Almería lies the Costa Tropical. It has escaped the worst excesses of the property developers, and its tourist onslaught has been mild. A flourishing farming center, this area earns its keep from tropical fruit, including avocados, mangoes, and papaws (also known as custard apples). Housing developments are generally inspired by Andalusian village architecture rather than bland high-rise design. You may find packed beaches and traffic-choked roads at the height of the season, but for most of the year the Costa Tropical is relatively free of tourists, if not also devoid of expatriates.

SALOBREÑA

❹ *102 km (63 mi) east of Málaga.*

You can reach Salobreña by descending through the mountains from Granada or by continuing west from Almería on N340. A detour to the left from the highway brings you to this unspoiled village of near-perpendicular streets and old white houses, slapped onto a steep hill beneath a Moorish fortress. It's a true Andalusian *pueblo,* separated from the beachfront restaurants and bars in the newer part of town.

ALMUÑECAR

❺ *85 km (53 mi) east of Málaga.*

Almuñecar has been a fishing village since Phoenician times, 3,000 years ago, when it was called Sexi. Later, the Moors built a castle here for the treasures of Granada's kings. Today Almuñecar is a small-time resort with a shingle beach, popular with Spanish and northern-European vacationers. The road west from Motril and Salobreña passes through the former empire of the sugar barons who brought prosperity to Málaga's province in the 19th century. The cane fields are now giving way to litchis, limes, mangoes, papaws, and olives; avocado groves line your route as you descend into Almuñecar. The village is actually two, separated by the dramatic rocky headland of Punta de la Mona. To the east is Almuñecar proper, and to the west is **La Herradura,** a quiet fishing community. Between the two is the Marina del Este yacht harbor, a popular diving center along with La Herradura.

Crowning Almuñecar is the **Castillo de San Miguel** *(St. Michael's Castle)*. A Roman fortress once stood here, later enlarged by the Moors, but the castle's present aspect owes more to 16th-century additions. The building was bombarded during the Peninsular War at the beginning of the 19th century, and what was left became initially a cemetery until the 1990s, when excavation and restoration began. You can wander the ramparts and peer into the dungeon; the skeleton at the bottom is a reproduction of human remains discovered on the spot. ☜€2, *includes admission to Cueva de Siete Palacios* ⊙ *July and Aug., Tues.–Sat. 10:30–1:30 and 6–9, Sun. 10–2; Sept.–June, Tues.–Sat. 10:30–1:30 and 4–6:30, Sun. 10:30–2.*

Beneath the Castillo de San Miguel is a large, vaulted stone cellar of Roman origin, the **Cueva de Siete Palacios** *(Cave of Seven Palaces)*, now Almuñecar's archaeological museum. The collection is small but interesting, with Phoenician, Roman, and Moorish artifacts. ☜€2, *includes admission to Castillo de San Miguel* ⊙ *July and Aug., Tues.–Sat. 10:30–1:30 and 6–9, Sun. 10–2; Sept.–June, Tues.–Sat. 10:30–1:30 and 4–6:30, Sun. 10:30–2.*

WHERE TO STAY & EAT

$$ ✕ **Jacquy-Cotobro.** One of the finest French restaurants on Spain's southern coast, Jacquy-Cotobro is cozy, with bare brick walls and green wicker chairs; a beachfront terrace is open in summer. Try the *menú de degustación,* with three courses plus dessert; it might include fresh pasta topped with oyster mushrooms and prawns, lobster salad with truffle oil, or duck in orange sauce. Finish with the calorific delight of strawberry mousse drizzled with Kirsch. ✉ *Edificio Río, Playa Cotobro* ☎958/631802 ▤*MC, V* ⊙*Closed Mon.*

$$$ ⌂ **Sol Los Fenicios.** Near the beach in La Herradura, this modern, Andalusian-style hotel has views of the bay and the cliffs of Punta de Mona to the east and the rocky headland of Cerro Gordo to the west. The rooms have recently benefited from a major revamp. They are set around a traditional interior patio, complete with pond; ask for a room with a sea view. ✉ *Paseo de Andrés Segovia s/n, La Herradura 18697* ☎958/827900 ☎958/827910 ⊕*www.sollosfenicios.solmelia. com* ⇋*42 rooms* ⌂*In-room: Wi-Fi. In-hotel: restaurant, pool, parking (fee)* ▤*AE, DC, MC, V* ⊠|*BP* ⊙*Closed late Nov.–early Mar.*

$–$$ ⌂ **Casablanca.** There's something quaint about this family-run hotel with its neo-Moorish façade sitting next to the beach and near the botanical park. The rooms, which are all different, have modern fittings juxtaposed with antiques and the occasional four-poster bed. All have private balconies or large picture windows. The restaurant specializes in traditional cuisine, such as *migas* (breadcrumbs fried with sausage and spices) and paella. ✉ *Pl. San Cristóbal 4, 18690* ☎958/635575 ⊕*www.almunecar.info/casablanca* ⇋*35 rooms* ⌂*In-hotel: restaurant, bar, public Internet, parking* ▤*D, MC, V.*

Continued on page 164

Sherry wine at the *Feria del Caballo* of Jerez de la Frontera, Cádiz.

THE WINES OF SPAIN

Copitas (traditional sherry wine glasses) and casks at González Byass winery.

After years of being in the shadows of other European wines, Spanish wines are finally gunning for the spotlight—and what has taken place is nothing short of a revolution. The wines of Spain, like its cuisine, are currently experiencing a firecracker explosion of both quality and variety that has brought a new level of interest, awareness, and recognition throughout the world, propelling them into superstar status. A generation of young, hot-to-trot winemakers has jolted dormant areas awake, rediscovered long-forgotten local grapes, and introduced top international varieties. Even the most established regions submitted to makeovers to keep up with these dramatic changes and compete in the global market.

THE ROAD TO GREAT WINE

(top) Vineyard in Navarra. (below) Men with *cunachos* (grape baskets) near Málaga.

In the beginning, it wasn't so rosy. Spanish wine has a long and agitated history dating back to the time when the Phoenicians introduced viticulture over 3,000 years ago. Some wines achieved fame in Roman times, and the Visigoths enacted wine laws, but in the regions under Muslim rule, winemaking slowed down for centuries. Starting in the 16th century, wine trade expanded along with the Spanish Empire, and by the 18th and 19th centuries the Sherry region *bodegas* (wineries) were already established.

In the middle of the 19th century, seeds of change blossomed throughout the Spanish wine industry. In 1846 the estate that was to become Vega Sicilia, Spain's most revered winery, was set up in Castile. Three years later the famous Tío Pepe brand was established to produce the excellent dry *Fino* wines. Marqués de Murrieta and the Marqués de Riscal wineries opened in the 1860s creating the modern Rioja region and clearing the way for many centenary wineries. *Cava*—Spain's white or pink sparkling wine—was created the following decade in Catalonia.

After this flurry of activity, Spanish wines languished for almost a century. Vines were hit hard by phylloxera, and then a civil war and a long dictatorship left the country stagnant and isolated. Just 30 short years ago, Spain's wines were somehow split between the same dominant trio of Sherry, Rioja, and Cava, and loads of cheap, watered-down wines made by local cooperatives with little gumption to improve and even less expertise.

However, starting in the 1970s, a wave of innovation crashed through Rioja and emergent regions like Ribera del Duero and Penedés. In the 1990s, it turned into a revolution that spread all over the landscape—and it's still going strong. Today, Spain is the third largest wine producer in the world, makes enticing wines at all price ranges, in never before seen levels of quality and variety. As a result, in 2006 Spain became the second wine exporting country by volume, beating out France and trailing just behind Italy.

TYPE OF WINES BY AGING

A unique feature of Spanish wines is their indication of aging. DO wines (see "A *Vino Primer*" on following page) show this on mandatory back labels. They apply to white, rose, and sparkling wines, but are much more prevalent among reds, whose requirements are the following:

Joven or Cosecha

A young wine with less than the legal *crianza* barrel-aging period. This is the basic category. But quality-oriented winemakers have begun to shun the traditional aging regulations and have produced new,

cutting-edge wines in this category. To distinguish the ambitious new reds from the charming, easy-drinking jovenés, check the price.

Crianza

A wine aged for at least 24 months, six of which are in

barrels (12 in Rioja, Ribera del Duero, and Navarra). A great bargain in top vintages from the most reliable wineries and regions.

Reserva

A wine aged for a minimum of 36 months, at least 12 of which are in oak.

Gran Reserva

Traditionally the top of the Spanish wine hierarchy, and the pride of the centenary Rioja wineries. A red wine aged for at least 24 months in oak, followed by at least an additional 36 in the bottle before release.

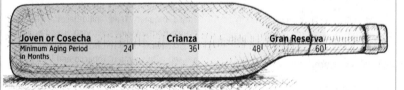

	Joven or Cosecha	Crianza		Gran Reserva	
Minimum Aging Period in Months	24	36	48	60	

READING LABELS LIKE A PRO

This term means that the wine has been bottled at the property.

Name of the wine

In some prestigious wines, each bottle is numbered.

Alcohol content

Name of the winery

ESTATE BOTTLED · PRODUCE OF SPAIN

SINGLE VINEYARD

CONTINO

RIOJA

DENOMINACION DE ORIGEN CALIFICADA

De esta cosecha se han embotellado
117.139 botellas de Reserva

13,5% Vol.   BOT.   75 cl. ℮
R.E.
N.°
5212 VI

Embotellado en la propiedad
VIÑEDOS DEL CONTINO, S. A.
LAGUARDIA - LASERNA, ESPAÑA

RESERVA 2002

This expression appears in wines always made from the same plot of land.

Name of the appellation (look for the expression "Denominación de Origen" displayed in small print just below the appellation's name)

Town where the winery is located

Aging category   Vintage year

A *VINO* PRIMER

Spain offers a daunting assortment of styles, regions, grapes, and terminology. But don't panic. A few guidelines can help you soldier through them. Save for a growing number of worthy exceptions, Spain's quality wines come from designated areas called *Denominaciones de Origen* (Appellations of Origin) or simply *DO* for short. Spain has more than 60, all of them with specific regulations designed to protect the personality of their wines. Four key elements account for the distinctive character in the best of them: diverse climates, varied soils, indigenous grape varieties, and winemaking practices.

1 The green and more humid areas of the Northwest deliver crisp, floral white albariños in Galicia's Rias Biaxas. In the Bierzo DO, the Mencía grape distills the essence of the schist slopes, where it grows into minerally infused red wines.

2 Moving east, in the iron-rich riverbanks of the Duero, Tempranillo grapes, here called "Tinto Fino," produces complex and age-worthy Ribera del Duero reds and hefty Toro wines. Close by, the Rueda DO adds aromatic and grassy whites from local Verdejo and adopted Sauvignon Blanc.

3 The Rioja region is a winemaker's paradise. Here a mild, nearly perfect vine-growing climate marries limestone and clay soils with Tempranillo, Spain's most noble grape, to deliver wines that possess the two main features of every great region: personality and quality. Tempranillo-based riojas evolve from a young cherry color and aromas of strawberries and red fruits, to a brick hue, infused with scents of tobacco and leather. Whether medium or full-bodied, tannic or velvety, these reds are some of the most versatile and food-friendly wines, and have set the standard for the country for over a century.

Nearby, Navarra and three small DOs in Aragón, deliver great wines made with the local Garnacha, Tempranillo, and international grape varieties.

4 South of Barcelona, a group of visionary winemakers, in less than a decade, revived the tiny and dormant medieval mountainous region of Priorat. Blending indigenous old Garnacha and Cariñena vines with mostly Cabernet and Syrah, they translated the brown

WINE + ARCHITECTURE

Calatrava's Ysios winery

Nothing symbolizes the current golden era of Spanish wines better than the winery projects completed by world-class architects. Just to name a few: Rafael Moneo built the new Chivite winery; Zaha Hadid is renovating the traditional López Heredia; Frank Gehry just opened the new Marqués de Riscal visitors center; Santiago Calatrava created Ysios with a curvy profile that mim-

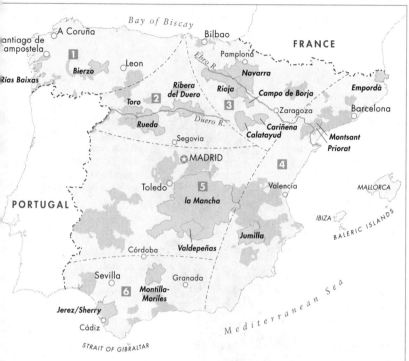

slate soils into fascinating and powerful red wines, deeply different from the Rioja and Ribera del Duero wines. Their immense success has energized the areas along the Mediterranean coast—notably *Montsant, Empordà,* and *Jumilla*—and has provoked the emergence of new bold, rich, full-bodied, packed with fruit, and immediately appealing wines.

5 In the central plateau south of Madrid, rapid investment, modernization, and replanting is resulting in medium bodied, easy drinking, and fairly priced wines made with Tempranillo (here called "Cencíbel"), Cabernet, Syrah, and even Petit Verdot, that are opening the doors to more ambitious endeavors.

6 In sun-drenched Andalusia, where the white albariza limestone soils reflect the powerful sunlight while trapping the scant humidity, the fortified Jerez (Sherry) and Montilla emerge. In all their different incarnations, from dry *finos, manzanillas, amontillados, palo cortados,* and *olorosos,* to sweet creams and Pedro Ximénez, they are the most original wines of Spain.

ics the nearby mountains; Philippe Mazières made the new barrel-shaped CVNE winery; Richard Rogers's new Protos winery sits in stark contrast to the medieval castle above the hill. These flashy wineries, set in picturesque vine landscapes and quaint villages, are adding a new attraction to the growing enotourism industry (wine-related tourism).

Gehry's Marqués de Riscal winery

JUST OFF THE VINE

Beyond Tempranillo: The current wine revolution has recovered many native varieties. Albariño, Godello, and Verdejo among the white, and Callet, Cariñena, Garnacha, Graciano, Mandó, Manto Negro, Mencía, and Monastrell among the red are currently gaining momentum and will become more popular over the years.

Cult Wines: For most of the past century, Vega Sicilia Unico was the only true cult wine from Spain. The current explosion has greatly expanded the roster: L'Ermita, Pingus, Clos Erasmus, Artadi, Cirsion, Terreus, and Termanthia are the leading names in a list that grows every year.

Vinos de Pagos: *Pago,* a word meaning plot or vineyard, is the new legal term chosen to create Spain's equivalent of a *Grand Cru* hierarchy, by protecting quality-oriented wine producers that make wine from their own estates.

V.O.S. and V.O.R.S.: Sherry's most dramatic change in over a century is the creation of the "Very Old Sherry" designation for wines over 20 years of age, and the addition of "Rare" for those over 30, to easier distinguish their best, oldest, and most complex wines.

Petit Verdot: Winemakers in Spain are discovering that Petit Verdot, the "little green" grape of Bordeaux, ripens much easier in warmer climates than in its birthplace. This is leading to a dramatic increase in the presence of Petit Verdot in blends, and even to the production of varietals.

Innovative New Blends: A few wine regions have strict regulations concerning the varieties used in their wines, but most allow for experimentation. All over the country, *bodegas* are crafting wines with unsuspecting blends that involve local varieties, Tempranillo, and famous international grapes.

Andalusia's New Wines: For centuries, scorching southern Andalusia has offered world-class Sherry and Montilla wines. Now trailblazing winemakers are making serious inroads in the production of quality white, red, and new dessert wines, something deemed impossible a few years back.

Island Wines: In both the Balearic and Canary Islands the strong tourist industry helped to revive local winemaking. Although hard to find, the best Callet and Manto Negro–based red wines of Majorca, and the sweet *malvasías* of Lanzarote will reward the adventurous drinker.

SUPERSTAR WINEMAKERS

Mariano García   Peter Sisseck   Alvaro Palacios   Josep Lluís Pérez

The current wine revolution has made superstars out of a group of dynamic, innovative, and visionary winemakers. Here are some of the top names:

Mariano García. His 30 years as winemaker of Vega Sicilia made him a legend. Now García displays his deft touch in the Duero and Bierzo through his four family projects: Mauro, Aalto, San Román, and Paixar.

Peter Sisseck. A Dane educated in Bordeaux, Sisseck found his calling in the old Ribera de Duero vineyards, where he crafted Pingus, Spain's quintessential new cult wine.

Alvaro Palacios. Palacios is the engine behind the current renaissance of Bierzo, and previously of Priorat, where he created L'Ermita, which is, along with Pingus, Spain's ultimate collector item.

Josep Lluís Pérez. From his base in Priorat and through his work as a winemaker, researcher, teacher, and consultant, Pérez (along with his daughter Sara Pérez) has become the main driving force in shaping the modern Mediterranean wines of Spain.

MATCHMAKING KNOW-HOW

A pairing of wine with *jamon* and Spanish olives.

Spain has a great array of regional products and cuisines, and its avant-garde chefs are culinary world leaders. As a general rule, you should match local food with local wines—but Spanish wines can be matched very well with some of the most unexpected dishes.

Albariños and the white wines of Galicia are ideal partners of seafood and fish. Dry sherries complement Serrano and Iberico hams, *lomo, chorizo,* and *salchichón* (white dry sausage), as well as olives and nuts. Pale, light, and dry *finos* and *manzanillas* are the perfect aperitif wines, and the ideal companion of fried fish. Fuller bodied *amontillados, palo cortados,* and *olorosos* go well with hearty soups. Ribera del Duero reds are the perfect match for the outstanding local lamb. Try Priorat and other Mediterranean reds with strong cheeses and barbecue meats. Traditional Rioja harmonizes well with fowl and game. But also take an adventure off the beaten path: *manzanilla* and *fino* are great with sushi and sashimi; Rioja *reserva* fit tuna steaks; and cream sherry will not be out of place with chocolate. ¡Salud!

NERJA

❻ *52 km (32 mi) east of Málaga, 22 km (14 mi) west of Almuñecar.*
★

Nerja—the name comes from the Moorish word *narixa*, meaning "abundant springs"—has a large foreign resident community living mainly outside town in *urbanizaciones* ("village" developments). The old village is on a headland above small beaches and rocky coves, which offer reasonable swimming despite the gray, gritty sand. In high season, Nerja is packed with tourists, but the rest of the year it's a pleasure to wander the old town's narrow streets. Nerja's highlight is the **Balcón de Europa**, a tree-lined promenade with magnificent views, on a promontory just off the central square. The **Cuevas de Nerja** *(Nerja Caves)* lie between Almuñecar and Nerja on a road surrounded by giant cliffs and dramatic seascapes. Signs point to the cave entrance above the village of Maro, 4 km (2½ mi) east of Nerja. Its spires and turrets created by millennia of dripping water are now floodlighted for better views. One suspended pinnacle, 200 feet long, is in fact the world's largest known stalactite. The awesome subterranean chambers create an evocative setting for concerts and ballets during the Nerja Festival of Music and Dance, held annually during the second and third weeks of July. ☎*952/529520* ⊕*www.cuevanerja.com* ⊠*€6* ⊙*Oct.–Apr., daily 10–2 and 4–6:30; May–Sept., daily 10–2 and 4–8.*

WHERE TO STAY & EAT

$$–$$$ ✕**Udo Heimer.** Your eponymous host, a genial German, welcomes you warmly to this stylish art deco villa in a development east of Nerja. The visual flair extends to the food, which mixes German and Spanish flavors. Try the rack of lamb with rosemary and thyme, or prawns wrapped in bacon with cayenne rice and a sweet curry sauce. The excellent wine list has rarities from all over Spain. ⊠*Pueblo Andaluz 27* ☎*952/520032* ⊟*MC, V* ⊙*Closed Wed. No lunch.*

$$ ✕**Casa Luque.** One of Nerja's most authentic Spanish restaurants, Casa Luque is in an old Andalusian house in a lovely square just off the Balcón de Europa. The menu has dishes from northern Spain, often of Basque or Navarrese origin, with an emphasis on meat and game; tapas and seafood are also on offer. Ask to sit on the patio in summer. ⊠*Pl. Cavana 2* ☎*952/521004* ⊟*AE, DC, MC, V* ⊙*Closed Wed. No dinner Sun.*

$$–$$$ 🏨**Hotel Carabeo.** Tucked away down a side street near the center
★ of town and the sea, this British-owned boutique hotel has bookshelves, antiques, and cozy overstuffed sofas in the downstairs sitting room. The walls throughout are hung with colorful oil paintings by local artist David Broadhead. In the main building there are seven rooms, five with sea views, and a private terrace overlooking the sea. In the newer annex there are six more rooms, plus a small gym and games room. ⊠*C. Hernando de Carabeo 34, 29780* ☎*952/525444* 🖷*952/522677* ⊕*www.hotelcarabeo.com* ⇋*20 rooms* ⅋*In-hotel: restaurant, bar, pool, gym, public Internet* ⊟*MC, V* ⊙*Closed end– Oct.-mid–Mar.* ⊚*CP.*

NIGHTLIFE & THE ARTS

El Colono (⊠ *Granada 6, Nerja* ☎ *952/521826*) is a flamenco club in the town center. Although the show is obviously geared toward tourists, the club has an authentic olé atmosphere. The food is good, and local specialties, including paella, are served. Dinner shows begin at 9 PM on Wednesday and Friday from February until the end of October.

FRIGILIANA

➐ *58 km (36 mi) east of Málaga.*

The village of Frigiliana, on a mountain ridge overlooking the sea, was the site of one of the last battles between the Christians and the Moors. The short drive off the highway rewards you with spectacular views and an old quarter of narrow, cobbled streets and dazzling white houses decorated with pots of geraniums. (If you don't have a car, take a bus here from Nerja.)

THE AXARQUÍA

➑ *Vélez-Málaga: 36 km (22 mi) east of Málaga.*

The Axarquía region is in the eastern third of Málaga's province, stretching from Nerja to Málaga. The area's charm lies in its mountainous interior, peppered with pueblos, vineyards, and tiny farms. Its coast consists of narrow, pebbly beaches and drab fishing villages on either side of the high-rise resort town of Torre del Mar. The four-lane E15 highway speeds across the region a few miles in from the coast; traffic on the old coastal road (N340) is slower. **Vélez-Málaga** is the capital of the Axarquía. A pleasant agricultural town of white houses, Vélez-Málaga is a center for strawberry fields and vineyards. Worth quick visits are the **Thursday market,** the ruins of a **Moorish castle,** and the church of **Santa María la Mayor,** built in Mudejar style on the site of a mosque that was destroyed when the town fell to the Christians in 1487.

If you have a car and an up-to-date road map, explore the Axarquía's inland villages. You can follow the **Ruta del Vino** *(Wine Route)* 22 km (14 mi) from the coast, stopping at villages that produce the sweet, earthy local wine, particularly Cómpeta. Alternatively you can take the **Ruta de la Pasa** *(Raisin Route)* through Moclinejo, El Borge, and Comares. Comares perches like an eagle's nest atop one of La Serrazuela's highest mountains and dates back to Moorish times. This area is especially spectacular during the late-summer grape-harvest season or in late autumn, when the leaves of the vines turn gold. A short detour to Macharaviaya (7 km [4 mi] north of Rincón de la Victoria) might lead you to ponder the past glory of this now sleepy village: in 1776 one of its sons, Bernardo de Gálvez, became Spanish governor of Louisiana and later fought in the American Revolution (Galveston, Texas, takes its name from the governor). Macharaviaya prospered under his heirs and for many years enjoyed a lucrative monopoly on the manufacture of playing cards for South America. Both the Ruta del Vino and the Ruta de la Pasa are signposted locally.

WHERE TO STAY & EAT

$$$ ✕▦**Molino de Santillán.** This small country hotel and restaurant is typi-
cally Andalusian, with arches, terra-cotta floors, and dark oak furni-
ture. There are superb countryside views from the rooms as well as
from the timbered restaurant ($$–$$$), where the cooks use organic
ingredients grown at the hotel (try the fresh quince salad with Burgos
cheese). At the end of a signposted dirt road north of the main highway,
the hotel is a short drive away from the Añoreta golf club and 5 km
(2½ mi) from the nearest beach. Pottery and woodcarving workshops
are regularly held here. ✉*Ctra. de Macharaviaya, Km 3, Rincón de la
Victoria, 29730* ☎*952/400949* 🖷*952/115782* ⊕*www.molinodesan-
tillan.es* 🛏*22 rooms* ⚒*In-hotel: restaurant, tennis, pool, public Wi-Fi,
some pets allowed* ▤*AE, DC, MC, V.*

¢–$ ▦**El Molino de los Abuelos.** Under a canopy of jasmine and bougainvil-
★ lea, this former olive mill has a cobbled courtyard where you can enjoy
a glass of *fino* (sherry) at sundown. The rooms are all different, vary-
ing from small and simple with shared bath to a sumptuous suite with
hot tub. The restaurant has fabulous views; its menu has an empha-
sis on fish—despite the fact that Axarquía sits some 3,000 feet above
sea level. ✉*Plaza 2, Comares, 29195* ☎*952/509309* 🖷*952/214220*
🛏*6 rooms* ⚒*In-room: no TV (some). In-hotel: restaurant, no eleva-
tor* ▤*AE, MC, V.*

MÁLAGA PROVINCE

The city of Málaga and the provin-
cial towns of the upland hills and
valleys to the north create the kind
of contrast that makes travel in
Spain so tantalizing. The region's
Moorish legacy is a unifying visual
theme, connecting the tiny streets
honeycombing the steamy depths of
Málaga, the rocky cliffs and gorges
between Alora and Archidona, the
layout of the farms, and the crops
themselves, including olives, grapes,
oranges, and lemons. Ronda and
the whitewashed villages of the
mountains behind the Costa del Sol
form one of Spain's most scenic and
emblematic driving routes.

> **GOLFING IN SUNSHINE**
>
> Nicknamed the Costa del Golf,
> the Sun Coast has some 40 golf
> courses within putting distance
> of the Mediterranean, making it a
> prime golfing destination. Most of
> the courses are between Rincón
> de la Victoria (east of Málaga) and
> Gibraltar. The best season is Octo-
> ber to June; greens fees are lower
> in summer. Pick up *Sun Golf*, a
> free magazine, at hotels and
> golf clubs.

To the west of Málaga along the coast, the sprawling outskirts of Tor-
remolinos signal that you're leaving the "real" Spain and entering, well,
the "real" Costa del Sol, with its beaches, high-rise hotels, and serious
tourist activity. On the far west, you can still see Estepona's fishing vil-
lage and Moorish old quarter amid its booming coastal development.
Just inland, Casares piles whitewashed houses over the bright-blue
Mediterranean below.

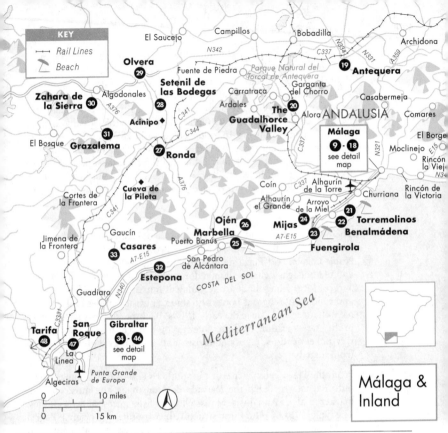

MÁLAGA

175 km (109 mi) southeast of Córdoba.

With about 550,000 residents, the city of Málaga is technically the capital of the Costa del Sol, though most travelers head straight for the beaches west of the city. Approaching Málaga from the airport, you'll be greeted by huge 1970s high-rises that march determinedly toward Torremolinos. But don't despair: in its center and its eastern suburbs, Málaga is a pleasant port city, with ancient streets and lovely villas amid exotic foliage. Blessed with a subtropical climate, it's covered in lush vegetation and averages some 324 days of sunshine a year.

Málaga has been spruced up with tastefully restored historic buildings and the gradual emergence of more sophisticated shops, bars, and restaurants. The opening of the prestigious Picasso Museum has similarly boosted tourism to this Costa capital, although there are still far fewer visitors here than in the other grand-slam Andalusian cities of Seville, Córdoba, and Granada. Most hotels organize sightseeing tours, and there's an inexpensive open-top tourist bus that travels to the major sights. Tickets (€13) allow you to hop on and off as many times as you like in 24 hours. ⚠ *Note that more tourists usually means more pickpockets, so stay alert, particularly around the historic city center.*

Arriving from Nerja, you'll enter Málaga through the suburbs of El Palo and Pedregalejo, once traditional fishing villages in their own right. Here you can eat fresh fish in the numerous *chiringuitos* (beach-side bars) and stroll Pedregalejos' seafront promenade or the tree-lined streets of El Limonar. At sunset, walk along the **Paseo Marítimo** and watch the lighthouse start its nightly vigil. A few blocks inland from here is Málaga's bullring, **La Malagueta,** built in 1874. Continuing west you soon reach the city center and inviting **Plaza de la Marina;** with cafés and an illuminated fountain overlooking the port, it's a pleasant place for a drink. From here, stroll through the shady, palm-lined gardens of the **Paseo del Parque** or browse on **Calle Marqués de Larios,** the elegant pedestrian-only main shopping street.

WHAT TO SEE

The narrow streets and alleys on each side of Calle Marqués de Larios have charms of their own. Wander the warren of passageways around
❾ **Pasaje Chinitas,** off Plaza de la Constitución, and peep into the dark, vaulted bodegas, where old men down glasses of *seco añejo* or *Málaga Virgen,* local wines made from Málaga's muscatel grapes. Silversmiths and vendors of religious books and statues ply their trades in shops that have changed little since the early 1900s. Backtrack across Larios, and, in the streets leading to Calle Nueva, you can see shoeshine boys, lottery-ticket vendors, Gypsy guitarists, and tapas bars with wine served from huge barrels.

❿ From the Plaza Felix Saenz, at the southern end of Calle Nueva, turn onto Sagasta to reach the **Mercado de Atarazanas,** the most colorful market in all of Andalusia. Stalls sell fresh fish, spices, and vegetables. The typical 19th-century iron structure incorporates the original **Puerta de Atarazanas,** the exquisitely crafted 14th-century Moorish gate that once connected the city with the port.

NEED A BREAK?

The Antigua Casa de Guardia (✉ *Alameda 18* ☎ *952/214680*), around the corner from the Mercado de Atarazanas, is Málaga's oldest bar, founded in 1840. Andalusian wines flow straight from the barrel, and the floor is ankle-deep in discarded shrimp shells.

⓫ Málaga's **cathedral,** built between 1528 and 1782, is a triumph, although a generally unappreciated one, having been left unfinished when funds ran out. Because it lacks one of its two towers, the building is nicknamed *La Manquita* (The One-Armed Lady). The enclosed choir, which miraculously survived the burnings of the civil war, is the work of 17th-century artist Pedro de Mena, who carved the wood wafer-thin in some places to express the fold of a robe or shape of a finger. The choir also has a pair of massive 18th-century pipe organs, one of which is still used for the occasional concert. Adjoining the cathedral is a small museum of religious art and artifacts, and a walk around the cathedral on Calle Cister will take you to the magnificent Gothic Puerta del Sagrario. ✉ *C. de Molina Larios* ☎ *952/215917* 🎫 *€3.50* ⏱ *Mon.–Sat. 10–6:45.*

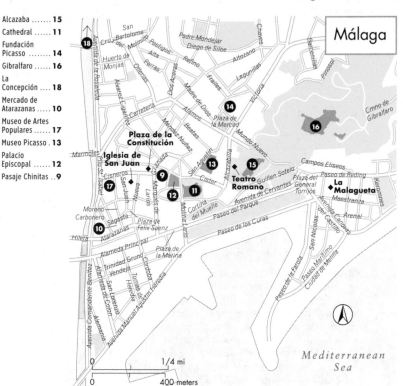

12 **Palacio Episcopal** *(Bishop's Palace),* which faces the cathedral's main entrance, has one of the most stunning facades in the city. It's now a venue for temporary art exhibitions. ⊠*Pl. Obispo 6* ☎*952/602722* ⊠*Free* ⊙*Tues.–Sun. 10–2 and 6–9.*

13 The charm of the **Museo Picasso,** the city's most prestigious museum, is that it's such a family affair. These are the works that Pablo Picasso kept for himself or gave to his family and include the heartfelt *Paulo con gorro blanco* (Paulo with a white cap), a portrait of his firstborn son painted in the early 1920s. The holdings were largely donated by two family members—Christine and Bernard Ruiz-Picasso, the artist's daughter-in-law and grandson. The works are displayed in chronological order according to the periods that marked his development as an artist, from Blue and Rose to Cubism, and beyond. The museum is housed in a former palace where, during restoration work, Roman and Moorish remains were discovered. These are now on display, together with the permanent collection of Picassos and temporary exhibitions. ⊠*C. de San Agustín* ☎*952/602731* ⊠*Permanent exhibition €6, combined permanent and temporary exhibition €8, last Sun. of every month free* ⊙*Tues.–Thurs. 10–8, Fri. and Sat. 10–9.*

FodorśChoice
★

⓮ On the Plaza de la Merced, No. 15 was the childhood home of Málaga's most famous native son, Pablo Picasso, born here in 1881. Now the **Fundación Picasso,** the building has been painted and furnished in the style of the era and houses a permanent exhibition of Picasso's early sketches and sculptures, as well as memorabilia, including the artist's christening robe and family photographs. ⊠*Pl. de la Merced 15* ☎*952/600215* ⬚*€1* ☽*Mon.–Sat. 10–8, Sun. 10–2.*

⓯ Just beyond the ruins of a Roman theater on Calle Alcazabilla, the Moorish **Alcazaba** is Málaga's greatest monument. This fortress was begun in the 8th century, when Málaga was the principal port of the Moorish kingdom, though most of the present structure dates from the 11th century. The inner palace was built between 1057 and 1063, when the Moorish emirs took up residence; and Ferdinand and Isabella lived here for a while after conquering Málaga in 1487. The ruins are dappled with orange trees and bougainvillea and include a small museum; from the highest point you can see over the park and port. ⊠*Entrance on Alcazabilla* ⬚*€1.90, €3.15 combined entry with Gibralfaro* ☽*Nov.–Mar., Tues.–Sun. 8.30–7; Apr.–Oct., Tues.–Sun. 9:30–8.*

⓰ Magnificent vistas beckon at **Gibralfaro,** which is floodlighted at night. The fortifications were built for Yusuf I in the 14th century; the Moors called them Jebelfaro, from the Arab word for "mount" and the Greek word for "lighthouse," after a beacon that stood here to guide ships into the harbor and warn of pirates. The beacon has been succeeded by a small parador. You can drive here by way of Calle Victoria or take a minibus that leaves 10 times a day between 11 and 7, or roughly every hour, from the bus stop in the park near the Plaza de la Marina. ⊠*Gibralfaro Mountain* ☎*952/220043* ⬚*€1.90, €3.15 combined entry with Alcazaba* ☽*Nov.–Mar., daily 9–5:45; Apr.–Oct., daily 9–7:45.*

⓱ In the old Mesón de la Victoria, a 17th-century inn, is the **Museo de Artes**
☽ **Populares** *(Arts and Crafts Museum).* On display are horse-drawn carriages and carts, old agricultural implements, folk costumes, a forge, a bakery, an ancient grape press, and Malagueño painted clay figures and ceramics. ⊠*Pasillo de Santa Isabel 10* ☎*952/217137* ⬚*€2* ☽*Oct.–May, weekdays 10–1:30 and 4–7, Sat. 10–1:30; June–Sept., weekdays 10–1:30 and 5–8, Sat., 10–1:30.*

⓲ A 150-year-old botanical garden, **La Concepción** was created by the daughter of the British consul, who married a Spanish shipping magnate—the captains of the Spaniard's fleet had standing orders to bring back seedlings and cuttings from every "exotic" port of call. The garden is just off the exit road to Granada—too far to walk, but well worth the cab fare from the city center. ⊠*Ctra. de las Pedrizas, Km 166* ☎*952/252148* ⬚*€3.15* ☽*Tues.–Sun. 10* AM*–dusk.*

WHERE TO STAY & EAT

$$–$$$ ✕**El Chinitas.** Decorated with traditional mosaic tiles and original paintings by Malagueño artists, this place sits at one end of Pasaje Chinitas, Málaga's most *típico* (typical) street. The tapas bar is popular, especially for its cured ham. The second floor has three private dining rooms—groups of 12 to 20 can reserve the Sala Antequera, with a Camelot-style round table—and a banquet hall. Try the *sopa castellana* (soup made with fresh garlic, bread, paprika, and egg), followed by *solomillo al vino de Málaga* (fillet steak in Málaga wine sauce). ⊠ *Moreno Monroy 4* ☎ *952/210972* ⊕ *www.chinitas.arrakis.es* ⊟ *AE, DC, MC, V.*

$$–$$$ ✕ **La Ménsula.** Head here if you want to sample traditional Andalusian cuisine in an elegant, yet cozy atmosphere. The setting is warm and woody, with arches, beams, and a barrel vault ceiling. Stone-cooked steak, warm fish salad, and king prawns with *setas* (oyster mushrooms) are included on the menu. The restaurant is between the port and the city center. ⊠ *C. Trinidad Grund 28* ☎ *952/221314* ⊟ *DC, MC, V* ⊘ *Closed Sun.*

$ ✕ **El Vegetariano de la Alcazabilla.** This restaurant is arguably the best of the handful of vegetarian restaurants on the carnivorous Costa. The location is pleasantly atmospheric, tucked up a side street just around the corner from the Roman amphitheater. Dishes include vegan options and more mainstream vegetarian choices, such as spinach cannelloni, Roquefort-and-celery turnovers, and plenty of salads. The daily set menu prices fluctuate from a reasonable €6.50 to €8.50, and refreshingly, this restaurant is not too pious to include a healthy wine list and some delicious calorie-laden desserts. ⊠ *Pozo del Rey 5* ☎ *952/214858* ⊟ *MC, V* ⊘ *Closed Sun.*

$ ✕ **Tintero.** Come to this sprawling and noisy restaurant for the entertainment rather than the food. There's no menu—the waiters circle the restaurant carrying various dishes, and you choose whatever looks good to you. The bill is totaled up according to the number and size of the plates on the table at the end of the meal. On the El Palo seafront, Tintero specializes in catch-of-the-day seafood, such as *boquerones* (fresh anchovies), *sepia* (cuttlefish), and the all-time familiar classic, *gambas* (prawns). ⊠ *Playa del Dedo, El Palo* ☎ *952/204464* ⊟ *No credit cards* ⊘ *No dinner.*

¢–$ ✕ **Logueno.** This traditional tapas bar has two dining spaces: the original well-loved bar shoehorned into a deceptively small space on a side street near Calle Larios and a more recent expansion across the street. Check out the original with its L-shape wooden bar crammed with a choice of more than 75 tantalizing tapas, including many Logueno originals, such as grilled oyster mushrooms with garlic, parsley, and goat cheese. There's an excellent selection of Rioja wines, and the service is fast and good, despite the lack of elbow room. ⊠ *Marin Garcia s/n* ☎ *No phone* ⊟ *No credit cards* ⊘ *Closed Sun.*

FodorśChoice
★

$$$ ✕🖪 **Parador de Málaga–Gibralfaro.** Surrounded by pine trees on top of Gibralfaro, 3 km (2 mi) above the city, this cozy, gray-stone parador has spectacular views of Málaga and the bay. Rooms are attractive—with blue curtains and bedspreads, and woven rugs on bare tile floors—and are some of the best in Málaga. Reserve well in advance. The restaurant ($–$$$) excels at such classic Mediterranean dishes as calamari and fried green peppers. ⊠ *Monte de Gibralfaro s/n, 29016* ☎ *952/221902* ⊟ *952/221904* ⊕ *www.parador.es* 🛏 *38 rooms* ⌂ *In-room: Ethernet. In-hotel: restaurant, bar, pool, parking (no fee)* ⊟ *AE, DC, MC, V.*

FodorśChoice
★

$$$$ ⌂**Larios.** On the central Plaza de la Constitución, Larios is inside a 19th-century building that's been elegantly restored. Black-and-white tile floors lend subdued elegance to the second-floor lobby; the rooms are furnished in art deco style with photographs and jazzy bedspreads. The roof terrace has views of the cathedral, and the restaurant has a Japanese menu. There are special discount weekend rates. ✉*Marqués de Larios 2, 29005* ☎*952/222200* 🖷*952/222407* ⊕*www.hotel-larios.com* ⤵*34 rooms, 6 suites* ♿*In-room: Wi-Fi. In-hotel: restaurant* ☰*AE, DC, MC, V* ⊺◯⎮*BP.*

$$ ⌂**Don Curro.** Just around the corner from the cathedral, this family classic is going through continual renovations, but an old-fashioned air permeates the wood-panel common rooms and fireplace lounge. The revamped rooms have parquet floors, spot lighting, and classy cream and white fabrics. The ground floor bingo parlor is a quirky surprise. Prices drop considerably on weekends. ✉*Sancha de Lara 9, 29015* ☎*952/227200* 🖷*952/215946* ⊕*www.hoteldoncurro.com* ⤵*112 rooms, 6 suites* ♿*In-room: dial-up. In-hotel: public Wi-Fi, restaurant, parking (fee)* ☰*AE, DC, MC, V.*

$$ ⌂**Humaina.** In this small hotel 16 km (10 mi) north of the city, the
Fodor'sChoice   rooms are painted a sunny yellow and are furnished with terra-cotta
★   tiled floors. Balconies overlook a thickly forested park of olive, pine, and oak trees. Solar energy, an organic garden, and serious recycling are part of the ecofriendly package; horseback riding, bird-watching, and rambling excursions can be arranged. The restaurant dishes up healthful, tasty dishes, and vegetarians are happily accommodated—a rarity in these parts. ✉*Parque Natural Montes de Málaga, Carretera del Colmenar s/n, 29013* ☎*952/641025* 🖷*952/640115* ⊕*www.hotelhumaina.es* ⤵*10 rooms, 4 suites* ♿*In-hotel: restaurant, pool, no elevator* ☰*MC, V* ⊺◯⎮*BP.*

$ ⌂**Lis.** This older hotel is housed in an elegant building in between the center and the port. The public areas, with original marble floors, have a scuffed, lived-in feel, but a planned renovation (no definite dates given) could change this. The rooms are butter-colored and have dark wood trim. The bathrooms have tubs, as well as showers. ✉*C. Cordoba 7, 29001* ☎*952/227300* ⤵*51 rooms* ♿*In-hotel: bar* ☰*MC, V* ⊺◯⎮*EP.*

NIGHTLIFE & THE ARTS

The region's main theater is the **Teatro Cervantes** (✉*Ramos Marín* ☎*952/224109 or 952/220237* ⊕*www.teatrocervantes.com*), whose programs include Spanish-language plays, concerts, and flamenco. The **Málaga Symphony Orchestra** has a winter season of orchestral concerts and chamber music, with most performances held at the Teatro Cervantes. In summer, larger concerts are staged in the bullring or the **Palacio Municipal de Deportes** (☎*952/176392* ⊕*www.palaciodeportesmalaga.com*); past big-name billings have included Bryan Ferry and Bob Dylan. Málaga's main nightlife districts are Maestranza, between the bullring and the Paseo Marítimo, and the beachfront in the suburb of Pedregalejos. Central Málaga also has a lively bar scene.

ANTEQUERA

⑲ *64 km (40 mi) northwest of Málaga and 108 km (67 mi) northeast of Ronda, via Pizarra.*

Antequera became a stronghold of the Moors after their defeat at Córdoba and Seville in the 13th century. Its fall to the Christians in 1410 paved the way for the reconquest of Granada—the Moors retreated, leaving a fortress on the town heights.

WHAT TO SEE

Next door to the town fortress is the former church of **Santa María la Mayor,** one of 27 churches, convents, and monasteries in Antequera. Built of sandstone in the 16th century, it has a fine ribbed vault and is now a concert hall. The church of **San Sebastián** has a brick baroque Mudejar tower topped by a winged figure called the Angelote ("big angel"), the symbol of Antequera. The church of **Nuestra Señora del Carmen** (Our Lady of Carmen) has an extraordinary baroque altarpiece that towers to the ceiling.

Antequera's pride and joy is *Efebo,* a beautiful bronze statue of a boy that dates back to Roman times. Standing almost 5 feet high, it's on display in the **Museo Municipal.** ⊠*Pl. Coso Vieja* ☎*952/704051* ⊠*€3* ⊙*Tues.–Fri. 10–1:30 and 4:30–6:30, Sat. 10–1:30, Sun. 11–1:30.*

The mysterious prehistoric **dolmens** are megalithic burial chambers, built some 4,000 years ago out of massive slabs of stone weighing more than 100 tons each. The best-preserved dolmen is La Menga. They're just outside Antequera. ⊠*Signposted off Málaga exit Rd.* ⊠*Free* ⊙*Tues. 9–3:30, Wed.–Sat. 9–6, Sun. 9:30–2:30.*

Europe's major nesting area for the greater flamingo is **Fuente de Piedra,** a shallow saltwater lagoon. In February and March, these birds arrive from Africa by the thousands to breed, returning to Africa in August when the water dries up. The visitor center has information on wildlife. Don't forget your binoculars. ⊠*10 km (6 mi) northwest of Antequera, off A92 to Seville* ☎*952/111715* ⊠*Free* ⊙*May–Sept., Wed.–Sun. 10–2 and 4–6; Oct.–Apr., Wed.–Sun. 10–2 and 6–8.*

East of Antequera, along N342, is the dramatic silhouette of the **Peña de los Enamorados** *(Lovers' Rock),* an Andalusian landmark. Legend has it that a Moorish princess and a Christian shepherd boy eloped here one night and cast themselves to their deaths from the peak the next morning. The rock's outline is often likened to the profile of the Córdoban bullfighter Manolete.

About 8 km (5 mi) from Antequera's Lovers' Rock, the village of **Archidona** winds its way up a steep mountain slope beneath the ruins of a Moorish castle. This unspoiled village is worth a detour for its **Plaza Ochavada,** a magnificent 17th-century square resplendent with contrasting red and ocher stone. ⊠*8 km (5 mi) beyond Peña de los Enamorados, along N342, Antequera.*

Well-marked walking trails guide you at the **Parque Natural del Torcal de Antequera** *(El Torcal Nature Park).* You can walk among eerie pillars of pink limestone sculpted by aeons of wind and rain. Keep to the well-marked paths. A guide can be arranged for longer hikes. The visitor center includes a small museum. ⊠ *Centro de Visitantes, Ctra. C3310, 10 km (6 mi) south of Antequera* ☎ *649/472688* 🖾 *Free* ☺ *Daily 10–5.*

WHERE TO STAY & EAT

$$ ✕ **El Angelote.** Across the square from the Museo Municipal, El Ange-
Fodor's Choice lote's two wood-beam dining rooms are usually packed. Try the *por-
★ rilla de setas* (wild mushrooms in an almond-and-wine sauce) or *perdiz hortelana* (stewed partridge). Antequera's typical dessert is *bienmes-abe* (literally, "tastes good to me"), a delicious concoction of almonds, chocolate, and apple custard. ⊠ *Pl. Coso Viejo* ☎ *952/703465* ▤ *DC, MC, V* ☺ *Closed Mon. No dinner Sun.*

$ ✕ **Caserío San Benito.** If it weren't for the cell-phone transmission tower looming next to this country restaurant 11 km (7 mi) north of Ante-quera, you might think you've stumbled into an 18th-century scene. Many of the items found during the renovation of this former farm-house fronted by a cobbled courtyard are displayed in a small adjacent museum. Popular dishes include *porra antequerana* (a thick version of gazpacho) and *migas* (fried bread crumbs with sausage and spices). ⊠ *Ctra. Málaga–Córdoba, Km 108* ☎ *952/111103* ▤ *AE, MC, V* ☺ *Closed Mon. and 1st 2 wks in July. No dinner Tues.–Thurs.*

$$–$$$$ 🏨 **La Posada del Torcal.** Surrounded by the lunar landscape of El Torcal, this small hotel is just the place to chill out and relax after a long day on the trail. There are king-size beds (a rarity in Spain!) and a fireplace in each room. You can find skillful copies of Spanish paintings through-out. The Posada's restaurant uses organic, locally produced ingredients to cook up Spanish dishes with an innovative twist. ⊠ *Partido de Jeva, Villanueva de la Concepción, 29230* ☎ *952/031177* 🖷 *952/031006* ⊕ *www.laposadadeltorcal.com* ➯ *10 rooms* ⚲ *In-hotel: restaurant, bar, tennis court, pool, gym, no elevator* ▤ *AE, MC, V* ☺ *Closed Dec. and Jan.* ⍾ *BP.*

$ 🏨 **Castillo.** Despite its name, this hotel is modern, although housed in an elegant building in the historic center. The rooms are not fancy, but they are bright and comfortable; try for one with a balcony overlooking the bustling street. The downstairs restaurant serves good traditional food, including tapas, *raciones,* (large tapa) and grilled meats. ⊠ *C. Don Fernando 40* ☎ *952/843090* ⊕ *www.castillahotel.com* ➯ *18 rooms* ⚲ *In hotel: restaurant* ▤ *MC, V* ⍾.

THE GUADALHORCE VALLEY

❷⓿ *Leave Antequera via the El Torcal exit and turn right onto A343.*

From the village of Alora, follow a small road north to the awe-inspir-ing **Garganta del Chorro** *(Gorge of the Stream),* a deep limestone chasm where the Guadalhorce River churns and snakes its way some 600 feet below the road. The railroad track that worms in and out of tunnels in the cleft is, amazingly, the main line heading north from Málaga for Bobadilla junction and, eventually, Madrid. Clinging to the cliff side is the **Caminito del Rey** *(King's Walk),* a suspended catwalk built for a

2

visit by King Alfonso XIII at the beginning of the 19th century. At this writing, the catwalk is closed for major construction and renovations.

North of the gorge, the Guadalhorce has been dammed to form a series of scenic reservoirs surrounded by piney hills, which constitute the **Parque de Ardales** nature area. Informal, open-air restaurants overlook the lakes and a number of picnic spots. Driving along the southern shore of the lake, you reach Ardales and, turning onto A357, the old spa town of **Carratraca.** Once a favorite watering hole for both Spanish and foreign aristocracy, it has a Moorish-style *ayuntamiento* (town hall) and an unusual **polygonal bullring.** Carratraca's old hotel, the **Hostal del Príncipe,** once sheltered Empress Eugénie, wife of Napoléon III; Lord Byron also came seeking the cure. The splendid Roman-style marble-and-tile **bathhouse** has benefited from extensive restoration.

TORREMOLINOS

㉑ *11 km (7 mi) west of Málaga, 16 km (10 mi) northeast of Fuengirola, 43 km (27 mi) east of Marbella.*

Torremolinos is all about fun in the sun. It may be more subdued than it was in the action-packed '60s and '70s, but scantily attired northern Europeans of all ages still jam its streets in season, shopping for bargains on Calle San Miguel, downing sangría in the bars of La Nogalera, and congregating in the karaoke bars and English pubs. By day, the sunseekers flock to the beaches El Bajondillo and La Carihuela, where, in high summer, it's hard to find towel space on the sand.

Torremolinos has two sections. The first, **Central Torremolinos,** is built around the Plaza Costa del Sol; Calle San Miguel, the main shopping street; and the brash Nogalera Plaza, which is full of overpriced bars and restaurants. The Pueblo Blanco area, off Calle Casablanca, is more pleasant; and the Cuesta del Tajo, at the far end of Calle San Miguel, winds down a steep slope to Bajondillo Beach. Here, crumbling walls, bougainvillea-clad patios, and old cottages hint at the quiet fishing village of bygone years. The second, much nicer, section of Torremolinos is **La Carihuela.** (To find it, head west out of town on Avenida Carlota Alessandri and turn left following the signs.) Far more authentically Spanish, the Carihuela still has a few fishermen's cottages and excellent seafood restaurants. The traffic-free esplanade makes for a pleasurable stroll, especially on a summer evening or Sunday at lunchtime, when it's packed with Spanish families.

☾ Just inland on the Churriana road, **Senda** bird park, botanical garden, and minizoo opened in 2005 in former historical gardens. Exhibits include an aquarium, reptile enclosure, and plenty of exotic birds, all viewed in a lush tropical setting. ✉ *Ctra. Coín, Km 88, Churriana* ☎ *952/623540* ⊕ *www.sendaelretiro.com* ✆ *€20* ☾ *May–Sept., daily 10–10; Oct.–Apr., daily 10–6.*

WHERE TO STAY & EAT

$$$ ✕ **Med.** Med is tucked away around
★ the corner from the car-free San
Miguel. An elevator whisks you
up to an elegant restaurant with
wooden beams, a blue-and-white
nautical setting, seamless Medi-
terranean views, and impeccable
service. The beautifully presented
food is from a menu (written in
Spanish) that changes every six
months, with dishes such as *solo-*

<table>
<tr><td>

SAVE YOUR
SWEET TOOTH

In seafood restaurants here, the
desserts tend to be disappoint-
ing: frozen, commercially made,
and overpriced. Skip dessert and
enjoy an ice-cream cone on the
beach instead.

</td></tr>
</table>

millo de ternero con setas, patata machacona y tempura de verduras
(braised veal with oyster mushrooms, creamed potatoes, and vegetable
tempura) followed by *sorbete de limón o mandarina con cava* (lemon
or orange sorbet with champagne). There's also an excellent wine
selection. ⊠ *Las Mercedes 12* ☎ *952/058830* ⌚ *Reservations essen-*
tial ⊟ *AE, DC, MC, V.*

$$ ✕ **Casa Juan.** This restaurant is an institution among malagueño
families, who flock here on weekends to sample the legendary
fresh seafood. Try for a table on the square overlooking the mer-
maid fountain. This is a good place to indulge in *fritura malagueña*
(fried seafood) or *arroz marinera* (seafood with rice), another specialty. ⊠ *Plaza San Gines, La Carihuela* ☎ *952/373512* ⊟ *MC, V*
☺ *Closed Mon.*

$ ✕ **Matahambre.** Opened in mid-2005, this restaurant has a stylish yet
rustic feel, with brick barrel-vault ceiling, terra-cotta tiles, and walls
washed in dark ocher and sky blue. There are outside tables on the
Plaza del Panorama—aptly named, as the views of the coast from here
are stunning. The affordable restaurant takes its wines seriously, with
more than 80 reds to choose from. To accompany your tipple choose
from dishes such as *carpaccio de salmón y espinacas con vinagreta*
pesto (carpaccio of salmon and spinach with pesto vinaigrette), or, for
lightweights, goat-cheese salad with bacon and walnuts. ⊠ *Las Mer-*
cedes 14 ☎ *952/381242* ⊟ *MC, V* ☺ *Closed Mon.*

$$$ ⌂ **Don Pedro.** Extremely comfortable and well maintained, this three-
story hotel was built in traditional low-rise Andalusian-style with
ocher-painted walls. The rooms are spacious and have balconies;
sea views get snapped up fast. The bodega-style bar gets popular at
happy hour; nightly entertainment there includes flamenco shows.
The hearty breakfast buffet should set you up for the day. ⊠ *Av. del*
Lido, 29620 ☎ *952/386844* 🖷 *952/386935* ⊕ *www.solmelia.com*
⌸ *524 rooms* ⌂ *In-hotel: restaurant, pools, beachfront* ⊟ *AE, DC,*
MC, V ⍱ *BP.*

$$$ ⌂ **Tropicana.** On the beach at the far end of the Carihuela, in one of
the most pleasant parts of Torremolinos, you'll find this low-rise resort
hotel, which has its own beach club. A tropical theme runs throughout, from the purple passion-flower climbers covering the brickwork to
the common areas, with exotic plants, raffia floor mats, and bamboo
furniture, to the rooms, with their warm color schemes complemented

2

by lashings of white linen. The hotel has a friendly, homey feel that keeps many guests returning year after year. ⊠*Trópico 6, La Cari-huela, 29620* ☎*952/386600* ⊟*952/380568* ⊕*www.hoteltropicana.es* ⇆*84 rooms* ♿*In-room: refrigerator. In-hotel: restaurant, bar, pool, public Wi-Fi, beach* ☰*AE, DC, MC, V* ⊚|*BP.*

$$ 🏨 **Miami.** Something of a find, this small hotel dates from 1950, when it was designed by Manolo Blascos, Picasso's cousin, for the well-known flamenco Gypsy dancer Lola Medina. Rooms are individually furnished, if a little dated, and there's a sitting area with a TV, cozy fireplace, and small library. The inn is surrounded by a shady garden west of the Cari-huela, making a stay here like visiting a private Spanish home. Reserve ahead. ⊠*Aladino 14, at C. Miami, 29620* ☎*952/385255* ⊕*www.residencia-miami.com* ⇆*26 rooms* ♿*In-room: no TV. In-hotel: bar, pool, some pets allowed* ☰*No credit cards* ⊚|*CP.*

$ 🏨 **Cabello.** The rooms at this small hotel have few frills, but most have impressive sea views—it's just a block from the beach, in La Carihuela. Near the ground-floor bar is a comfortable sitting area, with overstuffed chairs, a piano, and a pool table. The owners are friendly and helpful, though they speak only Spanish. ⊠*Calle Chiriva 28, 29620* ☎*952/384505* ⇆*19 rooms* ♿*In-hotel: bar, no elevator* ☰*No credit cards.*

NIGHTLIFE & THE ARTS

Most nocturnal action is in the center of town. Many of the better hotels stage flamenco shows, but you may also want to check out the **Taberna Flamenca Pepe López** (⊠*Pl. de la Gamba Alegre* ☎*952/381284*). There are nightly shows at 10 PM from April to October. The rest of the year shows are on weekends only.

BENALMÁDENA

㉒ *9 km (5½ mi) west of Torremolinos, 9 km (5½ mi) east of Mijas.*

★ **Benalmádena-Pueblo,** the village proper, is on the mountainside 7 km (4 mi) from the coast. It is surprisingly unspoiled and offers a glimpse of the old Andalusia. **Benalmádena-Costa,** the beach resort, is practically an extension of Torremolinos; it is run almost exclusively by package-tour operators, however the marina does have shops, restaurants, and bars aimed at a sophisticated clientele that may appeal to the independent traveler.

In Benalmádena-Costa's marina, **Sea Life Benalmádena** is an above-average aquarium with fish from local waters, including rays, sharks, and sunfish. Adjacent is a pirate-theme miniature golf course. ⊠€6 ⊠*Puerto Marina Benalmádena* ☎*952/560150* ⊕*www.sealife.es* ⊠€10.95 ⊙*May–Sept., daily 10* AM*–midnight; Oct.–Apr., daily 10–6.*

Ⓒ The Costa del Sol's leading amusement park is **Tivoli World,** with rides, Wild West shows, and 40-odd restaurants and snack bars. A 4,000-seat, open-air auditorium showcases international stars alongside can-can, flamenco, and Spanish ballet performances. Take a cable car to the top of Calamorro Mountain for hiking trails. ✉ *Av. Tivoli s/n, Arroyo de la Miel* ☎ *952/7577016* 🌐 *www.tivoli.es* 🎫 *€6, Sun. 11–2* ⏲ *May–Sept., daily 1 PM–1 AM; Oct.–Apr., weekends noon–8.*

WHERE TO STAY & EAT

$$$–$$$$ ✕ **Mar de Alborán.** Next to the yacht harbor, this restaurant has a touch more class than most of its peers, including a decent wine list. Fish dishes, such as the Basque-inspired *lomo de merluza con kokotxas y almejas* (hake stew with clams) or *bacalao al pil-pil* (salted cod in a spicy sauce) can be a welcome switch from standard Costa fare. ✉ *Av. de Alay 5* ☎ *952/446427* 💳 *AE, MC, V* ⏲ *Closed Mon. mid-Dec.–mid-Jan. No dinner Sun.*

$–$$ ✕ **Casa Fidel.** This Benalmádena-Pueblo restaurant is in a typical Andalusian house complete with arches, terra-cotta tiles, a large fireplace, and a small leafy patio. For a starter, try *crema fría de aguacate con salmón marinado* (cold avocado soup with marinated salmon) or *ensalada templada de setas y gambas* (warm salad with shrimp and wild mushrooms). Main courses include *langostinos con chalotas y puré de garbanzos* (king prawns with shallots and garbanzos) and T-bone steak for two. ✉ *Maestra Ayala 1* ☎ *952/449165* 💳 *AE, DC, MC, V* ⏲ *Closed Tues. and Aug. 1–15. No lunch Wed.*

$–$$ ★ ✕ **Ventorillo de la Perra.** If you've been scouring the coast for something typically Spanish, you may find it at this old inn, which dates from 1785. Outside, there's a leafy patio; inside is a cozy dining room and bar with hams hanging from the ceiling. Choose between local Malagueño cooking, including *gazpacuelo malagueño* (a warm gazpacho of potatoes, rice, and shrimp), and typical Spanish food, such as *conejo en salsa de almendras* (rabbit in almond sauce). The *ajo blanco* (a cold, garlicky almond-based soup) is particularly good. ✉ *Av. Constitución 115, Km 13, Arroyo de la Miel* ☎ *952/441966* 💳 *AE, DC, MC, V* ⏲ *Closed Mon. and Nov.*

$$ 🏨 **La Fonda.** You'll find a true taste of Andalusia at this small hotel on one of the prettiest streets in the pueblo. Rooms have white walls, marble floors, and bright floral fabrics. Some rooms have peerless views of the coast and the Mediterranean; others look onto the cool interior patio shaded by palms. In the same building, under different management, is an excellent restaurant run by Málaga's official hotel school; it's open for lunch on weekdays. ✉ *Santo Domingo 7, 29639* ☎ *952/568324* 📠 *952/568273* 🌐 *www.fondahotel.com* 🛏 *26 rooms* 👍 *In-hotel: bar, pool* 💳 *AE, DC, MC, V* 🍽 *BP.*

NIGHTLIFE

For discos, piano bars, and karaoke, head for the port. The **Fortuna Nightclub** in the **Casino Torrequebrada** (✉ *Av. del Sol s/n, Benalmádena-Costa* ☎ *952/446000* 🌐 *www.torrequebrada.com*) has flamenco and an international dance show with a live orchestra, starting at 10:30 PM. A passport, jacket, and tie are required in the casino, open daily 9 PM–4 AM.

FUENGIROLA

❷③ *16 km (10 mi) west of Torremolinos, 27 km (17 mi) east of Marbella.*

Fuengirola is less frenetic than Torremolinos. Many of its waterfront high-rises are vacation apartments that cater to budget-minded sun-seekers from northern Europe and, in summer, a large contingent from Córdoba and other parts of Spain. The town is also a haven for British retirees (with plenty of English and Irish pubs to serve them) and a shopping and business center for the rest of the Costa del Sol. Its Tuesday market is the largest on the coast, and a major tourist attraction.

The most prominent landmark in Fuengirola is **Castillo de Sohail**. The original structure dates from the 12th century, but the castle served as a military fortress until the early 19th century. Just west of town, the castle makes a dramatic performance venue for the annual summer season of music and dance. *⌧€1.30 ☉Tues.–Sun. 10–3.*

WHERE TO STAY & EAT

$$–$$$
Fodor'sChoice
★
✕**Guy Massey.** A celebrated chef from the United Kingdom, Guy Massey took over the helm of the acclaimed Patrick Bausier restaurant in fall 2006 and renamed it to reflect that change. The menu continues to be French-inspired. Starters include crab salad and vegetable soup with crispy beetroot. Main dishes like roast pheasant, Barbary duck, and turbot follow. The salmon and goat's cheese salad garnished with pomegranate seeds comes particularly recommended. There's complimentary champagne and hors d'oeuvres. *⌧Rotondade la Luna 1, Pueblo López ☎952/585120 ⌲Reservations essential ▤AE, MC, V ☉Closed Sun. No lunch.*

$–$$
✕**Bistro.** This restaurant is in the most charming part of Fuengirola, a neighborhood with low-rise buildings punctuated by the occasional fisherman's cottage. With a series of pine-clad rooms, the Bistro has a loyal following of foreign residents, who come for the reliably good food and reasonable prices. The cuisine caters to international palates with such dishes as chicken salad with Philadelphia cheese sauce, crepes stuffed with spinach, and fillet steak with a choice of sauces. The bow-tied waiters are charming and efficient. *⌧Calle Palangreros 30 ☎952/477701 ▤MC, V ☉Closed Sun.*

$–$$
✕**Mo Mo.** Tucked down a side street, this gem of a restaurant has a vegetarian menu that changes daily. Among the choices you might find are moussaka, tofu kebabs, and lentil and coriander patties. The soothing classical music combined with a pine interior and contemporary art for sale results in a mellow dining experience. There are additional tables outside on the attractive pedestrian street. *⌧Calle Marbella 8 ☎952/197321 ▤MC, V ☉Closed Sun. and Mon. dinner.*

$$
☷**Villa de Laredo.** At the quieter end of the promenade, just a Frisbee throw from the beach, this hotel has a mildy scuffed, old-fashioned feel, but it is excellently priced given the location and facilities. The rooms are washed in pale cream and have striped Regency-style fabrics. There are small terraces with sea views. Its restaurant ($–$$) offers an aquarium of catch-of-the-day options to choose from. *⌧Paseo Marítimo 42, Rey de España, 29640 ☎952/477689 ⎙952/477950 ⊕www.hotelvilladelaredo.com*

2

🗗*50 rooms* 🛏*In-room: dial-up. In-hotel: restaurant, pool* ▤*AE, DC, MC, V.*

$ ⍐ **Hostal Italia.** Right off the main plaza and near the beach, this small, family-run hotel is deservedly popular. People come here year after year, particularly during the October *feria*. The rooms are small yet comfy, and nearly all have balconies. There's a larger sun terrace for catching the rays. ✉*C. de la Cruz 1, 29640* ☎*952/474193* 🖷*952/461909* ⊕*www.hostal-italia.com* 🗗*40 rooms* ▤*MC, V.*

NIGHTLIFE & THE ARTS

Amateur local troupes regularly stage plays and musicals in English at the **Salón de Variétés Theater** (✉*Emancipación 30* ☎*952/474542*). For concerts—from classical to rock to jazz—check out the modern **Palacio de la Paz** (✉*Recinto Ferial, Av. Jesús Santo Rein* ☎*952/589349*) between Los Boliches and the town center.

MIJAS

24 *8 km (5 mi) north of Fuengirola, 18 km (11 mi) west of Torremolinos.*
★

Mijas is in the foothills of the sierra just north of the coast. Buses leave Fuengirola every half hour for the 20-minute drive through hills peppered with villas. If you have a car and don't mind a mildly hair-raising drive, take the more dramatic approach from Benalmádena-Pueblo, a winding mountain road with splendid views. Mijas was discovered long ago by foreign retirees, and though the large, touristy square may look like an extension of the Costa, beyond this are hilly residential streets with time-worn homes. Try to arrive late in the afternoon, after the tour buses have left. Park in the underground parking garage signposted on the approach to the village. The **Museo Mijas** occupies the former town hall. Themed rooms, including an old-fashioned bakery and bodega, surround a patio. Regular art exhibitions are mounted in the upstairs gallery. ✉*Plaza de la Libertad* ☎*952/590380* 🎟*Free* ⊙*Daily 10–2 and 5–8.*

Bullfights take place year-round, usually on Sunday at 4:30 PM, at Mijas's tiny **bullring.** One of the few square bullrings in Spain, it's off the Plaza Constitución—Mijas's old village square—and up the slope beside the Mirlo Blanco restaurant. ✉*Pl. Constitución* ☎*952/485248* 🎟*Museum entrance fee, €3* ⊙*June–Sept., daily 10–10; Oct.–Feb., daily 9:30–7; Mar., daily 10–7:30; Apr. and May, daily 10–8:30.*

Worth a visit is the delightful village church **Iglesia Parroquial de la Inmaculada Concepción** *(The Immaculate Conception).* It's impeccably decorated, especially at Easter, and the terrace and spacious gardens have a splendid panoramic view. The church is up the hill from the Mijas bullring. ✉*Pl. Constitución.*

NEED A BREAK?   **The Bar Porras** on Plaza de la Libertad (at the base of Calle San Sebastián—the most photographed street in the village) attracts a regular crowd of crusty locals with its good-value tasty tapas.

Mijas extends down to the coast, and the coastal strip between Fuengirola and Marbella is officially called **Mijas-Costa**. This area has several hotels, restaurants, and golf courses.

WHERE TO STAY & EAT

$$$–$$$$ ✕ **El Padrastro.** Perched on a cliff above the Plaza Virgen de la Peña, "The Stepfather" is accessible by an elevator from the square or, if you're energetic, by stairs. A view over Fuengirola and the coast is the restaurant's main draw. Dishes might include *lubina cocida con ragout de alcachofa y mantequilla al limón* (sea bass cooked with ragout of artichokes and lemon butter). When the weather's right, you can dine alfresco on the large terrace. ⊠ *Paseo del Compás 22* ☎ *952/485000* ⊟ *AE, DC, MC, V.*

$$$ ✕ **Mirlo Blanco.** In an old house on the pleasant Plaza de la Constitución, with a terrace for outdoor dining, this place is run by a Basque family that has been in the Costa del Sol restaurant business for decades. Good choices here are such Basque specialties as *txangurro* (spider crab) and *kokotxas de bacalau* (cod cheeks). ⊠ *Pl. de la Constitución 2* ☎ *952/485700* ⊟ *AE, MC, V* ☉ *Closed Jan.*

$$–$$$ ✕ **Valparaíso.** Halfway up the road from Fuengirola to Mijas, this sprawling villa stands in its own garden, complete with swimming pool. There's live music nightly ranging from flamenco to opera and jazz. Valparaíso is a favorite among local (mainly British) expatriates, some of whom come in full evening dress to celebrate their birthdays. In winter, logs burn in a cozy fireplace. Try the *pato a la naranja* (duck in orange sauce). ⊠ *Ctra. de Mijas–Fuengirola, Km 4* ☎ *952/485996* ⊟ *AE, DC, MC, V* ☉ *No dinner Sun. No lunch Oct.–June.*

$$$$ ✕⌂ **Gran Hotel Guadalpin Byblos.** On the edge of Mijas's golf course
★ (closer to Fuengirola than to Mijas) and in a huge garden of palms, cypresses, and fountains, this is one of the most exclusive hotels on the Costa del Sol. It's primarily a spa known for its thalassotherapy, a skin treatment using seawater and seaweed, which is applied in a Roman-like temple of cool, white-and-blue marble tiles. Three outstanding restaurants ($$$–$$$$) serve savory regional and international dishes. The menu changes according to season but may include such gourmet delights as roast duck breast flambéed with Jerez brandy. Check the Web site for reduced-price package deals. ⊠ *Urbanización Mijas-Golf, Mijas-Costa, 29640* ☎ *952/473050* ⊟ *952/476783* ⊕ *www.byblos-andaluz.com* ⤣ *109 rooms, 35 suites* ⌂ *In-room: Ethernet. In-hotel: 3 restaurants, bars, golf courses, tennis courts, pools, gym, spa, public Internet, public Wi-Fi, some pets allowed* ⊟ *AE, DC, MC, V* ⫾⎮ *BP.*

$$$ ⌂ **Beach House.** The epitomé of cool Mediterranean-inspired decor, the
Fodor'sChoice Beach House seems not so much like a hotel, but rather like a sumptu-
★ ous villa owned by a hospitable (and wealthy) friend. From the pleasing viewpoint of the bougainvillea-draped bar, the pool merges seamlessly with the sea. The interior is all clean lines, sparkling marble, and minimalist good taste. The town and restaurants of Fuengirola are 10 minutes due east on N340. ⊠ *Urbanización El Chaparral, CN340, Km 203, 19648* ☎ *952/494540* ⊕ *www.beachhouse.nu* ⤣ *10 rooms* ⌂ *In-room: Ethernet. In-hotel: pool, no elevator* ⊟ *MC, V* ⫾⎮ *CP.*

$$ ⊞ **TRH Mijas.** It's easy to unwind here, thanks to the poolside restaurant and bar, and the gardens with views of the hillsides stretching down to Fuengirola and the sea. The tasteful decor is marked by marble floors throughout, wrought-iron window grilles, and wooden shutters. The lobby is large and airy, and there's an attractive glass-roof terrace. All rooms are well furnished, with wood fittings and marble floors. TRH Mijas is at the entrance to Mijas village. ☒ *Urbanización Tamisa, 29650* ☎*952/485800* 📠*952/485825* ⊕*www.trhhoteles.es* ⇆*204 rooms, 2 suites* ⚒*In-room: dial-up. In-hotel: restaurant, tennis court, pool, gym* ⊟*AE, DC, MC, V.*

MARBELLA

㉕ *27 km (17 mi) west of Fuengirola, 28 km (17 mi) east of Estepona, 50 km (31 mi) southeast of Ronda.*

Playground of the rich and home of movie stars, rock musicians, and dispossessed royal families, Marbella has attained the top rung on Europe's social ladder. Dip into any Spanish gossip magazine and chances are the glittering parties that fill its pages are set in Marbella. Much of this action takes place on the fringes—grand hotels and luxury restaurants line the waterfront for 20 km (12 mi) on each side of the town center. In the town itself, you may well wonder how Marbella became so famous. The main thoroughfare, Avenida Ricardo Soriano, is distinctly charmless, and the Paseo Marítimo, though pleasant enough, with a mix of seafood restaurants and pizzerias overlooking an ordinary beach, is far from spectacular.

Marbella's appeal lies in the heart of the **old village,** which remains miraculously intact. Here, a block or two back from the main highway, narrow alleys of whitewashed houses cluster around the central **Plaza de los Naranjos** (Orange Square), where colorful, albeit pricey, restaurants vie for space under the orange trees. Climb onto what remains of the old fortifications and stroll along the Calle Virgen de los Dolores to the Plaza de Santo Cristo.

The **Museo del Grabado Español Contemporáneo,** in a restored 16th-century palace in the heart of the old town, has contemporary Spanish prints and temporary exhibitions. ☒*Hospital Bazán* ☎*952/765741* ⊕*www. museodelgrabado.com* 🎫*€2.50* ⊙*Tues.–Sat. 10–2 and 5:30–8:30.*

In a modern building just east of Marbella's old quarter, the **Museo de Bonsai** has a collection of miniature trees, including a 300-year-old olive tree from China. ☒*Parque Arroyo de la Repesa, Av. Dr. Maiz Viñal* ☎*952/862926* 🎫*€3* ⊙*June–Sept., daily 10:30–1:30 and 5–8:30; Oct.–May., daily 10:30–1:30 and 4–7.*

Marbella's wealth glitters most brightly along the Golden Mile, a tiara of star-studded clubs, restaurants, and hotels west of town stretching from Marbella to **Puerto Banús.** Here, a mosque, Arab banks, and the onetime residence of Saudi Arabia's King Fahd betray the influence of oil money in this wealthy enclave. About 7 km (4½ mi) west of central Marbella (between Km 175 and Km 174), a sign indicates the turnoff

2

leading down to Puerto Banús. Though now hemmed in by a belt of high-rises, Marbella's plush marina, with 915 berths, is a gem of ostentatious wealth, a Spanish answer to St. Tropez. Huge and flashy yachts, beautiful people, and countless expensive stores and restaurants make up the glittering parade that marches long into the night. The backdrop is an Andalusian pueblo—built in the 1960s to resemble the fishing villages that once lined this coast.

WHERE TO STAY & EAT

$$$–$$$$ ✕**La Hacienda.** In a large, pleasant villa 12 km (7 mi) east of Marbella, the Hacienda was founded in the early '70s by the late Belgian chef Paul Schiff, who helped transform the Costa del Sol culinary scene with his modern approach and judicious use of local ingredients. His legacy lives on here through his family. Schiff's signature dish, *pintada con pasas al vino de Málaga* (guinea fowl with raisins in Málaga wine sauce), is often available. ✉*Urbanización Las Chapas, N340, Km 193* ☎*952/831267* ✍*Reservations essential* ▤*AE, MC, V* ✪*Closed Mon. and Tues. mid-Nov.–mid-Dec. No lunch July and Aug.*

$$$–$$$$ ✕**Santiago.** Facing the seafront promenade, this busy place has long been considered the best fish restaurant in Marbella. Try the *ensalada de langosta* (lobster salad), followed by *besugo al horno* (baked red bream). The menu also has roasts, such as *cochinillo* (pig) and *cordero* (lamb) of the owner's native Castile. Around the corner from the original restaurant (and sharing the same phone number) is Santiago's popular tapas bar. ✉*Paseo Marítimo 5* ☎*952/770078* ▤*AE, DC, MC, V* ✪*Closed Nov.*

$$–$$$ ✕**Aquavit.** Cream-and-yellow paintwork, titanium cutlery, and handcrafted tables provide a sunny, snazzy look. Asian-style starters include nori rolls, Thai fish cakes, and fresh arugula salad; the signature dish just has to be the potato-and-anchovy gratin with a shot of (what else?) chilled aquavit. More than 35 different vodkas are available, as well as some unusual wines and liqueurs. ✉*Plaza del Puerto, Puerto Banús* ☎*952/819127* ▤*AE, MC, V* ✪*No lunch.*

$$–$$$ ✕**La Comedia.** This Swedish-run restaurant is on one of the old town's most traditional Andalusian plazas and has one of the most imaginative menus among Marbella's 600-plus restaurants. Starters include such delights as blue mussel carpaccio topped with grilled scallops and truffles. Entrées include avocado-and-salmon spring rolls with mango and marie rose sauce (a thousand island–style dressing) and tandoori sweet curried chicken. For dessert there's an unusual deep-fried apple-cinnamon wonton with vanilla and white chocolate mousse. ✉*Plaza de la Victoria* ☎*952/776478* ✍*Reservations essential* ▤*AE, DC, MC, V* ✪*Closed Mon. No lunch.*

$$–$$$
Fodor'sChoice
★

✕**Zozoi.** Tucked into the corner of one of the town's squares, upbeat, art deco Zozoi receives rave reviews from the local press. The fashionably Mediterranean menu makes little distinction between starters and main courses; all the portions are generous. Imaginative use of ingredients is shown in such dishes as grilled fillet of sea bass with saffron fettucini and green asparagus, and roasted duck breast with black cherries and pepper. For dessert, try the red forest fruits with *mille feuilles* (puff pastry) or lemon sorbet spiked with vodka. ⊠*Plaza Altamirano 1* ☎*952/858868* ⚐*Reservations essential* ▭*MC, V.*

$$$$
Fodor'sChoice
★
✕⊞ **Marbella Club.** The grande dame of Marbella hotels was a creation of the late Alfonso von Hohenlohe, a Mexican-Austrian aristocrat who turned Marbella into a playground for the rich and famous. The exquisite grounds have lofty palm trees, dazzling flower beds, and a beachside tropical pool area. The bungalow-style rooms vary in size; some have private pools. The main restaurant has a classy eclectic menu of modern Mediterranean cuisine. If you can't afford to stay, at least stop by for afternoon tea, served daily 4–6:30, with a selection of finger sandwiches, pastries, and strawberries and cream (in summer). ⊠*Blvd. Principe Alfonso von Hohenlohe at Ctra. de Cádiz, Km 178, 3 km (2 mi) west of Marbella, 29600* ☎*952/822211* ⛶*952/829884* ⊕*www. marbellaclub.com* ⬐*84 rooms, 37 suites, 16 bungalows* ⚐*In-room: Ethernet, dial-up, Wi-Fi. In-hotel: 3 restaurants, pools, gym, public Internet, parking (no fee)* ▭*AE, DC, MC, V* ⃝|*BP.*

$$$$
★
✕⊞ **Puente Romano.** West of Marbella, between the Marbella Club and Puerto Banús, is this palatial hotel designed like an Andalusian pueblo, complete with gardens and trickling fountains. As the name suggests, there's a genuine Roman bridge on the grounds running right down to the beach. There are four restaurants, including El Puente, and Roberto; the latter serves Italian food in the hotel's beach club, a popular summer nightlife venue. In summer there's a beachfront *chiringuito* (seafood restaurant), where you can sample fresh fish. ⊠*Ctra. Cádiz, Km 177, 29600* ☎*952/820900* ⛶*952/775766* ⊕*www.puenteromano.com* ⬐*149 rooms, 77 suites* ⚐*In-room: Wi-Fi. In-hotel: 4 restaurants, tennis courts, pools* ▭*AE, DC, MC, V* ⃝|*BP.*

$$$
Fodor'sChoice
★
⊞ **The Town House.** In a choice location in one of old town Marbella's prettiest squares, this former family house has been exquisitely transformed into a boutique hotel. A combination of antiques and modern fittings make for luxurious rooms, accentuated by earthy colors. The spacious bathrooms are decked out in shiny marble with plenty of complimentary suds to encourage pampering. There is an attractive bar and plenty of restaurants nearby. ⊠*C. Alderete 7, Plaza Tetuan, 29600* ☎*952/901791* ⊕*www.townhouse.nu* ⬐*9 rooms* ⚐*In-hotel: bar, no elevator* ▭*MC, V.*

$$
⊞ **Lima.** Here's a good midrange option in downtown Marbella, two blocks from the beach. The tastefully decorated rooms have dark-wood furniture, bright floral bedspreads, and balconies; corner rooms are the largest. Underground parking is available for a fee. ⊠*Av. Antonio Belón 2, 29600* ☎*952/770500* ⛶*952/863091* ⊕*www.hotellimamarbella.com* ⬐*64 rooms* ⚐*In-hotel: parking (fee)* ▭*AE, DC, MC, V.*

¢
⊞ **Juan.** On a quiet street, this no-frills cheapie with a small courtyard is a short stroll from the beach and Marbella's historic center. Because the rooms have refrigerators, this is a good place if you're economizing on eating out. ⊠*Calle Luna 18, 29600* ☎*952/779475* ⬐*4 rooms* ⚐*In-room: no a/c, refrigerator, no elevator* ▭*No credit cards* ⃝|*EP.*

NIGHTLIFE & THE ARTS

Art exhibits are held in private galleries and in several of Marbella's leading hotels, notably the Puente Romano. The **tourist office** (⊠ *Glorieta de la Fontanilla* ☎ *952/822818* ⊕ *www.pgb.es/marbella*) can provide a map of town and monthly calendar of exhibits and events.

Much of the nighttime action revolves around the **Puerto Banús**, in such bars as Sinatra's and Joy's Bar. Marbella's most famous nightspot is the **Olivia Valére disco** (⊠ *Ctra. de Istán, Km 0.8* ☎ *952/828861*), decorated to resemble a Moorish palace; head inland from the town's mosque (an easy-to-spot landmark).

FodorsChoice
★

The trendy **Dreamers** (⊠ *CN 340 km, Puerto Banús* ☎ *952/812080*) attracts a young, streetwise crowd with its live bands, go-go girls, and a massive dance space. The **Casino Nueva Andalucía** (⊠ *Bajos Hotel Andalucía Pl., N340* ☎ *952/814000*), open 8 PM to 6 AM May through October (until 5 AM November through April), is a chic gambling spot in the Hotel Andalucía Plaza, just west of Puerto Banús. Jacket and tie are required for men, and passports for all. In the center of Marbella, **Ana María** (⊠ *Pl. de Santo Cristo 5* ☎ *952/775646*) is a popular flamenco venue but open only from May to September.

OJÉN

㉖ *10 km (6 mi) north of Marbella.*

For a contrast to the glamour of the coast, drive up to Ojén, in the hills above Marbella. Take note of the beautiful pottery and, if you're here the first week in August, don't miss the **Fiesta de Flamenco,** which attracts some of Spain's most respected flamenco names, including the Juan Peña El Lebrijano, Chiquetete, and El Cabrero. Four kilometers (2½ mi) from Ojén is the **Refugio del Juanar,** a former hunting lodge in the heart of the Sierra Blanca, at the southern edge of the Serranía de Ronda, a mountainous wilderness. Not far from the Refugio, you might spot the wild ibex that dwell among the rocky crags; the best times to watch are dawn and dusk, when they descend from their hiding places. A bumpy trail takes you a mile from the Refugio to the **Mirador** (lookout), with a sweeping view of the Costa del Sol and the coast of northern Africa.

WHERE TO STAY & EAT

$$$ ✕⌂ **Castillo de Monda.** Designed to resemble a castle, this hotel incorporates the ruins of Monda's Moorish fortress, some of which date back to the 8th century. The interior is decorated with ceramic tiles, elaborate arches, and extensive use of Moorish-style stucco bas-relief. The guest rooms are sumptuous and fun, with four-poster beds, marble heated bathroom floors, and colorful fabrics. The main restaurant ($$–$$$), which resembles a medieval banquet hall, has terrific views of the surrounding countryside. There are weeklong relaxation skills courses available. ⊠ *Monda, 29110* ☎ *952/457142* 🖷 *952/457336* ⊕ *www. mondacastle.com* ⤳ *17 rooms, 6 suites* ⚲ *In-room: dial-up. In-hotel: restaurant, bar, pool, public Wi-Fi* ▤ *AE, MC, V.*

$$-$$$ ✕▦ **Refugio del Juanar.** Once an aristocratic hunting lodge (King Alfonso XIII came here), this secluded hotel and restaurant was sold to its staff in 1984 for the symbolic sum of 1 peseta. The hunting theme prevails, both in the common areas—where a log fire roars in winter—and on the restaurant menu, where game is emphasized. The rooms are simply decorated in a rustic style, and six (including the three suites) have their own fireplace. ✉*Sierra Blanca s/n, 29610* ☎☎952/881000 ⊕*www. juanar.com* ⇌*23 rooms, 3 suites* ♿*In-hotel: restaurant, tennis court, pool* ▭*AE, DC, MC, V.*

RONDA

❷⁷ *61 km (38 mi) northwest of Marbella, 108 km (67 mi) southwest of*
Fodor's Choice *Antequera (via Pizarra).*
★

Ronda, one of the oldest towns in Spain, is known for its spectacular position and views. Secure in its mountain fastness on a rock high over the River Guadalevín, the town was a stronghold for the legendary Andalusian bandits who held court here from the 18th to early 20th century. Ronda's most dramatic element is its ravine (360 feet deep and 210 feet across)—known as **El Tajo**—which divides La Ciudad, the old Moorish town, from El Mercadillo, the "new town," which sprang up after the Christian Reconquest of 1485. Tour buses roll in daily with sightseers from the coast 49 km (30 mi) away, and on weekends affluent Sevillanos flock to their second homes here. Stay overnight midweek to see this noble town's true colors.

The most attractive approach is from the south. The winding but well-maintained A376 from San Pedro de Alcántara travels north up through the mountains of the Serranía de Ronda. Take the first turnoff to Ronda from A376. Entering the lowest part of town, known as El Barrio, you can see parts of the old walls, including the 13th-century Puerta de Almocobar and the 16th-century Puerta de Carlos V gates. The road climbs past the Iglesia del Espíritu Santo (Church of the Holy Spirit) and up into the heart of town.

WHAT TO SEE

Begin in El Mercadillo, where the **tourist office** (✉*Paseo de Bas Infante s/n* ☎*952/187119* ⊕*www.andalucia.org* ⊗ *Weekdays 9:30–6:30, weekends 10–2*) in the Plaza de España can supply you with a map.

Immediately south of the Plaza de España is Ronda's most famous bridge, the **Puente Nuevo** *(New Bridge)*, an architectural marvel built between 1755 and 1793. The bridge's lantern-lighted parapet offers dizzying views of the awesome gorge. Just how many people have met their ends here nobody knows, but the architect of the Puente Nuevo fell to his death while inspecting work on the bridge. During the civil war, hundreds of victims were hurled from it.

Cross the Puente Nuevo into **La Ciudad,** the old Moorish town, and wander the twisting streets of white houses with birdcage balconies.

The so-called House of the Moorish King, **Casa del Rey Moro,** was actually built in 1709 on the site of an earlier Moorish residence. Despite the name and the *azulejo* (painted tile) plaque depicting a Moor on the facade, it's unlikely that Moorish rulers ever lived here. The garden has a great view of the gorge, and from here a stairway of some 365 steps, known as **La Mina,** descends to the river. However, the steps are steep and poorly lighted and should be tackled only by the agile. The house, across the Puente Nuevo on Calle Santo Domingo, is being converted into a luxury hotel due for completion in mid-2008, although you can visit the gardens and La Mina. ⊠*Calle Santo Domingo 17* ☎*952/187200* 🎟*€4* ⊙*May–Sept., daily 10–8; Oct.–Apr., daily 10–7.*

> ## PICASSO'S CUBES
>
> It's been suggested that Picasso, who was born in Málaga, was inspired to create cubism by the pueblos *blancos* of his youth. The story may or may not be apocryphal, but it's nonetheless easy to imagine—there *is* something wondrous and inspiring about Andalusia's whitewashed villages, with their dwellings that seem to tumble down the mountain slopes like giant dice. Perhaps it's the contrast in color: the bright white against the pine green. Or perhaps the mountaintop isolation: at these altitudes, the morning light breaks silently over the slopes, the only movement a far-off shepherd guiding his flock.

The excavated remains of the **Baños Arabes** *(Arab Baths)* date from Ronda's tenure as capital of a Moorish *taifa* (kingdom). The star-shape vents in the roof are an inferior imitation of the ceiling of the beautiful bathhouse in Granada's Alhambra. The baths are beneath the Puente Arabe (Arab Bridge) in a ravine below the Palacio del Marqués de Salvatierra. 🎟*€2* ⊙*Weekdays 10–6, weekends 10–3.*

The collegiate church of **Santa María la Mayor,** which serves as Ronda's cathedral, has roots in Moorish times: originally the Great Mosque of Ronda, the tower and adjacent galleries, built for viewing festivities in the square, retain their Islamic design. After the mosque was destroyed (when the Moors were overthrown), it was rebuilt as a church and dedicated to the Virgen de la Encarnacion after the Reconquest. The naves are late Gothic, and the main altar is heavy with baroque gold leaf. The church is around the corner from the remains of a mosque, Minarete Árabe (Moorish Minaret) at the end of the Marqués de Salvatierra. ⊠*Pl. Duquesa de Parcent* 🎟*€2* ⊙*May–Sept., daily 10–8; Oct.–Apr., daily 10–6.*

A stone palace with twin Mudejar towers, the **Palacio de Mondragón** *(Palace of Mondragón)* was probably the residence of Ronda's Moorish kings. Ferdinand and Isabella appropriated it after their victory in 1485. Today you can wander through the patios, with their brick arches and delicate, Mudejar stucco tracery, and admire the mosaics and *artesonado* (coffered) ceiling. The second floor holds a small museum with archaeological items found near Ronda, plus the reproduction of a dolmen. ⊠*Plaza Mondragón* ☎*952/878450* 🎟*€2* ⊙*Apr.–Oct.,* *weekdays 10–6, weekends 10–3; May–Sept., weekdays 10–8, weekends 10–3.*

The main sight in Ronda's commercial center, El Mercadillo, is the **Plaza de Toros.** Pedro Romero (1754–1839), the father of modern bullfighting and Ronda's most famous native son, is said to have killed 5,600 bulls here during his long career. In the museum beneath the plaza you can see posters for Ronda's very first fights, held here in 1785. The plaza was once owned by the late bullfighter Antonio Ordóñez, on whose nearby ranch Orson Welles's ashes were scattered (as directed in his will)—indeed, the ring has become a favorite of filmmakers. Every September, the bullring is the scene of Ronda's *corridas goyescas,* named after Francisco Goya, whose bullfight sketches (*tauromaquias*) were inspired by the skill and art of Pedro Romero. Both participants and the dignitaries in the audience don the costumes of Goya's time for the occasion. Seats for these fights cost a small fortune and are booked far in advance. Other than that, the plaza is rarely used for fights except during Ronda's May festival and sometimes in September. ☎952/874132 ⚎€5 ⊙*Daily 10–6; May–Sept. 10–8*

WHERE TO STAY & EAT

$$$$ ✕**Tragabuches.** Málagueño chef Benito Goméz is famed for his dar-
★ ingly innovative menu. The *menú de degustación,* a taster's menu of five courses and two desserts, includes imaginative choices, such as a casserole of noodles with octopus sashimi and butter and white-garlic ice cream with pine nuts. Traditional and modern furnishings blend in the two dining rooms (one with a picture window). The restaurant is around the corner from Ronda's parador and the tourist office. You can purchase a cookbook at the restaurant that contains some of its best-loved dishes. ⊠*José Aparicio 1* ☎*952/190291* ⊟*AE, DC, MC, V* ⊙*Closed Mon. No dinner Sun.*

$$ ✕**Pedro Romero.** Named after the father of modern bullfighting, this restaurant opposite the bullring is packed with colorful bullfight paraphernalia. Mounted bull heads peer down at you as you tuck into the *sopa de la casa* (house soup, made with ham and eggs), *rabo de toro,* (oxtail) or *perdiz estofada con salsa de vino blanco y hierbas* (stewed partridge with white-wine-and-herb sauce), and, for dessert, *helado de higos con chocolate* (fig ice cream topped with house-made chocolate sauce). ⊠*Virgen de la Paz 18* ☎*952/871110* ⊟*AE, DC, MC, V.*

$$$ ✕⊡ **Ancinipo.** The artistic legacy of its former owners, Ronda artist Téllez Loriguillo and acclaimed Japanese watercolor painter Miki Haruta, is evidenced throughout this boutique hotel. The interior has exposed stone panels, steel-and-glass fittings, and mosaic-tile bathrooms—and many murals and paintings. There are dramatic mountain views from most of the rooms, and the Atrium restaurant ($$) dishes up such traditional favorites as *migas* (fried breadcrumbs with sausage and spices) and oxtail stew, followed by chestnuts with brandy and cream. ⊠*José Aparicio 7, 29400* ☎*952/161002* ⊕*www.hotelacinipo.com* ⇆*14 rooms* ⌂*In-room: Wi-Fi. In-hotel: restaurant, bar* ⊟*AE, DC, MC, V.*

2

$$$ ✕▦ **El Molino del Santo.** In the now-converted "Saint's Mill" next to a rushing stream near Benaoján, 10 km (7 mi) from Ronda, this British-run establishment was one of Andalusia's first country hotels. Guest rooms are arranged around a pleasant patio and come in different sizes, some with a terrace. This is a good base for walks in the mountains, and the hotel rents mountain bikes as well. There's also a small station nearby with trains to Ronda and other villages. The restaurant ($–$$) has an excellent reputation and offers vegetarian options. The hotel uses solar panels for hot water and the pool. ⊠ *Estación de Benaoján s/n, Benaoján, 29370* ☎ *952/167151* 🖷 *952/167327* ⊕ *www.andalucia.com/molino* 🗪 *18 rooms* ♿ *In-hotel: restaurant, pool, bicycles, no elevator* ⊟ *AE, DC, MC, V* ⊘ *Closed mid-Nov.– mid-Feb.* ⧖| *BP.*

$$ ✕▦ **Alavera de los Baños.** This small, German-run hotel was used as a backdrop for the film classic *Carmen.* Fittingly, given its location next to the Moorish baths, there's an Arab-influenced theme throughout, with terra-cotta tiles, graceful arches, and pastel-color washes. The two rooms on the first floor have their own terraces, opening up onto the split-level garden. The restaurant is open for dinner and uses predominantly organic foods. ⊠ *Hoya San Miguel s/n, 29400* ☎🖷 *952/879143* ⊕ *www.andalucia.com/alavera* 🗪 *9 rooms* ♿ *In-room: no a/c. In-hotel: restaurant, bar, pool, no elevator* ⊟ *MC, V* ⧖| *BP.*

$$$ ▦ **Husa Reina Victoria.** Built in 1906 by the Gibraltar British as a weekend stop for passengers on the rail line between Algeciras and Bobadilla, this classic Spanish hotel rose to fame in 1912, when the ailing German poet Rainer Maria Rilke came here to convalesce. (His room has been preserved as a museum.) The Queen Victoria still exudes old-fashioned charm with large Edwardian-style windows, hunting prints, and gracious lounges. The views from the cliff-top gardens, hanging over a roughly 500-foot precipice, are particularly dramatic. ⊠ *Jerez 25, 29400* ☎ *952/871240* 🖷 *952/871075* ⊕ *www.husa.es* 🗪 *90 rooms* ♿ *In-hotel: restaurant, pool, parking (fee), some pets allowed* ⊟ *AE, DC, MC, V.*

$$ ▦ **Finca la Guzmana.** This traditional Andalusian *corijo* (cottage) 4 km (2½ mi) east of Ronda has been lovingly restored with bright, fresh decor to complement the original beams, the wood-burning stoves, and a sublime setting surrounded by olive trees and grapevines. Walkers, bird-watchers, and painters are frequent guests. The owners also organize trips (guided or unguided) through the white villages in a classic sports car. The breakfast is more generous than most, with homemade bread, preserves, and local cheeses. ⊠ *Aptdo de Correos 408, 29400* ☎ *600/006305* ⊕ *www.laguzmana.com* 🗪 *5 rooms* ♿ *In-hotel: pool, no elevator* ⊟ *No credit cards* ⧖| *CP.*

$$ ▦ **San Gabriel.** In the oldest part of Ronda, this hotel is run by a fam-★ ily who converted their 18th-century home into an elegant, informal hotel (the family still lives in part of the building). The common areas, furnished with antiques, are warm and cozy, and include a DVD screening room with autographed photos of actors. (John Lithgow, Isabella Rossellini, and Bob Hoskins, in town to film the 2000 television movie version of *Don Quixote,* were among the first to stay at the hotel.)

Olive Oil, the Golden Nectar

Inland from the Costa de Sol's clamor and crowds, the landscape is stunning. Far in the distance, tiny villages cling precariously to the mountainside like a tumble of sugar cubes, while in the foreground, brilliant red poppies and a blaze of yellow mimosa are set against a rippling quilt of cool green olive trees and burnt ocher soil.

Up close, most of the trees have dark twisted branches and gnarled trunks, which denote a lifetime that can span more than a century. It is believed that many of the olive trees here are born from seeds of the original crop brought to the Mediterranean shores in the 7th century BC by Greek and Phoenician traders. Since that time, the oil produced has been used for innumerable purposes, ranging from monetary to medicinal.

These days, the benefits of olive oil are well-known. The locals don't need convincing. Olive oil has long been an integral part of the traditional cuisine and is used lavishly in every meal, including breakfast. This is when the country bars fill up with old men wearing flat caps who start their day with coffee, brandy, and black tobacco along with slabs of toasted white bread generously laden with lashings of olive oil, garlic, and salt.

Spain's most southerly province produces a copious 653 metric tons of olive oil each year, or 90% of the entire Spanish production. The area currently exports to more than 95 countries, with the main buyers of bulk oil being Italy, France, Germany, Portugal, and the United Kingdom. The type and grade of oil varies according to the destination. Some oils taste sweet and smooth; others have great body and character, and varying intensities of bitterness. North Americans like their oil to be light, with little distinctive taste, while Mexicans prefer olive oil that is dark and strong.

It has been about 30 years since a published medical study revealed that people living in the southern Mediterranean countries had the lowest case of heart disease in the Western world. This has resulted in increased use of olive oil throughout the West, not only for salad dressing but also as a healthy and tasty substitute for butter and vegetable oil in almost every aspect of cooking—except, that is, as a spread for toast; it may take several decades more before olive oil on toast becomes standard breakfast fare anywhere else but in rural Andalucia!

Some guest rooms have small sitting areas; all are stylishly furnished with antiques. ⊠ *Marqués de Moctezuma 19, 29400* ☎ *952/190392* 🖷 *952/190117* ⊕ *www.hotelsangabriel.com* 🛏 *15 rooms, 1 suite* ⌂ *In-hotel: restaurant, parking (no fee), no elevator* ▤ *AE, MC, V.*

AROUND RONDA: CAVES, ROMANS & PUEBLOS BLANCOS

This area of spectacular gorges, remote mountain villages, and ancient caves is fascinating to explore and a dramatic contrast with the clamor and crowds of the coast.

About 20 km (12 mi) west of Ronda toward Seville is the prehistoric **Cueva de la Pileta** *(Pileta Cave)*. Exit left for the village of Benaoján—

from here the caves are well signposted. A Spanish-speaking guide will hand you a paraffin lamp and lead you on a roughly 90-minute walk that reveals prehistoric wall paintings of bison, deer, and horses outlined in black, red, and ocher. One highlight is the Cámara del Pescado (Chamber of the Fish), whose drawing of a huge fish is thought to be 15,000 years old. ☎952/167343 ⚊€6 ⊙Nov.–Apr., daily 10–1 and 4–6; May–Oct., daily 10–1 and 4–5.

Ronda la Vieja (Old Ronda), 20 km (12 mi) north of Ronda, is the site of the old Roman settlement of **Acinipo**. A thriving town in the 1st century AD, Acinipo was abandoned for reasons that still baffle historians. Today it's a windswept hillside with piles of stones, the foundations of a few Roman houses, and what remains of a theater. Excavations are often under way at the site, in which case it will be closed to the public. Call the tourist office in Setenil (see number below) before visiting to get an update. ⊠Take A376 toward Algodonales; turnoff for ruins is 9 km (5 mi) from Ronda on MA449 ☎956/134261 ⊕www.setenil.com ⚊Free ⊙ Weekdays 10–2:30 and 5–8, weekends noon–2 and 5–8.

28 **Setenil de las Bodegas**, 8 km (5 mi) north of Acinipo, is in a cleft in the rock cut by the Guadalporcín River. The streets resemble long, narrow caves, and on many houses the roof is formed by a projecting ledge of heavy rock.

29 In **Olvera**, 13 km (8 mi) north of Setenil, two imposing silhouettes dominate the crest of its hill: the 11th-century castle Vallehermoso, a legacy of the Moors, and the neoclassical church of La Encarnación, reconstructed in the 19th century on the foundations of the old Moorish mosque.

30 A solitary watchtower dominates a crag above the village of **Zahara de la Sierra**, its outline visible for miles around. The tower is all that remains of a Moorish castle where King Alfonso X once fought the emir of Morocco; the building remained a Moorish stronghold until it fell to the Christians in 1470. Along the streets you can see door knockers fashioned like the hand of Fatima: the fingers represent the five laws of the Koran and serve to ward off evil. ⊠From Olvera, drive 21 km (13 mi) southwest to village of Algodonales then south on A376 to Zahara de la Sierra 5 km (3 mi).

SIERRA DE GRAZALEMA

Village of Grazalema: 28 km (17 mi) northwest of Ronda, 23 km (14 mi) northeast of Ubrique.

The 323-square-km (125-square-mi) Sierra de Grazalema straddles the provinces of Málaga and Cádiz. These mountains trap the rain clouds that roll in from the Atlantic and thus have the distinction of being the wettest place in Spain, with an average annual rainfall of 88 inches. Thanks to the park's altitude and prevailing humidity, it's one of the last habitats for the rare fir tree Abies pinsapo; it's also home to ibex, vultures, and birds of prey. Parts of the park are restricted, accessible only on foot and accompanied by an official guide.

Continued on page 198

THE ART OF BULLFIGHTING

Whether you attend is your choice, but love it or hate it, you can't ignore it. Bullfighting in Spain is big. For all the animal-rights protests, attempted local bans, failed European parliamentary censures, and general world-wide antipathy, you'd be hard pressed to find a higher volume of fans than you would around Spain's bullrings between March and October.

Its opponents call it a blood sport, its admirers—Hemingway, Picasso, and Goya among them—an art form. The latter win when it comes to media placement: you won't find tales of a star matador's latest conquest on a newspaper's jump page with car racing stories; you'll spy bullfighting news alongside theater and film reviews. This is perhaps the secret to understanding bullfighting's powerful cultural significance and why its popularity has risen over the past decade.

Bullfighting is making certain people very, very rich, via million-dollar TV rights, fight broadcasts, and the 300-plus bull-breeding farms. The owners of these farms comprise a powerful lobby that receives subsidies from the EU and exemption from a 1998 amendment to the Treaty of Rome that covers animal welfare. The Spanish Ministry of Culture also provides considerable money to support bullfighting, as do local and regional governments.

The Spanish media thrive on it, too. The matador is perhaps Spain's last remaining stereotypical *macho hombre*, whose popularity outside the ring in the celebrity press is often dramatically disproportionate to what he achieves inside it.

How bullfighting came to Spain is an unsettled issue. It may have been introduced by the Moors in the 11th century or via ancient Rome, where human vs. animal events were held as a warm-up for the gladiators.

Historically speaking, the bull was fought from horseback with a javelin and was used by the noble classes as a substitute and preparation for war, like hunting and jousting. Religious festivities and royal weddings were celebrated by fights in the local plaza, where noblemen would ride competing for royal favor, with the populace enjoying the excitement. In the 18th century, the Spanish introduced the practice of fighting on foot. As bullfighting developed, men on foot started using capes to aid the horsemen in positioning the bulls. This type of fighting drew more attention from the crowds, thus the modern *corrida*, or fight, started to take form.

THE CASE AGAINST BULLFIGHTING

Animal welfare activists aggressively protest bullfighting for the cruelty it afflicts on both bulls and horses. They contend that the bulls die a cruel (usually slow and painful) death; in fact, activists argue, the bull is essentially butchered alive and bleeds to death. The horses involved are knocked around and sometimes die or are injured as they're used as shields for the picadors riding atop them.

Activists have had little success in banning the bullfight on a national level. However, while the sport is as popular as ever in the south of Spain and Madrid, it has been halted in several Catalonian towns, and in 2003, the Catalan regional parliament became the first in Spain to ban children under 14 from attending bullfights. Then, in 2004, the Barcelona City Council banned bullfighting altogether, a historic first in Spain. The decision still needs to be ratified by the regional government.

SUITING UP

Matadors are easily distinguished by their spectacular and quite costly *traje de luces* (suit of lights), inspired by 18th-century Andalusian clothing. This ensemble can run several thousand dollars, and a good matador uses at least six of them each season. The Matador's team covers the cost.

The custom-made jacket (*chaquetilla*) is heavily embroidered with silver or golden thread.

Matadors use two kinds of capes: the *capote*, which is magenta and gold and used at the start to test the ferocity of the bull, and the red cape or *muleta*, used in the third stage.

Bicorne hat (also called *montera*)

Tightly-fitting trousers (called *taleguilla*)

Black, ballet-like shoes (called *zapatillas*)

OTHER BULLFIGHTING TERMS

Alguacilillo—the title given to the two men in the arena who represent the presiding dignitary and apply his orders.

Banderilleros—the torero's team members who place a set of banderillas (barbed sticks mounted on colored shafts) into the bull's neck.

Corrida de toros—bullfight (literally, running of the bulls); sometimes just referred to as *corrida*.

Cuadrilla—the matador's team of three *banderilleros* and two *picadors*.

Matador or Torero—matador literally means "killer."

Paseíllo—the parade that the participants make when they enter the bullring.

Picador—lancers mounted on horseback.

Presidente—the presiding dignitary.

Varas—lances.

MATADOR LEGENDS, PAST AND PRESENT

YESTERDAY'S HEROES

Modern-day Spanish bullfighting's most famous son is **Juan Belmonte.** He's credited for the daring and revolutionary style that kept him and the bull always within inches of one another. **Manuel Rodríguez Sánchez** (Manolete), comes a close second. After hundreds of performances, and in Manolete's final year before retirement, he was mortally wounded in a *corrida* in Linares, Spain, resulting in a national mourning.

Manuel Rodríguez Sánchez

TODAY'S HOT MATADORS

SEBASTIAN CASTELLA

Age: 24
Hometown: Beziers, France
Experience: 8 years
Style: Intense, rapid, assured

"EL JULI" (JULIÁN LÓPEZ ESCOBAR)

Age: 25
Hometown: Madrid
Experience: 10 years
Style: Nothing short of Spain's best—a master of his craft

EL FANDI (DAVÍD FANDILA MARÍN)

Age: 26
Hometown: Granada
Experience: 9 years
Style: Powerful, sharp, decisive

CÉSAR JIMÉNEZ

Age: 23
Hometown: Madrid
Experience: 6 years
Style: Creative, effortless, courageous

2

WHAT YOU'LL SEE

Modern-day bullfights in Spain follow a very strict ritual that's played out in 3 stages ("*tercios*" or "thirds").

1ST STAGE: TERCIO DE VARAS

After the procession of the matador and his *cuadrilla* (entourage), the bull is released into the arena. A trumpet sounds and the *picadors* (lancers on horseback) encourage the bull to attack the heavily padded horse. They use the lances to pierce the bull's back and neck muscles.

2ND STAGE: TERCIO DE BANDERILLAS

Three *banderilleros* (hit squad) on foot each attempt to plant barbed sticks mounted on colored shafts into the bull's neck and back. These further weaken the enormous ridges of the bull's neck and shoulder in order to make it lower its head. Rather than use capes, the banderilleros use their bodies to attract the bull.

3RD STAGE: TERCIO DE MUERTE (DEATH)

The torero reenters with his red cape and, if he so chooses, dedicates the bull to an individual, or to the audience. The *faena* (work), which is the entire performance with the *muleta* (cape), ends with a series of passes in which the matador attempts to maneuver the bull into a position so he can drive his sword between the shoulder blades and through the heart.

Lancers astride heavily padded horses parade around the bullring near the beginning of a fight.

HOW TO BEHAVE

The consummate bullfighting fan is both passionate and knowledgeable. The more learned respond according to the minutest details that occur inside the ring. Audiences are in fact part of the spectacle and their intervention during the event is often an indicator of the quality of the *corrida*.

For instance, during the *tercio de varas* or first third of the fight, when the matador confronts his adversary and performs with art and courage, he will be rewarded with an ovation. If a picador is over-zealous in the stabbing of the bull and leaves it too weak to fight, the crowd will boo him.

Similarly, the *estocada*, the act of thrusting the sword by the matador, can generate boos from the crowd if it's done clumsily and doesn't achieve a quick and clean death. A *trofeo* (trophy) is the usual indicator of a job well done. When the records of bullfights are kept, *trofeos* earned by the matador are always mentioned. If the crowd demands, the matador is allowed to take a lap of victory around the ring. If half or more of the spectators petition the *presidente* by waving handkerchiefs, the presidente is obliged to award the matador with one ear of the bull.

If a matador performs particularly poorly, the audience may shift its support to the bull instead. A hapless matador may find himself being pelted with seat cushions as he makes his exit.

■ TIP→ **Many bullrings have eight or more entrances. It is always advisable to specify whether you want a seat in the sun (*sol*) or shade (*sombra*) or a mix of sun and shade as time passes (*sol y sombra*) as the bullfighting season coincides with the hot summer months. It's also recommended to take a cushion or rent one for €1 so you're not sitting on the hard concrete. Seats at the top rows in the sun can be as little as €5, whereas shaded bottom row seats can cost as much as €120. If you want tickets for a major bullfight, buy tickets well in advance—call 902/150025 or go online to www.taquillatoros.com.**

STAR GAZING

It's not uncommon for local Spanish celebrities to attend bullfights, and during the most prestigious summer carnival, the San Isidro in Madrid, King Juan Carlos often makes an appearance.

③ Standing dramatically at the entrance to the park, the village of **Graza-lema** is the prettiest of the pueblos blancos. Its cobblestone streets of houses with pink-and-ocher roofs wind up the hillside, red geraniums splash white walls, and black wrought-iron lanterns and grilles cling to the house fronts.

From Grazalema, A374 takes you to **Ubrique,** on the slopes of the Saltadero Mountains, and known for its leather tanning and emboss-ing industry. Look for the **Convento de los Capuchinos** (Capuchin Con-vent), the church of **San Pedro,** and 4 km (2½ mi) away the ruins of the Moorish castle **El Castillo de Fátima.**

Another excursion from Grazalema takes you through the heart of the nature park: follow the A344 west through dramatic mountain scenery, past Benamahoma, to **El Bosque,** home to a trout stream and information center.

WHERE TO STAY

$ 🏠 **La Mejorana.** This is the place to find rural simplicity. A mere 20 years old, the house has been cleverly designed and built to resemble an old-fashioned village home, complete with beams, tiled floors, and thick whitewashed walls. The rooms have simple wrought-iron beds, but the mountain views are stunning. There is a tranquil flower-filled garden for sunny days, and when temperatures drop, the cozy alternative of a fireplace in the communal sitting room. ✉ *C. Santa Clara 6, 11610* ☎ *956/132327* ⊕ *www.lamejorana.net* ↪ *5 rooms* ↯ *In-room: no TV. In-hotel: pool, no elevator* ⦿*CP.*

ESTEPONA

③ *17 km (11 mi) west of San Pedro de Alcántara and 22 km (13 mi) west of Marbella.*

Estepona is a pleasant and relatively tranquil seaside resort, despite being surrounded by an ever-increasing number of urban develop-ments. The beach, more than 1 km (½ mi) long, also has better-quality sand than the Costa norm, and the promenade is lined with well-kept, aromatic flower gardens. The gleaming white **Puerto Deportivo** is lively and packed with restaurants, serving everything from fresh fish to pizza and Chinese food. Back from the main Avenida de España, the old quarter of narrow streets and bars is surprisingly unspoiled.

WHERE TO STAY & EAT

$$–$$$ ✕**Alcaría de Ramos.** José Ramos, a winner of Spain's National Gas-tronomy Prize, opened this restaurant in the El Paraíso complex, between Estepona and San Pedro de Alcántara, and has watched it garner a large and enthusiastic following. Try the ensalada *de lente-jas con salmón ahumado* (with lentils and smoked salmon), followed by *zarzuela de pescados y mariscos* (seafood casserole), leaving room for Ramos's exemplary crêpes suzette with raspberry sauce. ✉*Urban-ización El Paraíso, Ctra. N340, Km 167* ☎*952/886178* ▭*MC, V* ⊗ *Closed Sun. No lunch.*

$ ✕ **La Escollera.** This cheerful, family-friendly seafood restaurant is appropriately located at the fishing boat end of the port. Expect no-frills decor and paper tablecloths but excellent fresh fish and seafood. This place is a favorite with locals—always a good sign. The menu changes according to the catch of the day. ⊠ *Puerto Pesquero de Estepona* ☎ *952/806354* ▭ *No credit cards* ⊘ *Closed Mon.*

$$$$ ✕▥ **Las Dunas.** Rising like a multicolor apparition next to the beach,
★ this spectacular hotel is halfway between Estepona and Marbella. Trickling fountains and copious exotic plants help create a sense of the palatial, and the large guest rooms are suitably sumptuous. Sea views command a premium. The El Lido Restaurant ($$$$) serves first-rate international cuisine; chef Juan Carlos Jiménez was awarded Best Chef 2005 by the Academia Gastronómica de Málaga. The health center offers several alternative therapies, and families will appreciate the well-organized children's club. ⊠ *La Boladilla Baja, Ctra. de Cádiz, Km 163.5, 29689* ☎ *952/794345* ▤ *952/794825* ⊕ *www.las-dunas. com* ⇌ *33 rooms, 39 suites, 33 apartments* ⚬ *In-room: Ethernet, Wi-Fi. In-hotel: 3 restaurants, pools, gym, spa, children's programs (ages 6–12), parking (no fee)* ▭ *AE, DC, MC, V* ¶⏴*BP.*

$$$$ ▥ **Kempinski.** From the outside, this luxury resort between the coastal highway and the beach looks like a cross between a Moroccan casbah and the Hanging Gardens of Babylon. Tropical gardens, with a succession of large swimming pools, meander down to the beach. The rooms are spacious, modern, and luxurious, with faux–North African furnishings and balconies overlooking the Mediterranean. The Sunday-afternoon jazz brunch, with a live band and lavish buffet, is something of a social occasion for locals. ⊠ *Playa El Padrón, Ctra. N340, Km 159, 29680* ☎ *952/809500* ▤ *952/809550* ⊕ *www.kempinski-spain. com* ⇌ *133 rooms, 16 suites* ⚬ *In-room: Ethernet, dial-up, Wi-Fi. In-hotel: 4 restaurants, pools, gym, children's programs (ages 5–12), some pets allowed* ▭ *AE, DC, MC, V* ¶⏴*BP.*

$$$ ▥ **Albero Lodge.** Owner Myriam Perez Torres' love for travel infuses
★ this boutique hotel, where each room is named after a city, with decor to match. Exotic Fez has rich fabrics and colors; European rooms, such as Florence and Berlin, are elegantly decorated with antiques. In playful contrast, the New York room is dramatically avant-garde with a black-and-white theme. There are private terraces, and a sandy path leads to the beach. Myriam can arrange hiking, horse riding, and boat trips, as well as therapeutic massages. ⊠ *Urb. Finca La Cancelada, Calle Támesis 16, 29689* ☎ *952/880700* ▤ *952/885238* ⊕ *www.alberolodge.com* ⇌ *9 rooms* ⚬ *In-hotel: pool, no elevator* ▭ *AE, DC, MC, V.*

CASARES

㉝ *20 km (12 mi) northwest of Estepona.*

The mountain village of Casares lies high above Estepona in the Sierra Bermeja. Streets of ancient white houses piled one on top of the other perch on the slopes beneath a ruined but impressive Moorish castle. The heights afford stunning views over orchards, olive groves, and cork woods to the Mediterranean, sparkling in the distance.

GIBRALTAR

The tiny British colony of Gibraltar—nicknamed Gib, or simply the Rock—whose impressive silhouette dominates the strait between Spain and Morocco, was one of the two Pillars of Hercules in ancient times, marking the western limits of the known world. Gibraltar today is a bizarre anomaly of Moorish, Spanish, and British influences in an ace position commanding the narrow pathway between the Mediterranean Sea and the Atlantic Ocean.

The Moors, headed by Tariq ibn Ziyad, seized the peninsula in 711 as a preliminary to the conquest of Spain. After the Moors had ruled for 750 years, the Spaniards recaptured Tariq's Rock in 1462. The English, heading an Anglo-Dutch fleet in the War of the Spanish Succession, gained control in 1704, and, after several years of local skirmishes, Gibraltar was finally ceded to Great Britain in 1713 by the Treaty of Utrecht. Spain has been trying to get it back ever since. In 1779 a combined French and Spanish force laid siege to the Rock for three years to no avail. During the Napoléonic Wars, Gibraltar served as Admiral Horatio Nelson's base for the decisive naval Battle of Trafalgar, and during the two World Wars, it served the Allies well as a naval and air base. In 1967 Franco closed the land border with Spain to strengthen his claims over the colony, and it remained closed until 1985.

The Rock is like Britain with a suntan. There are double-decker buses, policemen in helmets, and bright red mailboxes. Millions of dollars have been spent in developing the Rock's tourist potential, while a steady flow of expatriate Britons come here from Spain to shop at Morrisons supermarket and High Street shops. Gibraltar's economy is further boosted by its important status as an offshore financial center. Britain and Spain have been talking about joint Anglo-Spanish sovereignty, much to the ire of the majority of Gibraltarians, who remain fiercely patriotic to the crown. The relationship between the two traditional foes has relaxed a little with the introduction of flights from the Spanish mainland to Gibraltar in November 2006.

EXPLORING THE ROCK

20 km (12 mi) east of Algeciras, 77 km (48 mi) southwest of Marbella.

There are likely few places in the world that you enter by walking or driving across an airport runway, but that's what happens in Gibraltar. First, show your passport; then make your way out onto the narrow strip of land linking Spain's La Linea with Britain's Rock. Unless you have a good reason to take your car—such as loading up on cheap gas or duty-free goodies—you're best off leaving it in a guarded parking area in La Linea, the Spanish border town—and don't bother hanging around here; it's a seedy place. In Gibraltar you can hop on buses and taxis that expertly maneuver the narrow, congested streets. The Official Rock Tour—conducted either by minibus or, at a greater cost, taxi—takes about 90 minutes and includes all the major sights, allowing you to choose which places to come back to and linger at later. When you call Gibraltar from Spain, the area code is 9567; when you call from another country, the code is 350. Prices in this section are given in British pounds; Gibraltar permits the use of U.K. currency and its own sterling government notes and coins. Euros can also be used in most of the shops, but the exchange rate may be unfavorable.

WHAT TO SEE

③④ **Catalan Bay,** a fishing village founded by Genoese settlers, is now a resort on the eastern shores. The massive water catchments once supplied the colony's drinking water. ⊠ *From the Rock's eastern side, go left down Devil's Tower Rd. as you enter Gibraltar.*

③⑤ From **Europa Point,** have a look across the straits to Morocco, 23 km (14 mi) away. You're now standing on one of the two ancient Pillars of Hercules. In front of you, the lighthouse has dominated the meeting place of the Atlantic and the Mediterranean since 1841; sailors can see its light from a distance of 27 km (17 mi). ⊠ *Continue along coast road to the Rock's southern tip.*

③⑥ To the north of the lighthouse is the **Shrine of Our Lady of Europe,** venerated by seafarers since 1462. Once a mosque, the small Catholic chapel has a little museum with a 1462 statue of the Virgin and some documents. ⊠ *Just north of Europa Point and lighthouse, along Rock's southern tip* ☐ *Free* ☉ *Weekdays 10–7.*

③⑦ For a fine view, drive high above **Rosia Bay,** to which Nelson's flagship, HMS *Victory,* was towed after the Battle of Trafalgar in 1805. On board were the dead, who were buried in Trafalgar Cemetery on the southern edge of town—except for Admiral Nelson, whose body was returned to England preserved in a barrel of rum. ⊠ *From Europa Flats, follow Queensway back along the Rock's western slopes.*

③⑧ The **Upper Rock Nature Preserve,** accessible from Jews' Gate, includes St. Michael's Cave, the Apes' Den, the Great Siege Tunnels, the Moorish Castle, and the Military Heritage Center, which chronicles the British regiments who have served on the Rock. ⊠ *From Rosia Bay, drive along Queensway and Europa Rd. as far as Casino, above Alameda Gardens. Make a sharp right here up Engineer Rd. to Jews' Gate, a lookout over docks and Bay of Gibraltar toward Algeciras.* ☐ *£8, includes all attractions, plus £1.50 per vehicle* ☉ *Daily 9:30–6:30.*

③⑨ **St. Michael's Cave** is the largest of Gibraltar's 150 caves. A series of underground chambers hung with stalactites and stalagmites, it's an ideal performing-arts venue. Sound-and-light shows are held here most days at 11 AM and 4 PM. The skull of a Neanderthal woman (now in the British Museum) was found at nearby Forbes Quarry eight years *before* the world-famous discovery in Germany's Neander Valley in 1856; nobody paid much attention to it at the time, which is why this prehistoric race is called Neanderthals rather than *Homo calpensis* (literally, "Gibraltar Man"—after the Romans' name for the Rock, *Calpe*). St. Michael's is on Queens Road.

The Full Monty on Gibraltar's Past

Plenty of places in Spain are culturally a country apart, but Gibraltar is—literally—a country apart. As a little piece of Britain tucked onto the underside of Spain, Gibraltar has an amusing mix of tea-and-biscuits culture paired with the baking sun of its Mediterranean surroundings. This strategic spot, a quick skip into Africa and a perfect point of departure around the base of Europe, has inspired a fair amount of turf wars, ultimately placing it in the hands of the British. Today that relationship is amicable, however in the beginning it was anything but.

Although the Romans ruled the area from 500 BC to AD 475, it was left to the Moors to establish the first settlement here in 1160. The Duke of Medina Sidonia recaptured the Rock for Spain in 1462. In 1501 Isabel the Catholic declared Gibraltar a crown property and the following year it received the Royal Warrant that bestowed on it a coat-of-arms consisting of a castle and a key. In 1704 an Anglo-Dutch force eventually captured Gibraltar—and this developed into Spain's ceding of Gibraltar to Britain in 1713.

In 1779, combined Spanish and French forces totaling over 50,000 troops laid the final Great Siege against a mere 5,000 defenders. The attack highlighted all the unusual problems defending Gibraltar. The great north face of the Rock guarded the entrance to Gibraltar, but it seemed impossible to mount guns on it. Taking into account the characteristics of limestone, Sergeant Ince came up with an answer: tunnels. Of course the solution had one major problem: cannons are designed to fire upward, not down. They circumvented the problem

by digging tunnels that sloped downward. Later, in World War II, tunnels were used again to defend Gibraltar. General Eisenhower conducted the Allied invasion of North Africa from one of the tunnels—and all of them remain under military control today.

From 1963 to 1964 Gibraltar's future was debated at the United Nations, but in a referendum on September 10, 1967, which has now become Gibraltar's National Day, 99.9% of Gibraltarians voted to remain a part of Britain. In 1969 this resulted in a new constitution granting self-government. These events severely provoked General Franco and he closed the costal border that same year. It stayed closed until February 5, 1985. Despite this, Spain occasionally decided to make the crossing more difficult. In 2002, finally, the governments of the U.K. and Spain reached an agreement in principle on joint sovereignty. Another referendum resulted in 99% voting against the idea. Nevertheless, this led to the creation of a tripartite forum, including the Gibraltar government and, in turn, direct flights from Madrid were started in December 2006.

★ You can reach St. Michael's Cave—or ride all the way to the top of Gibraltar—on a **cable car.** The car doesn't go high off the ground, but the views of Spain and Africa from the Rock's pinnacle are superb. It leaves from a station at the southern end of Main Street. ✉ *Cable car £8 round-trip* ⊙ *Daily 9:30–5:45.*

The famous Barbary Apes are a breed of cinnamon-color, tailless monkeys native to Morocco's Atlas Mountains. Legend holds that as long as the apes remain in Gibraltar, the British will keep the Rock; Winston Churchill went so far as to issue an order for their preservation when the apes' numbers began to dwindle during World War II. They are publicly fed twice daily,
⓵ at 8 and 4, at **Apes' Den,** a rocky area down Old Queens Road and near the Wall of Charles V (this is the famous wall built in 1552 after an attack by Turkish pirates). Among the apes' mischievous talents are grabbing food, purses, and cameras.

> ### GIBRALTAR FACTS
>
> ■ Gibraltar has been a self-governing Crown Colony of the United Kingdom since 1830.
>
> ■ Currency on the rock is the pound sterling and although Gibraltar issues its own notes and coins, U.K. notes and coins are equally accepted, as are euros.
>
> ■ The official language is English, but a mixed English–Spanish dialect, known as Llanito is commonly used.
>
> ■ Century-old rituals such as the Changing of the Guard and the Ceremony of the Keys continue to draw the largest crowds of visitors.

⓶ The **Great Siege Tunnels,** formerly known as the Upper Galleries, were carved out during the Great Siege of 1779–82 at the northern end of Old Queen's Road. You can plainly see the openings from where the guns were pointed at the Spanish invaders. These tunnels form part of what is arguably the most impressive defense system anywhere in the world.

⓷ The **Moorish Castle** was built by the descendants of Tariq, who conquered the Rock in 711. The present Tower of Homage dates from 1333, and its besieged walls bear the scars of stones from medieval catapults (and, later, cannonballs). Admiral George Rooke hoisted the British flag from its summit when he captured the Rock in 1704, and it has flown here ever since. The castle is on Willis's Road but may be viewed from outside only.

⓸ **Casemates Square,** in the northern part of town, is Gibraltar's social hub. It has been pedestrianized, and there are plenty of places to sit out with a drink and watch the world go by. There's a **tourist office** (☎ *9567/50762* ⊙ *Weekdays 9–5:30, weekends 10–4 PM*) branch here.

⓹ The colorful, congested **town of Gibraltar** is where the dignified Regency architecture of Great Britain blends well with the shutters, balconies, and patios of southern Spain. Shops, restaurants, and pubs beckon on busy Main Street; at the Governor's Residence, the ceremonial Changing of the Guard takes place six times a year and the Ceremony of the Keys takes place twice a year. Also make sure you see the Law

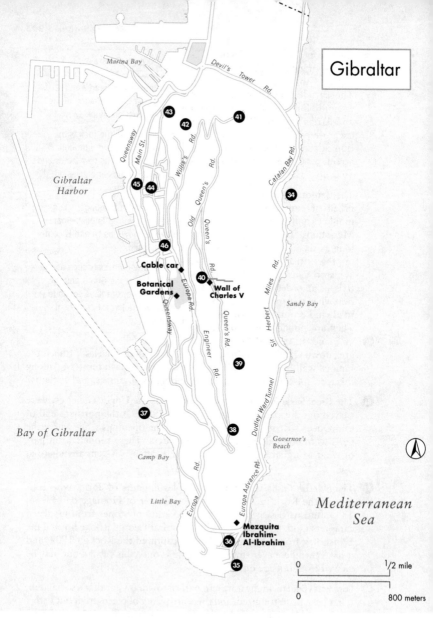

Gibraltar

Courts, where the famous case of the sailing ship *Mary Celeste* was heard in 1872; the Anglican Cathedral of the Holy Trinity; and the Catholic Cathedral of St. Mary the Crowned. The **main tourist office** (⊠ *Duke of Kent House, Cathedral Sq.* ☎ *9567/45000* ☉ *Weekdays 9– 5:30*) is on Cathedral Square.

45 The **Gibraltar Museum** houses a beautiful 14th-century Moorish bathhouse and an 1865 model of the Rock; it has displays that evoke the Great Siege and the Battle of Trafalgar. There's also a reproduction of the "Gibraltar Woman," the Neanderthal skull discovered here in 1848. ⊠ *Bomb House La.* ☎ *9567/74289* ☝ *£2* ☉ *Weekdays 10–6, Sat. 10–2.*

46 The 18th-century **Nefusot Yehudada Synagogue,** on Line Wall Road, is one of the oldest synagogues on the Iberian Peninsula, dating back to 1724. There are guided tours twice a day at 12:30 PM and 2:30 PM, accompanied by a short history of the Gibraltar Jewish community. ☎ *9567/78804.*

MONKEYING AROUND ON THE ROCK

The most privileged—and popular—residents of Gibraltar are the 200 or so tailless Barbary apes, the only wild primates in all of Europe. Treated with great respect, the apes receive health care at the local military hospital as if they were any other patient. They live in the Upper Rock Nature Reserve (although occasionally one is seen wandering into the town), and a popular stop for visitors is the Ape's Den. With their friendly, playful, and inquisitive nature, it's easy to forget they are semi-wild creatures. But remember: don't touch them, feed them, or go near the babies.

WHERE TO STAY & EAT

$$–$$$ ✕ **Terrace Restaurant.** Upstairs from the casino, this is one of the best restaurants for sea views. Tarifa's colorful kite-surfers and Africa's Atlas Mountains are visible on a clear day. The menu here is comfortably traditional and as good as the black bow-tie service. Dishes include beef Wellington, chicken Roquefort, and lobster thermidor. Afterward, choose from the diet-defying dessert trolley with classic English desserts, such as trifle, and fresh fruit tarts. ⊠ *7 Europa Rd.* ☎ *9567/76666* ☝ *Reservations essential* ▭ *AE, DC, MC, V* ☉ *Closed Sun. No lunch.*

$ ✕ **Sacarello's.** Right off Main Street, this place is as well known for its excellent coffee and cakes as it is for its adjacent restaurant. There's a daily lavish salad buffet, as well as filled baked potatoes; panfried noodles with broccoli, mussels, and chicken; and rack of lamb with wine and fine herbs. Top your meal off with a specialty coffee with cream and vanilla. The restaurant has several rooms warmly decorated in English-pub style, with cozy corners, dark-wood furnishings, and low ceilings. ⊠ *57 Irish Town* ☎ *9567/70625* ▭ *MC, V* ☉ *No dinner Sun.*

$$$$ ⌶ **The Eliott.** If you want to stay at the most slick and modern of the Rock's hotels, try this place right in the center of the town, in what used to be the Gibraltar Holiday Inn. Rooms have been revamped over the past couple of years, so you can expect all the extras. Ask for

a room at the top of the hotel, with a view over the Bay of Gibraltar. ✉2 *Governor's Parade* ☎9567/70500 🖷9567/70243 ⊕*www.ocal-laghanhotels.com* ⟿106 *rooms, 8 suites* ♿*In-room: dial-up, Wi-Fi. In-hotel: 2 restaurants, bars, pool, no-smoking rooms* ☰*AE, DC, MC, V* ⫶〇⫶*BP.*

$$$$ 🏨**The Rock.** Overlooking Gibraltar, this hotel first opened in 1932. Furnishings in the rooms and restaurants are modern and colorful, yet they manage to preserve something of the English colonial style—bamboo, ceiling fans, and a fine terrace bar with a wisteria-covered terrace. There's a 20% discount if you book online. ✉3 *Europa Rd.* ☎9567/73000 🖷9567/73513 ⊕*www.rockhotelgibraltar.com* ⟿101 *rooms, 2 suites* ♿*In-room: dial-up, Wi-Fi. In-hotel: restaurant, bar, pool* ☰*AE, DC, MC, V* ⫶〇⫶*BP.*

$ 🏨**Bristol.** This colonial-style hotel in the heart of town has splendid views of the bay and the cathedral. Rooms are spacious and comfortable, and the downstairs lounge exudes a faded elegance with sink-into sofas and chandeliers. The tropical garden is a haven. ✉10 *Cathedral Sq.* ☎9567/76800 🖷9567/77613 ⊕*www.bristolhotel.gi* ⟿60 *rooms* ♿*In-hotel: bar, pool, parking (no fee)* ☰*AE, DC, MC, V.*

NIGHTLIFE

At the **Ladbrokes Casino** (✉7 *Europa Rd.* ☎9567/76666) the gaming room is open 9 PM–4 AM, the cocktail bar 7:30 PM–4 AM. Dress is smart casual.

SPORTS & THE OUTDOORS

Bird- and dolphin-watching, diving, and fishing are popular activities on the Rock. For details on tours and outfitters, visit the Gibraltar government Web site's "On Holiday" page (⊕*www.gibraltar.gov.uk*) or call the local tourist office (☎9567/745000).

SIDE TRIPS FROM GIBRALTAR

SAN ROQUE

❹⓻ *92 km (57 mi) southwest of Ronda, 64 km (40 mi) west of Marbella, 40 km (25 mi) west of Estepona, 14 km (9 mi) east of Gibraltar, and 35 km (22 mi) east of Tarifa.*

The town of San Roque was founded within sight of Gibraltar by Spaniards who fled the Rock when the British captured it in 1704. Almost 300 years of British occupation have done little to diminish the ideals of San Roque's inhabitants, who still see themselves as the only genuine Gibraltarians. Fourteen kilometers (10 mi) east of San Roque is the luxury **Sotogrande** complex, a gated community with sprawling millionaires' villas, a yacht marina, and four golf courses, including the legendary Valderrama, which once hosted the Ryder Cup.

2

WHERE TO STAY & EAT

$$-$$$ ✕**Los Remos.** The dining room in this gracious colonial villa has peach-color walls with quasi-baroque adornments: gilt rococo mirrors, swirling cherubs, friezes of grapes, and crystal lamps. It overlooks a formal, leafy garden full of palms, cedars, and trailing ivy. Entrées include *potaje de sepia con garbanzos* (cuttlefish stew with chickpeas). All the seafood comes from the Bay of Algeciras area—the restaurant's name means "The Oars"—and the wine cellar contains some 20,000 bottles. ⊠ *Villa Victoria, Campomento de San Roque* ☎ *956/698412* ▤ *AE, DC, MC, V* ☾ *Closed Mon. No dinner Sun.*

$$$$ ▦**San Roque Club.** In this Moorish-Andalusian-style pueblo, the main building houses the reception area, golf clubhouse, and two restaurants, one specializing in Japanese food. The rooms and suites are in white houses scattered around a garden with fountains and exotic plants; each room has a little garden patio, and each suite has an enclosed courtyard as well. The houses are connected by paved paths, on which the cleaning staff tool around on golf carts. The hotel is next to the San Roque golf course, halfway between the village and Sotogrande. ⊠ *San Roque Club, N340, Km 127, 11360* ☎ *956/613030* 🖷 *956/613360* ⊕ *www.sanroqueclub.com* ➴ *50 rooms, 50 suites* ♿ *In-room: dial-up. In-hotel: 2 restaurants, golf course, tennis courts, pool, some pets allowed* ▤ *AE, DC, MC, V* ⏣ *BP.*

$$$ ▦**NH Almenara Golf Hotel & Spa.** This deluxe Sotogrande resort is a complex of semidetached Andalusian-style houses clustered around a main building on the edge of an 18-hole golf course, 6 km (4 mi) from the coast. Gardens surround each house, accessible via golf cart. Each house also has a private terrace or patio. Facilities at the marble-clad spa include a Finnish sauna, Turkish bath, and hydromassage pool. ⊠ *Av. Almenara s/n, Sotogrande, 11310* ☎ *956/582000* 🖷 *956/582001* ⊕ *www.sotogrande.com* ➴ *136 rooms, 12 suites* ♿ *In-room: dial-up, Wi-Fi. In-hotel: restaurant, bar, golf courses, pool, spa* ▤ *AE, DC, MC, V.*

NIGHTLIFE

The **Casino de San Roque** (⊠ *N340, Km 124* ☎ *956/780100* ☾ *Mar.–Sept., daily 8* PM*–5* AM; *Oct.–Feb., daily 9* PM*–5* AM) has a gaming room with roulette and blackjack tables and a less formal slot-machine area. Passports, and a jacket and tie for men, are required in the casino.

TARIFA

48 *35 km (21 mi) west of San Roque.*

Fodor'sChoice
★

On the Straits of Gibraltar at the southernmost tip of mainland Europe—where the Mediterranean and the Atlantic meet—Tarifa was one of the earliest Moorish settlements in Spain. Strong winds kept Tarifa off the tourist maps for years, but they have ultimately proven a source of wealth; the vast wind farm on the surrounding hills creates electricity, and the wide, white-sand beaches stretching north of the town have become Europe's biggest wind- and kite-surfing center. As a result, the town has continued to grow and prosper. Downtown cafés, which a couple of years ago were filled with men in flat caps playing dominoes and drinking *anís,* now serve croissants with their *café con leche* and make fancier tapas for a more cosmopolitan crowd.

Tarifa's 10th-century **castle** is famous for its siege of 1292, when the defender Guzmán el Bueno refused to surrender even though the attacking Moors threatened to kill his captive son. In defiance, he flung his own dagger down to them, shouting, "Here, use this"—or something to that effect. (And they did indeed kill his son afterward.) The Spanish military turned the castle over to the town in the mid-1990s, and it now has a **museum** on Guzmán and the sacrifice of his son. ⌫*€1.50* ☉*Tues.–Sun. 10–2 and 4–6.*

Ten kilometers (6 mi) north of Tarifa on the Atlantic coast are the Roman ruins of **Baelo Claudia.** This settlement was a thriving production center of *garum,* a salty fish paste appreciated in Rome. ☎*956/688530* ⌫*Free* ☉*July–mid-Sept., Tues.–Sat. 10–6, Sun. 10–2; mid-Sept.–June, Tues.–Sat. 10–5, Sun. 10–2.*

WHERE TO STAY & EAT

$$ ✕🖼 **100% Fun.** This funky hotel across from Tarifa's sandy strip is popular with the wind- and kite-surfing crowd. There's an exotic Amazonian theme here, with thatched roofs, bubbling fountains, and thick, exuberant greenery. In bungalows surrounding the pool, rooms are washed in shades of ocher, nicely complimented by crisp white bedding and terracotta tiles. The restaurant ($) serves Tex Mex dishes, including sizzling prawn fajitas, chilli con carne, and several vegetarian options. The predominantly young, fun-loving crowd makes peace and quiet hard to find. ✉*Ctra. Cádiz-Málaga, Km 76, 11380* ☎*956/680330* ⊕*www.tarifa.net/100fun* ⮐*22 rooms* ⚒*In-room: no a/c In-hotel: restaurant, bar, pool* ▭*MC, V* ⦿*EP.*

$$ 🖼 **Convento de San Francisco.** Rooms are comfortable and basic, but the main draw here is the setting: a restored 17th-century convent in the spectacular village of Vejer, just west of Tarifa, overlooking the coast. Breakfast is served in the former refectory. ✉*La Plazuela, 11150* ☎*956/451001* 🖷*956/451004* ⊕*www.tugasa.com* ⮐*25 rooms* ⚒*In-hotel: restaurant* ▭*MC, V* ⦿*EP.*

THE COSTA DEL SOL ESSENTIALS

To research prices, get advice from other travelers, and book travel arrangements, visit www.fodors.com.

TRANSPORTATION

For more on travel to and in Costa del Sol, see the Costa del Sol Planner at the beginning of this chapter.

BY AIR

Airports **Aeropuerto de Almería** (☎ 950/213700). **Aeropuerto de Málaga (AGP)** (*Pablo Picasso Airport* ⊠ *Av. García Morato s/n* ☎ 952/048804 ⊕ www.ccoo-agp.com). **Gibraltar Airport (GIB)** (⊠ *Winston Churchill Ave.* ☎ 9567/73026).

Carriers **Air Plus Comet** (☎ 212/983–1277 ⊕ www.airpluscomet.com). **British Airways** (☎ 800/247–9297 ⊕ www.ba.com). **easyJet** (⊕ www.easyjet.com). **Iberia** (☎ 952/136166 *at airport*, 902/400500 *inquiries* ⊕ www.iberia.com). **Monarch** (☎ 800/099260 ⊕ www.flymonarch.com).

BY BIKE

The Costa del Sol is famous for its sun and sand, but many people supplement their beach time with mountain-bike forays into the hilly interior, particularly around Ojén, near Marbella, and also along the mountain roads around Ronda. A popular route, which affords sweeping vistas, is via the mountain road from Ojén west to Istán. The Costa del Sol's temperate climate is ideal for biking, though it's best not to exert yourself on the trails in July and August, when temperatures soar. There are numerous bike-rental shops around the Costa del Sol, particularly in Marbella, Ronda, and Ojén; many shops can also arrange bike excursions. The cost to rent a mountain bike for the day ranges between €15 and €20. Guided bike excursions, which include the bikes and support staff and cars, generally start at about €62 a day.

Bike Rentals **Monte Aventura** (⊠ *Pl. de Andalucía 1, Ojén* ☎ 952/881519). **Sierra Cycling** (⊠ *Urbanization Pueblo Castillo No. 7, Fuengirola* ☎ 952/471720 ⊕ www.sierracycling.com). **Spanish Cycling Federation** (⊠ *Ferraz 16, 28008 Madrid* ☎ 91/542–0421).

BY BOAT & FERRY

ARRIVING & DEPARTING There are no direct ferries to Andalusia; the only possible option is to go to the northern Spanish coast from the United Kingdom (on P&O Ferries) via the Portsmouth-to-Bilboa route or the Plymouth-to-Santander route and then catch a train south.

GETTING AROUND If you opt for the P&O ferry from the United Kingdom to northern Spain, you can take the RENFE train from Bilboa to Málaga (journey time 14 hours, one daily). Alternatively, it is quicker to catch a train to Madrid (journey time 7 hours, 30 minutes, three daily) and catch a further train south to Málaga (journey time 4 hours).

Information **P&O Ferries** (☎ 944/234477 ⊕ www.poferries.com). **RENFE Trains** (☎ 942/360611 *or* 902/240202 ⊕ www.renfe.es).

BY BUS

During holidays it is wise to reserve your bus seat in advance for long-distance bus travel. On the Costa del Sol, the bus service connects Málaga with Cádiz (4 daily), with Córdoba (5 daily), with Granada (18 daily), and with Seville (12 daily). In Fuengirola you can catch buses for Mijas, Marbella, Estepona, and Algeciras. The Portillo bus company serves most of the Costa del Sol. Alsina Gräells serves Granada, Córdoba, Seville, and Nerja. Los Amarillos serves Cádiz, Jerez, Ronda, and Seville. Málaga's tourist office has details on other bus lines.

Bus Lines **Alsina Gräells** (☏ *952/318295*). **Los Amarillos** (✉ *Málaga bus station* ☏ *902/210317*). **Portillo** (✉ *Málaga bus station* ☏ *952/360191*).

Bus Stations **Algeciras** (✉ *Av. Virgen del Carmen 15* ☏ *956/51055*). **Estepona** (✉ *Av. de España* ☏ *952/800249*). **Fuengirola** (✉ *Av. Alfonso X111* ☏ *952/475066*). **Málaga** (✉ *Paseo de los Tilos* ☏ *952/350061*). **Marbella** (✉ *Av. Trapiche* ☏ *952/764400*). **Torremolinos** (✉ *Calle Hoyo* ☏ *952/382419*).

BY CAR

Málaga is 580 km (360 mi) from Madrid, taking the N–IV to Córdoba, then N331 to Antequera and the N321; 182 km (114 mi) from Córdoba via Antequera; 214 km (134 mi) from Seville; and 129 km (81 mi) from Granada by the shortest route of N342 to Loja, then N321 to Málaga.

There are some beautiful scenic drives here about which the respective tourist offices can advise you. The A369 heading southwest from Ronda to Guacín passes through stunning whitewashed villages. Another camera-clicking route is the N334 from Churriana to Coín, via Alhaurín de la Torre and Alhaurín el Grande. From here, continue on to Coín, then take the N337 toward Marbella, which travels via the villages of Monda and Ojen, finally ending at the coast just north of Marbella.

On major roads and motorways the speed limit is 120 kph (75 mph); in urban areas it is 50 kph (31 mph), and on other roads it is either 90 kph (55 mph) or 100 kph (63 mph).

Parking in the smaller villages can be fraught with danger (such as getting your vehicle sideswiped on winding, narrow streets), so it is advisable to park on the edge of the center and walk. In larger towns head for the nearest parking garage. The major resorts have improved their parking, and you should have no problem. You can expect to pay around €1.20 an hour. Blue lines on the street mean you must pay at the nearest meter to park during working hours, around €0.50 an hour. Yellow lines mean no parking. If your car is towed, you will be fined approximately €65 to claim it.

To take a car into Gibraltar you need, in theory, an insurance certificate and a logbook (a certificate of vehicle ownership). In practice, all you need is your passport. Prepare for parking problems on the Rock, as space is scarce.

Local car-rental agencies can be less expensive than the large chains (*See Essentials at the back of the book for contact information for international chains*).

Car-Rental Agencies **Autopro** (⊠ *Carril de Montañez 49, Málaga* ☎ *952/176030* ⊕ *www.autopro.es*). **Crown Car Hire** (⊠ *At Málaga Airport* ☎ *952/176486* ⊕ *www.crowncarhire.com*). **Niza Cars** (⊠ *At Málaga Airport* ☎ *952/236179* ⊕ *www.nizacars.com*).

BY TAXI

Taxis are plentiful throughout the Costa del Sol and may be hailed on the street or from specified taxi ranks marked TAXI. Restaurants are usually obliging and will call you a taxi, if requested. Fares are reasonable and meters are strictly used. There are extra charges for luggage. You are not required to tip taxi drivers, although rounding off the amount will be appreciated.

Taxi Companies **Morales Rodriguez–Málaga** (☎ *952/430077*). **Radio Taxi Torremolinos** (☎ *952/380600*) .**Radio Taxi Fuengirola** (☎ *952/471000*).

BY TRAIN

Most Madrid–Málaga trains leave Madrid from Atocha station (⇨ Chapter 2), though some leave from Chamartín. Travel time varies between 4½ and 10 hours; the best and fastest train is the daytime *Talgo 200* from Atocha. All Madrid–Málaga trains stop at Córdoba. A new AVE high-speed service is under construction that will connect Málaga to Madrid in around 2½ hours. The current date for completion is set for late 2007. From both Seville (4 hours, five daily) and Granada (3–3½ hours, three daily) to Málaga, you have to change at Bobadilla, making buses a more efficient mode of travel from those cities. In fact, aside from the direct Madrid–Córdoba–Málaga line, trains in Andalusia can be slow because of the hilly terrain. Málaga's train station is a 15-minute walk from the city center, across the river. Check the RENFE Web site for schedules and fares. You can book tickets online for most services.

RENFE connects Málaga, Torremolinos, and Fuengirola, stopping at the airport and all resorts along the way. The train leaves Málaga every half hour between 6 AM and 10:30 PM and Fuengirola every half hour from 6:35 AM to 11:35 PM. For the city center get off at the last stop—Centro-Alameda—not the previous stop, which will land you at Málaga's RENFE station. A daily train connects Málaga and Ronda via the dramatic Chorro gorge, with a change at Bobadilla. Travel time is about three hours. Three trains a day make the direct two-hour trip between Ronda and Algeciras on a spectacular mountain track. All routes are operated by RENFE.

Information **AVE** (☎ *902/240202* ⊕ *www.renfe.es*). **Málaga train station** (⊠ *Explanada de la Estación* ☎ *952/360202*). **RENFE** (☎ *902/240202* ⊕ *www.renfe.es*).

CONTACTS & RESOURCES

EMERGENCIES

In an emergency, call one of the Spain-wide emergency numbers for police, ambulance, or fire services. The local Red Cross (Cruz Roja) can also dispatch an ambulance in case of an emergency. Also, there are numerous private ambulance services, which are listed under *ambulancias* (ambulances) in the *Paginas Amarillas* (Yellow Pages). The Hospital Carlos Haya in Málaga has a 24-hour emergency department. For nonemergencies, there are private medical clinics throughout the Costa del Sol, which often have staff members who can speak some English. Every town has at least one pharmacy open 24 hours; the address of the on-duty pharmacy is posted on the front door of all pharmacies. You can also dial Spain's general information number for the location of a doctor's office or pharmacy that's open nearest you.

Emergency Services **Directory Enquiries** (☎ *11818*). **Emergencies** (☎ *112*). **Fire department** (☎ *080*). **Hospital Carlos Haya** (☎ *952/390400*). **Local police** (☎ *092*). **Medical service** (☎ *061*). **National police** (☎ *091*). **Red Cross** (☎ *952/443545*).

INTERNET, MAIL & SHIPPING

For shipping, most of the international couriers have representatives on the Costa del Sol, including MRW and Mail Boxes Etc.

Internet Cafés **Cristanet** (✉ *Cristamar Commercial Centre, Puerto Bánus, Marbella* ☎ *952/799591*). **Microfun** (✉ *Av. de Los Boliches, Fuengirola* ☎ *952/661424*). **Navegaweb** (✉ *Calle Molina Lario 11, Málaga* ☎ *952/352300*).

Courier Services **Mail Boxes Etc.** (✉ *C. Medellin 1, Málaga 29006* ☎ *952/311482*). **MRW** (✉ *C. Paris 45, Málaga 29006* ☎ *952/171760*).

TOUR OPTIONS

Many one- and two-day excursions from Costa del Sol resorts are run by the national company Pullmantur and by smaller firms. All local travel agents and most hotels can book you a tour; excursions leave from Málaga, Torremolinos, Fuengirola, Marbella, and Estepona, with prices varying by departure point. Most tours last half a day, and in most cases you can be picked up at your hotel. Popular tours include Málaga, Gibraltar, the Cuevas de Nerja, Mijas, Marbella, and Puerto Banús; a burro safari in Coín; and a countryside tour of Alhaurín de la Torre, Alhaurín el Grande, Coín, Ojén, and Ronda. Night tours include a barbecue evening, a bullfighting evening with dinner, and a night at the Casino Torrequebrada. The varied landscape here is also wonderful for hiking and walking, and several companies offer walking tours. All provide comprehensive information on their Web sites.

If you plan to visit Málaga independently, but are on a tight schedule, the colorful, open-topped Málaga Tour City Sightseeing Bus is a good way to view the city's attractions within a day. The bus stops at all the major sights in town, including the Gibralfaro and the cathedral.

Tour Operators Málaga Tour City Sightseeing Bus (✉ *Málaga* ☎ *952/363133* ⊕ *www.citysightseeing-spain.com*). **Pullmantur** (✉ *Av. Imperial, Torremolinos* ☎ *952/384400* ⊕ *www.pullmantur-spain.com*). **Walking Holidays** (☎ *0207/494–-2699* from U.K. ⊕ *www.walksinspain.com*).

VISITOR INFORMATION

The official Web site of the Andalucian government is www.andalucia.org; it has further information on sightseeing and events as well as contact details for the following regional and local tourist offices. Tourist offices are generally open 10–2 and 5–8 Monday–Saturday.

Regional Tourist Office Málaga (✉ *Pasaje de Chinitas 4* ☎ *952/213445*).

Local Tourist Offices Almuñecar (✉ *Palacete de La Najarra, Av. Europa* ☎ *958/631125*). **Antequera** (✉ *Palacio de Najera, Coso Viejo* ☎ *952/702505*). **Benalmádena Costa** (✉ *Av. Antonio Machado 14* ☎ *952/442494*). **Estepona** (✉ *Av. San Lorenzo 1* ☎ *952/802002*). **Fuengirola** (✉ *Av. Jesús Santos Rein 6* ☎ *952/467625*). **Gibraltar** (✉ *6 Duke of Kent House, Cathedral Sq.* ☎ *9567/45000*). **Málaga** (✉ *Av. Cervantes 1, Paseo del Parque* ☎ *952/604410*). **Marbella** (✉ *Glorieta de la Fontanilla* ☎ *952/822818* ⊕ *www.pgb.es/marbella*). **Nerja** (✉ *Puerta del Mar 2* ☎ *952/521531*). **Ronda** (✉ *Pl. de España 1* ☎ *952/871272*). **Ronda** (✉ *Paseo de Bas Infante s/n* ☎ *952/187119*). **Torremolinos** (✉ *Pl. Blas Infante 1* ☎ *952/379512*).

Andalusia Essentials

PLANNING TOOLS, EXPERT INSIGHT, GREAT CONTACTS

There are planners and there are those who, excuse the pun, fly by the seat of their pants. We happily place ourselves among the planners. Our writers and editors try to anticipate all the issues you may face before and during any journey, and then they do their research. This section is the product of their efforts. Use it to get excited about your trip to Andalusia, to inform your travel planning, or to guide you on the road should the seat of your pants start to feel threadbare.

GETTING STARTED

We're really proud of our Web site: fodors.com is a great place to begin any journey. Scan Travel Wire for restaurant and hotel openings, travel deals, and other up-to-the-minute information. Check out Booking to research prices and make reservations for flights, hotel rooms, and rental cars, as well as booking vacation packages. Head to Talk for on-the-ground pointers from travelers who frequent our message boards.

■ RESOURCES

ONLINE TRAVEL TOOLS

All kinds of information on Andalusia can be found at the region's official site, ⊕*www.andalusia.org*. For information about Spain, visit the Tourist Office of Spain's offical site at ⊕*www spain.info*. For a virtual brochure on Spain's paradores, go to ⊕*www.parador.es*.

Currency Conversion **Google** (⊕*www. google.com*) does currency conversion. Just type in the amount you want to convert and an explanation of how you want it converted (e.g., "14 Swiss francs in dollars"). **Oanda.com** (⊕*www.oanda.com*) allows you to print out a handy table with the current day's conversion rates. **XE.com** (⊕*www.xe.com*) is also a good currency conversion site.

Safety **Transportation Security Administration** (⊕*www.tsa.gov*).

Time Zones **Timeanddate.com** (⊕*www. timeanddate.com/worldclock*).

Weather **Accuweather.com** (⊕*www.accu-weather.com*) is an independent weather-forecasting service. **Weather.com** (⊕*www.weather.com*) is the Web site for the Weather Channel.

Other Resources **CIA World Factbook** (⊕*www. odci.gov/cia/publications/factbook/index. html*) has profiles of every country in the world. **U.S. Department of State** (⊕*www. travel.state.gov*) provides travel warnings and advisories as well as consular information sheets for every country, which feature general safety tips, entry requirements (but verify these with the country's embassy), and other useful information.

■ THINGS TO CONSIDER

GOVERNMENT ADVISORIES

Since different countries have different world views, it's helpful to look at travel advisories from a range of governments to get a more complete picture of what's going on in the region you're planning to visit. As you see different warnings, assess the language carefully. For example, a warning to "avoid all travel" carries more weight than one urging you to "avoid nonessential travel," and both are much stronger than a plea to "exercise caution." A U.S. government travel warning is more permanent (though not necessarily more serious) than a so-called public announcement, which carries an expiration date. When traveling abroad, consider registering online with the State Department (https://travelregistration.state.gov/ibrs), so the government will know to look for you should a crisis occur in the country you're visiting.

PASSPORTS & VISAS

In order to enter Spain, as well as any surrounding countries on your visit (such as France, Portugal, and Morocco), visitors from the United States need a passport valid for a minimum of six months.

PASSPORTS

U.S. passports are valid for 10 years. You must apply in person if you're getting a passport for the first time; if your previous passport was lost, stolen, or damaged; or if your previous passport has expired and was issued more than 15 years ago or when you were under 16. All children under 18 must appear in person to apply for or renew a passport. Both parents must accompany any child under 14 (or send a notarized statement with their permission) and provide proof of their relationship to the child.

■TIP➔ Before your trip, make two copies of your passport's data page (one for someone at home and another for you to carry separately from your passport). Another option is to scan the page and e-mail it to someone at home and/or yourself.

VISAS

Visas are not necessary for those with a U.S. passport valid for a minimum of six months and who plan to stay in Spain for up to 90 days. Should you need a visa to stay longer than this, contact the nearest Spanish Consulate office to you in the U.S. to apply for the appropriate documents.

U.S. Passport Information U.S. Department of State (☎877/487–2778 ⊕http://travel. state.gov/passport). Check for Spanish Consular office locations in the United States online at www.mae.es/en/home (note that the Web site is only partially in English; click on "Consular Services," then "Servicios Consulares," then "visas" on the far right box, and lastly "visados" to find visa information in English).

U.S. Passport & Visa Expediters A. Briggs Passport & Visa Expediters (☎800/806–0581 or 202/338–0111 ⊕www.abriggs. com). **American Passport Express** (☎800/455–5166 or 800/841–6778 ⊕www. americanpassport.com). **Passport Express** (☎800/362–8196 ⊕www.passportexpress. com). **Travel Document Systems** (☎800/874–5100 or 202/638–3800 ⊕www. traveldocs.com). **Travel the World Visas** (☎866/886–8472 or 301/495–7700 ⊕www. world-visa.com).

PACKING TIPS

■ **Make a list.** In a Fodor's survey, 29% of respondents said they make lists a week before a trip. You can use your list to pack and to repack at the end of your trip. It can also serve as record of the contents of your suitcase—in case it disappears in transit.

■ **Edit your wardrobe.** Plan to wear everything twice (better yet, thrice) and to do laundry along the way. Stick to one basic look—urban chic, sporty casual, etc. Build around one or two neutrals and an accent (e.g., black, white, and olive green).

■ **Be practical.** Put comfortable shoes on the top your list. Pack lightweight, wrinkle-resistent, compact, washable items. Stack and roll clothes, so they'll wrinkle less. Unless you're on a guided tour or a cruise, select luggage you can readily carry.

■ **Check weight and size limitations.** In the United States you may be charged extra for checked bags weighing more than 50 pounds. Abroad, some airlines don't allow you to check bags over 60 to 70 pounds, or they charge outrageous fees for every excess pound—or bag. Carry-on size limitations can be stringent, too.

■ **Check carry-on restrictions.** Research restrictions with the TSA. Rules vary abroad, so check them with your airline if you're traveling overseas on a foreign carrier. Consider packing all but essentials (travel documents, prescription meds, wallet) in checked luggage.

■ **Rethink valuables.** On U.S. flights, airlines are liable for only about $2,800 per person for bags. On international flights, the liability limit is around $635 per bag. But items like computers, cameras, and jewelry aren't covered, and as gadgetry can go on and off the list of carry-on no-no's, you can't count on keeping things safe by keeping them close. Comprehensive travel policies may cover luggage, but the liability limit is often a pittance.

BOOKING YOUR TRIP

Unless your cousin is a travel agent, you're probably among the millions of people who make most of their travel arrangements online. But have you ever wondered just what the differences are between an online travel agent (a Web site through which you make reservations instead of going directly to the airline, hotel, or car-rental company), a discounter (a firm that does a high volume of business with a hotel chain or airline and accordingly gets good prices), a wholesaler (one that makes cheap reservations in bulk and then resells them to people like you), and an aggregator (one that compares all the offerings so you don't have to)? Is it truly better to book directly on an airline or hotel Web site? And when does a real live travel agent come in handy?

ONLINE

You really have to shop around. A travel wholesaler such as Hotels.com or Hotel-Club.net can be a source of good rates, as can discounters such as Hotwire or Priceline, particularly if you can bid for your hotel room or airfare. Indeed, such sites sometimes have deals that are unavailable elsewhere. They do, however, tend to work only with hotel chains (which makes them just plain useless for getting hotel reservations outside of major cities) or big airlines (so that often leaves out upstarts like jetBlue and some foreign carriers like Air India). Also, with discounters and wholesalers you must generally prepay, and everything is nonrefundable. And before you fork over the dough, be sure to check the terms and conditions, so you know what a given company will do for you if there's a problem and what you'll have to deal with on your own.

■ TIP→ **To be absolutely sure everything was processed correctly, confirm reservations made through online travel agents, discounters, and wholesalers directly with your hotel or airline before leaving home.**

Booking engines like Expedia, Travelocity, and Orbitz are actually travel agents, albeit high-volume, online ones. And airline travel packagers like American Airlines Vacations and Virgin Vacations—well, they're travel agents, too. But they may still not work with all the world's hotels.

An aggregator site will search many sites and pull the best prices for airfares, hotels, and rental cars from them. Most aggregators compare the major travel-booking sites such as Expedia, Travelocity, and Orbitz; some also look at airline Web sites, though rarely the sites of smaller budget airlines. Some aggregators also compare other travel products, including complex packages—a good thing, as you can sometimes get the best overall deal by booking an air-and-hotel package.

Booking Engines **Cheap Tickets** (⊕ *www. cheaptickets.com*) is a discounter. **Expedia** (⊕ *www.expedia.com*) is a large online agency that charges a booking fee for airline tickets. **Hotwire** (⊕ *www.hotwire.com*) is a discounter. **lastminute.com** (⊕ *www.lastminute.com*) specializes in last-minute travel; the main site is for the U.K., but it has a link to a U.S. site. **Luxury Link** (⊕ *www.luxurylink.com*) has auctions (surprisingly good deals) as well as offers on the high-end side of travel. **Onetravel. com** (⊕ *www.onetravel.com*) is a discounter for hotels, car rentals, airfares, and packages. **Orbitz** (⊕ *www.orbitz.com*) charges a booking fee for airline tickets, but gives a clear breakdown of fees and taxes before you book. **Priceline.com** (⊕ *www.priceline.com*) is a discounter that also allows bidding. **Travel.com** (⊕ *www.travel.com*) allows you to compare its rates with those of other booking engines. **Travelocity** (⊕ *www.travelocity.com*) charges a booking fee for airline tickets, but promises good problem resolution.

Online Accommodations **Hotelbook.com** (⊕ *www.hotelbook.com*) focuses on independent hotels worldwide. **Hotel Club** (⊕ *www. hotelclub.net*) is good for major cities and some resort areas. **Hotels.com** (⊕ www.hotels.com) is a big Expedia-owned wholesaler that offers rooms in hotels all over the world. **Quikbook** (⊕ www.quikbook.com) offers "pay when you stay" reservations that allow you to settle your bill when you check out, not when you book; best for trips to U.S. and Canadian cities. **Reservator** (⊕ www.reservator.com) is one of the best online sources focusing purely on hotels in Spain.

Other Resources **Bidding For Travel** (⊕ www.biddingfortravel.com) is a good place to figure out what you can get and for how much before you start bidding on, say, Priceline.

WITH A TRAVEL AGENT

If you use an agent—brick-and-mortar or virtual—you'll pay a fee for the service. And know that the service you get from some online agents isn't comprehensive. For example Expedia and Travelocity don't search for prices on budget airlines like jetBlue, Southwest, or small foreign carriers. That said, some agents (online or not) *do* have access to fares that are difficult to find otherwise, and the savings can more than make up for any surcharge.

A knowledgeable brick-and-mortar travel agent can be a godsend if you're booking a cruise, a package trip that's not available to you directly, an air pass, or a complicated itinerary including several overseas flights. What's more, travel agents that specialize in a destination may have exclusive access to certain deals and insider information on things such as charter flights. Agents who specialize in types of travelers or types of trips can also be invaluable.

Agent Resources **American Society of Travel Agents** (☎ 703/739–2782 ⊕ www.travelsense.org).

■ ACCOMMODATIONS

By law, hotel prices must be posted at the reception desk and should indicate whether or not the value-added tax (I.V.A.;

7%) is included. Note that high-season rates prevail not only in summer but also during Holy Week and local fiestas.

In much of Spain, breakfast is normally *not* included. However, in the resort destinations of the Costa del Sol, a buffet breakfast is often included.

Most hotels and other lodgings require you to give your credit-card details before they will confirm your reservation. If you don't feel comfortable e-mailing this information, ask if you can fax it (some places even prefer faxes). However you book, get confirmation in writing and have a copy of it handy when you check in.

Be sure you understand the hotel's cancellation policy. Some places allow you to cancel without any kind of penalty—even if you prepaid to secure a discounted rate—if you cancel at least 24 hours in advance. Others require you to cancel a week in advance or penalize you the cost of one night. Small inns and B&Bs are most likely to require you to cancel far in advance. Most hotels allow children under a certain age to stay in their parents' room at no extra charge, but others charge for them as extra adults; find out the cutoff age for discounts.

■ TIP→ Assume that hotels operate on the European Plan (**EP**, no meals) unless we specify that they use the Breakfast Plan (**BP**, with full breakfast), Continental Plan (**CP**, continental breakfast), Full American Plan (**FAP**, all meals), Modified American Plan (**MAP**, breakfast and dinner) or are all-inclusive (**AI**, all meals and most activities).

APARTMENT & HOUSE RENTALS

If you are interested in a single-destination vacation, or are staying in one place and using it as a base for exploring the local area, renting an apartment or a house can be a good idea. However, it is not always possible to ensure the quality beforehand, and you may be responsible for supplying your own bed linen, towels, etc.

Contacts Barclay International Group
(☎ *516/364–0064* or *800/845–6636* ⊕ *www. barclayweb.com*). **Homes Away** (☎ *416/920– 1873* or *800/374–4637* ⊕ *www.homesaway. com*). **Hometours International** (☎ *865/690– 8484* ⊕ *thor.he.net/~hometour*). **Interhome** (☎ *954/791–8282* or *800/882–6864* ⊕ *www. interhome.us*). **Villanet** (☎ *206/417–3444* or *800/964–1891* ⊕ *www.rentavilla.com*). **Villas & Apartments Abroad** (☎ *212/213–6435* or *800/433–3020* ⊕ *www.vaanyc.com*). **Villas International** (☎ *415/499–9490* or *800/221– 2260* ⊕ *www.villasintl.com*).

HOME EXCHANGES

With a direct home exchange you stay in someone else's home while they stay in yours. Some outfits also deal with vacation homes, so you're not actually staying in someone's full-time residence, just their vacant weekend place.

Exchange Clubs Home Exchange.com
(☎ *800/877–8723* ⊕ *www.homeexchange. com*); $59.95 for a 1-year online listing. **HomeLink International** (☎ *800/638–3841* ⊕ *www.homelink.org*); $90 yearly for Web-only membership; $140 includes Web access and two catalogs. **Intervac U.S.** (☎ *800/756–4663* ⊕ *www.intervacus.com*); $78.88 for Web-only membership; $126 includes Web access and a catalog.

HOTELS & BED-AND-BREAKFASTS

The Spanish government classifies hotels with one to five stars, with an additional rating of five-star GL (Gran Luxo) indicating the highest quality. Although quality is a factor, **the rating is technically only an indication of how many facilities the hotel offers.** For example, a three-star hotel may be just as comfortable as a four-star hotel but may lack a swimming pool. Similarly, Fodor's price categories (¢–$$$$) indicate room rates only, so you might find a well-kept $$$ inn more charming than the famous $$$$ property down the street.

All hotel entrances are marked with a blue plaque bearing the letter H and the number of stars. The letter R (standing for *residencia*) after the letter H indicates

an establishment with no meal service, with the possible exception of breakfast. The designations *fonda* (F), *pensión* (P), *casa de huéspedes* (CH), and *hostal* (Hs) indicate budget accommodations. In most cases, especially in smaller villages, rooms in such buildings will be basic but clean; in large cities, these rooms can be downright dreary. Note that in Spain *hostales* are not the same as the dorm-style youth hostels common elsewhere in Europe— *hostales* are inexpensive hotels with individual rooms, not communal quarters.

All hotels listed have private bath and air-conditioning (*aire acondicionado*) unless otherwise noted. When inquiring in Spanish about whether a hotel has a private bath, ask if it's an *habitación con baño*.

Although a single room (*habitación sencilla*) is usually available, singles are often on the small side. Solo travelers might prefer to pay a bit extra for single occupancy of a double room (*habitación doble uso individual*.) Make sure you request a double bed (*matrimonial*) if you want one—if you don't ask, you may end up with two singles placed together.

Spain's major private hotel groups include the Sol Meliá, Tryp, and Hotusa. The NH chain, which is concentrated in major cities, appeals to business travelers. Dozens of reasonably priced beachside high-rises cater to package tours.

There's a growing trend in Spain toward small country hotels and agrotourism. Estancias de España is an association of more than 40 independently owned hotels in restored palaces, monasteries, mills, and estates, generally in rural Spain; contact them for a free directory. Similar associations serve individual regions, and tourist offices also provide lists of establishments.

A number of *casas rurales* (country houses similar to bed-and-breakfasts) offer pastoral lodging either in guest rooms or in self-catering cottages. You may also come across the term *finca*, which is a country estate house. Many of the accommodations designated agroturismo are fincas that people have inherited and converted to upscale B&Bs. Comfort and conveniences vary widely; it's best to book these types of accommodation through one of the appropriate regional associations. Ask the local tourist office about casas rurales and fincas in the area.

INFORMATION

Small Hotels **AHRA** (*Andalusian Association of Rural Hotels* ☎957/540801 ⊕*www. ahra.es*). **Estancias de España** (✉*Calle Luxemburgo, 4, Pozuelo de Alarcón, 28224* ☎91/3454141 ⊕*www.estancias.com*).

Major Spanish Chains **Hotusa** (☎93/268–1010 ⊕*www.hotusa.es*). **NH Hoteles** (☎902/115116 ⊕*www.nh-hoteles.es*). **Sol Meliá** (☎902/144444 ⊕*www.solmelia.com*).

PARADORES

The Spanish government runs 91 *paradores*—upmarket hotels in historic buildings or near significant sites. Some are in castles on a hill with sweeping views; others are in monasteries or convents filled with artistic treasures; still others are in modern buildings on choice beachfront, alpine, or pastoral property. Rates are reasonable, considering that most paradores have four- or five-star amenities; and the premises are invariably immaculate and tastefully furnished, often with antiques or reproductions. However, be advised that in most instances they do not offer many rooms with double beds (*matrimoniales*), so a special request is necessary. Each parador has a restaurant serving regional specialties, and you can stop in for a meal or a drink without spending the night. Breakfast, however, is an expensive buffet, so if you just want coffee and a roll, you'll do better to walk down the street to a local café.

Paradores are extremely popular with foreigners and Spaniards alike, so make reservations well in advance. If you plan to spend at least five nights in the paradores, the "five-night card" or *Tarjeta*

Cinco Noches in Spanish offers excellent savings. You can purchase and use the card at any parador within the valid calendar period; in most paradores, discounted nights aren't offered during the high-season months of June, July, and August, and are offered only Sunday through Thursday in spring. Note that you can still use the card during these periods, but you'll be paying the difference between the official and discounted rate. The card does not guarantee a room; you must make reservations in advance. The paradores offer 35% discounts to those 60 and over, usually in May and June, though the months may vary. Those 30 and under also qualify for special discounted deals "Young Person's Getaway" (with buffet breakfast included), that is valid throughout the year but with limited availability.

In Spain **Paradores de España** (✉*Central de Reservas, Requena 3, Madrid, 28013* ☎91/516–6666 ⊕*www.parador.es*).

▌AIRLINE TICKETS

Most domestic airline tickets are electronic; international tickets may be either electronic or paper. With an e-ticket the only thing you receive is an e-mailed receipt citing your itinerary and reservation and ticket numbers. The greatest advantage of an e-ticket is that if you lose your receipt, you can simply print out another copy or ask the airline to do it for you at check-in. You usually pay a surcharge (up to $50) to get a paper ticket, if you can get one at all. The sole advantage of a paper ticket is that it may be easier to endorse over to another airline if your flight is canceled and the airline with which you booked can't accommodate you on another flight.

The least expensive airfares to Spain are priced for round-trip travel and must usually be purchased in advance. Airlines generally allow you to change your return

10 WAYS TO SAVE

1. Nonrefundable is best. If saving money is more important than flexibility, then nonrefundable tickets work. Just remember that you'll pay dearly (as much as $200) if you change your plans.

2. Comparison shop. Web sites and travel agents can have different arrangements with the airlines and offer different prices for exactly the same flights.

3. Beware the listed prices. Many airline Web sites—and most ads—show prices *without* taxes and surcharges. Don't buy until you know the full price.

4. Stay loyal. Stick with one or two frequent-flier programs. You'll rack up free trips faster and you'll accumulate more quickly the perks that make trips easier. On some airlines these include a special reservations number, early boarding, access to upgrades, and more roomy seating.

5. Watch those ticketing fees. Surcharges are usually added when you buy your ticket anywhere but on an airline Web site. (That includes by phone—even if you call the airline directly—and paper tickets regardless of how you book).

6. Check often. Search for fares from three months to one month in advance. Look until you find a price you like.

7. Don't work alone. Some Web sites have tracking features that will e-mail you immediately when good deals are posted.

8. Jump on the good deals. Waiting even a few minutes might mean paying more.

9. Be flexible. Look for departures on Tuesday, Wednesday, and Saturday, typically the cheapest days to travel.

10. Weigh your options. What you get can be as important as what you save. A cheaper flight might have a long layover, or it might land at a secondary airport, where your ground transportation costs might be higher.

date for a fee; most low-fare tickets, however, are nonrefundable.

If you buy a round-trip transatlantic ticket on Iberia, you might want to purchase a **Visit Spain** Airpass, good for three or more domestic flights during your trip. The pass must be purchased before you arrive in Spain, and all flights must be booked in advance; the cost starts at $248. The maximum number of coupons you may purchase is nine, and the pass is valid for one year. On certain days of the week, Iberia also offers *minitarifas* (minifares), which can save you up to 40% on domestic flights. Tickets must be purchased at least two days in advance, and you must stay over Saturday night. Another option is to join the Iberia Plus Internet club, which can offer exceptionally low fares.

Air Pass Info **FlightPass** (☎ *888/387-2479 EuropebyAir* ⊕ *www.europebyair.com*). **Iberia** (☎ *800/772-4642* ⊕ *www.iberia.com*).

▌ RENTAL CARS

When you reserve a car, ask about cancellation penalties, taxes, drop-off charges (if you're planning to pick up the car in one city and leave it in another), and surcharges (for being under or over a certain age, for additional drivers, or for driving across state or country borders or beyond a specific distance from your point of rental). All these things can add substantially to your costs. Request car seats and extras such as GPS when you book.

Rates are sometimes—but not always—better if you book in advance or reserve through a rental agency's Web site. There are other reasons to book ahead, though: for popular destinations, during busy times of the year, or to ensure that you get certain types of cars (vans, SUVs, exotic sports cars).

■TIP→ **Make sure that a confirmed reservation guarantees you a car. Agencies sometimes overbook, particularly for busy weekends and holiday periods.**

Alamo, Avis, Budget, Europcar, Hertz, and National (partnered in Spain with the Spanish agency Atesa) have branches at major Spanish airports and in large cities. Smaller, regional companies and whole-salers offer lower rates. All agencies have a range of models, but virtually all cars in Spain have a manual transmission—if you don't want a stick shift, reserve weeks in advance and specify automatic transmission, then call to reconfirm your automatic car before you leave for Spain. Rates in Madrid begin at the equivalents of U.S. $65 a day and $300 a week for an economy car with air-conditioning, manual transmission, and unlimited mile-age. Add to this a 16% tax on car rentals. Consider renting a small car. Aside from saving you money, it's easier for Spain's many tiny roads and parking spaces.

Anyone over 18 with a valid license can drive in Spain, but some rental agencies will not rent cars to drivers under 21.

Your driver's license may not be recog-nized outside your home country. You may not be able to rent a car without an International Driving Permit (IDP), which can be used only in conjunction with a valid driver's license and which translates your license into 10 languages. Check AAA's Web site (www.aaa.com) for more information.

RENTAL AGENCIES

Major Agencies Alamo (☎800/522-9696 ⊕www.alamo.com). **Avis** (☎800/331-1084, 902/135531 in Spain ⊕www.avis.com). **Budget** (☎800/472-3325, 901/201212 in Spain ⊕www.budget.com). **Europcar** (☎902/105030 in Spain ⊕www.europcar.es). **Hertz** (☎800/654-3001, 902/402405 in Spain ⊕www.hertz.com). **National Car Rental/Atesa** (☎800/227-7368, 902/100101 in Spain ⊕www.nationalcar.com).

Wholesalers Mondialautos (☎971/453000 ⊕www.mondialautos.com). **Auto Europe** (☎888/223-5555 ⊕www.autoeurope.com). **Europe by Car** (☎800/223-1516, 212/581-3040 in New York ⊕www.europebycar.com).

Eurovacations (☎877/471-3876 ⊕www.eurovacations.com). **Kemwel** (☎877/820-0668 ⊕www.kemwel.com).

CAR-RENTAL INSURANCE

Everyone who rents a car wonders whether the insurance that the rental companies offer is worth the expense. No one—including us—has a simple answer. It all depends on how much regular insur-ance you have, how comfortable you are with risk, and whether money is an issue. More and more, companies are offering fully comprehensive insurance as an inte-gral part of the price—and this is far and away the most preferred option.

If you own a car, your personal auto insurance may cover a rental to some degree, though not all policies protect you abroad; always read your policy's fine print. If you don't have auto insur-ance, then seriously consider buying the collision- or loss-damage waiver (CDW or LDW) from the car-rental company, which eliminates your liability for dam-age to the car. Some credit cards offer CDW coverage, but it's usually supple-mental to your own insurance and rarely covers SUVs, minivans, luxury models, and the like. If your coverage is second-ary, you may still be liable for loss-of-use costs from the car-rental company. **But no credit-card insurance is valid unless you use that card for all transactions, from reserv-ing to paying the final bill.** All companies exclude car rental in some countries, so be sure to find out about the destination to which you are traveling.

■ TIP→ Diners Club offers primary CDW coverage on all rentals reserved and paid for with the card. This means that Din-ers Club's company—not your own car insurance—pays in case of an accident. It *doesn't* mean your car-insurance company won't raise your rates once it discovers you had an accident.

Some countries require you to purchase CDW coverage or require car-rental com-panies to include it in quoted rates. Ask your rental company about issues like these in your destination. In most cases it's cheaper to add a supplemental CDW plan to your comprehensive travel-insurance policy than to purchase it from a rental company. That said, you don't want to pay for a supplement if you're required to buy insurance from the rental company.

■ TIP→ **You can decline the insurance from the rental company and purchase it through a third-party provider such as Travel Guard (www.travelguard.com)—$9 per day for $35,000 of coverage. That's sometimes just under half the price of the CDW offered by some car-rental companies.**

▌CRUISES

Barcelona is the busiest cruise port in Spain and Europe. Other popular ports of call in the country are Málaga, Alicante, and Palma de Mallorca. Nearby Gibraltar is also a popular stop. Although cruise lines such as Silversea and Costa traditionally offer cruises that take in parts of Spain and other Mediterranean countries such as Italy and Greece, it is becoming increasingly common to package tours wholly within Spain. Two popular routes consist of island-hopping in the Balaerics or around the Canary Islands. Among the many cruise lines that call on Spain are Royal Caribbean, Holland America Line, the Norwegian Cruise Line, and Princess Cruises.

Cruise Lines **Celebrity Cruises** (☎ *800/647-2251* ⊕ *www.celebrity.com*). **Costa Cruises** (☎ *800/445–8020* ⊕ *www.costacruise. com*). **Crystal Cruises** (☎ *800/804–1500* ⊕ *www.crystalcruises.com*). **Cunard Line** (☎ *800/728–6273* ⊕ *www.cunard.com*). **Holland America Line** (☎ *206/281–3535* or *877/932–4259* ⊕ *www.hollandamerica. com*). **Mediterranean Shipping Cruises** (☎ *212/764–4800* or *800/666–9333* ⊕ *www. msccruises.com*). **Norwegian Cruise Line** (☎ *866/625–1166* ⊕ *www.ncl.com*). **Oceania Cruises** (☎ *305/514–2300* or *800/531–5659*

⊕ *www.oceaniacruises.com*). **Princess Cruises** (☎ *661/753–0000* or *800/774–6237* ⊕ *www.princess.com*). **Regent Seven Seas Cruises** (☎ *877/505–5370* ⊕ *www.rssc. com*). **Royal Caribbean International** (☎ *305/539–6000* or *800/327–6700* ⊕ *www. royalcaribbean.com*). **Seabourn Cruise Line** (☎ *305/463–3000* or *800/929–9391* ⊕ *www. seabourn.com*). **SeaDream Yacht Club** (☎ *800/707–4911* ⊕ *www.seadreamyachtclub. com*). **Silversea Cruises** (☎ *954/522–4477* or *800/722–9955* ⊕ *www.silversea.com*). **Star Clippers** (☎ *305/442–0550* or *800/442–0551* ⊕ *www.starclippers.com*). **Windstar Cruises** (☎ *877/827–7245* ⊕ *www.windstarcruises.com*).

TRANSPORTATION

■**TIP**→ Ask the local tourist board about hotel and local transportation packages that include tickets to major museum exhibits or other special events.

▌ BY AIR

Flying time from New York to Madrid is about 7 hours; from London, just over 2. Regular nonstop flights serve Spain from many major cities in the eastern United States; flying from other North American cities usually involves a stop. If you're coming from North America and would like to land in a city other than Madrid or Barcelona, consider flying a British or other European carrier, and know that you may have to stay overnight in London or another European city on your way home.

Since 2004, there's been a revolution in cheap flights from the United Kingdom to Spain, with the emergence of scores of new carriers such as Monarch and Flybmi providing competition to the market's main players—easyJet and Ryanair. All these carriers offer frequent flights, cover small cities as well as large ones, and have very competitive fares. Attitude Travel (⊕*www. attitudetravel.com/lowcostairlines*) is the most comprehensive site on the Internet for low-cost airlines worldwide.

There are no nonstop flights to Spain from Australia or New Zealand.

Smoking policies vary from carrier to carrier. Many airlines prohibit smoking on all of their flights; others allow smoking only on certain routes or departures. There is no smoking on domestic flights in Spain.

Airline Security Issues Transportation Security Administration (⊕*www.tsa.gov*) has answers for most questions related to secure air travel.

AIRPORTS

Most flights from the United States and Canada land in, or pass through, Madrid's Barajas (MAD). The other major gateway is Barcelona's El Prat de Llobregat (BCN). From England and elsewhere in Europe, regular flights also land in Málaga (AGP), Alicante (ALC), Palma de Mallorca (PMI), and many other smaller cities too.

AIRPORT INFORMATION

Madrid–Barajas (☎*91/305-8343* ⊕*www. aena.es*). **Barcelona–El Prat de Llobregat** (☎*93/298-3838* ⊕*www.aena.es*). **Girona–Girona** (☎*972/186600*). **Sagalés Buses** (☎*93/231-2756* ⊕*www.sagales.com*).

FLIGHTS

From North America, Air Europa, Continental, Spanair, and USAirways fly to Madrid; American, Delta, and Iberia fly to Madrid and Barcelona—note that some of these airlines use shared facilities and do not operate their own flights. Within Spain, Iberia is the main domestic airline, but Air Europa and Spanair fly most domestic routes at lower prices. The budget airline Vueling heavily promotes its Internet bookings, which are often the country's cheapest domestic flight prices. The airline is servicing more and more major Spanish cities on and off the mainland and outside of Spain offers cheap flights to Amsterdam, Brussels, Berlin, Lisbon, Milan, Rome, and Paris. The further from your travel date you purchase the ticket, the more bargains you're likely to find. Air Europa and Spanair also travel both within Spain and to the rest of Europe.

Airline Contacts Air Europa (☎*888/238-7672 and 902/401501* ⊕*www.air-europa. com*). **American Airlines** (☎*800/433-7300* ⊕*www.aa.com*). **Continental Airlines** (☎*800/523—3273 for U.S. and Mexico reservations, 800/231-0856 for international reservations* ⊕*www.continental.com*). **Delta Airlines** (☎*800/221-1212 for U.S. res-*

ervations, 800/241–4141 for international reservations ⊕ www.delta.com). **Iberia** (☎ 800/772–4642 ⊕ www.iberia.com). **Northwest Airlines** (☎ 800/225–2525 ⊕ www.nwa. com). **Spanair** (☎ 888/545–5757 ⊕ www. spanair.com). **United Airlines** (☎ 800/864–8331 for U.S. reservations, 800/538–2929 for international reservations ⊕ www.united.com). **USAirways** (☎ 800/428–4322 for U.S. and Canada reservations, 800/622–1015 for international reservations ⊕ www.usairways.com).

Within Spain **Air Europa** (☎ 902/401501 ⊕ www.air-europa.com). **Iberia** (☎ 902/400500 ⊕ www.iberia.com). **Spanair** (☎ 902/131415 ⊕ www.spanair.com). **Vueling** (☎ 902/333933 ⊕ www.vueling.com).

▌ BY BOAT

If you want to drive from Spain to Morocco directly (using the ferry) there are only two options, with one being much faster than the other. Otherwise, it is necessary to travel to either Ceuta or Melilla, two Spanish enclaves on the North African coast, and then move on to Morocco. Trasmediterránea operates services from Algeciras either to Ceuta or directly to Tangier, and from Málaga and Almería to Melilla. Buquebus operates fast ferries from Algeciras to Ceuta. However, the fastest and most direct route to Africa proper is from Tarifa to Tangier and operated by FRS.

INFORMATION

In Spain **Buquebus** (☎ 902/414242 ⊕ www. buquebus.es). **FRS** (☎ 956/681830 ⊕ www. frs.es). **Trasmediterránea** (☎ 902/454645 ⊕ www.trasmediterranea.com).

▌ BY BUS

Within Spain, a mix of private companies provide bus services that range from knee-crunchingly basic to luxurious. Fares are lower than the corresponding train fares, and service is more extensive: if you want to reach a town not served by train, you can be sure a bus goes there. Smaller towns don't usually have a cen-

tral bus depot, so ask the tourist office where to wait for the bus to your destination. Note that service is less frequent on weekends. Spain's major national long-haul bus line is Alsa-Enatcar. For a longer haul, you can travel to Spain by bus (Eurolines/National EXpress, for example) from London, Paris, Rome, Frankfurt, Prague, and other major European cities. It's a long journey, but the buses are modern. Although it may once have been the case that international bus travel was significantly cheaper than air travel, new budget airlines have changed the equation. For perhaps a little more money and a large savings of travel hours, flying is increasingly the better option.

Most of Spain's larger bus companies have buses with comfortable seats and adequate legroom; on longer journeys (two hours or longer), a movie is shown on board, and earphones are provided. Except for smaller, regional buses that travel only short hops, all buses have a bathroom on board. Nonetheless, most long-haul buses usually stop at least once every two to three hours for a snack and bathroom break. Smoking is prohibited on buses.

Road and traffic conditions can make or break the journey; Spain's highways, particularly along major routes, are well maintained. That may not be the case in the country's more rural areas, where you could be in for a bumpy ride—sometimes exacerbated by older buses with worn shock absorbers. Alsa-Enatcar has two luxury classes in addition to its regular seating. Supra Clase includes roomy leather seats and on-board meals; also, you have the option of *asientos individuales,* individual seats (with no other seat on either side) that line one side of the bus. The next class is the Eurobus, with comfortable seats and plenty of legroom. The Supra Clase and Eurobus usually cost, respectively, up to one-third and one-fourth more than the regular seats.

FLYING 101

Flying may not be as carefree as it once was, but there are some things you can do to make your trip smoother.

■ **Minimize the time spent standing line.** Buy an e-ticket, check in at an electronic kiosk, or—even better—check in on your airline's Web site before leaving home. Pack light and limit carry-on items to only the essentials.

■ **Arrive when you need to.** Research your airline's policy. It's usually at least an hour before domestic flights and two to three hours before international flights. But airlines at some busy airports have more stringent requirements. Check the TSA Web site for estimated security waiting times at major airports.

■ **Get to the gate.** If you aren't at the gate at least 10 minutes before your flight is scheduled to take off (sometimes earlier), you won't be allowed to board.

■ **Double-check your flight times.** Do this especially if you reserved far in advance. Schedules change, and alerts may not reach you.

■ **Don't go hungry.** Ask whether your airline offers anything to eat; even when it does, be prepared to pay.

■ **Get the seat you want.** Often, you can pick a seat when you buy your ticket on an airline Web site. But it's not guaranteed; the airline could change the plane after you book, so double-check. You can also select a seat if you check in electronically. Avoid seats on the aisle directly across from the lavatories. Frequent fliers say those are even worse than back-row seats that don't recline.

■ **Got kids? Get info.** Ask the airline about its children's menus, activities, and fares. Sometimes infants and toddlers fly free if they sit on a parent's lap, and older children fly for half price in their own seats. Also inquire about policies involving car seats; having one may limit seating options. Also

ask about seat-belt extenders for car seats. And note that you can't count on a flight attendant to produce an extender; you may have to ask for one when you board.

■ **Check your scheduling.** Don't buy a ticket if there's less than an hour between connecting flights. Although schedules are padded, if anything goes wrong you might miss your connection. If you're traveling to an important function, depart a day early.

■ **Bring paper.** Even when using an e-ticket, always carry a hard copy of your receipt; you may need it to get your boarding pass, which most airports require to get past security.

■ **Complain at the airport.** If your baggage goes astray or your flight goes awry, complain before leaving the airport. Most carriers require this.

■ **Beware of overbooked flights.** If a flight is oversold, the gate agent will usually ask for volunteers and offer some sort of compensation for taking a different flight. If you're bumped from a flight *involuntarily*, the airline must give you some kind of compensation if an alternate flight can't be found within one hour.

■ **Know your rights.** If your flight is delayed because of something within the airline's control (bad weather doesn't count), the airline must get you to your destination on the same day, even if they have to book you on another airline and in an upgraded class. Read the Contract of Carriage, which is usually buried on the airline's Web site.

■ **Be prepared.** The Boy Scout motto is especially important if you're traveling during a stormy season. To quickly adjust your plans, program a few numbers into your cell: your airline, an airport hotel or two, your destination hotel, your car service, and/or your travel agent.

If you plan to return to your initial destination, you can save by buying a round-trip ticket, instead of one-way. Also, some of Spain's smaller, regional bus lines offer multitrip bus passes, which are worthwhile if you plan to make multiple trips between two fixed destinations within the region. Generally, these tickets offer a savings of 20% per journey; you can buy these tickets only in the bus station (not on the bus). The general rule for children is that if they occupy a seat, they pay. Check the bus Web sites for deals (*ofertas*); you'll often find discounts for midweek and/or round-trip tickets to specific destinations.

In Spain's larger cities, you can pick up schedule and fare information at the bus station; smaller towns may not have a bus station but just a bus stop. Schedules are sometimes listed at the bus stop; otherwise, call the bus company directly or ask at the tourist office, which can usually supply all schedule and fare information.

At bus station ticket counters, generally all major credit cards (except American Express) are accepted. If you buy your ticket on the bus, it's cash only. Traveler's checks are almost never accepted. Big lines such as Enatcar are now encouraging online purchasing. Once your ticket is booked, there's no need to go to the terminal sales desk—it's simply a matter of showing up at the bus with your ticket number and ID. The smaller regional services are increasingly providing online purchasing, too, but will often require that your ticket be picked up at the terminal sales desk.

During peak travel times (Easter, August, and Christmas), it's a good idea to make a reservation at least a week in advance.

From the U.K. **Eurolines/National Express** (☎ 01582/404511 or 0990/143219 ⊕ www. eurolines.com).

In Spain **Alsa-Enatcar** (✉ *Estación Sur de Autobuses, Calle Méndez Álvaro, Madrid* ☎ 902/422242 ⊕ www.enatcar.com).

Bus Tours **Marsans** (✉ *Gran Vía 59, Madrid* ☎ 902/306090). **Pullmantur** (✉ *Pl. de Oriente 8, Madrid* ☎ 91/541–1805 ⊕ www. pullmantur-spain.com).

▌ BY CAR

Your own driver's license is valid in Spain, but you may want to get an International Driver's Permit for extra assurance, as having one may save you a problem with local authorities. Permits are available from the American or Canadian Automobile Association (AAA or CAA), or, in the United Kingdom, from the Automobile Association or Royal Automobile Club (AA or RAC). These international permits, valid only in conjunction with your regular driver's license (so have both on hand), are universally recognized.

Driving is the best way to see Spain's rural areas. The main cities are connected by a network of excellent four-lane *s* (freeways) and *autopistas* (toll freeways; "toll" is *peaje*), which are designated with the letter A and have speed limits of up to 120 km/h (74 mph). The letter N indicates a *carretera nacional* (basic national route), which may have four or two lanes, but these days they have largely been replaced with an E prefix, denoting the European route number, and an A prefix, denoting the new national route number. Smaller towns and villages are connected by a network of secondary roads maintained by regional, provincial, and local governments. Spain's major routes bear heavy traffic, especially during holidays. Drive with care: Spain has a yearly road toll that is ghastly—most accidents are speed related. The roads are shared by a potentially perilous mixture of local drivers and non-Spanish vacationers, some of whom are accustomed to driving on the left side of the road. Be prepared, too, for heavy truck traffic on national routes, which, in the case of two-lane roads, can have you creeping along for hours.

GASOLINE

Gas stations are plentiful, and most on major routes and in big cities are open 24 hours. On less-traveled routes, they're usually open 7 AM–11 PM. If a gas station is closed, it's required by law to post the address and directions to the nearest open station—but this is rarely adhered to. Most stations are self-service, though prices are the same as those at full-service stations. You punch in the amount of gas you want (in euros, not in liters), unhook the nozzle, pump the gas, and then pay. At night, however, you must pay before you fill up. Most pumps offer a choice of gas—leaded, unleaded, and diesel. All newer cars in Spain use *gasolina sin plomo* (unleaded gas), which is available in two grades, 95 and 98 octane. Prices vary little among stations and were at this writing €1 a liter for leaded, 97 octane; €1 a liter for unleaded, 95 octane; and €1.05 a liter for unleaded, 98 octane. Credit cards are widely accepted.

PARKING

Parking is, almost without exception, a nightmare in all Spanish cities and towns. Although parking meters are frequently used, finding an empty space to park in is another matter altogether. Parking lots are available, often underground, but spaces are at a premium. Another frequent problem is that many cities now have one-way systems, and it can be more than frustrating to drive around and around trying to find an empty space. The lesson is that if you don't need to go into a city or town center with your car then leave it at your hotel and take public transport or a taxi.

Although local drivers will park their cars just about anywhere, you should park only in legal spots. Parking fines are steep, and your car might well be towed, resulting in fines, hassles, and wasted time.

ROAD CONDITIONS

Spain's highway system includes some 3,600 mi (6,000 km) of beautifully maintained superhighways. Still, you'll find some stretches of major national highways that are only two lanes wide, where traffic often backs up behind slow, heavy trucks. *Autopista* tolls are steep, but as a result, these highways are often less crowded than the free ones. If you're driving down through Catalonia, be aware that there are more tolls here than anywhere else in Spain. This can result in a quicker journey, but at a sizeable cost. If you spring for the autopistas, you'll find that many of the rest stops are nicely landscaped and have cafeterias with reasonable but overpriced food. Rather than ordering a plate of food, you can pick up a cheese or ham *bocadillo* (baguette-style sandwich) for a much cheaper and often tastier alternative.

ROADSIDE EMERGENCIES

The rental agencies Hertz and Avis have 24-hour breakdown service. If you belong to an auto club (AAA, CAA, or AA), you can get emergency assistance from the Spanish counterpart, RACE.

Emergency Services RACE (⊠ *José Abascal 10, Madrid* ☎ *900/200093*).

RULES OF THE ROAD

Spaniards drive on the right; they pass on the left—so stay in the right-hand slow lane when not passing. Horns are banned in cities, but that doesn't keep people from blasting away. Children under 10 may not ride in the front seat, and seat belts are compulsory for the driver and all passengers. Speed limits are 50 km/h (31 mph) in cities, 100 km/h (62 mph) on N roads, 120 km/h (74 mph) on the *autopista* or *autovía,* and, unless otherwise signposted, 90 km/h (56 mph) on other roads.

Spanish highway police are increasingly vigilant about speeding and illegal passing. Fines start at €90, and police are empowered to demand payment from non-Spanish drivers on the spot. It is an unfortunate reality that rental-car drivers are disproportionately targeted by police for speeding and illegal passing.

▌ BY TRAIN

Spain's wonderful high-speed train, the 290-km/h (180-mph) AVE, travels between Madrid and Seville (with a stop in Córdoba) in less than three hours at prices starting around €86 each way. However, the rest of the state-run rail system (known as RENFE) remains below par by European standards. Train travel within cities is efficient, but many long-distance trips are tediously slow. Although some overnight trains have comfortable sleeper cars, first-class fares that include a sleeping compartment are comparable to, or more expensive than, airfares. In a nutshell: for shorter routes with convenient schedules, trains are the most economical way to go. First- and second-class seats are reasonably priced, and you can get a bunk in a compartment with five other people for a supplement of about €32.

Commuter trains and most long-distance trains forbid smoking, though some long-distance trains have smoking cars.

If you're coming from the United States or Canada and are planning extensive train travel throughout Europe, check Rail Europe for Eurail passes. Whichever of the many available passes you choose, remember that you must buy your pass before you leave for Europe.

Spain is one of 17 European countries in which you can use the Eurail Global Pass, which buys you unlimited first-class rail travel in all participating countries for the duration of the pass. If you plan to rack up the miles, get a standard pass. These are available for 15 days ($651), 21 days ($846), one month ($1,050), two months ($1,482), and three months ($1,829). If your needs are more limited, look into a Eurail Global Pass Flexi, which costs less than a Global Pass and buys you either 10 days in 2 months at $770 or 15 days in 2 months for $1,012.

In addition to these, Rail Europe sells the Eurail Global Pass Youth (you must be younger than 26), and a wide variety of other passes in different formats.

If Spain is your only destination, check into Rail Europe's Spain passes. Consider a Eurail Spain Pass that provides any 3 days of unlimited train travel in Spain in a 2-month period for $244 1st class and $190 2nd class, or the Eurail Spain Rail 'n Drive Pass that combines 3 days unlimited train travel and 2 days in a rental car. There are also combination passes for those visiting Spain and Portugal, Spain and France, and Spain and Italy.

You should also check for RENFE discounts in Spain. If you purchase a round-trip ticket on AVE or any of RENFE's Grandes Lineas, which are its faster, long-distance trains (including the Talgo) while in Spain, you'll get a 20% discount. You have up to 60 days to use the return portion of your ticket. Passengers with international airline tickets who are traveling on the AVE within 48 hours of their arrival receive a 25% discount on their AVE ticket. On regional trains, you receive a 10% discount on round-trip tickets, and you have up to 15 days to use the return portion. Children and students also receive good discounts. Note that even if you just buy a one-way ticket to your destination, you can still receive the round-trip discount if you present your ticket stub at the train station when buying your return (provided your return is within the allotted time frame, either 15 or 60 days).

Most Spaniards buy train tickets in advance at the train station's *taquilla* (ticket office). The lines can be long. For popular train routes, you will need to reserve tickets more than a few days in advance and pick them up at least a day before traveling; call RENFE to inquire. The ticket clerks at the stations rarely speak English, so if you need help or advice in planning a more complex train journey, you may be better off going to a travel agency that displays the blue-and-yellow RENFE sign. The price is the same. For shorter, regional train trips, you can often buy your tickets directly from machines in the main train stations. Note that if your itinerary is set in stone and has little room for error, you can buy RENFE tickets through Rail Europe before you leave home.

You can buy train tickets with a major credit card (except for American Express) at most city train stations. In the smaller towns and villages, it's cash only. Traveler's checks are no longer accepted.

Seat reservations are required on most long-distance and some other trains, particularly high-speed trains, and are recommended on any train that might be crowded. You'll also need a reservation if you want a sleeping berth. Many travelers assume that rail passes guarantee them seats on the trains they wish to ride: not so. Reserve seats in advance even if you're using a rail pass.

The easiest way to make reservations is to use the TIKNET service on the RENFE Web site. TIKNET involves registering and providing your credit-card information. When you make the reservation, you'll be given a car and seat assignment and a *localizador* (translated as "localizer" on the English version of the site; it is similar to a confirmation number). Print out the reservations page or write down the car number, seat number, and localizer. When traveling, go to your assigned seat on the train. When the conductor comes around, give him the localizer, and he will issue the ticket on the spot. You'll need your passport and, in most cases, the credit card you used for the reservation (in Spain, credit cards are often used for an additional form of ID). The AVE trains check you in at the gate to the platform, where you provide the localizer. You can review your pending reservations online at any time.

Caveats: the first time you use TIKNET, you must pick up the tickets at a RENFE station (most major airports have a RENFE booth, so you can retrieve your tickets as soon as you get off your plane). A 15% cancellation fee is charged if you cancel more than two hours after making the reservation. You cannot buy tickets online for certain regional lines or for commuter lines (*cercanias*). Station agents cannot alter TIKNET reservations: you must do this yourself online. If a train is booked, the TIKNET process doesn't reveal this until the final stage of the reservation attempt—then it gives you a cryptic error message in a little box—but if you reserve a few days in advance, it's unlikely you'll encounter this problem except at Easter, Christmas, or during the first week of August.

There's no line per se at the train station for advance tickets (and often for information); you take a number and wait until it's called. Ticket clerks at stations rarely speak English, so if you need help or advice in planning a more complex train journey, you may be better off going to a travel agency that displays the blue-and-yellow RENFE sign. A small commission (€3 perhaps) should be expected.

Information RENFE (☎902/240202 ⊕www.renfe.es). **Rail Europe** (☎877/456–7245 or 800/361–7245 ⊕www.raileurope.com). **RENFE** (☎902/157507 ⊕www.renfe.es).

FROM THE U.K.

Train services to Spain from the United Kingdom are not as frequent, fast, or affordable as flights, and you have to change trains—and stations—in Paris. Allow 2 hours for the changing process, then 13 hours for the trip from Paris to Madrid. It's worth paying extra for the Talgo or Puerta del Sol express trains to avoid changing trains again at the Spanish border. If you're under 26 years old, Eurotrain has excellent deals.

Information Eurotrain (✉52 Grosvenor Gardens, London SW1W OAG, U.K. ☎0207/730–8832). **Transalpino** (✉71–75 Buckingham Palace Rd., London SW1W ORE, U.K. ☎0207/834–9656).

ON THE GROUND

■ COMMUNICATIONS

INTERNET

The Internet boom came a bit late to Spain, with few or limited Internet cafés in the big cities at the turn of this century. But all that has changed, and the Internet is now in full swing. Huge increases in migration to the country's bigger cities means demand has skyrocketed for *locutorios* (cheap international phone centers), which double as places to get on the Internet. In addition to the locutorios, where Internet access is not always reliable, there are upmarket cafés and bars that provide Internet service, often at faster speeds. The most you're likely to pay for Internet access is about €3 an hour.

Internet cafés are most common in tourist and student precincts. If you can't find one easily, ask at either the tourist office or a hotel's front desk. There's no perfect guide to the many cybercafés in Spain, but Ocio Latino's Web site (⊕ *www.ociolatino. com*) is probably the best. Click on "Guía Latina" and then "locutorios."

Internet access within Spanish hotels is not widespread and tends to be offered only in the more expensive hotels. And those that do offer Internet access have varying services: Internet kiosks or rooms, in-room data ports or DSL, and/or Wi-Fi (either free or with a fee; sometimes in-room, sometimes in common areas).

Contacts **Cybercafes** (⊕ *www.cybercafes.com*) lists more than 4,000 Internet cafés worldwide.

PHONES

The good news is that you can now make a direct-dial telephone call from virtually any point on earth. The bad news? You can't always do so cheaply. Calling from a hotel is almost always the most expensive option; hotels usually add huge surcharges to all calls, particularly international ones. In some countries you can phone from call centers or even the post office. Calling cards usually keep costs to a minimum, but only if you purchase them locally. And then there are mobile phones (⇨ *below*)—as expensive as mobile phone calls can be, they are still usually a much cheaper option than calling from your hotel.

Spain's phone system is perfectly efficient but can be expensive. Direct dialing is the norm. Most travelers buy phone cards, which for €5 or €6 allows for about three hours of calls nationally and internationally. Phone cards can be used with any hotel, bar, or public telephone. Although some phone cards from Australia, the United Kingdom, and the United States can be used in Spain, those with the best value are found in Spain itself. There are many cards that work for only certain regions of the country, but the all-encompassing *Fantastic* card works for anywhere in the world. Phone cards can be bought at any tobacco shop or at most Internet cafés. Such cafés also often provide phone booths that allow you to call at cheaper rates. If you do use coins, be aware that the public phones in the street are cheaper than the green and blue phones found inside most bars and restaurants. Spain's main telephone company is Telefónica.

Note that only cell phones conforming to the European GSM standard will work in Spain. Buying a cell phone without a contract (i.e., paying for your calls by adding money to your phone either via a cell-phone card or at a cell-phone store) is popular in Spain. If you're going to be traveling in Spain for an extended period of time and plan on using a cell phone frequently to call within Spain, then buying a phone will often turn out to be a big money-saver. Using a Spanish cell phone means avoiding the hefty long-distance charges accrued when using your cell phone from home to call within Spain.

Prices fluctuate, but offers start at about €40 for a phone with about €30 worth of calls.

The country code for Spain is 34. The country code is 1 for the United States and Canada.

CALLING WITHIN SPAIN

For general information in Spain, dial 1003. International operators, who generally speak English, are at 025.

All area codes begin with a 9. To call within Spain—even locally—dial the area code first. Numbers preceded by a 900 code are no longer toll-free and often have long wait times, which can be expensive. Phone numbers starting with a 6 are going to a cellular phone. Note that when calling a cell phone, you do not need to dial the area code first; also, calls to cell phones are significantly more expensive than calls to regular phones.

You'll find pay phones in individual booths, in special telephone offices (*locutorios*), and in many bars and restaurants. Most have a digital readout so you can see your money ticking away. If you're calling with coins, you need at least €0.15 to call locally and €0.45 to call another province. Simply insert the coins and wait for a dial tone. (With older models, you line coins up in a groove on top of the dial and they drop down as needed.) Note that rates are reduced on weekends and after 8 PM during the week.

CALLING OUTSIDE SPAIN

International calls are awkward from coin-operated pay phones because of the many coins needed; and they can be expensive from hotels, as the hotel often adds a hefty surcharge. Your best bet is to use a public phone that accepts phone cards or go to the local telephone office, the *locutorio*: every town has one, and major cities have several. The locutorios near the center of town are generally more expensive; farther from the center, the rates are sometimes as much as one-third less. You converse in a quiet, private booth, and you're charged according to the meter. If the call ends up costing around €4 or more, you can usually pay with Visa or MasterCard.

To make an international call yourself, dial 00, then the country code, then the area code and number. GI id="d2e4419" The country code for the United States is 1.

Madrid's main telephone office is at Gran Vía 28. There's another at the main post office, and a third at Paseo Recoletos 43, just off Plaza Colón. In Barcelona you can phone overseas from the office at Carrer de Fontanella 4, off Plaça de Catalunya.

Before you leave home, find out your long-distance company's access code in Spain (⇨ *Access Codes, below*).

ACCESS CODES

AT&T Direct (☎ *900/990011*). **MCI World-Phone** (☎ *900/990014*). **Sprint International Access** (☎ *900/990013*).

General Information **AT&T** (☎ *800/222–0300*). **MCI WorldCom** (☎ *800/444–4444*). **Sprint** (☎ *800/793–1153*).

CALLING CARDS

To use a newer pay phone you need a special phone card (*tarjeta telefónica*), which you can buy at any tobacco shop or newsstand, in various denominations. Some such phones also accept credit cards, but phone cards are more reliable.

MOBILE PHONES

If you have a multiband phone (some countries use different frequencies than what's used in the United States) and your service provider uses the world-standard GSM network (as do T-Mobile, Cingular, and Verizon), you can probably use your phone abroad. Roaming fees can be steep, however: 99¢ a minute is considered reasonable. And overseas you normally pay the toll charges for incoming calls. It's almost always cheaper to send a text message than to make a call, since

LOCAL DO'S & TABOOS

GREETINGS

When addressing Spaniards with whom you are not well acquainted or who are elderly, use the formal *usted* rather than the familiar *tu* (⇨ *Language, below*).

OUT ON THE TOWN

These days, the Spanish are generally very informal, and casual-smart dress is accepted in most places.

DOING BUSINESS

Spanish office hours can be confusing to the uninitiated. Some offices stay open more or less continuously from 9 to 3, with a very short lunch break. Others open in the morning, break up the day with a long lunch break of two to three hours, then reopen at 4 or 5 until 7 or 8. Spaniards enjoy a certain notoriety for their lack of punctuality, but this has changed dramatically in recent years, and you are expected to show up for meetings on time. Smart dress is the norm.

Spaniards in international fields tend to conduct business with foreigners in English. If you speak Spanish, address new colleagues with the formal *usted* and the corresponding verb conjugations, then follow their lead in switching to the familiar *tu* once a working relationship has been established.

LANGUAGE

One of the best ways to avoid being an "Ugly American" is to learn a little of the local language. You need not be fluent; even mastering a few basic expressions is bound to make a difference with the locals.

Although Spaniards exported their language to all of Central and South America, Spanish is not the principal language in all of Spain. Outside their big cities, the Basques speak Euskera. In Catalonia, you'll hear Catalan throughout the region, just as you'll hear Gallego in Galicia and Valenciano in Valencia (the latter, as with Mallorquín in Majorca and Menorquín in Menorca, are considered Catalan dialects). Although almost everyone in these regions also speaks and understands Spanish, local radio and television stations may broadcast in their respective languages, and road signs may be printed (or spray-painted over) with the preferred regional language. Spanish is referred to as Castellano, or Castilian.

Fortunately, Spanish is fairly easy to pick up, and your efforts to speak it will be graciously received. Learn at least the following basic phrases: *buenos días* (hello—until 2 PM), *buenas tardes* (good afternoon—until 8 PM), *buenas noches* (hello—after dark), *por favor* (please), *gracias* (thank you), *adiós* (good-bye), *sí* (yes), *no* (no), *los servicios* (the toilets), *la cuenta* (bill/check), and *habla inglés?* (do you speak English?), *no comprendo* (I don't understand).

If your Spanish breaks down, you should have no trouble finding people who speak English in major cities and coastal resorts, but you won't necessarily be able to count on the bus driver or the passerby on the street. It's much more likely that you'll find an English-language speaker if you approach people under age 30. Those who do speak English may speak the British variety, so don't be surprised if you're told to queue (line up) or take the lift (elevator) to the loo (toilet). Many guided tours at museums and historic sites are in Spanish; ask which language will be spoken before you sign up. Alternatively, you can request a multilingual headset that guides you around a gallery or museum—these days they are fairly standard in the bigger establishments.

A phrase book and language-tape set can help get you started.

Fodor's Spanish for Travelers (available at bookstores everywhere) is excellent. Living Language sells comprehensive language programs: *Spanish Complete Course; Ultimate Spanish; All Audio Spanish;* and *Spanish Without the Fuss.*

text messages have a very low set fee (often less than 5¢).

If you just want to make local calls, consider buying a new SIM card (note that your provider may have to unlock your phone for you to use a different SIM card) and a prepaid service plan in the destination. You'll then have a local number and can make local calls at local rates. If your trip is extensive, you could also simply buy a new cell phone in your destination, as the initial cost will be offset over time.

■TIP→ If you travel internationally frequently, save one of your old mobile phones or buy a cheap one on the Internet; ask your cell phone company to unlock it for you, and take it with you as a travel phone, buying a new SIM card with pay-as-you-go service in each destination.

Contacts **Cellular Abroad** (☎ 800/287–5072 ⊕ www.cellularabroad.com) rents and sells GMS phones and sells SIM cards that work in many countries. **Mobal** (☎ 888/888–9162 ⊕ www.mobalrental.com) rents mobiles and sells GSM phones (starting at $49) that will operate in 140 countries. Per-call rates vary throughout the world. **Planet Fone** (☎ 888/988–4777 ⊕ www.planetfone.com) rents cell phones, but the per-minute rates are expensive.

■ CUSTOMS & DUTIES

You're always allowed to bring goods of a certain value back home without having to pay any duty or import tax. But there's a limit on the amount of tobacco and liquor you can bring back duty-free, and some countries have separate limits for perfumes; for exact figures, check with your customs department. The values of so-called "duty-free" goods are included in these amounts. When you shop abroad, save all your receipts, as customs inspectors may ask to see them as well as the items you purchased. If the total value of your goods is more than the duty-free limit, you'll have to pay a tax

(most often a flat percentage) on the value of everything beyond that limit.

From countries that are not part of the European Union, visitors age 15 and over may *enter* Spain duty-free with up to 200 cigarettes or 50 cigars, up to 1 liter of alcohol over 22 proof, and up to 2 liters of wine.

U.S. Information **U.S. Customs and Border Protection** (⊕ www.cbp.gov).

■ EATING OUT

Sitting around a table eating and talking is a huge part of Spanish culture, defining much of people's daily routines. Sitting in the middle of a typical bustling restaurant here goes a long way toward showing how fundamental food can be to Spanish lives.

Although Spain has always had an extraordinary range of regional cuisine, in the past decade or so its restaurants have won it international recognition at the highest levels. A new generation of Spanish chefs—led by the revolutionary Ferran Adrià—has transformed classic dishes to suit contemporary tastes, drawing on some of the freshest ingredients in Europe.

One of the major drawbacks of drinking and eating in Spanish bars and restaurants has been the unbridled smoking in almost all of them. The new antismoking laws introduced by the national government at the beginning of 2006 is changing all that. Establishments within shopping malls, theaters, and cinemas are now strictly non-smoking. All establishments that measure 100 meters squared or more are obliged to provide a non-smoking section. Children may not eat outside this section. However, establishments smaller than this size retain the option for the time being to permit smoking across the board or to ban it altogether. With a few exceptions, the proprietors of these establishments have maintained the status quo, presumably because of the fact that one in three Spaniards smoke, and they are fearful of losing clients. This may change over time as locals become more accustomed to the new regulations forbidding smoking in public places, shops, and places of work. All eating and drinking establishments are obliged to inform clients by posting a sign at the entrance. *Se permite fumar* means you can smoke, *No se permite fumar* means you can't, and *Sala habilitada para no fumadores* means a nonsmoking section is available.

For information on food-related health issues, see Health below.

MEALS & MEALTIMES

Most restaurants in Spain do not serve breakfast (*desayuno*); for coffee and carbs, head to a bar or *cafetería*. Outside major hotels, which serve morning buffets, breakfast in Spain is usually limited to coffee and toast or a roll. Lunch (*comida* or *almuerzo*) traditionally consists of an appetizer, a main course, and dessert, followed by coffee and perhaps a liqueur. Between lunch and dinner the best way to snack is to sample some tapas (appetizers) at a bar; normally you can choose from quite a variety. Dinner (*cena*) is somewhat lighter, with perhaps only one course. In addition to an à la carte menu, most restaurants offer a daily fixed-price menu (*menú del día*), consisting of two courses, wine, and dessert at an attractive price (usually between €6 and €12). Coffee usually costs extra. If your waiter does not suggest the menú del día when you're seated, ask for it—"*Hay menú del día, por favor?*" Restaurants in many of the larger tourist areas will have the menú del día posted outside. The menú del día is traditionally offered only at lunch, but increasingly it's also offered at dinner in popular tourist destinations.

Mealtimes in Spain are later than elsewhere in Europe, and later still in Madrid and Andalusia. Lunch starts around 2:30 or 3, and dinner after 9:30 or 10. Weekend eating times, especially din-

ner, can begin upward of about an hour later. In areas with heavy tourist traffic, some restaurants open a bit earlier. GI id="d2e4718" Unless otherwise noted, the restaurants listed in this guide are open daily for lunch and dinner.

PAYING

Credit cards are widely accepted in Spanish restaurants, but beware that smaller establishments often do not take them. If you pay by credit card and you want to leave a small tip above and beyond the service charge, leave the tip in cash. (For tipping guidelines, ⇨ *Tipping, below.*)

RESERVATIONS & DRESS

Regardless of where you are, it's a good idea to make a reservation if you can. In some places, it's expected. We only mention them specifically when reservations are essential (there's no other way you'll ever get a table) or when they are not accepted. For popular restaurants, book as far ahead as you can (often 30 days), and reconfirm as soon as you arrive. (Large parties should always call ahead to check the reservations policy.) We mention dress only when men are required to wear a jacket or a jacket and tie.

WINES, BEER & SPIRITS

Apart from its famous wines, Spain produces many brands of lager, the most popular of which are San Miguel, Cruzcampo, Aguila, Mahou, and Estrella. Jerez de la Frontera is Europe's largest producer of brandy and is a major source of sherry. Spanish law prohibits the sale of alcohol to people under 18.

▌ ELECTRICITY

Spain's electrical current is 220 volts, 50 cycles alternating current (AC); wall outlets take Continental-type plugs, with two round prongs.

Consider making a small investment in a universal adapter, which has several types of plugs in one lightweight, compact unit. Most laptops and mobile phone chargers are dual voltage (i.e., they operate equally well on 110 and 220 volts), therefore requiring only an adapter. These days the same is true of small appliances such as hair dryers. Always check labels and manufacturer instructions to be sure. Don't use 110-volt outlets marked FOR SHAVERS ONLY for high-wattage appliances such as hair-dryers.

▌EMERGENCIES

The pan-European emergency phone number (☎112) is operative in some parts of Spain, but not all. If it doesn't work, dial the emergency numbers below for the national police, local police, fire department, or medical services. On the road, there are emergency phones marked SOS at regular intervals on *autovías* (freeways) and *autopistas* (toll highways). If your documents are stolen, contact both the local police and your embassy. If you lose a credit card, phone the issuer immediately *(⇨ Money Matters)*.

Foreign Embassies **Fuengirola** (⊠ *Av. Juan Goméz 8, Apt. 1c* ☎ *952/474891*). **Madrid** (⊠ *C. Serrano 75, Salamanca* ☎ *91/587–2200*). **Seville** (⊠ *Paseo de las Delicias 7, Arenal* ☎ *95/423–1885*).

General Emergency Contacts **National police** (☎ *091*). **Local police** (☎ *092*). **Fire department** (☎ *080*). **Medical service** (☎ *061*).

▌HEALTH

The most common types of illnesses are caused by contaminated food and water. Make sure food has been thoroughly cooked and is served to you fresh and hot; avoid vegetables and fruits that you haven't washed (in bottled or purified water) or peeled yourself. If you have problems, mild cases of traveler's diarrhea may respond to Imodium (known generically as loperamide) or Pepto-Bismol. Be sure to drink plenty of fluids;

if you can't keep fluids down, seek medical help immediately.

Infectious diseases can be airborne or passed via mosquitoes and ticks and through direct or indirect physical contact with animals or people. Some, including Norwalk-like viruses that affect your digestive tract, can be passed along through contaminated food. Speak with your physician and/or check the CDC or World Health Organization Web sites for health alerts, particularly if you're pregnant, traveling with children, or have a chronic illness.

For information on travel insurance, shots and medications, and medical-assistance companies see Shots & Medications under Things to Consider in Before You Go, above.

▌**TIP→ If you travel a lot internationally— particularly to developing nations—refer to the CDC's** *Health Information for International Travel* **(aka Traveler's Health Yellow Book). Info from it is posted on the CDC Web site (www.cdc.gov/travel/yb), or you can buy a copy from your local bookstore for $24.95.**

SPECIFIC ISSUES IN SPAIN

Medical care is good in Spain, but nursing is perfunctory, as relatives are expected to stop by and look after patients' needs. In some popular destinations, such as the Costa del Sol, there are volunteer English interpreters on hand. In 2004, Spain was documented by the World Health Organization as having the highest number of cumulative AIDS cases in Europe, and like many European countries, it is once again experiencing increased rate of HIV infections. If you're applying for a work permit, you'll be asked for proof that you are HIV-negative.

In the summer, sunburn and sunstroke are real risks in Spain. On the hottest sunny days, even if you're not normally bothered by strong sun, you should cover yourself up, carry sunblock lotion (*protector solar*), drink plenty of fluids, and limit sun time for the first few days. If you require medical attention for any problem, ask your hotel's front desk for assistance or go to the nearest public **Centro de Salud** (day hospital); in serious cases, you'll be referred to the regional hospital.

OVER-THE-COUNTER REMEDIES

Over-the-counter remedies are available at any *farmacia* (pharmacy), recognizable by the large green crosses outside. Some will look familiar, such as *aspirina* (aspirin), and other medications are sold under various brand names. If you get traveler's diarrhea, ask for *un antidiarreico* (the general term for antidiarrheal medicine); Fortasec is a well-known brand. Mild cases may respond to Imodium (known generically as loperamide) or Pepto-Bismol. To keep from getting dehydrated, drink plenty of purified water or herbal tea. In severe cases, rehydrate yourself with a salt-sugar solution—½ teaspoon salt (*sal*) and 4 tablespoons sugar (*azúcar*) per quart of water.

If you regularly take a nonprescription medicine, take a sample box or bottle with you, and the Spanish pharmacist will provide you with its local equivalent.

▌HOURS OF OPERATION

The ritual of a long afternoon siesta is no longer as ubiquitous as it once was, but the tradition does remain, especially outside the larger cities, and many people take a postlunch nap before returning to work or continuing on with their day. Traditionally, Spain's climate created the siesta as a time to preserve energy while afternoon temperatures spiked. After the sun began setting, Spaniards went back to working, shopping, and taking their leisurely *paseo,* or stroll. In the big cities—particularly with the advent of air-conditioning—the heat has less of an effect on the population; in Andalusia's small towns, however, many still use a siesta as a way to escape the heat.

The two- to three-hour lunch "hour" makes it possible to eat and then snooze. Siestas generally begin at 1 or 2 and end between 4 and 5, depending on the city and the sort of business. The midafternoon siesta—often a half-hour power nap in front of the TV—fits naturally into the workday cycle, since Spaniards tend to work until 7 or 8 PM.

Until a decade or so ago, it was common for many businesses to close for a month in the July/August period. Europeanization, changing trading hours, and a booming consumerism are gradually altering that custom. These days many small businesses are more likely to close down for two weeks only, maybe three. When open, they often run on a summer schedule, which can mean a longer-than-usual siesta (sometimes up to four hours), a shorter working day (until 3 PM only), and/or no Saturday afternoon trading at all.

Banks are generally open weekdays from 8:30 or 9 until 2 or 2:30. From October to May the major banks open on Saturday from 8:30 or 9 until 2 or 2:30, and savings banks are also open Thursday 4:30 to 8. Currency exchanges at airports, train stations, and in the city center stay open later; you can also cash traveler's checks at El Corte Inglés department stores until 10 PM (some branches close at 9 PM or 9:30 PM). Most government offices are open weekdays 9 to 2.

Most museums are open from 9:30 to 2 and 4 to 7 six days a week—every day but Monday. Schedules are subject to change, particularly between the high and low seasons, so confirm opening hours before you make plans. A few large museums, such as Madrid's Prado and Reina Sofía and Barcelona's Picasso Museum, stay open all day, without a siesta.

Pharmacies keep normal business hours (9 to 1:30 and 5 to 8), but every midsize town (or city neighborhood) has a duty pharmacy that stays open 24 hours. The location of the duty pharmacy is usually posted on the front door of all pharmacies.

When planning a shopping trip, remember that almost all shops in Spain close at 1 or 2 PM for at least two hours. The only exceptions are large supermarkets and the department-store chain El Corte Inglés. Stores are generally open somewhere between 9 or 10 to 1:30 or 2 and from somewhere between 4 and 5 to 7:30 or 8. Most shops are closed on Sunday, and in several other places they're also closed Saturday afternoon. Larger shops in tourist areas may stay open Sunday in summer and during the Christmas holiday.

HOLIDAYS

Spain's national holidays are January 1, January 6 (Epiphany), Good Friday, Easter, May 1 (May Day), August 15 (Assumption), October 12 (National Day), November 1 (All Saints' Day), December 6 (Constitution), December 8 (Immaculate Conception), and December 25. In addition, each region, city, and town has its own holidays honoring political events and patron saints. Many stores close during *Semana Santa* (Holy Week—also sometimes translated as Easter Week); it is the week that preceeds Easter.

If a public holiday falls on a Tuesday or Thursday, remember that many businesses also close on the nearest Monday or Friday for a long weekend, called a *puente* (bridge). If a major holiday falls on a Sunday, businesses close on Monday.

▮ MAIL

Spain's postal system, the *correos*, does work, but delivery times can vary widely. An airmail letter to the United States may take anywhere from four days to two weeks; delivery to other destinations is equally unpredictable. Sending your letters by priority mail (*urgente*) or the cheaper registered mail *certificado* ensures speedier and safer arrival.

Airmail letters to the United States and Canada cost €0.78 up to 20 grams. Letters to the United Kingdom and other EU countries cost €0.57 up to 20 grams. Letters within Spain are €0.29. Postcards carry the same rates as letters. You can buy stamps at post offices and at licensed tobacco shops.

Want to receive mail while you're in Andalusia? Mail delivery in Spain can often be slow and unreliable, so it's best to have your mail held at a Spanish post office; have it addressed to LISTA DE CORREOS (the equivalent of poste restante) in a town you'll be visiting. Postal addresses should include the name of the province in parentheses, for example, Marbella (Málaga).

SHIPPING PACKAGES

When time is of the essence, or when you're sending valuable items or documents overseas, you can use a courier (*mensajero*). The major international agencies, such as Federal Express, UPS, and DHL, have representatives in Spain; the biggest Spanish courier service is Seur. MRW is another local courier that provides express delivery worldwide.

EXPRESS SERVICES

DHL (☎ *902/122424*). **Federal Express** (☎ *900/100871*). **MRW** (☎ *900/300400*). **Seur** (☎ *902/101010*). **UPS** (☎ *902/888820*).

▮ MONEY

Spain is no longer a budget destination. However, prices still compare slightly favorably with those elsewhere in Europe. Coffee (depending if it's a smaller espresso or a latte) in a bar generally costs anywhere from €0.80 to €2, again, depending on if you're standing or sitting at a bar, sitting at an inside table, or sitting at an outside terrace table. The latter is always the most expensive option—whether you're ordering coffee, a beer, or a packet of chips. Tap beer (regular size) in a bar: €1 standing or sitting at a bar, €1.50–€2 seated inside, and €1.50–€2.50

sitting outside. Small glass of wine in a bar: €1–€2.50. Soft drink: €1.20–€1.80 a bottle. Ham-and-cheese sandwich: €1.80–€2.70. Two-kilometer (1-mi) taxi ride: €2.40, but the meter keeps ticking in traffic jams. Local bus or subway ride: €0.90–€1.30. Movie ticket: €4–€6. Foreign newspaper: €2.

Prices throughout this guide are given for adults. Substantially reduced fees are almost always available for children, students, and senior citizens.

■TIP➡ Banks never have every foreign currency on hand, and it may take as long as a week to order. If you're planning to exchange funds before leaving home, don't wait until the last minute.

ATMS & BANKS

Your own bank will probably charge a fee for using ATMs abroad; the foreign bank you use may also charge a fee. Nevertheless, you'll usually get a better rate of exchange at an ATM than you will at a currency-exchange office or even when changing money in a bank. And extracting funds as you need them is a safer option than carrying around a large amount of cash.

■TIP➡ PIN numbers with more than four digits are not recognized at ATMs in many countries. If yours has five or more, remember to change it before you leave.

You'll find ATMs in every major city in Spain, as well as most smaller cities. ATMs will be part of the Cirrus and/or Plus networks, and will allow you to withdraw euros with your credit or debit card, provided you have a valid PIN (pronounced *peen*). Make sure your PIN code is four digits. Also, if you tend to rely on alphabetic memory to punch in your code, memorize the numerical equivalents before going to Spain; at some ATMs the keyboard is reverse from the American keyboard starting with a 9 in the top left.

The Spanish banking system has been hailed as Europe's most efficient on several occasions. Banks are generally located in the town and city centers, and the majority will have an ATM. Major banks in Spain are Banco Popular (⊕*www.banco popular.es*), Banesto (⊕*www.banesto. es*), BBVA (Banco Bilbao-Vizcaya Argentara ⊕*www.bbva.es*), and BSCH (Banco Santander Central Hispano ⊕*www. gruposantander.com*). *See Operation of Hours, above.*

CREDIT CARDS

Throughout this guide, the following abbreviations are used: **AE**, American Express; **DC**, Diners Club; **MC**, MasterCard; and **V**, Visa.

It's a good idea to inform your credit-card company before you travel, especially if you're going abroad and don't travel internationally very often. Otherwise, the credit-card company might put a hold on your card owing to unusual activity—not a good thing halfway through your trip. Record all your credit-card numbers—as well as the phone numbers to call if your cards are lost or stolen—in a safe place, so you're prepared should something go wrong. Both MasterCard and Visa have general numbers you can call (collect if you're abroad) if your card is lost, but you're better off calling the number of your issuing bank, since MasterCard and Visa usually just transfer you to your bank; your bank's number is usually printed on your card.

If you plan to use your credit card for cash advances, you'll need to apply for a PIN at least two weeks before your trip. Although it's usually cheaper (and safer) to use a credit card abroad for large purchases (so you can cancel payments or be reimbursed if there's a problem), note that some credit-card companies *and* the banks that issue them add substantial percentages to all foreign transactions, whether they're in a foreign currency or not. If you don't want any surprises on your bill, check on these fees before leaving home.

■TIP➜ **Before you charge something, ask the merchant whether or not he or she plans to do a dynamic currency conversion (DCC). In such a transaction the credit-card** *processor* **(shop, restaurant, or hotel, not Visa or MasterCard) converts the currency and charges you in dollars. In most cases you'll pay the merchant a 3% fee for this service in addition to any credit-card company and issuing-bank foreign-transaction surcharges.**

Dynamic currency conversion programs are becoming increasingly widespread. Merchants who participate in them are supposed to ask whether you want to be charged in dollars or the local currency, but they don't always do so. And even if they do offer you a choice, they may well avoid mentioning the additional surcharges. The good news is that you *do* have a choice. And if this practice really gets your goat, you can avoid it entirely with American Express cards—with them, DCC simply isn't an option.

Reporting Lost Cards **American Express**
(☎ *800/528–4800 in the U.S., 336/393–1111 collect from abroad* ⊕ *www.american-express.com*). **Diners Club** (☎ *800/234–6377 in the U.S., 303/799–1504 collect from abroad* ⊕ *www.dinersclub.com*). **MasterCard** (☎ *800/627–8372 in the U.S., 636/722–7111 collect from abroad* ⊕ *www.mastercard.com*). **Visa** (☎ *800/847–2911 in the U.S.* ⊕ *www.visa.com*).

Use these toll-free numbers in Spain. **American Express** (☎ *917/437000*). **Diners Club** (☎ *901/101011*). **MasterCard** (☎ *900/971231*). **Visa** (☎ *900/991124*).

CURRENCY & EXCHANGE
Since 2002, Spain has used the European monetary unit, the euro; other countries that also have adopted it are Austria, Belgium, Finland, France, Germany, Greece, Ireland, Italy, Luxembourg, the Netherlands, and Portugal. Euro notes come in denominations of 5, 10, 20, 50, 100, 200, and 500; coins are worth 1 cent of a euro, 2 cents, 5 cents, 10 cents, 20 cents, 50 cents, 1 euro, and 2 euros. Forgery is quite commonplace in parts of Spain, especially with 50-euro notes. You can generally tell a forgery by the feel of the paper: they tend to be smoother than the legal notes, and the metalic line down the middle is darker than those in real bills.

At this writing the euro is fairly strong against the U.S. dollar and other currencies: €0.84 to the U.S. dollar, €1.46 to the pound sterling, €0.72 to the Canadian dollar, €0.62 to the Australian dollar, €0.56 to the New Zealand dollar, and €0.14 to the South African rand.

■TIP➜ **Even if a currency-exchange booth has a sign promising no commission, rest assured that there's some kind of huge, hidden fee. (Oh…that's right. The sign didn't say no** *fee***.). And as for rates, you're almost always better off getting foreign currency at an ATM or exchanging money at a bank.**

TRAVELER'S CHECKS & CARDS
Some consider this the currency of the cave man, and it's true that fewer establishments accept traveler's checks these days. Nevertheless, they're a cheap and secure way to carry extra money, particularly on trips to urban areas. Both Citibank (under the Visa brand) and American Express issue traveler's checks in the United States, but Amex is better known and more widely accepted; you can also avoid hefty surcharges by cashing Amex checks at Amex offices. Whatever you do, keep track of all the serial numbers in case the checks are lost or stolen.

American Express now offers a stored-value card called a Travelers Cheque Card, which you can use wherever American Express credit cards are accepted, including ATMs. The card can carry a minimum of $300 and a maximum of $2,750. You can get replacement funds in 24 hours if your card is lost or stolen. Although it's a very safe way to carry your funds it doesn't strike us as a very good deal. In addition to a high initial cost ($14.95 to set up the card, plus $5 each time you "reload"), you still have to pay a 2% fee for each purchase in a foreign currency (similar to that of any credit card). Further, each time you use the card in an ATM you pay a transaction fee of $2.50 on top of the 2% transaction fee for the conversion—add it all up and it can be considerably more than you would pay when simply using your own ATM card. Regular traveler's checks are just as secure and cost less.

Contacts **American Express** (☎ 888/412–6945 in the U.S., 801/945–9450 collect outside of the U.S. to add value or speak to customer service ⊕ www.americanexpress.com).

▌RESTROOMS

Spain has some public restrooms (*servicios*), including, in larger cities, small coin-operated booths, but they are few and far between. Your best option is to use the facilities in a bar or cafeteria, remembering that at the discretion of the establishment you may have to order something. Gas stations have restrooms (you usually have to request the key to use them), but they are more often than not in terrible condition.

▌SAFETY

Petty crime is a huge problem in Spain's most popular tourist destinations. The most frequent offenses are pickpocketing (particularly in Madrid and Barcelona) and theft from cars (all over the country). Never leave anything valuable in a parked car, no matter how friendly the area feels, how quickly you'll return, or how invisible the item seems once you lock it in the trunk. Thieves can spot rental cars a mile away, and they work very efficiently. In airports, laptop computers are choice prey. Except when traveling between the airport or train station and your hotel, don't wear a money belt or a waist pack,

both of which peg you as a tourist. (If you do use a money belt while traveling, opt for a concealed one and don't reach into it once you're in public.) Distribute your cash and any valuables (including your credit cards and passport) between a deep front pocket or an inside jacket or vest pocket. When walking the streets, particularly in large cities, carry as little cash as possible. Men should carry their wallets in the front pocket; women who need to carry purses should strap them across the front of their bodies. Another alternative is to carry money or important documents in both your front pockets. Leave the rest of your valuables in the safe at your hotel. On the beach, in cafés, restaurants (particularly in the well-touristed areas), and in Internet centers, always keep your belongings on your lap or tied to your person in some way.

It's not advisable to sleep on beaches—no matter how well you store your possessions, you are an easy target for those who prey there in the early morning. Additionally, be cautious of any odd or unnecessary human contact, verbal or physical, whether it's a tap on the shoulder, someone asking you for a light for their cigarette, someone spilling their drink at your table, and so on. Thieves often work in twos, so while one is attracting your attention, the other could be swiping your wallet.

In the tourist areas of Madrid and Barcelona you'll sometimes see a raucous group standing around a makeshift cardboard table and cheering on a guy who appears to be playing the ancient game of hiding the seed under one of three walnut shells. He goads passersby to pick a shell, any shell, to see if they can guess where the seed is; someone takes the bait, and the con game has begun. You'll choose correctly and "win" at the beginning. The moment you start handing over betting money, it becomes noticeably more difficult—and all but impossible—to guess the right shell. This is a scam, through and through, and the people standing around cheering the guy on are his friends or paid accomplices.

Be cautious when a group of gypsy women approaches you in tourist areas to sell flowers. While you're admiring the flowers and bargaining a price, they'll often be picking your pocket—or that of the person you're with. Alternatively they'll insist you pay them something for the flower even if you haven't asked for it.

TAXES

Value-added tax, similar to sales tax, is called I.V.A. in Spain (pronounced "ee-vah," for *impuesto sobre el valor añadido*). It's levied on both products and services, such as hotel rooms and restaurant meals. When in doubt about whether tax is included, ask, "*Está incluido el I.V.A.*"?

The I.V.A. rate for hotels and restaurants is 7%, regardless of their number of stars. Menus will generally say at the bottom whether tax is included (*I.V.A. incluido*) or not (*más 7% I.V.A.*).

Although food, pharmaceuticals, and household items are taxed at the lowest rate, most consumer goods are taxed at 16%. A number of shops participate in Global Refund (formerly Europe Tax-Free Shopping), a V.A.T. refund service that makes getting your money back relatively hassle-free. You cannot get a refund on the V.A.T. for such items as meals or services such as hotel accommodation, or taxi fares. There are also some taxable goods for which the refund doesn't apply, such as consumable items like perfume.

When making a purchase, ask for a V.A.T. refund form and find out whether the merchant gives refunds—not all stores do, nor are they required to. Have the form stamped like any customs form by customs officials when you leave the country or, if you're visiting several European Union countries, when you leave the EU. After you're through passport control, take the form to a refund-service counter for an on-the-spot refund (which is usually the quickest and easiest option), or mail it to the address on the form (or the envelope with it) after you arrive home. You receive the total refund stated on the form, but the processing time can be long, especially if you request a credit-card adjustment.

Global Refund is a Europe-wide service with 225,000 affiliated stores and more than 700 refund counters at major airports and border crossings. Its refund form, called a Tax Free Check, is the most common across the European continent. The service issues refunds in the form of cash, check, or credit-card adjustment.

V.A.T. Refunds **Global Refund** (☎ *800/566–9828* ⊕ *www.globalrefund.com*).

TIME

Spain is on central European time, one hour ahead of Greenwich mean time, and six hours ahead of eastern standard time. Like the rest of the European Union, Spain switches to daylight saving time on the last weekend in March and switches back on the last weekend in October.

TIPPING

Service staff expect to be tipped, and you can be sure that your contribution will be appreciated. On the other hand, if you experience bad or surly service, don't feel obligated to leave a tip.

Restaurant checks do not list a service charge on the bill, but consider the tip included. If you want to leave a small tip in addition to the bill, do not tip more than 10% of the bill, and leave less if you eat tapas or sandwiches at a bar—just enough to round out the bill to the nearest €1. Tip cocktail servers €0.30–€0.50 a drink, depending on the bar.

Tip taxi drivers about 10% of the total fare, plus a supplement to help with luggage. Note that rides from airports carry an official surcharge plus a small handling fee for each piece of luggage.

Tip hotel porters €0.50 a bag, and the bearer of room service €0.50. A doorman who calls a taxi for you gets €0.50. If you stay in a hotel for more than two nights, tip the maid about €0.50 per night. The concierge should receive a tip for any additional help he or she provides.

Tour guides should be tipped about €2, ushers in theaters or at bullfights €0.15–€0.20, barbers €0.50, and women's hairdressers at least €1 for a wash and style. Restroom attendants are tipped €0.15.

INDEX

NOTES

NOTES

NOTES

NOTES

ABOUT OUR WRITERS

Journalist Michael Kessler writes almost exclusively on Spanish music, food, theater, film, travel, art, sports, and politics for the Australian press and a range of Spanish, American, and British magazines. He wrote the paradores and bullfighting in-focus features.

Journalist Mary McLean is from England and has worked in California, the Middle East, and—since 1990—Spain. Mary writes for many magazines and travel publications, including in-flight magazines and guidebooks. She has covered Portugal, Italy, and various regions of Spain and contributes to travel-related Web sites. In her spare time she likes nothing better than exploring the wilder regions of the Iberian Peninsula. She covered the Costa del Sol.

Norman Renouf was born in London and educated at Charlton Secondary School, Greenwich. He started writing travel guides, articles, and newspaper contributions in the early 1990s and has written about numerous European destinations, with particular emphasis on the Costa Tropical in Southern Spain, and on Portugal, Switzerland, and the Nordic countries. He updated the Andalusia Essentials.

Helio San Miguel is a wine and food writer and educator. He was born in Madrid and lives in New York, where he created and teaches the Wines of Spain Program at Instituto Cervantes. He is the New York correspondent of *Club de Gourmets,* Spain's leading wine and food magazine. He has a PhD in Philosophy and teaches at The New School. He wrote the in-focus feature on wine.

Writer and journalist George Semler has lived in Spain for the last 30-odd years. During that time he has written on Spain, France, Morocco, Cuba, and the Mediterranean region for *Forbes,* *Sky, Saveur,* the *International Herald Tribune,* and the *Los Angeles Times* and has published walking guides to Madrid and Barcelona. When not sampling Catalonia's hottest restaurants, this James Beard Journalism Awards Finalist forges ahead on his magnum opus about the Pyrenees. He covered Seville, Granada, and mainland Andalusia.

Kip Tobin is a freelance writer, journalist, music critic, English teacher, and DJ living in Madrid. He writes Spain-themed short stories, scripts, and blogs, and a slew of articles covering Spain-related travel, literature, music, film, and human interest. He currently is working on a script he's mulled over for years and a children's story for his nieces. He wrote the tapas in-focus feature.